The
Constitutional Bases
of Political and Social Change
in the United States

The
Constitutional Bases
of
Political and Social Change
in the
United States

Edited by SHLOMO SLONIM

PRAEGER

New York
Westport, Connecticut
London

To the Honorable
AMBASSADOR WALTER H. ANNENBERG,
whose commitment to American Studies
at The Hebrew University of Jerusalem
made this volume possible.

Library of Congress Cataloging-in-Publication Data

The Constitutional bases of political and social change in the United
    States / Shlomo Slonim, editor.
      p. cm.
    ISBN 0–275–93071–8 (alk. paper)
    1. Civil rights—United States. 2. United States—Constitutional
law. 3. Civil rights—Israel. 4. Sociological jurisprudence.
I. Slonim, Shlomo, 1931–
KF4749.C646   1990
342.73'085—dc20
[347.30285]   89–16215

Library of Congress Catalog Card Number: 89–16215
ISBN: 0–275–93071–8

First published in 1990

Praeger Publishers, One Madison Avenue, New York, NY   10010
A division of Greenwood Press, Inc.

Printed in the United States of America

The paper used in this book complies with the
Permanent Paper Standard issued by the National
Information Standards Organization (Z39.48–1984).

10 9 8 7 6 5 4 3 2 1

Contents

Preface

The years 1987–91 mark the bicentennial of the framing and adoption of the United States Constitution and of the appended Bill of Rights. This instrument of government has been a source of pride to Americans and a focus of admiration and respect for the nations of the world. It has both reflected and promoted the growth of U.S. democracy over the course of the past two centuries. The freedoms and liberties which Americans enjoy are essentially a product of the genius which underlies the Constitution and the Bill of Rights. Freedom-loving people all over the world have drawn inspiration from the U.S. experience. As a result, the bicentennial of the Constitution has been a cause for celebration not only for Americans but for other peoples as well.

Israel especially has much to celebrate in this constitutional milestone attained by the world's foremost democracy. For one thing, Jews, in the long night of their exile, have never enjoyed as much equality and freedom as has been their right and privilege under the federal Constitution. But furthermore, the special role of the United States in both the founding and survival of the State of Israel has generated unique ties between Jerusalem and Washington. The United States, as is well known, was the first country to extend diplomatic recognition to the State of Israel in May 1948. In his letter to President Harry Truman requesting recognition, Dr. Chaim Weizmann had written: "The world, I think, would regard it as especially appropriate that the greatest living democracy should be the first to welcome the newest into the family of nations."[1] Truman readily complied eleven minutes after the independence proclamation was issued and a strong bond of association has linked the two countries ever since. The coincidence of the fortieth anniversary of the establishment of the Jewish state occurring during the same period that the United States marks the bicentennial of its constitution, highlights the special affinity that binds the two countries. A key element in the affinity governing relations between the two nations is the firm commitment to shared values, above all to a democratic system of government—albeit, in the one case there is a written constitution and in the other there is not.

In recognition of the importance of the bicentennial of the Constitution, the Department of American Studies at the Hebrew University of Jerusalem resolved to convene a conference which would seek to explore the nature of the Constitution's influence upon the course of U.S. history. Thus was born the idea of a conference to be held in Jerusalem on the subject, "The Constitutional Bases of Political and Social Development in the United States of America." This topic would also allow room for examining the impact of the U.S. constitutional experience on the development of Israeli jurisprudence and Israeli democracy.

The conference was held at the Hebrew University from May 18–20, 1987. Distinguished members of the U.S. judiciary, bar, and academia joined their Israeli counterparts in an intensive debate on the part the Constitution has assumed in American life. Appropriately enough, the conference opened with a dinner session at the Knesset, Israel's parliament. Chairing the session was Mr. Abba Eban, former Foreign Minister of Israel. The session was also graced by the presence of the then U.S. Ambassador to Israel, Mr. Thomas Pickering. The papers assembled in this volume are a product of the conference.

The first two papers provide the backdrop to the constitutional debate. The first paper, by Professor Shlomo Slonim of the Hebrew University, is entitled "The Constitution and the Rise of an Ideological Court in a Nonideological Polity" (Chapter 1), and focuses on the factors which have contributed to the emergence of the Supreme Court as a strong force for change in the United States. According to the argument presented in this paper, because the provisions of the Constitution foster a nonideological polity, the Court has felt it necessary to move into the breach and to assume an ideologically activist role. In this context, the current debate over original intent is seen as a challenge to the ideological role of the Court.

The paper presented by Professor Gordon Wood of Brown University (Chapter 2) reviews the historical background. He undertakes an analysis of the views of the Founding Fathers in an attempt to determine to what extent they regarded the charter of government drafted at Philadelphia as a vehicle for political and social change.

The issue of executive-legislative relations and the impact of the Constitution on these relations over the years is analyzed in the papers of Professor Louis Henkin of Columbia University and Dr. Louis Fisher of the Congressional Reference Service. Professor Henkin focuses on the conduct of foreign affairs and notes that this is one of the "twilight zones" of the Constitution in which President and Congress vie for mastery (Chapter 3). Dr. Louis Fisher of the Library of Congress considers the domestic side of executive-legislative relations and maintains that recent rulings of the Supreme Court, especially Chadha and Gramm-Rudman, demonstrate a lack of appreciation for the mutually satisfactory accommodations that the other two branches of government have reached (Chapter 4). These judicial decisions, he claims, reflect an ignorance of political realities. In her comments, Professor Michla Pomerance of the Hebrew University analyzes the aftermath of the War Powers Resolution and the Chadha case for congressional-executive relations. Professor Donald Robinson of Smith College questions whether any change in the conduct of foreign affairs can be expected in the absence of a constitutional amendment, modifying the executive-congressional relationship.

Under the next heading, the inherent tensions that exist between the establishment and free exercise clauses in the First Amendment religion phrase are considered. Professor Jesse Choper, Dean of the University of California at Berkeley Law School, proposes a novel rule for determining which clause to sustain in any given issue that arises before the courts (Chapter 5). Dr. Nathan Lewin, prominent Washington attorney, decries the recent failure of the Supreme Court to respect and tolerate divergent religious principles and practices (Chapter 6). In his comments, Professor Slonim endorses the Choper thesis in part but questions the scope of its applicability.

The next topic under consideration is that of minority rights—both as relates to race and gender. Professor Glen Loury of Harvard University argues against the whole notion of affirmative action (Chapter 7). He maintains that it is demeaning to blacks and forestalls their proper integration into U.S. society. Dr. Frances Raday of the Hebrew University presents an original theory on the role of the adversarial process as a means of advancing minority rights under the Fourteenth Amendment (Chapter 8).

Professor Norma Basch of Rutgers University spotlights the harshly conservative role of the Supreme Court in denying women's rights in the nineteenth century (Chapter 9). Judge Ruth Bader Ginsburg of the Federal Court of Appeals analyzes recent use of the Constitution as a means to ensure equal rights for women (Chapter 10).

The newly discovered right of privacy under the Constitution is the subject matter of the next debate. Professor Wallace Mendelson of the University of Texas charges that in enunciating this right the Supreme Court has failed to establish either its constitutional origins or scope (Chapter 11). Professor Walter Murphy of Princeton University, on the other hand, seeks to delineate the constitutional bases of the right of privacy (Chapter 12). Comments by Professor Jacob Landynski of the

New School for Social Research challenge Murphy's attempt at classification.

The question of whether the Constitution at this bicentennial stage
needs amending is the next issue to be considered. Dr. James Sundquist
of the Brookings Institution argues that technical and minor amendments
such as a four-year term for Congressmen and an eight-year term for
Senators would help prevent divided government in the United States
(Chapter 13). Professor Theodore Lowi of Cornell University argues for
retaining the present arrangements but for bringing about greater political responsibility in the political parties and for opening up procedures
for the emergence of more parties in the political arena (Chapter 14). In
his comments, Professor Dan Elazar of Bar Ilan and Temple Universities
maintains that any radical changes would jeopardize the balance of relations ordered under the Constitution. Likewise, Professor Robert Goldwin of the American Enterprise Institute warns against tampering with
the present system of government.

The impact of the U.S. Constitution on Israeli jurisprudence is reviewed in the next two papers. Judge Aaron Barak of the Israeli Supreme
Court argues that Israeli courts are slowly but surely detaching themselves from British precedents and are increasingly guided by U.S. constitutional precedents (Chapter 15). Professor David Kretzmer of the
Hebrew University illustrates this point by highlighting the trend of
Americanization in Israeli judicial treatment of civil rights issues (Chapter 16).

The final group of papers deals with the possible assumption by the
United States Supreme Court of a new role—a more forthright involvement in promoting social justice. The twentieth century, it is noted, has
seen the Supreme Court adopt the Constitution as a vehicle for the
promotion of equality in the spheres of civil liberties and civil rights, at
the same time as it has denied that the Constitution bars economic
innovation by federal and state governments. With the battle for political
and civil equality nearly won will the Court now strike out to assume
a greater role in the search for social justice, and can the Constitution
be fashioned as an instrument to attain that goal? Professor Henry Abraham of the University of Virginia addresses this question by stressing
the positive role of the Court in asserting a civil-libertarian role for itself
after the Roosevelt court packing crisis of 1937 (Chapter 17). Professor
Martin Shapiro of the University of California at Berkeley argues that
the Court has already declined to become more actively involved in the
search for social justice (Chapter 18). Professor Michael Walzer of the
Institute for Advanced Study at Princeton analyzes the broader philosophical implications of the search for social justice under the Constitution (Chapter 19). He highlights the difficulty of reconciling judicial
initiatives, taken with the aim of ensuring greater liberty, with the fun-

damental concept of democracy. Professor Walzer's comments are a fitting close to the papers presented in this volume since it brings the debate, in a very real sense, full circle in the attempt to assess the impact of the Constitution and judicial interpretation of the Constitution, upon the United States' political and social development.

In conclusion, it is my pleasant task to thank all those who made it possible to stage the bicentennial conference and who contributed to the appearance of the present volume. First and foremost, I wish to acknowledge the debt owed by all of us at the Hebrew University to the doyen of American studies in Israel, Professor Yehoshua Arieli. His commitment to the project inspired the first steps toward the study presented herein. Secondly, I gladly acknowledge the help and support received from the members of the Hebrew University Bicentennial Committee—Professor Stephen Goldstein, currently Dean of the Law School, and Professors Aryeh Goren, Michla Pomerance, and David Ricci. Professor Jacob Landynski of the New School, who was at the Hebrew University during 1986–87 as a Fulbright scholar, contributed in innumerable ways to the success of our endeavors. His invaluable help is gratefully acknowledged.

No project can succeed without efficient, devoted administrative and secretarial assistance, and I am happy to express my deep appreciation to Mrs. Hana Hoffman and the staff of Te'um, together with Ms. Revital Adir, for their vital contribution at each step of the way.

I also wish to acknowledge with deep gratitude the generosity of the following organizations toward the Hebrew University bicentennial project. The United States Embassy in Israel; the United States Cultural Center in Jerusalem (whose director, Mr. Arthur Green and staff were involved in the project from the beginning); the Walter H. Annenberg Fund for American Studies at the Hebrew University (under the chairmanship of Dean Yochanan Friedman of the Faculty of Humanities); and the United States-Israel Educational Foundation (under the directorship of Mr. Dan Krauskopf).

And finally, I wish to thank Ms. Susan C. Pazourek and Ms. Mary Glenn, editors at Praeger Publishers, for their patience and assistance in the appearance of the present volume.

NOTE

1. Letter dated May 13, 1948 in *The Near East, South Asia and Africa*, Foreign Relations of the United States 1948, vol. 5, part 2 (Washington, DC: Government Printing Office, 1976), p. 983.

I THE CONSTITUTIONAL SETTING

1 The Constitution and the Rise of an Ideological Court in a Nonideological Polity

Shlomo Slonim

As the United States marks the two hundredth anniversary of the drafting of its Constitution, Israel enters upon the fortieth year of its renewed statehood. There are some parallels between the two historic events, that of 1787 and 1948. In each case there were those who predicted that the experiment would not last. In the case of Israel, of course, many did more than predict; they strove to ensure that their dire prediction would be realized.[1] But, even with regard to that document which emerged from Constitution Hall in Philadelphia after three and a half months of labor, some foresaw a dire end to the constitutional experiment. For instance, here are the words of George Mason of Virginia, a foremost architect of the Constitution, who, because of certain reservations, could not bring himself to sign the completed document:

This government will set out a moderate aristocracy: it is at present impossible to foresee whether it will in its operation, produce a monarchy, or a corrupt, tyrannical aristocracy; it will most probably vibrate some years between the two; and then terminate in the one or the other.[2]

Even a delegate like Nathaniel Gorham of New Hampshire, who signed the document, was led during the course of the debate to declare, "Can it be supposed that this vast Country including the Western territory will 150 years hence remain one nation?"[3] In both cases, that of the United States and Israel, the experiment survived and thrived.

Not only were Mason's and Gorham's predictions not realized, but the U.S. Constitution has become a focus of universal admiration mixed with puzzlement. Observers from abroad have been impressed by numerous features of the U.S. constitutional system but by none more than by the unique role which the Supreme Court has assumed. The role of the Court is remarkable precisely because it is so political. Disputes which in other systems of government would be settled within the political arena are, in the United States, ultimately resolved by a ruling of the U.S. Supreme Court.

While its decisions often confirm legislative policy, not infrequently the Court pronounces legislation—national or state—unconstitutional. And on occasion the court has forged ahead of the legislative will and the public opinion that sustains it. Decisions in such fields as busing, birth control, and abortion have stirred deep emotions among the U.S. public. The phenomenon of the Court is especially puzzling because, with all its vast power, it is a nondemocratic body. In fact, it is the only federal institution that in the Constitution's two hundred–year history has undergone no structural change toward democratization. In contrast, the process of electing a president has been significantly democratized so that now, notwithstanding the presence of the electoral college, it is a popular election in all but name. The Seventeenth Amendment ensured that senators would no longer be appointed as state legislators saw fit, but would be chosen in democratic elections. The House of Representatives was from the very beginning elected by popular vote and in a 1964 decision the Supreme Court ruled that congressional districts must be equal in population so that the most representative organ of government has been further democratized.[4] But the courts, as noted, have undergone no change. They remain as undemocratic today in their structure as they were upon adoption of the Constitution. Normally one is not concerned about the democratic character of a court, and that is the way it should be. Concern should be shown only for the independence and security of the judicial branch. But where a court engages in what is commonly regarded as a legislative function, initiating and implementing original policies, then naturally the question arises—How representative is the court in fulfilling its self-assigned legislative task?

It is puzzling too that, in general, U.S. public opinion not only accepts this political role of a nondemocratic body with equanimity but the very thought of tampering with it—as FDR attempted to do—evokes a sense of deep horror in the American public. The Supreme Court is the organ which is expected to cure the ills of the other organs of the U.S. political system, while it itself remains, overall, infallible and relatively speaking, above reproach.

The question might be asked, was such enormous power for judges intended by the Founding Fathers? Is the Court currently exercising its power of judicial review in accordance with "original intention?" In approaching this topic I realize that many have been grappling with these issues for years, and perhaps decades, and I am reminded of one of Joseph Sisco's favorite stories when addressing Israelis on the problems of the Middle East. He told of a man who miraculously survived the 1889 Johnstown, Pennsylvania flood and spent the rest of his days recounting how he did so. When his time came and he entered the gates of paradise, he was greeted by the angel Gabriel who explained to him the rules of his new abode. Every new entrant is invited to relate an outstanding event in his life. "What would you like to talk about?" he asked. "I'll tell everyone how I survived the Johnstown River flood," the man replied. "That's allright with me," said the angel Gabriel, "but just remember Noah will be in the audience!"

On the question of judicial review Charles Beard, for one, was certain that the Founding Fathers *had* intended endowing the Court with such power[5] and, for his part, Frankfurter was certain that Beard had settled the question, once and for all.[6] But from the present perspective, reliance on Beard's history and historiography is highly questionable. Beard was intent on demonstrating the economic motives of the Founding Fathers in drafting the Constitution. His work on the Court preceded by just one year his monumental study *An Economic Interpretation of the Constitution of the United States*[7] and by three years his book *Economic Origins of Jeffersonian Democracy.*[8] In fact, though this fact is little appreciated, these three studies formed a trilogy intended to demonstrate the economic character of the system of government drafted at Philadelphia in 1787.[9] Judicial review, according to Beard, was the "keystone of the whole structure" of government designed to curb popular majorities and protect property. The "sanctity and mystery of the law" was to serve "as a foil to democratic attacks."[10] The struggle over the Constitution that marked the years 1787–1788 was, according to Beard, a contest between personalty as opposed to land.[11] Beard saw in personalty the rise of the bourgeoisie to power in the United States. In accordance with his economic determinist interpretation of the Convention, which he claimed to have discovered in Madison's *Federalist* No. 10, this economic class drafted the constitution to serve its particular economic needs in an age of capitalist development. His three books formed one package of economic determinist interpretation. His 1912 book sought to prove that the founders premised the Constitution on the basis of judicial review; the 1913 study examined in more detail the whole structure of the Constitution including such principles as the separation of powers, and explained its features as economically motivated; and the 1915 work on Jefferson highlighted the division between the Federalists and anti-Federalists in inaugurating the capitalist development of a modern America.

Given the tendentious nature of Beard's evidence, one should treat his conclusions on judicial review with supreme caution. Since Beard's time the debate among historians has not abated, and researchers free of Beard's biases have reached opposite conclusions on the matter.[12] But regardless of their conclusions on original intention, and regardless, indeed, of the original intention, judicial review is here to stay and is not now open to challenge. Nevertheless, how the Court should exercise the power of judicial review remains a matter of continuing debate. Attorney General Meese's complaints are only the latest chapter in a perennial controversy over the judicial function. Neither the Meese viewpoint calling for a return to "original intention"[13] nor the thesis of Justice Brennan that "original intention" is largely irrelevant in constitutional interpretation[14] would satisfy most constitutional lawyers today. On the one hand, most would agree that it is quite unreasonable to fix a rigid, static meaning to words without the possibility of adjusting the meaning to modern circumstances. Even the framers repeatedly stressed that they were creating a constitution for generations to come.[15] No doubt they contemplated a constitution that could be adapted to satisfy the exigencies of each age by means of normal constitutional interpretation and application. But, if it is impossible to accept a call to return to original intention literally, it is no less difficult to accept the Brennan concept of an evanescent constitution that guides not by its text, but by its spirit. Was a constitution carefully formulated, provision by provision, phrase after phrase, with meticulous, even agonizing care, only to be cast to the winds as a vague, nebulous prescription for human dignity? Was it ever intended, either by the framers or the succeeding generations, that the Constitution would merely serve as a blank slate upon which judges would be free at any given time to write anything they felt the slate would bear?

Apart from the unique status of the Supreme Court, there are, as noted, other features of the U.S. political system that set the United States apart from other modern democracies. Properly understood, these features may help explain why the Supreme Court is what it is today. Unlike most parliamentary democracies the American polity has not spawned major ideological political parties, such as a labor party. Does this fact connect in any way with the role of the Court? Various writers have felt that it does. Their argument runs briefly as follows. Because of the absence of ideological parties, party discipline is weak. Therefore, any view that the Court adopts will inevitably muster sufficient support in Congress so as to allow the Court "to get away with it" so to speak.[16] I would like to go a step further and suggest that the Constitution itself creates a link between these two phenomena—namely, the absence of ideologically committed political parties subject to firm party discipline and the role of the Court as a vigorous ideological organ of government espousing new programs of public policy.

The reason for the absence of ideologically committed parties in the United States has long been a subject of debate.[17] Numerous explanations have been offered. Some writers have attributed the nonemergence of ideological parties to the United States' social tradition, others to the federal system, and yet others to the egalitarian nature of U.S. society or the absence of marked class divisions. In fact, a further critical reason, often overlooked, is the institutional one, and it derives from the very Constitution, whose bicentennial we are now celebrating.

As is well known, the Founding Fathers, in drafting the Constitution, sought to establish a system of government that would preclude the vice of factions and of factional disputes. The antifactional design of the Constitution was analyzed by Madison both at the Convention[18] and in *Federalist* No. 10. Since the new system of government would be "republican" in form, he argued, it would have "a tendency to break and control the violence of faction." Madison defined a faction as "a number of citizens whether amounting to a majority or minority of the whole, who are united and actuated by some common impulse of passion, or of interest, adverse to the rights of other citizens; or to the permanent and aggregate interests of a community."[19] Thus, the evil of faction, in Madison's eyes, arises from the a priori commitment of a group to a given ideology or political platform. Madison maintained that the members of the legislature should not be bound by the constraints which a set ideology imposes. The system of government provided for in the new constitution would, because of its republican form, attenuate the force of factions. This would be so for two reasons, Madison argued. First, representative democracy, unlike direct democracy, would "refine and enlarge the public views. . . . The medium of a chosen body of citizens" would be less likely to be swayed by "temporary or partial considerations." Second, in an extended republic a greater number and variety of groups would vie with one another and thus preclude domination by any single group or faction. The more factions competing with one another, the less probable "that a majority of the whole will have a common motive to invade the rights of others."[20]

Madison notwithstanding, there is no evidence that these features of republican government, separately or together, prevent the rise of factions or of ideological conflict. For example, Australia and Canada, despite their size and their systems of representative government, have not been spared the tensions arising from the clash of ideological political parties. The absence of ideological factions in the American polity, therefore, must rest on some other cause.

It would seem that the institution of fixed terms of office for the president and members of Congress, coupled with the division separating the executive from the legislature, foreclosed the rise of parliamentary democracy and its concomitant, party discipline, in the United States. Since no government could be toppled by an adverse vote and no congressman needed to fear a new election if he declined to toe the party line, party responsibility was effectively undermined. Absent party discipline, no ideological parties could take root in the American polity.

This situation has produced the atomization of U.S. politics. Members of the Senate or the House are spared the shackles of party in deciding which way to vote. The wishes of constituents take precedence over the policy line of the party. Congress is today that free and independent body of elitists which Madison espoused—a body voting to the merits of each issue. Every stage of a bill's passage requires the creation of a new coalition. In short, there are no a priori factions in the U.S. Congress; a new faction must be forged each time a matter comes up for a vote. A Madisonian factionless Congress is thus in operation, but not for the reasons suggested by Madison. Given the relative independence of members of Congress it can also be appreciated why they are such easy prey for pressure groups. The power of lobbyists under the U.S. system of government emerges as a natural product of the institutional arrangements.

In the absence of ideological politics in the legislature, due to the special ties that elected officials bear to their electorates, it is easier to understand the Court's emergence as an organ of government that takes initiatives that elected officials prefer to avoid. In effect, the constitutional arrangements that make for a nonideological legislature lend themselves to the emergence of an ideologically committed Court. Ideological programs that might form the political platform of political parties in other counties become the hallmark of the Supreme Court agenda.

Our analysis of *Federalist* No. 10 and of the "pluralism" arising from the extended republic which Madison believed would help safeguard minority rights, affords us now a fresh perspective on the current debate over original intention. At base, of course, the debate revolves around the purpose of the Constitution. In addition to unifying the nation and serving as a vehicle for expressing majority will, how far was the Constitution designed as an instrument to protect minorities? In short, the question of the purpose of the Constitution relates to the fundamental question of the nature of democratic government, a question that has engaged philosophers and political scientists since Aristotle: If democracy means "the rule of the people"—the majority of the people—how far must the majority go in deferring to minority rights? Furthermore who is qualified to rank as a minority? For Justice Brennan, in order to protect minority rights properly, the Court must be guided not so much by the language of the Constitution but by the needs of contemporary society in the light of such supreme values as "human dignity" and "individual autonomy."

The interpretivist school, on the other hand, claims that greater emphasis should be placed on the rights of the majority. By setting itself up as the final and absolute arbiter of claims against the majority, the Court, in this view, is exercising a power that departs from the original design of the Constitution. That design emerges from the views expressed by Madison in the Convention debates on the Council of Revision[21] and in *Federalist* No. 10. The pluralism which Madison advocated meant that a consensus must sustain public policy.[22] It did not mean that the minority, however defined, could hold the majority for ransom interminably. By highlighting the concept of the extended republic as the best guarantee of minority rights, Madison clearly did not intend conferring an absolute veto on each and every minority. Likewise, his proposal for a veto to be exercised by the judiciary in conjunction with the executive entailed only a relative veto. A two-thirds majority of Congress would be able to override the veto.[23] Thus, from this viewpoint, the Court, in arrogating to itself the function of final arbiter of the rights of the minority, has, in a sense, departed from the majoritarian principle that underlies the Constitution. Nor was this principle discarded with the adoption of the Bill of Rights. The interpretivist school does not take issue with the need for the Court to supervise and protect clearly defined rights. It is the self-appointed role of the Court to enunciate new rights, by means of substantive due process, in defiance of majority interests and values that are, in their view, contrary to the constitutional blueprint. They question the mandate of the Court to initiate policy where such policy initiatives are not rooted in the Constitution—its text, structure, or long-standing interpretation.[24]

It may be true, as the well-known adage has it, that the Court represents a continuous Constitutional Convention. Nonetheless, even the original Constitutional Convention which met in Philadelphia in 1787 merely produced a *draft* constitution—it was only after ratification by the people, in popular state conventions, that the Constitution entered into force.

In truth, the present debate is in certain key features but an extension of the earlier debate between Justice Black and his colleagues on the Court. As is well known, Justice Black was concerned that in identifying "new" rights the Court, at some future date and composed differently from the way it is today, may "redefine" old rights so as to vitiate their force.[25] Thus, even liberals celebrating the Court's capture by the non-interpretivist school might be wary lest the hitherto recognized and protected rights embodied in the constitutional text disappear one day in common with those amorphous rights emanating from the penumbra of the Constitution.

In the absence of the Constitution there is little else to hold onto. The story of Daniel Webster's last days may be instructive. When this great American lawyer was on his deathbed he was visited by a friend who said to him, "Cheer up Senator, I believe your constitution will pull you through." "Not at all," Webster replied, "My constitution was gone long ago, and I am living on my by-laws now."[26]

We in Israel may ponder the American experience. From time to time there are calls for us to take more guidance from the example of the U.S. Constitution. We should learn, some say, that a constitution can unify a nation, can provide and confirm rights for the people, and can strengthen the processes of democracy. No doubt all of these lessons can be drawn from the American experiment and we should study them carefully and appreciate their significance. At the same time it might be prudent to heed the counsel of Mr. Charles Pinckney at the Constitutional Convention:

No two people are so exactly alike in their situation or circumstances as to admit the exercise of the same government with equal benefit. . . . a system [of government] must be suited to the habits and genius of the People it is to govern, & must grow out of them.[27]

A constitution should be a truly indigenous product if it is to command the support and obedience of the people. It must express the soul of a nation. Two hundred years of U.S. constitutional history teaches us no less.

NOTES

1. On this topic see Nadav Safran, *Israel—The Embattled Ally* (Cambridge, MA: Harvard University Press, 1978), ch. 5.

2. Max Farrand, ed., *The Records of the Constitutional Convention*, 4 vols., rev. ed. (New Haven, CT, Yale University Press, 1937), vol 2, p. 640.

3. Ibid., p. 221.

4. Wesberry v. Sanders, 376 U.S. 1. (1964).

5. Charles A. Beard, *The Supreme Court and the Constitution* (New York: The Macmillan Co., 1912).

6. "One would suppose that, at least, after the publication of Beard's *The Supreme Court and the Constitution*, there would be an end to this empty controversy." Felix Franfurter, "A Note on Advisory Opinions," 37 *Harv. L. Rev.* 1002 (1924), p. 1003. Cited in 1962 Introduction by Alan F. Westin to Charles A. Beard, *The Supreme Court and the Constitution* (Englewood Cliffs, NJ: Prentice-Hall Inc., 1962), p. 1.

7. Charles A. Beard, *An Economic Interpretation of the Constitution of the United States* (New York: Macmillan Publishing Co., 1913).

8. Charles A. Beard, *The Economic Origins of Jeffersonian Democracy* (New York: Macmillan, 1915).

9. See Shlomo Slonim, "Beard's Historiography and the Constitutional Convention" *Perspectives in American History*, New Series, vol. 3, 1987, pp. 173–206.

10. Beard, *An Economic Interpretation of the Constitution*, pp. 161–62.

11. Ibid., p. 63.

12. See Westin's Introduction to Beard, *An Economic Interpretation of the Constitution*.

13. Address by Attorney General Meese to the American Bar Association (July

9, 1986). Reprinted in "The Great Debate: Interpreting our Written Constitution," the Federalist Society, 1986.

14. Address by Associate Justice William J. Brennan, (October 12, 1985) Reprinted in ibid.

15. See the remarks of James Madison at the Convention. Farrand, *Records of Convention*, Vol. 1, pp. 421–23, 430–31.

16. See the discussion in Robert A. Dahl, *Pluralist Democracy in the United States: Conflict and Consent* (Chicago: Rand McNally & Co., 1967), pp. 168–69.

17. Ibid., pp. 436–56.

18. Farrand, *Records of Convention*, Vol. 1, pp. 421–23.

19. *Federalist* No. 10.

20. Ibid.

21. See Farrand, *Records of Convention*, Vol. 1., pp. 95, 99–104; Vol. 2, pp. 74, 77.

22. See discussion of Federalist No. 10 in Dahl, *Pluralist Democracy*, chap. 2.

23. See Farrand, *Records of Convention*, Vol. 2, pp. 71–80.

24. See the debate between Judge Robert H. Bork and Professor Laurence H. Tribe, "Interpreting the Constitution," in *Humanities*. See also Henry Steel Commager, *Majority Rule and Minority Rights* (New York: Oxford University Press, 1943).

25. See the dissenting opinion of Justice Hugo Black in Griswold v. Connecticut, 381 U.S. 479.

26. Cited in Stephen J. Markman, "The Jurisprudence of Constitutional Amendments," in Joseph S. McNamara (ed.), *Still the Law of the Land? Essays on Changing Interpretations of the Constitution*. (Hillsdale, MI: Hillsdale College Press, 1987), p. 79.

27. Farrand, *Records of Convention*, Vol. 1, p. 402.

II THE HISTORICAL BACKGROUND

2 The Founding Fathers and the Constitution as a Vehicle for Change

Gordon S. Wood

Why was the U.S. Constitution created? What did the framers hope to accomplish by its formation? Did they expect the Constitution to be a vehicle for political and social change? Or did they expect it to inhibit such change? And finally did the Constitution have the immediate effects the framers intended? These are basic questions about the formation of the Constitution, and they are as alive and provocative now as they were two hundred years ago. Historians and political scientists have spent lifetimes trying to answer them.

At first glance it seems very easy to explain the formation of the Constitution. From the perspective of the last quarter of the twentieth century the Constitution and a strong national government seem inevitable. We Americans today can scarcely conceive of the United States without a huge dominating federal government that controls everything from the lunch money in our schools to the speed limit on our highways. We today take the federal Constitution and the powerful national government it created so much for granted that we often telescope the time between the Declaration of Independence and the actual writing of the Constitution a decade later. We wonder why the Americans in 1776 did not go at once to the creation of the Constitution. Why did they even bother with the Articles of Confederation? Wasn't the United States destined to be a single integrated nation with a powerful central government?

It may look that way from the vantage point of the late twentieth century, but from the vantage point of 1776, a strong central government such as the Constitution created did not look inevitable at all. At the time of the Declaration of Independence no American even contemplated the kind of strong national government that was formed a mere decade later. The American colonists had had too much despairing experience with the far-removed governmental power of the British Empire to think about erecting a strong distant government for themselves. If they had learned anything under the empire it was that the closer the government was to the people, the more local the government, the safer and less tyrannical it was likely to be. Besides, the best minds of the eighteenth century, including Montesquieu, had repeatedly told the world that a republic could exist only in a small territory. A monarchy with its centralized authority and its hierarchical social ligaments and its standing army could maintain itself over a large heterogeneous population. But a republic that depended on consent from below, from the people, needed a small homogeneous population. Too many diverse interests and a republic would fly apart. Therefore it was natural and inevitable that Americans in 1776 would create separate independent republics tied together only in a confederation or alliance. At the moment of revolution the Articles of Confederation, proposed by the Continental Congress in 1777, were about as far as most Americans were willing to go in creating a central government.

The Articles were an alliance of 13 sovereign states, a binding together of separate states in a manner not all that different from the present-day European community of nation-states. Each state had separate and equal representation in the Confederation Congress, and no changes could be made in the Articles without the agreement of every state. Although this Confederation was given some substantial powers concerning war and diplomacy, the borrowing of money, and the requisitions of troops, it lacked the crucial authority to tax and to regulate the commerce of the United States. Indeed, all final lawmaking authority remained with the individual states. Congressional resolutions were merely recommendations to be left to the states to enforce. The Confederation had no real executive or judicial authority. To remove any doubts of the decentralized nature of this Confederation, Article 2 of this first national constitution for America stated bluntly that "each State retains its sovereignty, freedom and independence, and every power jurisdiction, and right, which is not by this confederation expressly delegated to the United States, in Congress assembled." The Confederation was in fact less a national constitution than it was a treaty among independent states. It was intended to be and remained, as Article 3 declared, "a firm league of friendship" among states very jealous of their individual sovereignty.

The Confederation achieved a good deal, including the winning of the war and independence from Great Britain and the organizing of the new territories in the West. But scarcely a half-dozen years after their final ratification by all 13 states in 1781, the Articles were virtually moribund, and nearly all Americans were calling for their amendment.

The weaknesses of the Articles had become apparent early. The lack of a taxing power meant that the Confederation was unable to pay its debts. The Confederation's inability to regulate international commerce caused confusion and conflict among the states. And in foreign affairs, the United States seemed incapable of even maintaining its territorial integrity in the face of British and Spanish incursions. By 1786–1787, these weaknesses had become so glaring that nearly all Americans were prepared to amend the Articles and to add some powers to the Confederation government. This is what made most Americans remarkably accepting and casual about the calling of the Philadelphia Convention in the summer of 1787. They expected the Convention to amend the Articles. They did not expect it to do what it did however.

What the Convention did was not just amend the Articles but scrap them entirely. It did not just add a few needed powers to the Confederation, but it destroyed the Confederation completely. It created an altogether new government—one that utterly transformed the structure of central authority and greatly diminished the power of the several states. The Constitution that the Convention wrote created a national republic in its own right with a government organized as most of the states were, with a single executive, a bicameral legislature, and an independent judiciary operating directly on individuals over half a continent. It sought to displace the state constitutions as the center of public attention. It created, in fact, what a decade earlier in 1776 had seemed theoretically impossible and virtually inconceivable—a single continental-wide republic.

The radicalness of this change makes explaining the creation of the Constitution a much more difficult problem than it at first appears. The impotence of the Confederation, which could have been dealt with by amendments, is not enough to explain the Constitution. Only the most profound crisis could have forced Americans to change their minds so radically in such a short period of time.

In the end, it was not problems of taxation or commercial regulation or foreign policy in the Confederation that explain the formation of the Constitution of 1787; it was rather problems of democracy in the states. The representative state legislatures, in which the revolutionaries had placed so much faith and were to be the testing grounds for popular government, had behaved in unexpected ways. Since 1776 they had continually usurped executive and judicial functions in violation of the constitutions and had swallowed up all power. Annual elections and the very representativeness of the state legislatures had led to rapid turnovers of seats and a chaos of lawmaking. Law, as the Vermont Council of Censors said in 1786, was "altered—realtered—made better—made worse, and kept in such a fluctuating position that persons in civil commission scarce know what is law."[1] In fact, noted James Madison, who emerged in the mid-eighties as the most astute and important critic of the state legislatures, more laws were enacted by the states in the decade following independence that in the entire colonial period—all in response to the scrambling among different shifting narrow interests in the society. Everywhere, the national interest and even the states' interests were being eaten away by localism. In all the states the representatives, noted Ezra Stiles president of Yale College, were concerned with only the special interests of their electors. Whenever a bill was read in the legislature, said Stiles, "everyone instantly thinks how it will affect his constituents."[2] Appealing to the people therefore had none of the beneficial effects that good republicans had expected. A bill in Virginia having to do with court reform was "to be printed for consideration of the public," said Madison; but "instead of calling forth the sanction of the wise and virtuous," this appeal to the public, Madison feared, would only "be a signal to interested men to redouble their efforts to get into the Legislature."[3] Democracy, in other words, was no solution to the problem; it was the problem.

By the mid–1780s, many American leaders were convinced that the abuses of majority will by popular factions had become the greatest source of tyranny in America. The legislatures were passing stay laws, paper money bills, and other debtor relief legislation in violation of the property rights of creditors and other minorities. None of the revolutionary leaders in 1776 had anticipated such tyranny by popular majorities. Kings and governors were tyrannical, but the people, who loved liberty, could never tyrannize over themselves. The idea, said John Adams in 1775, was illogical: "a democratical despotism is a contradiction in terms."[4] But experience since the Revolution had taught American leaders that legislatures, however representative, however popularly elected, could indeed be tyrannical. It did not matter, wrote Jefferson, that such legislative representatives were numerous: "173 despots would surely be as oppressive as one." Nor did it matter that such representatives were "chosen by ourselves": "An elective *despotism* was not the government we fought for."[5]

This was one of those crucial moments in the history of Western political thought. There in the newly created United States, in these provincial outposts three thousand miles from the centers of civilization, the great modern division between the two kinds of liberty—public and private, positive and negative—first became apparent in the English-speaking world.[6] Liberty was not unitary and indivisible as men had thought for over two thousand years. Public or positive liberty—the right of the people to participate in their political affairs—was no guarantee after all of private or negative liberty—the right of individuals to live their lives unmolested by government. This was but one of the issues over which American and British political thought split during these momentous years.

It was not the defects of the Confederation, but what Madison called the "multiplicity," "mutability," and "injustice" of the laws of the states that lay behind the crisis of the 1780s and the creation of the Constitution in 1787.[7] To be sure, the impotence of the Confederation was important in the calling of the Philadelphia Convention, but the weaknesses of the Confederation were only embarrassing vexations requiring some pragmatic adjustments compared to the legislative abuses of the states. For such popular legislative abuses were not simple problems to be solved by patchwork or the adding of a few amendments to the Articles. They struck at the heart of what the Revolution was about. They, said Madison, "brought into question the fundamental principle of republican Government, that the majority who rule in such governments are the safest Guardians both of public good and private rights."[8] The crisis facing the Philadelphia Convention could not have been more profound: the very success of the revolutionary experiment in popular government was at stake.

Many of the 55 delegates representing 12 states who attended the Philadelphia Convention in the summer of 1787 proposed at the outset a plan for a powerful national government that would weaken if not destroy the states altogether. Then the states, in John Jay's words, would stand in relation to the central government "in the same light in which countries stand to the State of which they are parts, viz., merely as districts to facilitate the purpose of domestic order and good government."[9] At the heart of the original proposal was the power granted to the national government to veto all state legislation it disliked. The nationalists in the Convention hoped that this newly enlarged republic would inhibit or control the democratic forces that were expressing themselves so powerfully in the representative state legislatures. They hoped that this newly enlarged republic would contain so many popular interests and factions that no one of them could dominate. They hoped too that this newly elevated republic would be high and restricted enough to keep out of national office most of those parochial and narrow-minded men who were responsible for the majoritarian abuses in the state legislatures.

But the nationalists in the Convention were not seeking simply to stymie change. They expected their new national government, dominated, as Madison put it, by "men who possess the most attractive merit, and the most diffusive and established characters," would become a positive force for political and commercial change.[10] It would exist above the multiplicity of popular interests and act not only, in Madison's words, as a "disinterested umpire" among these competing interests, but also as a powerful promoter of national honor and prosperity.[11]

But there were others in the Convention who prized the states too much and were not ready to see them become mere administrative units. And although the Convention discarded the Articles of Confederation, in its deliberations and debates over three and a half months it did ultimately decide to do away with the right of the national government to veto all state legislation and to retain something of the states' individual sovereignty in the Senate. So much state sovereignty was retained, in fact, that Madison at the end of the Convention despaired for the future of the document he more than any other single figure had brought about.

And well he might have despaired, for the new national government was scarcely capable of restraining the popular energies unleashed by the Revolution. In fact, by helping to create a political and legal environment conducive to commercial expansion—by making possible a national market and the uniform regulation of trade with foreign states— it only accelerated these popular forces. Within a decade's time the efforts of the framers of the 1780s to stabilize politics and control the popular forces of enterprise and interest coming out of the Revolution were simply overwhelmed. Particularly in the north the very popular, narrow-minded, interested men that the framers had hoped to keep out of the elevated national government were winning election to Congress. By 1800 it was becoming clear that the best thing that governments, both federal and state, could do in the face of these surging popular interests was get out of the way. When governments did not get out of the way, they were simply bypassed or engulfed by the people's newly awakened aspirations to move, to make money, and to "get ahead."

In the decades following the Revolution the Americans spread themselves over half a continent at speeds that astonished everyone; and the federal government made repeated efforts to control the phenomenal sprawl of settlement westward. In order to fill up America's vast space in an orderly manner, the government priced the land high, limited the credit available, and kept the plots that could be bought large in size. But people on the move simply ignored these restrictions. They swarmed around the speculative holdings of land companies or squatted where they wanted, preempted land and refused to pay for it. And consequently over the next half century or so the national government was repeatedly forced to lower prices, expand credit, and decrease the size of plots of land that could be purchased in its desperate efforts to catch up with what people were doing. Finally at mid-century the government threw up its hands and simply gave the western land away free to anyone who would settle on it.

No constitution, no legal or political institution, could have stood in the way of these explosive popular forces. The restrictions imposed on these entrepreneurial interests by the Constitution simply did not matter. Article I, Section 10, of the Constitution prohibited the states from emitting bills of credit, but such a technical legal restraint could never have held back the burgeoning forces of popular enterprise. The people wanted money, and so they pressed their state legislatures to charter banks, hundreds of them, which in turn emitted the paper money the people wanted and needed for their commercial activities.

What all this tells us is that there is a limit to what constitutions and governmental institutions can do to change people's lives. Constitutions in the end do not make people; people make constitutions. Yet the Constitution of 1787 has endured and has managed better than most governments to do what the framers wanted it to do—reconcile majority will and the general good with the rights and liberties of individuals and minorities. The great achievement of American constitutionalism has not been simply the creation of institutions responsive to the momentary will of democratic majorities. Such institutions are often easy to create. Rather the Americans' constitutional achievement has been the creation of institutions that protect individual and minority liberties while remaining within the framework and spirit of popular government. This, wrote Madison in the *Federalist*, No. 10, was "the great desideratum" by which alone popular government could be "rescued from the opprobrium under which it has so long labored, and be recommended to the esteem and adoption of mankind."[12] This goal, this legacy, has never been lost.

NOTES

1. "Address of the Council of Censors," February 14, 1786, William Slade, ed., *Vermont State Papers* (Middlebury, VT, 1823), p. 540.

2. Stiles, quoted in Gordon S. Wood, *The Creation of the American Republic, 1776–1787* (Chapel Hill, NC: University of North Carolina Press, 1969), p. 195.

3. James Madison, "Vices of the Political System of the United States," in William T. Hutchinson, et al., eds, *The Papers of James Madison* (Chicago, Charlottesville: University of Chicago Press, 1962-), vol. IX, p. 346.

4. John Adams, "Novanglus" (1775), in Charles Francis Adams, ed., *The Works of John Adams* (Boston: Little, Brown, 1850–56), vol. IV, p. 79.

5. Thomas Jefferson, *Notes on the State of Virginia*, ed. William Peden (Chapel Hill, NC: University of North Carolina Press, 1955), p. 120.

6. On the two concepts of liberty see Isaiah Berlin, *Four Essays on Liberty* (New York: Oxford University Press, 1969).

7. Madison, "Vices," Hutchinson, et al., eds., *Papers of Madison*, vol. IX (1975), pp. 353–354.

8. Madison, quoted in Wood, *Creation of American Republic*, p. 140.

9. Jay to John Adams, May 4, 1786, in Henry P. Johnston, ed., *The Correspondence and Public Papers of John Jay* (New York: Putnam, 1890–1893), vol. III, p. 195.

10. Madison, *The Federalist*, No. 10.

11. Madison to George Washington, April 16, 1787, Hutchinson, et al., eds., *Papers of Madison*, vol. IX, p. 384.

12. Madison, *The Federalist*, No. 10.

III EXECUTIVE-LEGISLATIVE RELATIONS

3 Tension in the Twilight Zone: The President and Congress in Foreign Affairs

Louis Henkin

INTRODUCTION

For Israelis, the United States Constitution and its jurisprudence have particular significance. American ideas of liberty and individual rights have influenced Israel's Basic Law, and continue to punctuate the deliberations of the Knesset, the opinions of Israel's courts, and the pages of Israel's scholarly journals. The constitutional dispositions that shape the conduct of foreign relations by the United States are surely no less significant for Israel and for its special relationship with the United States.

The topic of the Bicentennial of the United States Constitution invites a particular emphasis: "Constitutional bases for political and social change in the United States." The constitutional allocations of political power in respect of foreign affairs affect the political process in the United States, U.S. foreign policy, and world affairs; they have effected political and social change in the United States and elsewhere.

After two hundred years, difficult constitutional issues arise from the so-called "separation of powers" and the various checks and balances between Congress and the president. Some of the divisions of authority between the two political branches that apply generally have evoked special dissatisfaction as they operate in foreign affairs. Some of the allocations of authority that relate to foreign affairs in particular have sometimes left either the president or the Congress—or both—unhappy. Above all, the constitutional blueprint has proved to be unclear and incomplete, and there is no agreed guiding principle to help make clear, or to fill the lacunae. National experience has filled some of them, but Congress and president continue to tug for more of the foreign policy blanket.

In 1954, in a famous essay on the distribution of political authority under the Constitution, Justice Jackson said: "there is a zone of twilight in which [the president] and Congress may have concurrent authority, or in which its distribution is uncertain."[1] Many aspects of the conduct of foreign affairs are in that twilight zone where the division of authority is concurrent or uncertain. Indeed, in few other respects is our constitutional system as troubled by uncertainty in principle and by conflict between Congress and the president in practice.

I shall indicate briefly what is clear about my subject under contemporary constitutional jurisprudence and what is disputed. Then I shall suggest—even more briefly—the implications of the distribution and of the uncertainties for the United States and for the world, not least for the State of Israel.

The Constitution does not use the term *foreign affairs*. It does not establish foreign and domestic categories and draw distinctions between them. Authority to conduct what we have learned to call foreign affairs is interspersed with domestic authority. Some general powers apply equally to domestic and foreign matters. Many powers that are surely foreign affairs powers are not mentioned at all.

In some respects, the constitutional blueprint for the conduct of U.S. foreign relations is clear. Congress is given the power to regulate commerce with foreign nations; to define offenses against the law of nations; to declare war; to raise an army and navy. Other powers of Congress— for example, the power to levy taxes to provide for the common defense and the general welfare, to borrow money, to create and regulate a federal bureaucracy, or to make laws necessary and proper for carrying out other powers of Congress or of the president[2]—have important applications in foreign as in domestic affairs. That no money may be drawn from the Treasury except pursuant to appropriations made by law[3] applies to money to be used for the conduct of foreign affairs as for other purposes.

It is relevant to note that the power of Congress to regulate commerce with foreign nations has been interpreted broadly.[4] In addition, Congress has an unenumerated "foreign affairs power" also interpreted broadly.[5]

For his part, the president is given power to make treaties and to appoint ambassadors, both subject to the advice and consent of the Senate. The president is authorized to receive ambassadors. He is designated commander-in-chief of the army and navy of the United States. It is the president's duty to take care that the laws be faithfully executed, laws relating to foreign as well as to domestic matters.[6]

That brief enumeration, it will be obvious, leaves much unsaid. The Constitution says nothing, surely nothing explicit and clear, about much else that has stirred controversy in our day: Does the president have the power, without congressional authorization or approval, to terminate a defense treaty with Taiwan—as President Carter did in the face of substantial congressional opposition? To send troops to Lebanon or Grenada, as President Reagan did, evoking significant congressional criticism on constitutional grounds and some citizen suits in the courts? To conclude base agreements with various countries, as several presidents have done? Is there an "executive privilege" to withhold information from Congress, or a presidential right to impound and not spend funds appropriated by Congress? Could the president—some unthinkable day—on his own authority, convert conventional war to nuclear war by "first use," retaliate against an enemy that had dropped nuclear bombs on an ally, initiate a nuclear "first strike" to preempt an anticipated attack or for other reasons of perceived national interest?

The Constitution does not provide any general principle or clear guideline for answering the questions or for supplying other "missing powers." Some have suggested that large questions of constitutional authority should be decided not by parsing particular clauses and phrases of constitutional text, but by looking to the "grand design." Resort to "grand design," I note, is usually urged by those who are not content with what the provisions of the text might be deemed to require. In any event, no theory of constitutional interpretation would warrant resort to grand design to contradict clear provisions of the text or their most plausible interpretation. Moreover, if the framers had a grand design, the only persuasive evidence of that design is in the specific clauses. The fact is that there is no clear grand design, though, we shall see, there is an executive view of grand design, and a congressional view of grand design.

Champions of Congress have sometimes suggested that since the Constitution grants legislative power to Congress and the executive power to the president, in principle Congress has the authority to "legislate" foreign policy and the president only the authority to conduct foreign relations in execution of congressional policy. The division between legislative and executive function in fact pertains generally in domestic affairs, but that principle of division is not one which the Constitution applies to foreign affairs. The president, we know, makes some foreign policy when he makes a treaty (with the consent of the Senate), or when he makes certain international agreements other than treaties on his own authority. The president makes foreign policy also in representing the United States in the international arena—by recognizing states or governments and deciding on the character of relations with them; by making or responding to international claims; by declaring the attitudes of the United States, which we call "foreign policy"—to particular countries, on particular matters, in particular contexts—attitudes many of which he can implement by actions on his own authority. Inevitably, the president makes foreign policy also by the manner in which he conducts foreign relations. Foreign policy is sometimes made also by authority which the president exercises as commander-in-chief. For their part, proponents of executive power have assumed an intention by the framers to establish a powerful president, dominant in foreign affairs. Often they have invoked Alexander Hamilton.

There was a sharp debate between Alexander Hamilton and James Madison in the eighteenth century as to President George Washington's authority to issue a proclamation of neutrality in the war between England and France. Alexander Hamilton (writing as "Pacificus") read the clause in the Constitution that "The executive power shall be vested in a President" as a grant to him of all of the executive power of the United States—which for Hamilton included all foreign affairs power—except as otherwise expressly provided.[7] James Madison ("Helvidius") reacted sharply, with Thomas Jefferson's encouragement. Power was in Congress, he wrote, except as the Constitution expressly and specifically granted modest amounts of it to the president.[8] Madison, I think, had the better of the argument from text and intent, though history, we shall see, has tilted toward Hamilton.

During the ensuing two hundred years, presidents have prominently and frequently invoked powers as commander-in-chief. In terms, "the President shall be Commander in Chief of the Army and Navy" is a designation not a grant of power (though some powers are necessarily implied in the function). Having learned the lesson of the Revolutionary War, the framers determined that there shall be a single, civilian commander-in-chief, not command by Congress or by congressional committee. The evidence is that in the contemplation of the framers the armed forces would be under the command of the president but at the disposition of Congress. Principally, the president would command the forces in wars declared by Congress. As an exception, the framers agreed to leave to "the executive the power to repel sudden attacks":[9] authorization by Congress might not be possible to obtain promptly, or at all, and could be assumed. There is no evidence that the framers contemplated any significant independent role—or authority—for the president as Commander-in Chief when there was no war.

The framers, I am persuaded, had a reasonably clear idea of the powers they were conferring upon Congress: in general, they saw Congress as the principal "policy-making" organ (our term, not theirs) in foreign as in domestic affairs, and Congress was to dominate the political process. They had a much less clear view about the Presidency. They allocated to the president particular functions but these did not add up to a comprehensive, coherent conception of the office, and of the division of authority between Congress and president, in the mind of any of the framers; surely there was no consensus about it.

Issues of power between Congress and the president in foreign affairs have not been resolved and are not soon likely to be. The courts, to which U.S. citizens look for constitutional resolution, promise little help. The Supreme Court has developed an armory of reasons for not hearing issues: a federal court will hear only a "case or controversy" (technically defined), at the behest of a petitioner with "standing" (technically defined), when the issue is "ripe," but not moot; those requirements are particularly difficult to meet in foreign affairs. In addition, the courts have declared certain issues to be political questions (not meaningfully defined) and therefore not justiciable, and foreign affairs issues have been particularly vulnerable to being declared nonjusticiable.[10]

The obvious lacunae, and the lack of an agreed general principle for filling them, have been a source of uncertainty and of competition and dispute between president and Congress from the national beginnings. Constitutional history, however, has supplied answers to some questions that constitutional principle has left unanswered. From the beginning, many powers not expressly allocated by the Constitution have flowed to the president and have made his the predominant part in the foreign policy process. Many problems called for ad hoc judgment, and for particular measures tailored to the case, of the kind that can be applied by the executive branch, not for a general policy best reflected in formal legislation or resolution by Congress. Sometimes decision was urgent, and the president was always "in session" while Congress was not. The president could act quickly and informally, often discreetly or secretly, while action by Congress would have to be public and formal, slow and sometimes unduly dramatic. In many circumstances, unless the president acted, the United States could not act at all.

Congress contributed to the steady growth of presidential power. Congress early recognized and confirmed the president's control of day-to-day foreign intercourse, and the resulting monopoly of information and experience promoted the president's claim of expertise and Congress's sense of inadequacy. A growing practice of informal consultations between the president and congressional leaders disarmed them as well as members of Congress generally, and helped confirm presidential authority to act without formal congressional participation. Often Congress later ratified or confirmed what the president had done, such as the decision in 1950 to fight in Korea. And repeatedly Congress delegated its own huge powers to the president in broad terms, so that he could later claim to act under the authority of Congress as well as his own, as in the Tonkin Gulf Resolution of 1964, which, in effect, legitimated the Vietnam War.[11]

Practice was early confirmed by doctrine. Before the turn of the eighteenth century, John Marshall, while still a member of the House of Representatives, declared that the president was the "sole organ of the nation in its external relations, and its sole representative with foreign nations."[12] That characterization was expressly approved in 1936 by the Supreme Court, which referred to the "very delicate, plenary and exclusive power of the president as the sole organ of the federal government in the field of international relations."[13]

The president's express authority to appoint and receive ambassadors, and the president's agreed role as "sole organ," have firmly established some foreign policy decisions as the exclusive responsibility of the president. It is not disputed that the president has authority to recognize or not to recognize states or governments, or to maintain or not to maintain diplomatic relations with particular countries. He can condition such relations on the settlement of claims and other disputes between the United States and the foreign state. Ambassadors appointed by the president have, from the beginning, received instruction only from the president, not from Congress, and have reported only to the president, not to Congress. That, it has been said, has made the president the eyes and ears of the United States. As the "sole organ," the president is also the voice of the United States. As commander-in-chief he is the arms of the United States.

So much is agreed. But presidents have often claimed more. Following Alexander Hamilton, presidents have asserted that when the Constitution vested "the Executive Power" in the president, it gave him control of the country's foreign relations, except as some authority is expressly denied to him, or some role for Congress (or for the Senate) is expressly provided. The president then, it has sometimes been claimed, can himself determine the foreign policy of the United States, communicate the policy as "sole organ," implement it as executive, and enforce it as commander-in-chief. Presidents have indeed often asserted authority to engage in various "foreign affairs activities," such as covert intelligence activities. Presidents have made international agreements on their sole authority, not as treaties with Senate consent. In response to events, presidents asserted authority to use the armed forces: early in his presidency, all know, Jefferson ordered the navy to defend U.S. vessels against the Barbary pirates. As their "foreign relations power" took root and grew, presidents found themselves with two hats. In limited, uncertain steps, the president as commander-in-chief began to carry out what the president as foreign affairs executive determined. In time, precedents accumulated and presidents gained confidence and claimed more authority. In several hundred instances of varying scope and significance presidents have deployed armed forces of the United States for foreign policy purposes determined by the president on his own authority.

Congress has challenged many such presidential claims of authority. Congress does not deny that the president is the sole organ of communication, but insists that it is Congress that largely decides the policies to be communicated. Congress agrees that the president can make international agreements, but insists that his authority to make agreements without the consent of the Senate or the approval of Congress is small. (In the "National Commitments Resolution" of 1969, the Senate declared that the president cannot commit the resources or the armed forces of the United States without the consent of the Senate to a treaty or authorization by act of Congress.[14]) Congress recognizes that the president is the commander-in-chief, but insists that it is Congress that decides not only whether the United States shall go to war, but also whether the arms and armies of the United States shall otherwise be deployed and, if so, where and for what purpose.

Congress has been more successful when it argued not constitutional limits on the president's initiatives, but rather the breadth of its own powers, and their supremacy. Congress has insisted that whatever the president may do on his own initiative when Congress is silent, he may not act contrary to the wishes of Congress when it expressed them by law in the exercise of Congress's broad powers over war and over commerce with foreign nations, and its power to spend for the common defense and the general welfare. Both Hamilton and Marshall, it has been stressed, made only limited claims for presidential power. Marshall asserted only that the president was the sole organ of communication with foreign nations; he did not claim for the president authority to determine the substance of what was to be communicated. Hamilton asserted power for the president to initiate foreign policy in some areas not within the expressed powers of Congress, when Congress was silent; he did not claim any authority for the president to exclude Congress, or to act contrary to direction by Congress.

These are the principal elements in what Justice Jackson has described as a "twilight zone" in which the allocation of authority between the president and Congress is uncertain. The emphasis on unresolved issues should not divert attention from the fact that large dispositions are not in dispute. Even in the twilight zone, moreover, powers may be concurrent: Either the president or Congress can act—and if their actions conflict, Congress will usually prevail. For in general, I stress, the president has claimed power to act on his own authority when Congress was silent; he has rarely asserted power to act when Congress has directed him not to, or without regard to conditions imposed by Congress on his action.

In principle, it would seem, the president's power to act inconsistently with congressional directive is limited to small areas where the president's constitutional authority is exclusive. Justice Jackson's essay from which I quoted says:

When the President takes measures incompatible with the expressed or implied will of Congress, his power is at its lowest ebb, for then he can rely only upon his own constitutional powers minus any constitutional powers of Congress over the matter.[15]

Congress cannot tell the president to recognize or not to recognize a foreign state or government; whom to appoint as ambassador; whether to negotiate or make a treaty (with Senate consent) or an executive agreement intimately related to the diplomatic function; or how to conduct a campaign even in a war authorized by Congress. For the rest, it is commonly accepted (by scholars if not always by Presidents) that even if the president may act when Congress is silent, Congress can prohibit or regulate what he does, and he may not flout congressional directives.

Those guidelines also help explain the scope and significance of Congress's power of the purse. The president cannot spend a penny unless Congress has authorized and appropriated the money. Where the president has independent constitutional authority to act, Congress is constitutionally bound to implement his actions, notably by appropriating the necessary funds. For example, Congress may not properly refuse to appropriate funds, as reasonably necessary, to pay for an embassy to a government the president has recognized. Where the president's authority to act is not exclusive but is subject to regulation by Congress, Congress may prohibit or limit the president's activity directly by legislation, or indirectly by denying him funds. Where Congress is of the view that a presidential act is outside his constitutional authority, it may challenge his action in various ways, including a refusal to appropriate funds to implement the action. Surely, the president cannot expend funds or transfer U.S. property contrary to Congressional instructions.

This, I believe, is what two hundred years have done to an eighteenth century blueprint which has never been replaced or formally amended in respects here relevant.

"The president" is now a huge bureaucracy of several million persons. Acting on the constitutional invitation to the president to recommend to the Congress "such measures as he shall judge necessary and expedient" (U.S. Constitution, Article II, section 3), much of the legislative program of Congress originates in the executive branch. But the outlines of the respective power of the two branches today are, in principle, not radically different from what they have long been. The twilight zone continues to have both uncertainty and competition but when Congress is moved to act it can generally prevail. The powers which Congress plausibly claims, it can enforce either by legislation or by withholding funds.

Consider what these constitutional divisions have meant in our day. The president determined—over significant congressional opposition—to recognize the Chinese Communist regime in Beijing and to terminate the defense treaty with the regime on Taiwan. He settled the Iran hostage crisis by executive agreement.[16] The president determines the intelligence-gathering activities of the CIA. But for much else he has not been independent of Congress. The president negotiated a North Atlantic treaty, but he had to involve the Senate intimately in that negotiation, and he could conclude the treaty only when the Senate consented, and subject to any limits and conditions the Senate imposed. Later other presidents concluded an ABM treaty, the Panama Canal treaties and a Strategic Arms Limitation treaty, but they were only ratified after Senate scrutiny and consent, and only subject to conditions which the Senate imposed. Congress exercises authority to regulate and oversee "covert activities" (for purposes other than gathering intelligence); in the Iran-contra mess, there apparently were gross violations of the law, but no one has seriously challenged the constitutionality of those laws. Some presidents have not liked congressional human rights policies, whether sanctions against South Africa on account of apartheid, or restrictions on aid to other gross violators of human rights, but no president has seriously questioned the constitutional authority of Congress to determine that policy. Congress insists on a voice in the deployment of U.S. forces where they might become involved in hostilities. The president promises financial or military aid, but he—and the recipients—are aware that Congress will determine whether that promise will be kept, within what limits, and on what terms and conditions. The president plans military policy, but only Congress can appropriate funds for research in and development of weapons, for acquiring weapons, and for the cost of deploying them. When Congress decides whether to appropriate funds for particular weapons it decides whether to acquiesce in the strategy which those weapons imply, whether a policy of deterrence, second strike, or perhaps even a preemptive first strike. Congress has not yet worked out the proper balance between its need to delegate and its desire to maintain oversight, but it is Congress that will decide.

Important matters, however, remain in the twilight zone. Members of Congress continue to question every new presidential deployment of armed forces and to assert the applicability of the War Powers Resolution; presidents continue to challenge the constitutionality of the Resolution or to circumvent it in fact. There are recurrent demands that Congress examine unexamined assumptions about the president's authority to act in unthinkable ways in unthinkable circumstances—if nuclear deterrence fails. The Senate periodically questions the president's power to conclude an international agreement without Senate consent. In the twilight zone, too, are general issues between president and Congress that have important applications in foreign affairs, notably claims of executive privilege which Congress challenges, and congressional strings attached to laws or appropriations that presidents resent and sometimes resist.

I have emphasized what the Constitution makes explicit, and adumbrated powers whose allocation as between Congress and president is uncertain, or perhaps jointly held. Students of constitutional law and politics might add that the foreign affairs issues that agitate congressional-presidential relations in the bicentennial year reflect more than the uncertainties of the twilight zone. There are issues of constitutional interpretation as to the scope of the powers that are explicitly allocated to one branch or the other. Some tensions between Congress and the president are not strictly constitutional issues but are the inevitable (and perhaps desirable) consequences of the separation of powers—frictions and inefficiencies which separation engenders, failures in the cooperation which separation demands but which is not easy to achieve.[17] Acute tensions in constitutional politics, including those reflected in the Iran-contra shame, derive not from constitutional uncertainties but from unhappiness with, even resistance to, what the Constitution prescribes. Presidents in particular, I think, often see the constitutional blueprint as being out of date for the country we have become, in the world in which we live.

In the wake of Watergate and Vietnam there were stray suggestions that we consider abandoning or radically modifying the separation of powers, and even that we replace our presidential system with some variation of the "Westminster model." But there have been no serious moves in this direction, and even less radical constitutional amendments are not likely. (And I, for my part, would not favor any that have been suggested.) Short of constitutional amendment, we can only hope to clarify and improve the interpretation of the Constitution we have. Some of the issues and tensions can be alleviated, I think, by the paying of greater attention, principally by Congress, to the use of the powers intended for the legislature by the framers.

The War Power

In the War Powers Resolution, Congress declared its view that the constitutional authority of the president to use the armed forces in "hostilities" is strictly limited: He can do so only when there is an attack on the United States or its armed forces. In addition, Congress commanded advance consultation and prompt reporting of any engagement of U.S. forces, and automatic termination after 60 (or 90) days, or at any time when Congress so directs by resolution (not subject to presidential veto).[18] Presidents have challenged the resolution in principle, have sometimes made gestures of acquiescence, and have generally disregarded it.

I think that the War Powers Resolution is sound in constitutional principle but that it demands rethinking and rewriting. The resolution does not make clear whether the regulatory provisions apply when the president is acting within his sole constitutional authority (as Congress sees it), or only when the president has exceeded his constitutional authority. The Resolution seems to require advance formal consultation with both Houses of Congress, not merely with leaders, committee chairmen, or specially designated agents of Congress. It requires such consultation "in every possible instance," but there is no indication as to what is meant by "possible."

Above all, the resolution suffers gravely from a lack of any definition of "hostilities"; yet the accuracy of Congress's statement of presidential power and the constitutionality of the regulatory provisions and their practical application may hang on how that term is defined. It is late in the day for Congress to challenge any deployment of troops whatsoever by the commander-in-chief, and in today's world any unit of U.S. armed forces anywhere may be an object of hostility and become involved in "hostilities." On the other hand, in invading Grenada, in putting the navy into the Persian Gulf, perhaps even in sending advisers to El Salvador and Honduras (to give some contemporary examples), the president has engaged in or risked war and placed himself, I think, within the purview of the war powers of Congress. If the Resolution is to survive and flourish, Congress will have to redefine its scope as well as some of its regulations, and establish institutions and procedures to make it work.

Nuclear Strategy

It seems to be commonly assumed that under the Constitution the issues of deterrence and of what to do if deterrence fails, are "executive altogether." Congress has not challenged that assumption; a few citizens have, making claims on Congress's behalf. There has been little discussion of these issues in constitutional terms either in Congress, in scholarly circles, or in the public domain.

The framers gave the powers over war and peace to Congress. It may seem hopelessly anachronistic to attempt to squeeze the issues of response to a first strike, or of the possibility of an anticipatory strike by the United States, into a constitutional framework designed for eighteenth century wars. But the original framework and its allocations of authority are all we have to work with and live by.

If we take the Constitution seriously, it is not unreasonable to conclude that the original reasons for leaving the powers of war to Congress apply, a fortiori, to nuclear exchange. Assumptions of presidential authority (other than by delegation by Congress), then, must derive from the accepted "exception," in which the framers contemplated that the president could act to "repel sudden attacks" on the United States. A first strike or a strike in response to action other than an attack on the United States (or its armed forces) is not within the authority of the president under the framers' exception, and not within Congress's statement of the president's constitutional authority in the War Powers Resolution. Moreover, the framers' acceptance of such exceptional presidential authority, I am satisfied, assumed the need to act promptly, took congressional consent for granted, and thought of presidential action as an emergency measure providing Congress the opportunity to act. But the assumption that Congress necessarily approves of a nuclear strike to defend an ally, or even for retaliation for an attack on the United States (as distinguished from "defense" of the United States), may not be obvious to all—not, say, to the Catholic bishops who reluctantly accepted deterrence but not the use of nuclear weapons if deterrence fails. In any event, that question, as an issue of principle, is not an emergency issue, but one that Congress could address in advance.

The assumption of the need for instant response, moreover, may apply to certain scenarios but not to some others. One can readily suggest situations in which there would be no need to respond instantly, and which are therefore not subject to the assumptions that might justify response by the executive without congressional authorization. In some circumstances, surely, there is both opportunity and justification for the operation of the original constitutional conception: consideration and decision by Congress. Should not Congress be exploring and planning for different contingencies, distinguishing those in which decision must be left to the president from those in which doing so contradicts the constitutional conception, and provide for congressional decision in some form wherever possible?

A constitutional issue of different dimension is raised by scenarios in which there would be no presidential finger available to press "the button." As applied in such circumstances, the authority contemplated by the framers for emergency response by the president would become authority not for presidential judgment but for virtually automatic response, and not by the president but by lower-ranking levels of civilian or military authority, unnamed, and unknown even to the president. Such dispositions raise grave constitutional issues of delegation and of presidential succession. Again, if there is to be a provision for automatic response in a particular contingency, if there are to be dispositions as to delegation, or as to presidential succession (other than those contemplated by the twenty-fifth Amendment), should they not be designed by Congress?

Congress has not explicitly made such dispositions. There is perhaps some level of involvement in strategic planning when the Senate consents to treaty arrangements such as the North Atlantic Treaty, including the institutions for strategic planning implied in NATO. When Congress approves and appropriates funds for development of particular weapons, there is some degree of congressional involvement in determining the strategies that different weapons systems might imply. Perhaps it is assumed that by providing the weapons Congress in effect approves the different strategies they make possible, and delegates to the president the authority to implement them. But there is an important—and constitutionally critical—difference between congressional authorization of weapons systems and their deployment, and decisions as to their use. It is far from obvious that the power to make war can be delegated, especially without guidelines, especially to unknown persons.

Reluctance to consider and discuss issues of nuclear strategy may be due in part to unwillingness to alarm the people, in part to a fear that public discussion of the issue might weaken deterrence, but even the question whether those consequences are inevitable has not been responsibly discussed or considered. And is it clear that Congress could not discharge its constitutional responsibility without publicity?

Have nuclear weapons effectively eliminated any meaningful role for Congress in decisions regarding nuclear strategy? If so, our celebrated Constitution is no longer relevant for our most compelling concerns.

The Spending Power

Issues of defense spending and foreign aid are essentially not differences as to what the Constitution provides, but unhappinesses with what is provided. The Constitution expressly gives Congress the power to tax and provide for the common defense and the general welfare. The president can only "recommend" to the Congress "such measures as he shall judge necessary and expedient"; the president can propose, Congress disposes (subject to presidential veto, which it can override).

Spending for the common defense, for "raising and supporting" the armed forces, allows the president's experts, military and civilian, to develop weapons and plan deployments and strategies—but Congress has to be persuaded to enact and implement them. Congress, for its part, is unhappy being a mere rubber stamp, particularly for spending huge sums requiring high taxes and competing with other societal demands. To provide itself some minimal role, Congress has had to develop its own experts and expertise. Inevitably, however, the role of Congress is often marginal, hardly what the framers contemplated. Presidents resent even that marginal restraint.

Similar, though less acute, is presidential impatience with the power of Congress to spend for the general welfare. In foreign relations, it is accepted that providing for the general welfare includes the appropriation of large sums for foreign aid. Again, presidents plan and promise, but Congress has to be persuaded, in general or in particular cases. Again, the roles are substantially reversed from what I think the framers intended.

Tensions as to the applications of the spending power are the inevitable consequences of the separation of powers, as it impinges on complex government in today's world. The tensions may even be desirable. I see no "remedy" other than more authentic consultation by improved procedures, at earlier as well as later stages.

Covert Activities

The framers recognized the need to seek intelligence information, and doubtless saw it as an aspect of maintaining diplomatic relations. They may even have understood and contemplated other "covert activities," even some kinds of "dirty tricks," but these would have been questions of policy to be determined by Congress, then to be executed by the president.

The distinction between intelligence-gathering activities and "covert actions" having other purposes is recognized by Congress, which has regulated the latter only. Presidents have been less willing to accept that distinction. As regards covert activities for purposes other than intelligence-gathering information, presidents have resisted even the requirement to inform Congress, in part from principle about executive privilege, but even more because presidents know that knowledge is power, that the need to report and inform deters and circumscribes, that requests for information are a form of congressional regulation, and that information will engender further regulation. The executive branch has acquiesced in requirements to report to Congress or congressional committees, especially if Congress provides loopholes for special circumstances. In practice, we have learned, the president has been less acquiescent when Congress regulates, as by forbidding the use of funds for certain kinds of covert activities or the sale of weapons to certain governments, such as states supporting terrorism.

From a constitutional perspective, it is difficult to make a persuasive argument that Congress cannot regulate these covert activities, whether under its power to regulate commerce with foreign nations, to deal with the issues of war and peace, to define offenses against the law of nations—or under the unarticulated "foreign affairs power" which the Supreme Court found implied for Congress in the notion of the national sovereignty of the United States.[19] In my view, the president has not made a case for "liberating" the intelligence agencies from restraints such as those Congress has imposed.

The Treaty Power

The president cannot make a treaty without Senate consent; the Senate has sometimes sold that consent dear. Increasingly—since the disasters of the Versailles treaty and other interwar agreements—the executive branch has learned to attempt to determine in advance what the Senate will buy, to consult particular Senators, to involve them in negotiations. But the Senate's perspectives on world affairs and the national interest are often different from those of the executive. The constitutional bifurcation of the treaty power is inefficient, and often frustrating to presidents and to the foreign governments we deal with. That is not an issue of the interpretation of the Constitution, but a complaint against it. More, better, earlier consultation with the Senate will surely improve the treaty-making process. I do not see an answer to these tensions in an expansion of the use of sole executive agreements.

The Senate's consent to a treaty is constitutionally necessary, and for that purpose the Senate is entitled to know what the treaty means; often it will insist on articulating explicit understandings as to what it means. When, as has recently happened in respect of the ABM treaty, the executive branch later seeks to interpret a treaty to an effect different from what it had told the Senate in seeking its consent, the executive would seem to be violating the constitutional conception.[20] Surely, such attempts by the executive invite the Senate in the future to probe ambiguities and to express understandings with nearly paranoid scrupulousness, from fear not only of what other states may make of a treaty but what a future executive branch will make of it. The president must be candid; the Senate must restrain itself.

How much social and political change is attributable to these constitutional dispositions?

In general, foreign affairs have not been a major impetus to political change. Domestic politics in the United States do not usually turn on issues of foreign affairs, and rarely on issues of competition for authority between president and Congress. In general, presidents and Congress have worked together in foreign affairs, even when the majority in Congress is not of the president's political party. The common impression that party politics "stop at the water's edge" and do not trouble U.S. foreign relations is not wholly true, and in the view of many would not be desirable. But during most of our recent history the dominant voices in the two major parties have not differed sharply in foreign policy.

Congress has more or less willingly followed the president's lead, while presidents have tried to lead where Congress would not be too reluctant to follow. Sometimes division between the two branches serves as a brake, to keep some things from happening, as when Congress refuses aid to rebels against the Nicaraguan government, or the president tries to veto sanctions against the Republic of South Africa; but these divisions have not necessarily reflected political divisions or effected significant political change. But Congress is more susceptible to the influence of constituencies, whether economic pressure groups—farmers, labor, the business community—or ethnic minorities who identify with other countries—Greece, Ireland, Israel, Italy, Poland—or with particular issues, such as human rights in South Africa or in the U.S.S.R. Particular constituencies and some particular issues have sometimes cumulated to achieve major political effect.

The distribution of foreign affairs powers, as conceived and as it has become, has left many matters in congressional control, with important political and social consequences. Trade regulation is subject to congressional control and has important significance for the U.S. economy; both labor and business follow closely such issues as protectionism or free trade. It is Congress that determines immigration and refugee policy, and thereby the changing demography of the United States. The Senate, whose consent is necessary for a treaty, exercises a veto on arms control policy—which has economic as well as political significance, or on ratification of international human rights agreements.

Students of the U.S. Constitution, particularly foreign students, have often found the so-called presidential system incomprehensible. Foreign governments have sometimes found it—and particularly the tensions in the twilight zone—unmanageable if not incredible. In the United States, it is widely thought that the system has worked with a substantial measure of success. It has not been too inefficient; it has prevented concentration of power.

The Constitution was not a perfect realization of ideals, principles and plans but a "mosaic of everyone's second choices." As a result, ours is a strange system, the strangest in the world. It was strange when it was conceived; it is stranger in the nuclear age. It blends different notions of democracy; a democracy represented to the world by the president; an internal democracy represented by Congress, closer to the people, to constituents, to individuals, to issues. It also blends respect for representation with concern for effectiveness, for different kinds of effectiveness. The president provides leadership, commands information, expertise, speed, efficiency. Congress represents the people, its wider, soberer (more cautious) long-term values and judgments. Two hundred years have given us separation of powers cum democracy or, perhaps more accurately, differentiation of function mixed for democracy. Ideally, the representatives of our different kinds of democracy work together. Good government as well as democracy demand fewer decisions by one representative alone, for war or in peace.

Constitutional development, even in foreign affairs, has responded to and has in turn shaped what the United States has become since 1787. Constitutional dispositions reflect—and shape—the identity and the character of the people of the United States, and their values, their friendships, their actions on the world stage.

NOTES

1. Youngstown Sheet & Tube Co. v. Sawyer, 343 U.S. 579, 637 (1952).
2. U.S. Constitution, Article I, section 8.
3. Id., Article I, section 9.
4. Congress has the power to regulate commerce with foreign nations and among the several states of the United States. The commerce clause has been interpreted as giving Congress power to regulate anything that is in or affects commerce—defined by John Marshall as any form of intercourse. Nothing has been held to be beyond the commerce power of Congress in more than 50 years. The breadth of that power is represented by such cases as Gibbons v. Ogden, 9 Wheat.1 (U.S. 1824); United States v. Darby, 312 U.S. 100 (1941); Wickard v. Filburn, 317 U.S. 111 (1942); Heart of Atlanta Motel v. United States, 379 U.S. 241 (1964). The cases that established the reach of the commerce power involved interstate commerce, but the power is at least as broad as it relates to foreign commerce. Compare Buttfield v. Stranahan, 192 U.S. 470 (1904); Kelly v. Washington, 302 U.S. 1 (1937); Huron Portland Cement Co. v. City of Detroit, 362 U.S. 440 (1960); also Japan Line Ltd. v. County of Los Angeles, 441 U.S. 434, 456 (1979).
5. See United States v. Curtiss-Wright Export Corp., 299 U.S. 304 (1936); Perez v. Brownell, 356 U.S. 44 (1959), *overruled on other grounds*, Afroyim v. Rusk, 387 U.S. 253 (1967).
6. U.S. Constitution, Article II, sections 2 and 3.
7. A. Hamilton, *Works*, 76, 81 (Hamilton ed. 1851).
8. J. Madison, *Writings* 138, 147–50 (Hunt ed. 1910).
9. Motion by James Madison and Elbridge Gerry. See *The Records of the Federal*

Convention of 1787, ed. Max Farrand, vol. 2. (New Haven, CT: Yale University Press, (1937), p. 318.

10. See, generally, Baker v. Carr, 369 U.S. 186 (1962).

11. See, P.L. No. 88–408, H.J. Res. 1145, 73 Stat. 384 (1964); Henkin, *Foreign Affairs and the Constitution* (Mineola, NY: Foundation Press 1972), pp. 101–102.

12. See 10 *Annals of Congress* 613 (1800) reprinted in 5 Wheat. Appendix note 1 at 26 (U.S. 1820). Marshall is quoted in Curtiss-Wright, cited in note 13.

13. United States v. Curtis-Wright Export Corp., note 5 above, at 320.

14. See 115 Cong. Rec. 17245 (1969).

15. 347 U.S. at 637.

16. The Supreme Court upheld the agreement, finding that Congress had long acquiesced in and accepted the president's authority to settle international claims by executive agreement. Dames & Moore v. Regan, 453 U.S. 654 (1981).

17. See Justice Brandeis dissenting in Myers v. United States, 272 U.S. 52, 293 (1926): "The doctrine of the separation of powers was adopted by the Convention of 1787, not to promote efficiency but to preclude the exercise of arbitrary power. The purpose was, not to avoid friction, but, by means of the inevitable friction incident to the distribution of the governmental powers among three departments, to save the people from autocracy."

18. 87 Stat. 555, P.L. 93–148, 93d. Cong. (1973), 50 U.S.C. §§1541–48 (1982). Some commentators have suggested that the use of such a congressional veto to control the president's use of armed force may be distinguishable from the "legislative veto" which the Supreme Court has invalidated. I.N.S. v. Chadha, 462 U.S. 919 (1983). But Congress has to reconsider that section of the resolution.

19. See United States v. Curtiss-Wright Export Corp., and Perez v. Brownell, note 5, supra.

20. The position of the Executive Branch changed somewhat during the course of the controversy. See, for example, *Statement and testimony of Abraham D. Sofaer, Legal Adviser, Department of State,* in *The ABM Treaty and the Constitution,* Joint Hearings before the Committee on Foreign Relations and the Committee on the Judiciary, U.S. Senate, 100th Cong., 1st sess., March-April 1987, p. 122.

4 Congressional Supervision of the Executive Branch: The Necessity for Legislative Controls

*Louis Fisher**

Advocates of a strict separation of power frequently complain that Congress oversteps the boundaries and interferes with administrative details. Vice-President George Bush (as he then was) developed this theme in an address to the Federalist Society, claiming that Congress has asserted an "increasingly influential role in the micro-management of foreign policy."[1] The same objection is raised with regard to congressional "meddling" in domestic affairs. In a veto message in 1920, President Woodrow Wilson warned that Congress and the Executive "should function within their respective spheres." Otherwise, he said, "efficient and responsible management will be impossible and progress impeded by wasteful forces of disorganization and obstruction." He acknowledged the authority of Congress to grant or deny appropriations, and to enact or refuse to enact a law, "but once an appropriation is made or a law is passed the appropriation should be administered or the law executed by the executive branch of the Government."[2]

This Wilsonian scheme is an overly rigid and impractical partitioning of powers between Congress and the executive branch, and yet two recent decisions by the Supreme Court have advocated the same compartmentalized view of government, confining Congress to legislative matters and leaving administration solely to the executive branch. In both the legislative veto case of 1983 and the Gramm-Rudman decision last year, the Court presented a highly formalistic model of the relationship between Congress and the president.

The customary role of Congress in supervising the work of executive agencies is therefore challenged from the highest quarters. My own view is that the Court is putting its weight behind a structural revamping that

*The views expressed in this chapter are those solely of the author.

is not in the interest either of Congress or the agencies. Efforts to concentrate all administrative power in the executive branch will necessarily fail because they run counter to a long tradition of spreading power and instituting checks. Such efforts contradict established patterns of executive-legislative cooperation, practical needs of government, and even previous decisions by the Supreme Court. For reasons set forth in this chapter, these two Court decisions will be largely ignored not only by Congress but also by executive agencies and lower courts.

THE CHADHA-BOWSHER DOCTRINE

In 1983 the Supreme Court ruled the legislative veto invalid in all its forms. For over 50 years Congress had relied on this instrument to control power it had delegated to executive agencies and to the president. Under this procedure, Congress granted power on the condition that it could, within a set number of days, disapprove an administrative action without having to pass another public law. Disapproval took the form of a two-house veto, a one-house veto, and even a committee veto.

The Court, in *INS* v. *Chadha* (1983), held that future congressional efforts to alter "the legal rights, duties, and relations of persons" outside the legislative branch must follow the full lawmaking process: passing a bill or joint resolution by both Houses and presenting that bill to the president for his signature or veto.[3] The Court lectured Congress that it could no longer rely on the legislative veto as "a convenient shortcut" to control executive agencies.[4] Instead, "legislation by the national Congress [must] be a step-by-step, deliberate and deliberative process."[5] According to the Court, the framers insisted that "the legislative power of the Federal Government be exercised in accord with a single, finely wrought and exhaustively considered, procedure."[6]

Anyone remotely familiar with the operations of Congress will recognize how much the Court exaggerates the rigors of the legislative process. Both houses of Congress regularly use "shortcuts" that pose no problems under *Chadha*: suspending the rules in the House of Representatives, asking for unanimous consent in the Senate, attaching legislative riders to appropriations bills, and even passing bills that have never been sent to committee. Nothing prevents Congress from using its constitutional power to adopt rules and regulations that offer the functional equivalent of the legislative veto. These techniques are covered in this chapter.

The Court implied that the legislative veto existed solely as a means by which Congress encroached upon the executive branch. The history of the legislative veto is more complicated. The record shows that executive officials wanted to make law without going to Congress. They proposed that the president or an executive official propose a certain action to Congress, wait a set number of days, and the proposal would become law just as if Congress had passed it. To obtain this extraordinary power, executive officials agreed to let Congress disapprove the proposal with a legislative veto.[7]

Clearly, both sides looked for shortcuts. Executive officials wanted to make law without obtaining the approval of both houses. Congress insisted that it control delegated power without having to pass another law. This accommodation lasted decades because it satisfied the needs of both branches. Despite the Court's ruling, some other form of accommodation must come forward because the conditions that created the legislative veto still exist: administrators want latitude and discretion; legislators want to control agency activities without passing a public law.

More interesting than the result in *Chadha* is the constitutional doctrine announced by the Court. The message is clear: once a bill is enacted into law, the only constitutional method of congressional influence or intervention is to pass another public law. Otherwise, administrators are free to carry out the law in accordance with their judgment about the statutory language and the legislative history. This degree of separation between the branches did not exist before *Chadha*. It will not exist after *Chadha*.

The 1986 Gramm-Rudman decision by the Supreme Court promotes the same mechanical model of separated powers. If anything, *Bowsher* v. *Synar* (1986) advances an even more rigid model. The Constitution, according to the Court, "does not contemplate an active role for Congress in the supervision of officers charged with the execution of the laws it enacts."[8] Of course the Constitution does not contemplate a number of things, including the president's active role in the legislative process or the president's ability to make law unilaterally by issuing executive orders and proclamations.

The Court also insisted that the "structure of the Constitution does not permit Congress to execute the laws; it follows that Congress cannot grant to an officer under its control what it does not possess."[9] Although Congress cannot execute the laws, that does not prevent it from intervening in agency affairs. For two centuries, congressional oversight of executive agencies has been a legitimate and longstanding constitutional responsibility.

Grounding itself on the legislative veto decision, the Court claimed in *Bowsher* that "once Congress makes its choice in enacting legislation, its participation ends. Congress can thereafter control the execution of its enactment only indirectly—by passing new legislation."[10] This is a caricature of Congress, offering a description of executive-legislative relations heretofore found only in the most sophomoric texts on U.S. government. The Court contradicts everything we know about the ability of Congress to control the execution of laws by means short of passing another public law: through hearings, committee investigations, actions by the General Accounting Office, informal contacts between members of Congress and agency officials, committee subpoenas, the contempt power, and nonstatutory controls. These devices will be reviewed in this chapter.

I do not disagree with the result in *Bowsher* v. *Synar*. The Gramm-Rudman law was constitutionally flawed and I testified to that effect during hearings in 1985.[11] I do not even object to using the separation of power doctrine as a kind of Platonic ideal of what we should strive for, invoking it as a standard against which to measure necessary departures.

The problem with *Bowsher* is that it encourages an ideal that has no basis in reality. For example, in seeking precedents for its ruling, the Court reached back to a passage in a 1935 decision which declared the "fundamental necessity of maintaining each of the three general departments of government entirely free from the control of coercive influence, direct or indirect, or either of the others."[12] Entirely free? Neither direct nor indirect? What happened to our system of checks and balances and the fear of concentrated power? The framers who spoke on separated powers rejected the purist formula adopted by the Court in 1935 and in the Gramm-Rudman case.

To support its wooden interpretation of the separation of power doctrine, the majority opinion in *Bowsher* v. *Synar* misrepresents the writings of James Madison and Justice Jackson. It accomplishes this by leapfrogging across the views of Jackson, Montesquieu, and Madison. Consider the following passage in *Bowsher*:

The declared purpose of separating and dividing the powers of government, of course, was to "diffus[e] power the better to secure liberty." *Youngstown Sheet & Tube Co.* v. *Sawyer*, 343 U.S. 579, 635, 72 S.Ct. 863, 870, 96 L.Ed. 1153 (1952) (Jackson, J., concurring). Justice Jackson's words echo the famous warning of Montesquieu, quoted by James Madison in The Federalist No. 47, that " 'there can be no liberty where the legislative and executive powers are united in the same person, or body of magistrates'. . . . "[13]

This is an extraordinary wrenching of thoughts out of context. Jackson's full statement in the Steel Seizure Case of 1952 demonstrates his conviction that powers must be shared, not totally separated: "While the Constitution diffused power the better to secure liberty, it also contemplates that practice will integrate the dispersed powers into a workable government. It enjoins upon its branches separateness but interdependence, autonomy but reciprocity."[14] The Court also seriously distorted Madison's position. Immediately after quoting Montesquieu's statement, Madison went on to explain that the French philosopher did not mean that "these departments ought to have no *partial agency* in, or no *control* over, the acts of each other." The meaning of Montesquieu, said Madison, "can amount to no more than this, that where the *whole* power of one department is exercised by the same hands which possess the *whole* power of another department, the fundamental principles of a free constitution are subverted."[15] Gramm-Rudman had many defects, but clearly it was never the intention of Congress to place the whole of the executive power within the legislative branch.

The framers sought an overlapping, not a separation, of powers. A partial intermixture was needed to give each branch the power to resist encroachments. A mixture of powers also made government more workable. Alexander Hamilton had little patience for critics who objected that the Constitution failed to keep the powers separate. In Federalist 66, he responded to complaints that the impeachment process combined legislative and judicial powers in the same department. He replied that the true meaning of the separation maxim was "entirely compatible with a partial intermixture." Overlapping was not only "proper, but necessary to the mutual defence of the several members of the government, against each other." A merely nominal separation, he warned in Federalist 71 and 73, was futile "if both the executive and the judiciary are so constituted as to be at the absolute devotion of the legislative." In Federalist 75 he responded to critics who challenged the treaty process because it mixed the executive with the Senate. He found this level of debate plainly annoying, dismissing it as "the trite topic of the intermixture of powers."

By the time of the Philadelphia Convention and the ratification debates, the doctrine of separated powers had given ground to allow for checks and balances. One contemporary pamphleteer called the separation doctrine, in its pure form, a "hackneyed principle" and a "trite maxim."[16] Three states—Virginia, North Carolina, and Pennsylvania—wanted to add a separation clause to the national bill of rights.[17] The proposed language read as follows: "The powers delegated by this constitution are appropriated to the departments to which they are respectively distributed: so that the legislative department shall never exercise the powers vested in the executive or judicial[,] nor the executive exercise the powers vested in the legislative or judicial, nor the judicial exercise the powers vested in the legislative or executive departments."[18] Congress rejected this proposal, as well as a substitute amendment to make the three departments "separate and distinct."[19]

METHODS OF CONGRESSIONAL OVERSIGHT

Ever since 1789, Congress has deliberately and persistently insulated certain administrative decisions from political (including presidential) control. It has also reserved to itself the tools needed to supervise executive agencies, thereby assuring that laws are executed in accordance with legislative intent. Through these techniques, Congress necessarily shares in administrative decisions. Nothing in *Chadha* or *Bowsher* will prevent Congress from continuing to exercise its oversight function.

To understand the tenacity with which Congress insists on the power to supervise and control executive actions, it is necessary to review some of the administrative history prior to 1789. Members of the Continental Congress found it impossible to exercise all the functions of government: legislative, executive, and judicial. In 1781 the Congress created single executives to carry out the laws. The secretary for Foreign Affairs and the secretary at War gained a fair amount of independence, but Congress kept tighter control on the Superintendent of Finance, even sharing in the power to appoint and remove such officials as the comptroller, the treasurer, the register, and the auditors.[20]

In 1789, when Madison strongly defended the President's prerogative to remove executive officials, he made an exception for the comptroller in the Treasury Department. He said its properties were not "purely of an Executive nature." It seemed to him that "they partake of a Judiciary quality as well as Executive; perhaps the latter obtains in the greatest degree." Because of the mixed nature of the office, "there may be strong reasons why an officer of this kind should not hold his office at the pleasure of the Executive branch of the Government."[21] Only by understanding the history of the comptroller during the Continental Congress could Madison have had such an insight.

Legislation in 1795 made the comptroller's decision on certain matters "final and conclusive."[22] This power, along with other executive and judicial duties, would later be transferred to the comptroller general in 1921 when Congress created the General Accounting Office. The dispute in *Gramm-Rudman* concerning the Comptroller General's functions in sequestering funds as part of the deficit reduction exercise thus has its roots in patterns and practices that had taken shape before 1787.

The Investigative Power

It was not until 1927 that the Supreme Court formally recognized the implied power of Congress to investigate agencies. The Court reasoned that a legislative body "cannot legislate wisely or effectively in the absence of information respecting the conditions which the legislation is intended to affect or change. . . . "[23] The Court merely blessed what Congress had been doing ever since 1789. When the House of Representatives ordered its first major investigation in 1792, regarding the disastrous expedition by Major General St. Clair, it empowered a committee "to call for such persons, papers, and records, as may be necessary to assist their inquiries." Washington's Cabinet agreed that the House was "an inquest, and therefore might institute inquiries [and] . . . might call for papers generally." The Cabinet also agreed the executive "ought to communicate such papers as the public good would permit, and ought to refuse those, the disclosure of which would injure the public." It concluded that there was not a paper "which might not be properly produced."[24] The committee examined papers furnished by the executive branch, listened to explanations from departments heads and other witnesses, and received a written statement from General St. Clair.[25]

President Andrew Jackson told Congress that if it could "point to any case where there is the slightest reason to suspect corruption or abuse of trust, no obstacle which I can remove shall be interposed to prevent the fullest scrutiny by all legal means. The offices of all the departments will be opened to you, and every proper facility furnished for this purpose."[26] The power of impeachment, said President Polk, gives to the House of Representatives "the right to investigate the conduct of all public officers under the Government. . . . the power of the House in the pursuit of this object would penetrate into the most secret recesses of the Executive Departments. It could command the attendance of any and every agent of the Government, and compel them to produce all papers, public or private, official or unofficial, and to testify on oath to all facts within their knowledge."[27]

In 1957, the Supreme Court noted that the power of Congress to conduct investigations "comprehends probes into departments of the Federal Government to expose corruption, inefficiency or waste."[28] There are occasions where congressional committees will defer their investigation so as not to interfere with the government's prosecution of a criminal case. For example, the Senate suspended its investigation of Senator Harrison A. Williams, Jr., until he was found guilty of criminal conduct in 1981.[29] On other occasions, Congress may decide to investigate agency activities even if it results in publicity that is prejudicial to a defendant and requires postponement of a trial.[30] When Congress seeks a document that it could have had in the absence of a lawsuit, the mere existence of a suit or a grand jury action is inadequate reason for the Justice Department to withhold information from Congress.[31]

In 1981, Attorney General William French Smith displayed an extraordinary misconception about the power of Congress to investigate. He said that "the interest of Congress in obtaining information for oversight purposes is, I believe, considerably weaker than its interest when specific legislative proposals are in question."[32] There is no merit to this distinction between oversight and legislation, giving the latter some superior leverage in obtaining agency documents. Such artificial distinctions could easily be circumvented by Congress simply by introducing legislation whenever it wants to perform its oversight role.

The courts have consistently held that the power to investigate is available not merely to legislate, or when a "potential" for legislation exists,[33] but even covers committee efforts to oversee executive agencies that take researchers up "blind alleys" and into nonproductive enterprises: "To be a valid legislative inquiry there need be no predictable end result."[34]

The Subpoena Power

To reinforce the power to investigate, congressional committees may issue subpoenas to compel the production of witnesses and documents. The Supreme Court has held that the issuance of a subpoena pursuant to an authorized investigation is "an indispensable ingredient of law-making." Without the power to issue subpoenas, the Court's recognition that the act of authorizing an investigation is a protected legislative activity "would be meaningless."[35]

The Contempt Power

Congress exercised its inherent power to punish for contempt in 1796 and 1812.[36] The Court upheld this power in 1821, provided that Congress exercise the least possible power adequate to the objective sought and that the punishment may not exceed the life of the legislative body (requiring imprisonment to cease with the adjournment of Congress).[37] For longer sentences, Congress may rely on the courts to determine punishment for contempt of Congress.[38]

When executive officials refuse to comply with a congressional request for information, the contempt power is an effective way to get the person's attention and cooperation. A 1975 tug of war between the branches, with Congress the eventual victor, concerned Arab boycott reports compiled by the Department of Commerce. Secretary Rogers Morton initially refused to comply with a committee subpoena, but the prospect of contempt proceedings forced him to release the material. In 1980, President Carter threatened to withhold documents concerning his oil import fee. Secretary Charles W. Duncan, Jr., with a contempt citation hanging over his head, yielded the documents to a House subcommittee.[39]

The contempt power has been used repeatedly against executive officials in the Reagan administration. Energy Secretary James B. Edwards narrowly escaped a contempt citation by agreeing to provide information on the synthetic fuels program to a House committee.[40] After Interior Secretary James Watt withheld documents from a House subcommittee in 1981, the subcommittee issued a subpoena and the House considered citing Watt for contempt. The documents were made available to Congress.[41] The effort of Congress to investigate the administration of the

"Superfund" program by the Environmental Protection Agency was thwarted when President Reagan invoked executive privilege. With bipartisan support, the House of Representatives voted EPA Administrator Ann Gorsuch in contempt. Following this confrontation, the necessary documents were supplied to Congress.[42]

Informal Contacts

Despite the Court's announcement in *Chadha* and *Bowsher* that Congress may affect the administration of a law only by passing another public law, agencies and congressional committees maintain informal clearance procedures. The General Services Administration (GSA) is required by statute to notify appropriate committees of Congress in advance of a negotiated sale of surplus government property valued in excess of $10,000. The review panels are the House Government Operations and Senate Governmental Affairs Committees. Agency regulations further provide that in the "absence of adverse comment" by a committee or subcommittee, an agency may sell the property on or after 35 days.[43] The U.S. Claims Court found "compelling similarities" between the GSA procedure and the practices prohibited by *Chadha*. It regarded the combination of congressional statute, agency regulation, and agency deference to committee objections as tantamount to a legislative veto and therefore an unconstitutional violation of the doctrine of separated powers.[44]

Congressmen Jack Brooks and Frank Horton, the chairman and ranking minority member of the House Government Operations Committee, filed an amicus curiae brief in which they argued that it was improper to characterize as a legislative veto the self-imposed agency deference to congressional sentiment. Such reasoning, they said, would render virtually every statute requiring notification an unconstitutional interference with agency decisions. Their brief also cited instances in which GSA had proceeded despite committee objections to proposed sales.

The Claims Court was reversed on appeal. The U.S. Court of Appeals for the Federal Circuit found nothing unconstitutional about the decision of agencies to defer to committee objections. The appeals court noted those committee chairmen and members of Congress "naturally develop interest and expertise in the subjects entrusted to their continuing surveillance." Executive officials have to take these committees "into account and keep them informed, respond to their inquiries, and it may be, flatter and please them when necessary." As a result, committees develop "enormous influence" over executive branch activities. The appeals court found "nothing unconstitutional about this: indeed, our separation of powers makes such informal cooperation much more necessary than it would be in a pure system of parliamentary government."[45]

Legislative Vetoes

Although *Chadha* supposedly sounded the "death knell" for the legislative veto, Congress continues to place legislative vetoes in bills and President Reagan continues to sign them into law. From the Court's decision on June 23, 1983, to the adjournment of the Ninety-ninth Congress in October 1986, an additional 102 legislative vetoes have been added to the books.

A flagrant case of noncompliance? A sign of disrespect for the Court? An alarming challenge to the time-honored belief that the Supreme Court has the last word on constitutional questions? Perhaps, but the Court painted with too broad a brush and offered a simplistic solution that is unacceptable not only to Congress but to executive agencies as well. In declaring the legislative veto unconstitutional, the Court did not eliminate the conditions that gave birth to the legislative veto. The two branches still need a way to reconcile administrative flexibility with congressional control.

Most of the new legislative vetoes require agencies to obtain the approval of the Appropriations Committees before taking certain actions. The agencies continue to comply with these committee vetoes because the arrangement gives administrators a substantial amount of discretion in moving funds around and taking other managerial actions. If the agencies refused to comply, Congress would stop granting the authority and force agencies to come to Congress and seek approval through the regular legislative process: passage by both Houses and presentment of a bill to the president. Since neither side wants that, the legislative veto survives despite the Court's ruling.

Nonstatutory Controls

If the legislative veto were ever to disappear entirely, there are any number of informal, nonstatutory substitutes that would give Congress and the agencies the functional equivalent of the legislative veto. The White House and the courts may wring their hands and shake their heads about the constitutional issue, but agencies and committees will discover new techniques of sharing power because they find that government works best that way. Rigidity and ideological warfare are in no one's interest.

Informal agency-committee agreements were solidly in place before *Chadha* and will be maintained regardless of the Court's strictures about the proper steps for lawmaking and the impropriety of congressional involvement in administration. A typical example is the reprogramming procedure, which allows agencies to shift funds within an appropriation account provided they obtain committee approval for significant actions. The arrangement is mutually beneficial to both branches. Without such an understanding and working relationship, Congress would have to appropriate with far greater itemization. With it, Congress can appropriate in lump sums and monitor major deviations through the reprogramming process. Line itemization is an unattractive solution because neither branch can forecast expenditures with sufficient precision. Flexibility is needed to adjust to new circumstances as the fiscal year unfolds.

Reprogramming is called nonstatutory because the procedures are not included in public laws. They are spelled out in committee reports, committee hearings, and correspondence between the committees and the agencies. Executive officials place these understandings in their instructions, directives, and financial management manuals, alerting agency personnel to the types of reprogrammings that may be done internally with only periodic reports to Congress and those that require prior approval by designated committees.

In 1984, President Reagan received the HUD-Independent Agencies Appropriations bill which contained a number of committee vetoes. In his signing statement, he took note of these legislative vetoes and asked Congress to stop adding provisions held to be unconstitutional by the Supreme Court. He said that the administration did not feel bound by the statutory requirements that directed agencies to seek committee approval before implementing certain actions.[46]

In response, the House Appropriations Committee reviewed an agreement it had entered into four years previously with the National Aeronautics and Space Administration (NASA). Dollar caps were set on various NASA programs, usually at the level requested in the president's budget. The agreement allowed NASA to exceed the caps with the approval of the Appropriations Committees. Because of Reagan's threat to ignore committee controls, the House Appropriations Committee said that it would repeal both the committee veto and NASA's authority to exceed the dollar caps. If NASA needed to exceed those levels in the future, it would have to do what the Court said in *Chadha*: get a public law.[47]

NASA did not want to jump the entire legislative hurdle to make these midyear adjustments. The administrator of NASA, James M. Beggs, wrote to both Appropriations Committees and suggested a nonstatutory approach. His letter reveals the pragmatic sense of give-and-take that is customary between executive agencies and congressional committees. The letter also underscores the impracticality and unreality of the doctrines announced in *Chadha* and *Bowsher*. Beggs proposed that future public laws delete the committee veto and the dollar caps. The caps would be placed in the conference report accompanying the appropriations bill. In return, NASA would agree that it would not exceed those caps "without the prior approval of the Committees."[48] What could not be done directly by statute was achieved indirectly by informal agreement.

Chadha does not affect these nonstatutory "legislative vetoes." They are not legal in effect. They are, however, in effect legal. Agencies are aware of the penalties that Congress can invoke if they decide to violate understandings with their review committees.

Internal Congressional Rules

What is now prohibited directly by *Chadha* can be accomplished indirectly through House and Senate rules. As highlighted by a dispute in the 1950s, rules governing authorizations and appropriations can serve as the functional equivalent of the legislative veto. President Eisenhower had objected to statutory provisions that required agencies to "come into agreement" with committees before implementing an administrative action. Such provisions, claimed the Justice Department, violated the principle of separated powers.[49]

Congress retaliated by changing its internal procedures so that funds could be appropriated for a project only after the authorizing committees had passed a resolution of approval. Previously the authorizing committees would have to approve a prospectus submitted by an agency. Now if they failed to approve a resolution approving the prospectus, a member of Congress could raise a point of order against appropriations for the agency project. The form had changed; the substance of the committee veto remained unscathed. The Justice Department accepted the new procedure as a valid form of action because it was directed at the internal workings of Congress (the Appropriations Committees) rather than at the executive branch.[50] By relying on the authorization-appropriation distinction, Congress retained its committee veto. Despite *Chadha*, this technique can be used to control executive activities.

Congress retains the right to place language in an appropriations bill to deny funds for agency actions. Although House and Senate rules generally prohibit the insertion of substantive language in appropriations bills, these rules are not self-enforcing. Members of both Houses frequently find it convenient to attach legislation and limitations to the most available appropriations bill. A president is unlikely to veto an appropriations bill simply because it contains an offensive rider. Thus, the practical effect is at least a two-House veto. Because of accommodations and comity between the House and the Senate, the reality in many cases is a one-House veto.

Joint Resolutions

After the Court's decision in *INS* v. *Chadha*, Congress rewrote a number of statutes by repealing one-House and two-House legislative vetoes and adopting a joint resolution to control agency activities. The joint resolution complies with *Chadha* because it meets the twin requirements of bicameralism and presentment. Like an ordinary bill, joint resolutions must pass both Houses of Congress and be presented to the president for his signature or veto.

Depending on the type of joint resolution, the practical result may be identical to the legislative veto. Before *Chadha*, the president would submit proposals to reorganize the executive branch and Congress could disapprove by a one-House veto. If one House failed to disapprove within a specific number of days, the reorganization plan became law. In response to *Chadha*, Congress amended the Reorganization Act to require that plans could not take effect unless Congress passed a joint resolution of approval within 90 days. Because the burden is on the president to obtain the support of both Houses within a limited time period, the effect is essentially a one-House veto. In fact, the new one-House veto is worse for the president than before. Under the old system, one House had to act to kill a reorganization plan. Under the 1984 statute, either House could "disapprove" simply by not acting.[51]

The authority in the 1984 law expired and no effort has been made to renew it. The Reagan administration finds the legislative hurdle of a joint resolution of approval too daunting. It may face it, however, if Congress adopts proposed changes in arms sales legislation. Before *Chadha*, Congress had to adopt a concurrent resolution of disapproval to stop an arms sale. After *Chadha*, Congress amended the law to require a joint resolution of disapproval. For example, in 1986 Congress passed a joint resolution to disapprove the sale of arms to Saudi Arabia. President Reagan vetoed the resolution and Congress was unable to override. This means that a president may enter into arms sales so long as he has the support of one-third plus one in either the House or the Senate. Partly as a result of this experience, Congress is now considering legislation that would require a joint resolution of approval for certain types of arms sales.

THE BID-PROTEST CASE

The complexities and subtleties of separation of powers are nicely captured in a 1986 case involving the power of the comptroller general of the General Accounting Office. The case illustrates how the separation doctrine is affected by all levels of government: Congress, the president, the attorney general, the director of the Office of Management and Budget, the Supreme Court, and the lower courts.

Congress passed the Competition in Contracting Act of 1984 as a way of encouraging more competition in the award of billions of dollars of contracts dispensed by executive agencies. The statute gives the comptroller general the power to stay, or delay, the award of a contract. In what is called the "bid-protest procedure," a disappointed bidder of an agency contract may submit a protest to the GAO and the comptroller general is authorized to delay the award of the contract.

When President Reagan signed the bill, he objected that the procedure unconstitutionally delegated to the comptroller general, "an officer of Congress, the power to perform duties and responsibilities that in our constitutional system may be performed only by officials of the executive branch."[52] Attorney General Smith instructed agencies not to comply with that part of the statute. The director of the Office of Management and Budget, David Stockman, issued a bulletin instructing all agencies to proceed with procurement decisions as though no stay provisions were contained in the Competition in Contracting Act.[53] Through this chain of events, President Reagan exercised the equivalent of an item veto by nullifying a portion of a statute.

The peculiar legal status of the General Accounting Office has generated cases in the past that attempted to answer whether the comptroller general is an executive or a legislative officer. Although generally considered part of the legislative branch, the comptroller general is also an "Officer of the United States" by virtue of being nominated by the president and confirmed by the Senate. The anomalous nature of this officer goes back to the establishment of GAO in 1921 and even to the creation of the comptroller's office in 1789. Court decisions have treated the Comptroller General as a hybrid officer who wears two hats, carrying out legislative functions when he audits accounts and performing executive duties when he approves payments and settles and adjusts accounts.[54]

Congressional committees held hearings to protest the Reagan administration's selective enforcement of the Competition in Contracting Act. In 1985, a federal district court upheld the bid-protest powers of the comptroller general by accepting the theory that this officer possesses both executive and legislative duties. The judge regarded the stay provision as unlike the legislative veto struck down in *Chadha*, since congressional influence in the bid-protest process "is completely excluded."[55]

Attorney General Edwin Meese III argued that there was no need to follow a decision by a district judge. Claiming that district judges do not make constitutional law, he said that the administration would await a decision by an appellate court.[56] In a second decision, the district court repudiated Meese's theory: "Such a position by the Executive Branch, I feel, flatly violates the express instruction of the Constitution that the President shall 'take care that the laws be faithfully executed.' . . . It has been one of the bedrocks of our system of government that *only* the Judiciary has the power to say what the law is."[57]

If this second ruling by the district court was insufficient to get the point across, Congress stepped in with a two-by-four. In its action on the Justice Department authorization bill, the House Judiciary Committee deleted all funds for the Office of Attorney General "unless and until he instructs all executive officials to comply fully with the provisions of the Competition in Contracting Act."[58] Here is where the abstract doctrine of separated powers receives concrete meaning: two branches ganging up on a third. At stake was $4.7 million for Meese's office and the far more important principle of how the powers of government are divided, shared, and checked.

The district court's decision was upheld in 1986 by the Third Circuit, which called the comptroller general "an independent official with duties involving both the legislative and executive branches of the United States government."[59] The fact that the comptroller general "is not under executive control does not necessarily mean that he is under legislative control."[60] Instead, GAO is a "hybrid agency."[61]

The iconoclast, Fred Rodell, once remarked that there are two things wrong with legal writing: one is the style; the other is the content. Some judges, however, have exceptional skills in turning a phrase. The decision of the Third Circuit to treat GAO as a "fourth branch" of government did not sit well with Judge Becker, who said in his concurrence that the Constitution establishes three branches of government, not four. Then came this sparkling sentence: "Even a living constitution cannot grow a new branch."[62]

Becker insisted that the comptroller general be placed in one of the three branches; the most likely spot to him was the legislative branch. He then asked what kind of power was involved in the bid-protest procedure and determined that it was executive or even quasi-judicial. Finally, asking whether it was unconstitutional for a legislative officer to carry out these executive or quasi-judicial duties, he decided that the powers exercised by the comptroller general did not threaten executive power or individual liberties.

Several months after the Third Circuit's decision, the Supreme Court handed down *Bowsher* v. *Synar* with its very strict reading of the doctrine of separation of powers. The Third Circuit reheard the bid-protest case in light of *Bowsher*. Fortunately, on the same day that the Court decided Gramm-Rudman it announced a more flexible interpretation of the separation doctrine. The second case involved the authority of the Commodity Futures Trading Commission to adjudicate certain matters. Those who brought the suit claimed that adjudication by an executive agency violated the principle of separated powers.

The Court found no merit to this claim. It refused to adopt "formalistic and unbending rules" to decide the separation of power issue.[63] Such rules, said the Supreme Court, might "unduly constrict Congress' ability to take needed and innovative action."[64] The Court weighed a number of factors "with an eye to the practical effect" that the congressional action would have on the structure and powers of government.[65]

It has been said that the Constitution is what the Supreme Court says it is, but Supreme Court decisions mean what lower courts say they mean. In the bid-protest case, the Third Circuit was able to move down the cafeteria line of Supreme Court cases and pick one it liked. The choice was ample, ranging from the simplistic model of separated powers in *Bowsher* to the more sophisticated reading in the Commodity Futures Trading Commission case. And both cases handed down on the same day!

The Third Circuit opted for the latter ruling. In doing so, it reviewed the many legitimate methods used by Congress to oversee agency activities. Congressional interference in the contract case was "entirely justified."[66] The Third Circuit correctly described the "subtle interplay between the branches which the founders hoped for and which the Constitution fosters."[67] The Competition in Contracting Act "diffuses and divides power, giving final control over procurement decisions to the executive but permitting meaningful oversight by an agent of Congress."[68] The statute therefore "encourages the branches to work together without enabling either branch to bind or compel the other. That is the way a government of divided and separated powers is supposed to work."[69]

The investigation of the Iran-contra affair only underscores what should be common knowledge: the right of Congress to intervene in agency matters when laws are violated or poorly administered. To call this "micromanagement" adds nothing to our understanding. We need to look behind such labels to see why Congress decides to intervene.

When I am asked by people from other countries whether we have a system of separated powers, and I have no time to develop a response, I prefer giving the short answer: "Not really." To say yes, I fear, would communicate wrong images of compartmentalized powers, much as Woodrow Wilson suggested in his veto message and the Court encourages in its *Chadha* and *Bowsher* decisions. Given time, I follow up my "not-really" response with a short list of powers that are truly exclusive to one branch and the much longer list of powers that are essentially shared. If someone from another country were to ask if this is a government of checks and balances, I could in good conscience give an unqualified "Yes." The notion of checks and balances better captures the sense of overlap and cooperation necessary for our system.

NOTES

1. "Bush Urges Lawmakers, Judges Not to Interfere in Foreign Policy," *Washington Post*, January 31, 1987, at A16. The speech is reprinted at 133 Cong. Rec. E493 (daily ed. February 18, 1987).

2. 19 Compilation of the Messages and Papers of the Presidents 405 (J. Richardson ed.).

3. 462 U.S. 919, 952 (1983).

4. Id. at 958.

5. Id. at 959.

6. Id. at 951.

7. Louis Fisher, Constitutional Conflicts between Congress and the President 162–173 (1985).

8. 106 S.Ct. 3181, 3187 (1986).

9. Id. at 3188.

10. Id. at 3192.

11. "The Balanced Budget and Emergency Deficit Control Act of 1985," hearing before the House Committee on Government Operations, 99th Cong., 1st Sess. 197–232 (1985).

12. Id. at 3188, quoting Humphrey's Executor v. United States, 295 U.S. 602, 629–630 (1935).

13. Id. at 3186.

14. Youngstown Co. v. Sawyer, 343 U.S. 579, 635 (1952).

15. The Federalist 338 (B. Wright ed. 1961).

16. M.J.C. Vile, Constitutionalism and the Separation of Powers 153 (1966).

17. 3 Debates in the Several State Conventions on the Adoption of the Federal Constitution 280 (J. Elliot ed.); 4 id. 116, 121; John Bach McMaster and Frederick D. Stone, eds., Pennsylvania and the Federal Constitution 475–477 (1888).

18. Edward Dumbauld, The Bill of Rights and What It Means Today 174–175, 183, 199 (1957).

19. 1 Annals of Congress 453–454 (June 8, 1789) and 789–790 (August 18, 1789); 1 Senate Journals 64, 73–74 (1820).

20. 19 Journals of the Continental Congress 290–291, 326–327, 337–338, 429, 431–433; 21 id. 949–950; 27 id. 437–438, 440–442. For greater detail, see my article "The Administrative World of *Chadha* and *Bowsher*," 47 Public Administration Review 213 (May/June 1987).

21. 1 Annals of Congress 611–612 (June 27, 1789).

22. 1 Stat. 441–442 (1795).

23. McGrain v. Daugherty, 273 U.S. 135, 175 (1927).

24. 1 Writings of Thomas Jefferson 303–305 (Mem. ed. 1903).

25. Annals of Congress, 2d Cong., 1–2 Sess. 493–494, 1113 (1792).

26. Cong. Debates, 24th Cong., 2d Sess., Vol. 17, Pt. 2, Appendix, at 202, but see entire discussion at 188–225.

27. 5 Compilation of the Messages and Papers of the Presidents 2284 (J. Richardson ed.)

28. Watkins v. United States, 354 U.S. 178, 187 (1957).

29. S. Rept. No. 187, 97th Cong., 1st Sess. 2 (1981).

30. Delaney v. United States, 199 F.2d 107, 114–115 (1st Cir. 1952). See also Hutcheson v. United States, 369 U.S. 599, 612–613, 623–625 (1962) and Sinclair v. United States, 279 U.S. 263, 295 (1929).

31. In re Hearings before the Committee on Banking and Currency of the United States Senate, 19 F.R.D. 410, 412 (N.D. Ill. 1956).

32. "Executive Privilege: Legal Opinions Regarding Claim of President Ronald Reagan in Response to a Subpoena Issued to James G. Watt, Secretary of the Interior," prepared for the use of the House Committee on Energy and Commerce, 97th Cong., 1st Sess. 3 (Committee Print, November 1981).

33. Kilbourn v. Thompson, 103 U.S. 168, 194–195 (1881); McGrain v. Daugherty, 273 U.S. at 177.

34. Eastland v. United States Servicemen's Fund, 421 U.S. 491, 509 (1975).

35. Id. at 505.

36. Fisher, Constitutional Conflicts between Congress and the President, at 186–187.

37. Anderson v. Dunn, 6 Wheat. 204 (1821).

38. 2 U.S.C. §§ 191–194 (1982); 28 U.S.C. § 1364 (1982).

39. "Contempt Proceedings Against Secretary of Commerce, Rogers C. B. Morton," hearings before the House Committee on Interstate and Foreign Commerce, 94th Cong., 1st Sess. (1975) and 121 Cong. Rec. 40768–40769 (1975); Duncan: Cong. Q. Wkly Rept., May 17, 1980, at 1352.

40. Washington Post, July 30, 1981, at A2.

41. Fisher, Constitutional Conflicts between Congress and the President, at 209–211.

42. Id. at 211–213.

43. 40 U.S.C. § 484 (e)(6) (1982); 41 C.F.R. § 101–47–304–12(f) (1982).

44. City of Alexandria v. United States, 3 Ct. Cl. 667, 675–678 (1983).

45. City of Alexandria v. United States, 737 F.2d 1022, 1026 (C.A.F.C. 1984).

46. 20 Wkly Comp. Pres. Doc. 1040 (July 18, 1984).

47. H. Rept. No. 916, 98th Cong., 2d Sess. 48 (1984).

48. Letter from NASA Administrator James M. Beggs to the House and Senate Appropriations Committees, August 9, 1984.

49. 41 Op. Att'y Gen. 230 (1955); 41 Op. Att'y Gen. 300 (1957).

50. In 1972 President Nixon stated: "Under section 7(a) of the Public Buildings Act of 1959, as it would be amended by this bill, no appropriations may be made to construct, alter, purchase, or acquire a public building, or to lease any space at an average annual rental in excess of $500,000, until the Public Works Committees have approved GSA's prospectuses for such projects. I understand that Congress regards this 'no appropriation may be made' provision as internal Congressional rulemaking which does not affect the executive branch. This Administration has acquiesced in that construction." Public Papers of the Presidents, 1972, at 687. See also Joseph P. Harris, Congressional Control of Administration 230–231 (1964).

51. 98 Stat. 3192 (1984).

52. 20 Wkly Comp. Pres. Doc. 1037 (July 18, 1984).

53. Office of Management and Budget, Bulletin No. 85–8 (December 17, 1984), at 2. See also Office of Legal Counsel, Department of Justice, Memorandum for the Attorney General, "Implementation of the Bid Protest Provisions of the Competition in Contracting Act" (October 17, 1984), at 15.

54. United States ex rel. Brookfield Const. Co., Inc. v. Stewart, 234 F.Supp. 94, 99–100 (D.D.C. 1964), aff'd, 339 F.2d 754 (D.C. Cir. 1964).

55. Ameron, Inc. v. U.S. Army Corps of Engineers, 607 F.Supp. 962, 973 (D. N.J. 1985).

56. H. Rept. No. 113, 99th Cong., 1st Sess. 12 (1985).

57. Ameron, Inc. v. U.S. Army Corps of Engineers, 610 F.Supp. 750, 755 (D. NJ 1985). Emphasis in original.

58. H. Rept. No. 113, 99th Cong., 1st Sess. 11 (1985).

59. Ameron, Inc. v. U.S. Army Corps of Engineers, 787 F.2d 875, 878 (3d Cir. 1986).

60. Id. at 885.

61. Id. at 886.

62. Id. at 892.

63. Commodity Futures Trading Com'n v. Schor, 106 S.Ct. 3245, 3258 (1986).

64. Id.

65. Id.

66. Ameron, Inc. v. U.S. Army Corps of Engineers, 809 F.2d 979, 997 (3d Cir. 1986).

67. Id. at 998.

68. Id.

69. Id.

Comments

ON THE AFTERMATHS OF THE WAR POWERS RESOLUTION AND *CHADHA*

Michla Pomerance

Both of the chapters in this section have illustrated incisively the manner in which the U.S. Constitution dictates both confrontation and cooperation between the legislative and executive branches of government. This is true in the domestic sphere and even more in the foreign relations sphere—and nowhere more than in the so-called "twilight zone."

That the relations between the two branches of government should be both confrontational and cooperational is perhaps as it should be. Both organs are engaged in the job of governing, and, as Daryl Zanuck once observed, "If two people on the same job agree *all* the time, then *one* is superfluous. If they *dis*agree all the time, then *both* are superfluous."

But in the course of getting their job done, the president and Congress seem to engage in a game with rules which are uncertain, evolving, and often baffling to the participants as well as to the spectators. The game is replete with paradoxes.

Not too long ago, the *New York Times* listed six paradoxes of the Soviet Union, as described by local wags. They were:

1. Nobody is unemployed, but nobody works.

2. Nobody works, but everybody is paid.

3. Everybody is paid, but there is nothing to buy.

4. There is nothing to buy, but nobody lacks for what he needs.

5. Nobody lacks for what he needs, but everybody complains.

6. Everybody complains, but when it comes time to vote, everybody votes yes![1]

I would like to suggest nine paradoxes of the executive-legislative game in the United States. Numerous illustrations of these paradoxes can be given (and many are given in the two papers presented in this chapter). I will briefly illustrate a few more by reference to the War

Powers Resolution, the *Chadha* (legislative veto) case, and their aftermaths.

1. When Congress wins, it sometimes loses.
2. When Congress loses and the president wins, he sometimes loses too.
3. When the dust settles, Congress and the president sometimes find that they did not *really* want what they *thought* they wanted.
4. Not only do they not always want what they thought they wanted; they sometimes find that they already *had* what they thought they wanted and were fighting to obtain.
5. It is sometimes not clear who won and who lost, and sometimes both win and both lose.
6. As the contestants fight and conquer in the twilight battle zone, they often create new twilight battle zones.
7. The rules of the game are not clear because the game is most often not refereed.
8. The rules of the game sometimes change in the middle of the game.
9. Though the game is usually played without a referee, both contestants sometimes join to outwit the referee.

With respect to several of the paradoxes, it seems that at times people's problems begin when their dreams *do* come true.

Let us take the War Powers Resolution as an example. It was long in coming, and it was passed only over President Nixon's veto. Did Congress, then, really get what it wanted and had fought so long to achieve?

It wanted, or so it said, merely to codify the constitutional scheme for congressional participation in the use of force abroad. It wanted to prevent another Vietnam. While the president deemed the act an encroachment on his constitutional prerogatives,[2] some congressional critics of the act, such as Senator Thomas Eagleton, felt that Congress had, in fact, *lost* rather than won. The act, they said, gave the president the *un*constitutional competence to commit armed forces abroad for 60 to 90 days unless *dis*approved by Congress, whereas the Constitution required *affirmative* congressional action for such a commitment.[3]

Furthermore, covert military actions were not covered. There was a paramilitary loophole which was never totally plugged.[4] Even the 1974 Hughes-Ryan amendment[5] and its subsequent 1980 revision[6] did not go the full length of requiring congressional authorization of covert activities.

In application, the War Powers Resolution seemed even less of a triumph than originally supposed. Not only had *Chadha* knocked out, to all intents and purposes, the provision allowing Congress to withdraw troops at any time, but the so-called "automatic" 60–90 day-clock proved not to be so automatic after all. To get it ticking for the multinational force in Lebanon, Congress had to adopt a further resolution setting the clock by agreement with the president.[7] And for this agreement, it conceded to the president a full 18-month period (which in the end, of course, he had no occasion to use). Thus the *implementation* of the War Powers Resolution required a further act of legislation. And if vetoed by the president, Congress would have needed to mobilize a two-thirds majority yet again. Who won then? In the Lebanon case, each side did what the United States was often advised to do in Vietnam—declare victory and pull out![8]

And how was the War Powers Resolution to be *interpreted*? When was there a requirement to consult? When did the reporting requirement begin? What is a situation where "involvement in hostilities is clearly indicated by the circumstances"? Carter's abortive attempt to rescue the hostages in Iran, the cases of Grenada, El Salvador, and many others—all demonstrated some of the difficulties. And also the difficulty of getting the difficulties judicially refereed. Inevitably, new twilight zones were created by legislation.

But was the War Powers Resolution (and was the legislative veto which it incorporated) really so necessary? Senator Frank Church, for one, had second thoughts on the matter. He wondered aloud whether the War Powers Resolution had accomplished anything at all. Swift successful actions (such as the subsequent Grenada invasion) Congress would naturally applaud. Swift unsuccessful actions might, at most, evoke congressional rebuke. And as for large and sustained actions, it seemed to him that "the argument that the War Powers Resolution forces Congress to confront the decision is an argument that overlooks the fact that Congress in any case must confront the decision, because it is Congress that must appropriate the money to make it possible for the sustained action to be sustained."[9] Congress could always have refused to appropriate money for Vietnam or legislated to bring the boys back home. As Senator Gaylord Nelson once said, it was wrong to see in the Gulf of Tonkin Resolution the key to U.S. involvement in Vietnam. "If there had never been a Tonkin Resolution . . . the same events would have occurred. Tonkin did not authorize it, Congress did."[10]

Why, then, does Congress *not* utilize its admitted powers of appropriations to stop unwanted commitments? A partial answer, at least, is that Congress is sometimes "more bark than bite," and when offered the bite, it runs the other way. President Coolidge once explained his habit of silence by saying: "I have discovered that you do not have to explain what you haven't said"; and Congress sometimes operates on the assumption that you do not have to accept responsibility for what you haven't done. And as Mr. Dooley recognized, if you are not an author, you can be a *great* critic.

Now to turn to one of the president's supposed great "triumphs"— the *Chadha* decision in which the legislative veto in all its forms was emphatically judicially vetoed.[11] Presidents had sometimes acquiesced in its use but basically, and especially as these vetoes proliferated, presidents had urged their unconstitutionality.

Did the president win? As Louis Fisher has so ably shown—not really. Congress can always adopt more onerous restrictions, as it has done with respect to reorganization and is threatening to do with regard to arms sales. By requiring a joint resolution of *approval*, Congress may substitute the functional equivalent of a "one-House" veto for the earlier, far less burdensome "two-House" veto. Thus, the president may reap a strategic defeat from the jaws of a tactical judicial victory.

But, in any case, there is no limit to the ingenuity of man—and of Congress, as Fisher has shown. Moreover, in reading his paper, I began to wonder whether Kissinger had it right after all. He once said— and as it turned out, only *half* in jest: "The illegal we do at once; the unconstitutional takes a little longer." It seems it has not been taking Congress all that long, although it must be admitted that the post-*Chadha* legislative vetoes have been committee, rather than full House vetoes.

Like the War Powers Resolution, *Chadha* too has introduced new uncertainties. But these (which include questions of severability) will more readily be judicially refereed.

There is another sense in which one may question whether *Chadha* was really so necessary for the president. While legislative vetoes began to be routinely included in much legislation, like legal boilerplate in contracts, the actual *use* of the legislative vetoes presented a different and less menacing picture. Especially in the field of foreign relations, including arms sales, it was perhaps all bark and no bite (although the threat of the bite did induce changes in some of the terms of the arms sales contracts).[12] Without the legislative veto, as Fisher has noted, new rules of the game will evolve which all of the players will have to learn to use to their own advantage.

And so the game goes on. But for many foreign states, and most notably Israel, the game is no mere spectator sport. Though far away from the geographical arena of action, Israel must learn to understand and to operate with more delicacy the rules of the game—the old, the new, and the evolving. For in the field of foreign relations, as Louis Henkin has observed, congressional-executive relations may not have so much of an impact on political and social change in the United States.

But their impact on political and social change abroad can be immediate and compelling—and nowhere more than in Israel.

NOTES

1. *New York Times*, Weekly Review, February 6, 1983.

2. See President Nixon's Veto Message of October 24, 1973, in *Public Papers of the Presidents, Richard M. Nixon*, (Washington, D.C.: Government Printing Office, 1973), pp. 893–95.

3. See the views of Senator Eagleton, as reported in the *New York Times*, November 8, 1973, p. 20.

4. See Newell L. Highsmith, "Policing Executive Adventurism: Congressional Oversight of Military and Paramilitary Operations," *Harvard Journal on Legislation* 19 (1982): 327–92. The Senate rebuffed the attempt of Senator Eagleton to get a "CIA Amendment" incorporated in the War Powers Resolution. It was feared, inter alia, that the entire resolution might thereby be defeated. Ibid., pp. 353–54.

5. 22 U.S.C. § 2422 (1976).

6. See Intelligence Authorization Act for Fiscal Year 1981, Pub. L. No. 96–450, 94 Stat. 1975 (1980) (adding "Title V—Accountability for Intelligence Activities" to the National Security Act of 1947, 50 U.S.C. § 401–405 (1980).

7. Multinational Force in Lebanon Resolution, Pub. L. No. 98–119, 97 Stat. 805 (1983), signed into law on October 12, 1983.

8. The bill represented a compromise, and upon signing, President Reagan expressed reservations regarding the constitutionality of the War Powers Resolution. *Weekly Compilation of Presidential Documents*, Vol. 19, pp. 1422–23 (October 17, 1983). From a congressional perspective, as explained in a memorandum transmitted on September 22, 1983, by former Senator Jacob K. Javits to the Senate Foreign Relations Committee, "Congress has established the proposition that it may set the clock running under the [War Powers] resolution even if the President does not trigger it. . . . The President has gained the point that for the situation in Lebanon the authority Congress gives him to continue their [the Marines'] involvement must be by joint, not concurring resolution." U.S. Congress, Senate, *War Powers Resolution: Markup*, Hearing before the Committee on Foreign Relations, 98th Cong., 1st Sess. (1983), p. 2.

9. See U.S. Congress, House of Representatives, *The War Powers Resolution: Relevant Documents, Correspondence, Reports*, Subcommittee on International Security and Scientific Affairs of the Committee on International Relations, 94th Cong., 2nd Sess. (January 1976), p. 172.

10. *Congressional Record*, Vol. 121, p. 32678 (1975).

11. 103 S. Ct. 2764 (1983). For a discussion of the effect of the *Chadha* decision on the law of U.S. foreign relations, see Michla Pomerance, "United States Foreign Relations Law After *Chadha*," *California Western International Law Journal* 15, No. 2 (Spring 1985), pp. 201–302.

12. See ibid., pp. 262–75; and see, generally, Richard F. Grimmett, *Executive-*

Legislative Consultation on U.S. Arms Sales, U.S. Congress, House of Representatives, Committee on Foreign Affairs, Committee Print (1982).

APPENDIX

The following bicentennial limericks deal, respectively, with the aftermath of *Chadha*, the aftermath of the War Powers Resolution, and the aftermath of the Iran-contra affair.

BICENTENNIAL LIMERICKS © MICHLA POMERANCE

I.

When over the legislative veto the Court no longer glossed,
Two hundred provisions out the window it tossed.
Congress said: "We're in quite a fix!
But we have our *own* bag of tricks.
And the President will wish Chadha had *lost*!"

"We shall pester him over arms sales.
Riders we'll attach in bales.
And if *that's* not enough,
There's investigation stuff
Which can always tip the scales."

"So even if gone is our veto
In no way have we said *finito*.
We'll appropriate more sparingly
And delegate more caringly
And not be a Congress of 'me too'!"

II.

When in getting a War Powers Act Congress succeeded,
And *still* its advice went so largely unheeded,
Some said: "We were wrong
When we thought all along
That it was legislation we needed."

"True, in Vietnam we had sunken
And we blamed it on the Gulf of Tonkin.
But we should have known
That in the 'twilight zone'
It was the wrong horn we were honkin'."

"It was not a matter of powers.
We might have *saved* precious hours.
Had we closed the purse
We'd have ended the curse.
But we did not—for we were such cowards!"

III.

On the other end of Pennsylvania,
They thought: "It's only a passing mania.
Why we are not Caesars,
We're only poor geezers
Trying to use our best crania!"

"And why rant against Presidents imperial
And move on to matters ethereal
When recent events
Give so much of a sense
That the emperor's clothes have less material?"

FOREIGN RELATIONS AND THE RULE OF LAW: THE CASE FOR CONSTITUTIONAL REVISION

Donald L. Robinson

The United States' coming of age as a world power has revealed an ominous weakness in our constitutional structure. The framers insisted that officers of government must be directed by the law equally in domestic and foreign governance. Experience, however, has revealed that the power of government operates quite differently in these two arenas.

In domestic governance, a president administers and enforces laws made by a representative assembly and interpreted by judges. If people in the United States feel that the president is acting in an unlawful manner, the press instantly takes notice of the complaint, citizens go to court, and senators and representatives in Congress spring into action. The president is called to account and can defend himself only by persuading his critics that he is acting lawfully.

The constitutional system exercises far less control over a president's governance in foreign policy. Foreign nations that feel a president's power do not elect representatives in the U.S. government, and U.S. journalists may not be present when the action takes place. It took 15 months, for example, before U.S. citizens found out that their government was trying to exchange arms for hostages in Iran.

The U.S. constitutional tradition is rooted in a philosophical tradition. Influential theorists in that tradition, particularly Locke, Montesquieu, and Blackstone, make a clear distinction between the work of an executive in domestic governance and his actions toward other nations. Locke, for example, in chapter 12 of his *Second Treatise*, distinguishes three basic powers of government: not executive, legislative and judicial, but executive, legislative, and *federative*. The federative power, he writes, is the "power of war and peace, leagues and alliances, and all the transactions with all persons and communities without the commonwealth. . . . " Locke notes that this power is "almost always united in the hands of the executive," but that "it is much less capable to be directed by antecedent, standing, positive laws than the executive." In other words, in foreign policy, the executive necessarily employs prerogative, to use another of Locke's terms. Prerogative is the power to govern in the absence of law and sometimes even against it.

The framers of the U.S. Constitution rejected this tradition. The importance of this fact cannot be exaggerated. The rule of law, said the lawyers who framed our Constitution, must control everything a president does. Most of them were familiar with Locke's teaching—and Blackstone's and Montesquieu's to the same effect—so we must assume that, on this point, they were determined to be naive. The president's principal responsibility, they insisted, was to *"take care* that the laws be *faithfully* executed." It is almost as if the framers were wagging their fingers at the presidents and saying, "You shall not think that you have prerogative, as the tradition has taught. You are bound to execute the laws, even in foreign affairs—yes, especially in foreign affairs."

Nevertheless, from the very beginning of our national existence, presidents have in practice followed the philosophical tradition and moved beyond the Constitution. Abraham Sofaer's excellent book on the early precedents in foreign relations amply illustrates this point. So does Arthur Schlesinger's *Imperial Presidency*. Thomas Jefferson in the purchase of Louisiana, James K. Polk in provoking war with Mexico by stationing troops in a contested zone—in these cases and in so many others, presidents were not executing any laws. They were using their powers under the Constitution—and indeed, in some cases, those not in the Constitution at all, as in Jefferson's purchase of Louisiana—to do what the national interest required, as they saw it.

Abraham Lincoln was terribly concerned about this "war power" of presidents. His response to Polk's action in the Mexican war came in a letter to his law partner back in Illinois. The power of kings to take their people to war was "the most oppressive of all Kingly oppressions," Lincoln wrote. The framers gave Congress the power to initiate military conflict so that "no one man should hold the power to take this nation to war."

In our own time, it has become routine for one person to take the

United States to war. In Libya and Grenada, in Korea and Vietnam, one person, aided by those who serve at his pleasure, has made the decisions that took us to war.

In foreign relations, the actions of presidents are not directed by the rule of law. Nor do the checks and balances work, in most cases, until after commitments have been made. The War Powers Resolution of 1973 is not the answer to the problem, either. As an attempt to bring the foreign policy power under the rule of law, it has manifestly failed.

These deficiencies of our constitutional system were masked for the first 150 years by two facts: our isolation geographically and the lack of a standing army between wars. After World War II, these two facts suddenly changed. We entered into mutual defense treaties ("entangling alliances") with over 40 nations around the world, which oblige us to respond to attacks on foreign countries as if they were attacks on our own territory. (How do we respond to attacks on our own territory? The commander-in-chief rallies our military forces to immediate action.) And we mobilized a permanent standing army of awesome capability.

These changes have greatly altered the constitutional powers of the person who serves as commander-in-chief. He now has authority and capability to act in foreign relations that presidents did not have before the middle of the twentieth century.

In these new circumstances, if we are to preserve constitutional democracy, we must revise our constitutional system. One way to meet the problem, as James Sundquist has suggested, would be to build dissolution and special elections into our Constitution as an incentive to hold presidential power politically accountable. Another way, as Theodore Lowi has argued, would be to repeal Article I, Section 6 of the Constitution so as to permit members of Congress to serve in the president's cabinet. Those changes and others would help to meet the essential need: to broaden the political foundations of the executive power, which the Constitution vests in a single individual.

IV THE ESTABLISHMENT AND FREE EXERCISE CLAUSES: RESOLVING THE INHERENT TENSION

5 The Religion Clauses of the First Amendment: Reconciling the Conflict*

Jesse H. Choper

The religion clauses of the First Amendment, having been held fully applicable to the states[1] as well as to the national government, forbid government from enacting laws "respecting an establishment of religion, or prohibiting the free exercise thereof."[2] In this chapter, I wish to confront the ineluctable tension that exists between the two provisions—a conflict that the Court has conceded in observing that the religion clauses "are cast in absolute terms, and either. . . . , if expanded to a logical extreme, would tend to clash with the other."[3]

In the main, the Court has tended to view the religion clauses as embodying two independent mandates. Consequently, it has developed separate tests for determining whether government action violates either provision. As for the establishment clause, the three-prong test that has evolved is that, in order to pass constitutional muster, government action (1) must have a secular, rather than a religious, purpose, (2) may not have the principal or primary effect of advancing or inhibiting religion, and (3) may not involve "excessive entanglement" between government and religion.[4]

As for the free exercise clause, the Court has made clear that if the purpose of a law "is to impede the observance of one or all religions or is to discriminate invidiously between religions, that law is constitu-

*Parts of the material contained in this paper have been published either in Choper, The Religion Clauses of the First Amendment: Reconciling the Conflict, 41 U. Pitt. L. Rev. 673 (1980) or Choper, Church, State and the Supreme Court: Current Controversy, 29 Ariz. L. Rev. 551 (1987). Copyright (c) 1987 by the Arizona Board of Regents. Reprinted by permission.

tionally invalid."[5] It is equally plain that a law that attempts to regulate religious beliefs is unqualifiedly forbidden.[6] Very few laws, however, single out religion for adverse treatment,[7] deliberately prejudice persons because of their particular religious scruples, or penalize religious beliefs.[8] Rather, most issues under the free exercise clause arise when a general government regulation, undertaken for genuinely secular purposes, either penalizes (or otherwise burdens) conduct that is dictated by some religious belief or specifically requires (or otherwise encourages) conduct that is forbidden by some religious belief. The Court has recognized that while "[the freedom to believe] is absolute . . . , in the nature of things, the . . . [freedom to act] cannot be."[9] In this context, the Court has employed "a balancing process"[10] and ruled that if a government regulation of general applicability burdens the exercise of religion then, in the absence of a state interest "of the highest order,"[11] government must accommodate the religious interest by granting it an exemption from the general rule.

Thus, the seemingly irreconcilable conflict: on the one hand the Court has said that the establishment clause forbids government action the purpose of which is to aid religion, but on the other hand the Court has held that the free exercise clause may require government action to accommodate religion. Unfortunately, the Court's separate tests for the religion clauses have provided virtually no guidance for determining when an accommodation for religion, seemingly required under the free exercise clause, constitutes impermissible aid to religion under the establishment clause.[12] Nor has the Court adequately explained why aid to religion, seemingly violative of the establishment clause, is not actually required by the free exercise clause.[13]

More than 20 years ago, I proposed an interpretation of the establishment clause for testing the validity of religious practices in the public schools.[14] The interpretation was that such activities should be held unconstitutional if (1) they were solely religious, that is, if their "primary" purpose was religious even if "derivative" secular benefits might flow from their promotion of religion,[15] and if (2) they were likely to compromise or influence students' religious beliefs. Under this test, students' religious beliefs are "compromised" if they do something that is forbidden by their religion; their religious beliefs are "influenced" if they engage in religious activities that, although not contrary to their religion, they would not otherwise undertake.

Several years later, I proposed a rule for testing the validity of government financial aid to religious institutions, particularly parochial schools.[16] It reasoned that government expenditures for "solely religious" purposes—as ordinarily evidenced by their "primary" effect even if "derivative" public goals were advanced[17]—result in coercing taxpayers to support religion and thereby infringe religious liberty. My approach concluded that government assistance to parochial schools should not be held violative of the establishment clause so long as it did not exceed the value of the secular educational services provided by the schools because, in such case, the primary purpose and effect was nonreligious.

Taken together, both proposals encompass a single principle: *The establishment clause should forbid only government action whose purpose is solely religious and that is likely to impair religious freedom by coercing, compromising, or influencing religious beliefs.* My main goal in this chapter is to suggest why I believe this principle should also be used to resolve the conflict between the establishment and free exercise clauses.

It is both appropriate and useful to begin all constitutional interpretation by consulting the historical intent of the framers. Indeed, perhaps "[n]o provision of the Constitution is more closely tied to or given content by its generating history than the religious clause of the First Amendment."[18] But, as is so often true, "[a] too literal quest for the advice of the Founding Fathers [may be] futile and misdirected,"[19] because there is no clear record as to the framers' intent, and such history as there is reflects several varying purposes.[20]

For example, a number of states retained established churches until long after the Revolution.[21] There is some evidence that an original purpose of the establishment clause was to immunize these state-sponsored churches from the authority of the newly ordained national government.[22] After application of the establishment clause to the states through the Fourteenth Amendment,[23] the fulfillment of this original purpose becomes painfully complicated. Thus, dogmatic insistence on implementing the framers' precise intent, if such is discernible, might jeopardize values that we now perceive as unconditionally protected by the establishment clause. Perhaps because our nation has become far more religiously heterogeneous, "practices which may have been objectionable to no one in the time of Jefferson and Madison may today be highly offensive to . . . the deeply devout and the nonbelievers alike."[24]

Moreover, even if the framers' intent were unanimous, unambiguous, and totally in accord with contemporary values, it could provide no ready answers for the resolution of many of today's church-state problems. For example, since public education was virtually nonexistent until long after the Revolution,[25] the framers could have no specific position on the subject of religious activities in the public schools—one of the most frequently litigated and emotionally charged modern establishment clause questions. Nor did the framers foresee the development of such social and regulatory programs as unemployment insurance,[26] antidiscrimination laws,[27] or the National Labor Relations Act,[28] all of which have generated thorny church-state issues.

Nonetheless, history does "divulge a broad philosophy of church-state relations."[29] One tenet that emerges most clearly is that a central purpose of the establishment clause (as well as of the free exercise clause) was to protect religious liberty—to prohibit the coercion of religious practice or conscience,[30] a goal that remains paramount today.[31] "Cruel persecutions," observed the Court in its first major establishment clause decision, "were the inevitable result of government established religions."[32] As Justice Brennan concluded in his influential examination of the religion clauses, "[the establishment and free exercise clauses], although distinct in their objectives and their applicability, emerged together from a common panorama of history. The inclusion of both restraints . . . show unmistakably that the Framers of the First Amendment were not content to rest the protection of religious liberty exclusively upon either clause."[33]

The practice perceived by the framers as perhaps the most serious infringement of religious liberty sought to be corrected by the establishment clause was forcing the people to support religion by the use of compulsory taxes for purely sectarian purposes.[34] Thus, Madison abhorred obliging "a citizen to contribute three pence only of his property"[35] for nonsecular ends; Jefferson insisted that "to compel a man to furnish contributions of money for the propagation of opinions which he disbelieves, is sinful and tyrannical;"[36] and the Court has repeatedly expressed this basic ideal by confirming that the establishment clause means at least that "[n]o tax in any amount, large or small, can be levied to support any religious activities or institutions, whatever they may be called, or whatever form they may adopt to teach or practice religion."[37] While public subsidy of religion may not directly influence people's beliefs or practices, it plainly coerces taxpayers either to contribute indirectly to their own religions, or, worse, to support sectarian doctrines and causes that are antithetical to their own convictions. As a matter of both historical design and present constitutional policy, the establishment clause forbids so basic an infringement of religious liberty.

I believe that the major weakness in the Court's approach, one both of logic and policy, lies in the first prong of its test, the proviso that if government action has a religious purpose, that alone makes it unconstitutional. First, as a matter of policy, this principle casts substantial doubt on many deeply engrained practices in U.S. society. For example, our national motto is "In God We Trust." It appears on all coins and currency and in a number of other places. It seems to me that no one can seriously argue that our national motto has anything but a religious purpose. Yet, under the Supreme Court's doctrine that a religious purpose alone produces a violation of the establishment clause, "In God We Trust," our national motto, is unconstitutional.

Since the days of President Washington, U.S. presidents have proclaimed a national day of thanksgiving. It has been quite clear that the thanksgiving urged is to the deity. Again, no one can seriously argue that the purpose is other than religious. But, under the Supreme Court's doctrine that a religious purpose alone produces a violation of the establishment clause, this practice is also unconstitutional.

How does the Court reconcile this tension between its doctrine and these deeply engrained national practices? As I will illustrate, when the Supreme Court's doctrine conflicts with one of these deeply engrained practices that the Court feels uncomfortable about striking down as being violative of the establishment clause, the Court simply ignores its own doctrine and upholds the practice.

There have been two important Supreme Court cases on this point in the last four years. In 1983, in *Marsh* v. *Chambers*,[38] Nebraska paid a chaplain $320 for each month that the legislature was in session to open each legislative day with a prayer. The Court held that this was not a violation of the establishment clause, quite frankly acknowledging that it was ignoring its own doctrine. If it had relied on its three-part test, it would have held the practice unconstitutional. After all, what purpose but a religious one is there in having a clergyman open each legislative session with a prayer? In approving this practice, the Court instead relied on history, on longstanding tradition in this country at both the federal and state levels, and on the specific intent of the framers.[39]

How do I think this problem ought to be resolved? First, as indicated, I think that it is plain that Nebraska's practice had a religious purpose. Second, since there was a meaningful expenditure of tax-raised funds for religious purposes ($320 a month), that poses a danger to religious liberty. Thus, I would have found a violation of the establishment clause.

A year later, in *Lynch* v. *Donnelly*,[40] the city of Pawtucket, Rhode Island had erected a large Christmas display each holiday season in a privately owned park. This display included a Santa Clause house, reindeer, a Christmas tree, and carolers, as well as a nativity scene depicting the birth of Christ. The total cost of the creche, paid for 10 years earlier, was about $1365. It currently cost the city $20 each year to erect the creche and to take it down. There was no maintenance cost involved at all. The inclusion of the nativity scene in this otherwise overall secularly oriented Christmas display was challenged as being unconstitutional. The Court again found no violation of the establishment clause, reasoning that the purpose was not exclusively religious.[41]

How would I resolve the question? Although I would conclude that inclusion of the creche was for a religious purpose, I would not find a violation of the establishment clause because I am not persuaded that there was any meaningful danger to religious liberty. No one was forced to do anything, and to the extent that there were any tax funds presently used, it seems to me to be de minimis. Since I can find no coercing, compromising, or influencing of anyone's religious beliefs, I would find no violation of the establishment clause. It is true that this creche was offensive to people who believe in the strict separation of church and state. But it does not seem to me that the establishment clause was meant to protect against offense. Rather, in my judgement, it was intended to protect against dangers to religious liberty and, in the absence of such dangers, I would find no violation of the establishment clause despite the existence of a religious purpose.

As a matter of logic, because this first prong of the Court's test flatly prohibits any government action that has a religious purpose, it would make virtually all accommodations for religion unconstitutional. Since, as we shall see,[42] the primary goal of nearly all accommodations for religion is to avoid burdening religious activity, it is plain that their purpose is to assist religion. Thus, taken literally, the "secular purpose" requirement of the Court's establishment clause test would, for example, forbid the exemption of conscientious objectors from military service[43] and Amish schoolchildren from compulsory education laws.[44] As we have seen,[45] the Court's interpretation of the free exercise clause rejects these implications of its establishment clause test. Indeed, the Court has not only mandated religious exemptions under the free exercise clause but has also strongly indicated its approval of a number of government accommodations for religion that were not constitutionally required.[46]

The Court's apparent inconsistency may be rationalized by concluding that its establishment clause principles simply give way in the face of a serious (or even arguably substantial) free exercise clause claim.[47] Indeed, this approach may be endorsed as wisely fulfilling the historic and contemporary aims of both clauses to further religious liberty. But while I do not believe that the establishment clause should be read to bar all exemptions for religion, I am also unwilling to totally ignore the establishment Clause simply because government's purpose is to accommodate religion. Precisely because the establishment clause is designed to protect religious liberty, I believe that it should not be automatically read as subordinate to the free exercise clause, but rather as limiting the extent to which government may act on behalf of religion.

My discussion will focus on the establishment clause. It makes no attempt to determine, once it is found that a religious accommodation is *permissible* under the Establishment Clause, when such accommodation may be *required* under the Free Exercise Clause. Rather, it concerns the Free Exercise Clause only by confining its scope.

My proposal, once again, is that the establishment clause should forbid government action that is undertaken for a religious purpose and that is likely to result in coercing, compromising, or influencing religious beliefs. Thus, I disagree with the Court's articulated view that religious purpose alone renders government action invalid. Rather, it is only when religious purpose is coupled with threatened impairment of religious freedom that government action should be held to violate the establishment clause.

I wish to make clear that my position is not grounded in the idea that government promotion of religion serves secular ends by producing public benefits. If legislation designed to assist religion jeopardizes religious freedom, no public benefit should save it. Conversely, if state satisfaction of the religious needs of either the majority or a minority does not jeopardize any establishment clause values that have been identified, it should be held constitutionally permissible regardless of whether it serves some independent secular goal. Thus, the key to an establishment clause violation should be whether the government action endangers religious freedom.

Let me provide several illustrations of my view and specifically contrast it with prevailing judicial doctrine. In 1980, the Burger Court had its first significant case on the topic of religion in the public schools. In *Stone* v. *Graham*,[48] a Kentucky statute required that a copy of the Ten Commandments, paid for by private funds, be posted in every public classroom. The Court held that this violated the establishment clause. Taking its own doctrine seriously, something that it does not do all the time, the Court reasoned that posting the Ten Commandments plainly serves a religious purpose, and that produces a violation of the establishment clause.[49]

I disagree with the Court's conclusion. I agree that posting the Ten Commandments in public school classrooms had "no secular legislative purpose."[50] But I do not find that this poses any serious threat to religious liberty. Since this program was paid for by private money, there was no use of tax-raised funds to support religion. Moreover, I am not persuaded that anyone's religious beliefs are coerced, compromised, or even influenced in any significant way by simply having this religious message posted in the public schools.

Similarly, I disagree with the Warren Court's earlier decision in *Epperson* v. *Arkansas*,[51] holding that Arkansas's "anti-evolution" statute, which made it unlawful to teach the theory of Charles Darwin in the public schools, violated the religion clauses. The Court rested its conclusion on the ground that it was "clear that fundamentalist sectarian conviction was and is the law's reason for existence."[52] I would not dispute the Court's finding that the statute had a solely religious purpose even if it could be shown that it produced derivative secular benefits such as the promotion of classroom harmony.[53] But to rely on the non-establishment precept to invalidate a religiously motivated law that creates none of the dangers the establishment clause was designed to prevent represents, in my view, an "untutored devotion to the concept of neutrality"[54] between church and state. Conceding that the law in *Epperson* "aided" fundamentalist religions, there was no evidence that religious beliefs were coerced, compromised, or influenced. That is, it was not shown, nor do I believe that it could be persuasively argued, that the anti-evolution law either (1) induced children of fundamentalist religions to accept the biblical theory of creation, or (2) conditioned other children for conversion to fundamentalism. In contrast to other situations to be discussed below,[55] those whose religious interests were not advanced by the law appeared to suffer no *religious* harm. Therefore, while the accommodation for religion in *Epperson* may not have been constitutionally required by the free exercise clause,[56] the law should have survived the establishment clause challenge. Even though it satisfied a private religious need, it did not, given the above factual premises, threaten religious liberty.

A case decided several years ago, *Wallace v. Jaffree*,[57] was the Burger Court's second effort in the area of religion in the public schools. It concerned an Alabama statute requiring a minute of silence for "meditation or voluntary prayer" at the beginning of every public school day. In a 6–3 decision, the Court found that this law was motivated solely by religious purposes. There was powerful support in the record for this conclusion. Statements by the bill's sponsor in the Alabama legislature made plain that its purpose was to enable voluntary prayer to be reintroduced into the Alabama public schools. Thus, the Court reasoned, since government action undertaken for a religious purpose violates the establishment clause, the law was unconstitutional.[58]

Second, I think that *Wallace v. Jaffree*[59] was an unfortunate decision. It was wrongly decided. I agree that the Alabama statute was passed for one reason only: to give children in public schools an opportunity to pray. (Indeed, at least within current vision, I believe this to be the purpose of all moment of silence statutes.) But since I do not find that a minute of silence for prayer poses any meaningful danger to religious liberty, I would not find a violation of the establishment clause.[60] I think that there is a critical difference between an opportunity for silent prayer in the schools and a program of oral prayer or Bible reading. In the latter situations, even if children are given the opportunity to be excused, they are going to feel peer pressure to participate despite the fact that, at least for some children, this is contrary to their religious beliefs. But there is nothing in a moment of silence situation that is going to make any child feel pressure to do something contrary to his or her religion. Those who want to pray can do so. Those who are atheists can think that there is no God. Others can simply meditate during the moment of silence period. My guess is that many, if not most, elementary and secondary school children will turn their thoughts to matters having nothing to do with religion during the period of silence.

It merits reemphasis that I understand and appreciate the fact that some people find a moment of silence for prayer at the beginning of the school day offensive. But I think that almost all governmental accommodations for religion may be offensive to some people. That does not make them unconstitutional. Indeed, under some circumstances, accommodations for religion have been held by the Supreme Court to be constitutionally required by the free exercise clause.[61]

Although the Court has seldom explored the tension between the religion clauses, the problem has by no means gone unnoticed. It should be helpful in defining the contours of my proposal to contrast it with some of the major scholarly attempts to reconcile the conflict.

Twenty-five years ago, an influential article by Philip Kurland urged that the religion clauses be read together to state a single principle of neutrality, mandating that "government cannot utilize religion as a standard for action or inaction because these clauses prohibit classification in terms of religion either to confer a benefit or to impose a burden."[62] Although there is much to be said for this rule of "religion-blindness," it has, in my view, two serious shortcomings. In requiring government impartiality respecting religion, the rule produces results hostile to religion without serving nonestablishment values and permits forms of aid that subvert historical and contemporary aims of the establishment clause.

The neutrality principle produces hostility to religion by flatly prohibiting all solely religious exemptions from general regulations no matter how greatly they burden religious exercise and no matter how insubstantial the competing state interest may be. In advancing the admirable goals of government neutrality and impartiality, it downgrades the positive value that both religion clauses assign to religious liberty.

Consider a simple illustration: Suppose that a school regulation requires pupils to wear shorts during gym class for the aesthetic effect of uniform dress and that one child requests an exemption because her religious scruples forbid her to bare her legs.[63] The religion-blindness rule would allow a broadly worded exemption for "all children whose modesty makes the wearing of shorts uncomfortable" or "for all children whose parents request exemption." Either of these would protect the religious objector, but so many other children might also take advantage of the exemption that the regulation's aesthetic goal would be destroyed. Even if the school believed that it could exempt children who objected on religious grounds and still achieve its overall aesthetic purpose, such an exemption would constitute an impermissible classification under the neutrality principle. Thus, the school board would seemingly be faced with the choice of either protecting the religious child by abandoning its concededly valid purpose, or compromising the religious child's beliefs even though denying the exemption is unnecessary to serve its purpose. The religion-blindness rule would appear to demand these equally unsatisfying alternatives even though granting a religious exemption would neither coerce, compromise, nor influence the religious beliefs of any schoolchildren. I doubt that it could plausibly be argued that children would change their religions in order to obtain an exemption, or that the beliefs of those granted the religious exemption would thereby be intensified. Therefore, a religious exemption—admittedly undertaken for nonsecular purposes—would in no way impair religious freedom. Pursuant to my proposal, it would be permitted by the establishment clause.

Paradoxically, the neutrality principle not only requires hostility to religion at odds with the values of the free exercise clause, but also permits aid to religion in conflict with values of the establishment clause. It would apparently allow the use of tax funds for the purely religious functions of church organizations, so long as the legislative classification were broad enough. For example, suppose the state allocated public funds to all private associations for the purpose of distributing replicas of their insignia to their members. The Rotary Club, the League of Women Voters, and religious groups would all be beneficiaries. Under the religion-blindness rule, denial of funds to religious groups would constitute an impermissible religious classification, yet including such groups would designate tax funds to be used to purchase crosses and Stars of David. If our economy were to reach such a stage of collectivization that government fiscal policies so shrank private sources of funds as to make voluntary support of religion impracticable, there might well then be merit in reevaluating the historically rooted and contemporarily valued prohibition against state support of strictly sectarian activities.[64] But I do not believe that it has yet been persuasively shown that that time has come.

Several scholars have urged that the establishment clause is largely designed to implement the free exercise clause, so that when the religion clauses clash, the establishment clause must be subordinated to the free exercise clause.[65] The leading decision of *Sherbert* v. *Verner*[66] may be read as supporting this view. In that case, Mrs. Sherbert, a mill worker and a Seventh Day Adventist, was discharged by her employer when she would not work on Saturday, the Sabbath day of her faith, after all the mills in her area adopted a six-day workweek. South Carolina denied her unemployment compensation benefits for refusing to accept "suitable work," even though that would require her to work on Saturday. The Court held that this violated the free exercise clause because "to condition the availability of benefits upon [her] willingness to violate a cardinal principle of her religious faith effectively penalizes the free exercise of her constitutional liberties."[67] Under the Court's establishment clause test, however, any government action that has a religious purpose is forbidden, and, therefore, a Sabbatarian exemption would appear to be unconstitutional. It seems indisputable that when the state excuses Mrs. Sherbert from taking otherwise suitable work because of her religious scruples, the purpose of the exemption is solely to facilitate her religious exercise.

To avoid the stark impact of its establishment clause approach, the Court may have either totally subordinated the establishment clause's "no-aid" mandate to the free exercise clause, or simply balanced Mrs. Sherbert's right to Sabbatarianism under the Free Exercise Clause against the no-aid principle of the establishment clause and found the former weightier. Justice Brennan, author of the *Sherbert* opinion, had previously advocated this approach for resolving the establishment-free exercise conflict: "[T]he logical interrelationship between the Establishment and Free Exercise Clauses may produce situations where an injunction against an apparent establishment must be withheld in order to avoid infringement of rights of free exercise."[68]

If, in a balancing process, the establishment clause's prohibition of aid to religion is viewed only as an abstract principle rather than as a means for securing religious liberty, then it is not surprising that the Court found it wanting in *Sherbert*. On the other side of the balance was Mrs. Sherbert's grave, immediate, and concrete injury—the very type of injury that the free exercise clause was meant to prevent. Indeed, if the establishment clause is so abstractly viewed, then it is difficult to imagine any situation where it would not be subordinated or outweighed when measured against a colorable free exercise claim.

Under my proposal, the establishment clause would not be so viewed. Rather it would serve the underlying values of both religion clauses by forbidding laws the purpose of which is to aid religion—including exemptions for religion from general government regulations— if such laws tended to coerce, compromise, or influence religious beliefs.

Mrs. Sherbert's exemption would fail this test. First, since those who refused to work on Saturdays for nonreligious reasons, such as watching football games or spending the day with their children, would be denied unemployment benefits under South Carolina's scheme (and could constitutionally be denied them under the Court's ruling), the sole purpose of Mrs. Sherbert's exemption was to aid religion. Second, the exemption results in impairment of religious liberty because compulsorily raised tax funds must be used to subsidize Mrs. Sherbert's exercise of religion.

The situation produced by the Court's decision in *Sherbert* is distinguishable from that in which the state allows all unemployment compensation claimants to refuse to work on one day of their choosing in order to pursue whatever outside interests they might have. Even though some claimants might use the day for religious exercise, government has not conditioned the grant of public funds on a religious use, nor in any other way restricted freedom of choice as to how the money will be spent. While taxpayers may rightfully complain if Mrs. Sherbert's exemption is granted on condition that she use it for religious purposes, they may not object to Mrs. Sherbert's religious use of her leisure time. This is analytically the same as a welfare recipient's contributing part of his benefits to his church. Even though the state's money finds its way into the church's coffers, there is no violation of the establishment clause because the government has not conditioned the grant on the recipient's promise to use it for religious purposes. The government's secular goal of providing for the basic needs of indigents is served even though a particular recipient decides that one of his basic needs is religion.[69]

Does my proposal—which forbids a religious exemption for Mrs. Sherbert because it would coerce taxpayer's religious beliefs—simply subordinate the free exercise clause to the establishment clause? I think not, because the religious liberty value at the core of both religion clauses demands that Mrs. Sherbert's right to freely exercise her religion not encompass the right to governmental assistance which infringes the religious freedom of others.

In a provocative article published two decades ago, Marc Galanter sought to justify exemptions for religious minorities from general government regulations on the ground that they do not constitute preferential aid to religion forbidden by the establishment clause but rather amount to no more than equalizing the position of these minorities with that of the majority.[70] He based his thesis on the persuasive premise that "[w]hatever seriously interferes with majority religious beliefs and practices is unlikely to become a legal requirement—for example, work on Sunday or Christmas."[71] Indeed, the statute involved in *Sherbert* is illustrative because, by prohibiting any disadvantage against employees who refused to work on Sunday because of their religion,[72] it "expressly save[d] the Sunday worshiper from having to make the kind of choice"[73] imposed on Mrs. Sherbert. Thus, special treatment for religious minorities, Galanter contended, is restorative or equalizing, granting them only "what majorities have by virtue of suffrage and representative government."[74]

One difficulty that I have with this view is that it assumes the validity of certain advantages that religious majorities may create for themselves. But if what the majority obtains "by virtue of suffrage" itself contravenes the establishment clause, then providing the same benefit to religious minorities compounds the violation rather than eliminates it. Thus, the devotional Bible reading and Lord's Prayer programs struck down by the Court[75] could not have been cured, in my judgement, by reading from the Torah, the Koran, and works of secular philosophy on selected days of the month. In *Sherbert*, since the exemption for Sunday worshipers granted by South Carolina, as much as the exemption for Mrs. Sherbert mandated by the Supreme Court, served a religious purpose and involved religious coercion in the form of a tax subsidy for religious practice, it too would violate the establishment clause under my proposal.

But if the government policy that imposes burdens on minority religions has a secular purpose (as most such regulatory and tax programs do), and is thus itself immune to challenge under the establishment clause, I do not believe that establishment clause values should be ignored in situations where alleviating the burden or "restoring" the minority to a position of "equality" with the majority results in impairment of religious liberty. For example, even if members of a particular church demonstrated that, largely because of the financial burdens of government taxation, they had inadequate funds to buy vestments, it appears beyond dispute—at least in the absence of the wholly collectivized society hypothesized earlier[76]—that the establishment clause should forbid a state subsidy for this purpose. Moreover, even if a zoning ordinance, enacted to serve substantial public goals, excluded churches within many miles of a particular indigent person's home, it is plain that the historical and contemporary establishment clause command to avoid taxation in aid of religion should forbid the state's funding his weekly transportation to church.

Similarly, the establishment clause should be held to forbid the government's paying chaplains to minister to the religious needs of prisoners and military personnel. It may be that, under a free exercise clause balancing test,[77] the state could not exclude chaplains who volunteer for these purposes. But the establishment clause makes it the financial responsibility of the church and not the state to attend to its members' religious needs.

I agree, however, that "restorative or equalizing" accommodations for religion that do not tend to interfere with religious freedom should be permissible, even when such accommodations impose substantial costs of other kinds on those who are not their beneficiaries. For example, if a state were to grant a Sabbatarian exemption from a Sunday closing law, a non-Sabbatarian merchant might well object on the ground that the religiously motivated exemption caused him financial injury because, being forced to close on Sundays, he lost business to Sabbatarian competitors.[78] But even though the non-Sabbatarian store owner probably suffers a far greater monetary loss than any individual taxpayer would suffer from most tax subsidies of religious activities, this alone would not produce a violation of the establishment clause under my proposal. Similarly, that other accommodations of religious exercise would impose substantial non-monetary costs on nonrecipients would not itself invalidate them. For example, granting a draft exemption to a religious objector probably means that a nonbeliever who would otherwise avoid being drafted will be required to serve. Exempting a religious child from the school requirement that she wear shorts in gym class deprives her nonbelieving classmates of the desired total uniformity of dress. Excising evolutionary theory from public school curricula in order to avoid offending devout believers in a religious theory of creation deprives nonbelieving children of meaningful knowledge.

However, these indirect social costs of religious accommodation—in contrast to the tax cost of a religious subsidy—do not themselves threaten the values undergirding the establishment clause. They do not tend to coerce, compromise, or influence the nonbeliever's religious beliefs. Unlike the tax cost in *Sherbert*, these indirect social costs are not required to satisfy the believer's needs. The Sabbatarian store owner who seeks to remain open on Sunday does not demand that the non-Sabbatarian be closed on Sunday so that the Sabbatarian may acquire the non-Sabbatarian's customers; they are an unsought benefit, and the Sabbatarian's free exercise claim could be fully satisfied without them. Nor does the religious pacifist need to have another serve in his place; the cost imposed on the nonbelieving draftee does not aid the exempted person's religious beliefs at all. Nor, on the factual premises discussed earlier,[79] is it necessary to the religious tenets of the fundamentalist that nonbelieving children fail to learn about Darwin. In contrast, Mrs. Sherbert claimed a constitutional right to tax funds to subsidize the observance of her Sabbath. The pocketbook injury to nonbelieving taxpayers was required to accomplish this religious end. The cost itself served a religious purpose, rather than resulting incidentally from the accommodation of religious exercise. If accommodations for religion impose religious costs on nonbelievers, then, under my proposal, they are forbidden by the establishment clause. But if such accommodations impose only nonreligious costs, then the establishment clause should be held to permit—or, indeed, the free exercise clause may be interpreted to demand—that these costs of religious tolerance be paid.

In a most sophisticated effort to resolve the tension between the religion clauses, Alan Schwartz nearly two decades ago urged that accommodations for religious exercise should survive establishment clause challenge unless they result in the "imposition of religion,"[80] that is, they *actually influence* individuals to change their religious beliefs. His approach differs from mine in several important respects. First, it would apparently not invalidate a tax subsidy of religion unless it met this criterion. But, as we have seen, the framers considered taxation in support of churches to be an especially reprehensible form of religious coercion,[81] a view confirmed by the contemporary value of protecting religious freedom. Under the "no imposition" approach, many such subsidies would seemingly be permissible, thus enabling government to finance most private religious activities—as opposed to public activities such as school prayers, which undoubtedly influence religious belief[82]—free of establishment clause constraints.[83]

Second, under Schwartz's approach, government action that merely "helps implement a religious or irreligious choice independently made,"[84] rather than actually influences religious beliefs, does not amount to imposition of religion, and thus passes the establishment clause hurdle. I believe that government programs with no secular purpose that intensifies or meaningfully encourages even independently chosen beliefs should be held to violate the establishment clause. Otherwise, a modest public reward for regular attendance at the church of one's faith would be permissible.

Finally, Schwartz contends that although aid to religion may induce false claims of religious belief, "the Establishment Clause is not concerned with false claims of belief, only with induced belief."[85] But, as we shall see,[86] at least some initially false claims of belief, particularly those which require for their proof participation in religious exercise, will probably ripen into sincere belief.[87] Indeed, it also seems likely that strong temptations to adopt a particular religion will sometimes produce a sincere belief without any initial bad faith. Thus, government temptations that tend to influence religious choice, like other forms of religiously motivated action that tend to coerce or compromise religious freedom, jeopardize establishment clause values and should be proscribed.

As indicated earlier, my proposal to reconcile the tension between the religion clauses focuses on when the establishment clause permits or prohibits government accommodations for religion. Although it does not speak to when the free exercise clause mandates religious exemptions from secular government regulations, it does assist in the balancing process traditionally employed under the free exercise clause by identifying the state interest that must be weighed against the religious burden imposed. If the establishment clause *permits* a religious exemption, the state interest to be balanced against the free exercise claim is that of *maintaining its program without religious exemptions.* If, however, the establishment clause *prohibits* a religious exemption, the state interest to be balanced is that of *preserving its entire program*, because only by abandoning it altogether could the free exercise claim be satisfied.

To illustrate, consider the hypothetical regulation requiring school-children to wear gym shorts. We have already observed that a religious exemption would in no way coerce, compromise, or influence religious choice and is thus permissible under the establishment clause. In balancing the child's claim for exemption under the free exercise clause, the state's interest would be that of complete uniformity of dress. The free exercise balancing process necessarily involves value judgements that may often be difficult. Whether a more refined analysis than naked interest balancing can be developed is beyond the scope of this discussion. Whatever the optimal approach may be, it would seem most unlikely that the aesthetic interest in complete uniformity could overcome the child's interest in not being compelled to violate her religious beliefs.

Similarly, in *Wisconsin* v. *Yoder*,[88] which held that the free exercise clause demanded an exemption for Amish children from the state's requirement of school attendance until age 16, the Court correctly identified the relevant state interest as that of denying religious exemption. Unless it could be shown that relieving the Amish of this government-created impediment to fulfillment of their religious tenets would tend to coerce, compromise, or influence religious choice—and it is extremely doubtful that it could—the exemption was permissible under the establishment clause. In contrast, in *Sherbert* v. *Verner* we have seen that my proposal would prohibit the state from granting a religious exemption from the "suitable work" requirement. Therefore, only by abandoning this requirement for *all* claimants as applied to Saturdays (or a day of the claimant's choice) could the state have satisfied Mrs. Sherbert's free exercise claim without running afoul of the establishment clause. Under the appropriate free exercise clause balancing test, it seems likely under these circumstances that the state's interest in maintaining its requirements intact would have prevailed.

The draft exemption cases present a further problem. The Court has never held that the free exercise clause requires an exemption for those who object to military service on religious grounds. Indeed, as recently as 1971 in *Gillette* v. *United States*[89]—holding that the free exercise clause does not require excuse of those whose religious beliefs prohibit participation only in particular wars—the Court strongly suggested that "relief for conscientious objectors is not mandated by the Constitution."[90] The central question for our purposes, however, is whether, contrary to prevailing doctrine,[91] Congress may grant a religious exemption without violating the establishment clause.

First, the Court's efforts in *Gillette* to the contrary notwithstanding, an exemption for persons whose objection to military service is based on "religious training and belief" cannot be found to have other than a religious purpose. In *Gillette*, the Court contended that this exemption had a "neutral, secular basis"[92] grounded in "considerations of a pragmatic nature, such as the hopelessness of converting a sincere conscientious objector into an effective fighting man. . . . "[93] But if Congress's aim were simply to exclude those who were especially poor risks for military combat, then its making "religious belief" an absolute ground of incapacity was plainly both under- and over-inclusive. Rather, the Selective Service Act's specific limitation to religious objectors demonstrated on its face—as the Court conceded—Congress's "attempt to accommodate free exercise values"[94] and its "respect for the value of conscientious action and for the principle of supremacy of conscience."[95]

Second, we have already observed that religious exemptions from conscription impose substantial costs on nonbelieving draftees who must take the religious objector's place, but that these "nonreligious" social costs are not themselves enough to condemn the exemption under the establishment clause.[96] Nonetheless, they do serve as a warning signal that the advantage for religion may be so great as to impermissibly induce nonbelievers to profess religious belief and ultimately undergo genuine conversions.

The Selective Service Law of 1917, which exempted from combat duty only those religious objectors who belonged to "well-recognized" religious sects,[97] strikingly posed the danger of influencing people to adopt particular religions. The more broadly worded exemption in effect during the Vietnam War era—applying to any person "who, by reason of religious training and belief, is conscientiously opposed to participation in war in any form"[98] —was significantly less likely to induce people to join established churches. In addition, the Court's expansive reading of that provision[99] —making it available "if an individual . . . holds beliefs that are purely ethical or moral in source and content but . . . nevertheless impose upon him a duty of conscience to refrain from participating in any war at any time"[100] —minimized that danger still further. Still, professing a personal "religion" (as opposed to "essentially political, sociological, or philosophical considerations")[101] was enough to gain the enormous advantage of avoiding combat duty, and therefore would likely influence religious choice. Indeed, since the government was authorized to examine the sincerity of a claimant's religious beliefs,[102] it seems that at least some claimants would be induced to join established churches to corroborate their claims.[103] Even if not, potential draftees seeking exemption would have to formulate a statement of personal doctrine that would pass muster. This endeavor would involve deep and careful thought, and perhaps reading in philosophy and religion. Some undoubtedly would be persuaded by what they read. Moreover, the theory of "cognitive dissonance"[104] —which posits that to avoid madness we tend to become what we hold ourselves to be and what others believe us to be—also suggests that some initially fraudulent claims of belief in a personal religion would develop into true belief. Thus, a draft exemption for religious objectors threatens values of religious freedom by encouraging the adoption of religious beliefs by those who seek to qualify for the benefit.

Finally, in contrast to draft exemption, recall the case of the non-Sabbatarian merchant who coveted the Sabbatarian exemption from the Sunday closing laws because he felt that it was more profitable to be open on Sundays than on Saturdays.[105] Perhaps it is possible that some such non-Sabbatarian would be led to misrepresent his religious beliefs to obtain the exemption. But I believe that the intrinsic motivational difference between conscientious opposition to war and the comparatively crass desire to obtain pecuniary gain makes it extremely unlikely that the non-Sabbatarian's actual beliefs would be influenced in the process. Therefore, the establishment clause should not bar the accommodation for religion.

CONCLUSION

My proposal for resolving the conflict between the two religion clauses seeks to implement their historically and contemporarily acknowledged common goal: to safeguard religious liberty. It surely does not produce ready answers for every case involving instances of government action the purposes of which are to aid religion—either because such aid is claimed under the free exercise clause, because the state wishes to avoid antagonizing or burdening religious groups, or simply because the state otherwise wishes to assist religion as a private means. The proposal requires that a number of delicate, factual judgements be made—and some that I have advanced herein may well be subject to dispute. Nor have I attempted to set forth criteria for determining when an advantage to religion is so great as to influence impermissibly religious choice: That is left for case-by-case adjudication on developed factual records leavened by common sense. I have urged, however, that the establishment clause forbids such influence if accompanied by government action for a religious purpose.

Although the proposal will invalidate some accommodations for religion, I do not believe that it improperly diminishes the religious freedom guaranteed by the Constitution. For it is only when an accommodation would jeopardize religious liberty—when it would coerce, compromise, or influence religious choice—that it would fail. To subordinate the establishment clause in such circumstances would be to permit—or, indeed, sometimes require—government to implement one person's religious liberty at the expense of another's.

NOTES

1. See, generally, School Dist. of Abington Twp. v. Schempp, 374 U.S. 203, 215–17 (1963).

2. U.S. CONST. Amend. I.

3. See Walz v. Tax Comm'n 397 U.S. 664, 668–69 (1970).

4. See, for example, Lemon v. Kurtzman, 403 U.S. 602, 612–13 (1971).

5. Braunfield v. Brown, 366 U.S. 599, 607 (1961).

6. Cantwell v. Connecticut, 310 U.S. 296, 303 (1940).

7. But see McDaniel v. Paty, 435 U.S. 618 (1978).

8. But see West Virginia State Bd. of Educ. v. Barnette, 319 U.S. 624 (1943).

9. Cantwell v. Connecticut, 310 U.S. 296, 303–04 (1940).

10. Wisconsin v. Yoder, 406 U.S. 205, 214 (1972).

11. Id. at 215.

12. See, for example, Wisconsin v. Yoder, 406 U.S. 205 (1972); Sherbert v. Verner, 374 U.S. 398 (1963).

13. See, for example, Lemon v. Kurtzman, 403 U.S. 602 (1971); School Dist. of Abington Twp. v. Schempp, 374 U.S. 203 (1963); McCollum v. Board of Educ., 333 U.S. 203 (1948).

14. Choper, "Religion in the Public Schools: A Proposed Constitutional Standard," 47 Minn. L. Rev. 329 (1963).

15. Id. at 334–38.

16. Choper, "The Establishment Clause and Aid to Parochial Schools," 56 Calif. L. Rev. 260 (1968).

17. Id. at 277–78.

18. Everson v. Board of Educ. 330 U.S. 1, 33 (1947) (Rutledge J., dissenting).

19. School Dist. of Abington Twp. v. Schempp, 374 U.S. 203, 237 (Brennan concurring).

20. See L. Tribe, American Constitutional Law, Sect. 14–3 (1978).

21. L. Pfeffer, Church, State and Freedom 141 (rev. ed. 1967).

22. Compare W. Katz, Religion and American Constitutions 8–10 (1964) with Howe, The Garden and the Wilderness 23 (1965).

23. See Everson v. Board of Educ. 330 U.S. 1 (1947).

24. School Dist. of Abington Twp. v. Schempp, 374 U.S. 203, 241 (1963) (Brennan concurring).

25. See id. at 238 N.7.

26. See Sherbert v. Verner, 374 U.S. 398 (1963).

27. See Trans-World Airlines, Inc. v. Hardison, 432 U.S. 63 (1977).

28. See NLRB v. Catholic Bishop of Chicago, 440 U.S. 490 (1979).

29. C. Antieau, A. Downey, & E. Roberts, Freedom from Federal Establishment at xi (1964).

30. See Engel v. Vitale, 370 U.S. 421, 429–30 (1962); Zorach v. Clauson, 343 U.S. 306, 313–14 (1952); Everson v. Board of Educ., 330 U.S. 1, 8–11 (1947); Id at 53–54 (Rutledge, J., dissenting); L. Pfeffer, Church, State, and Freedom 122 (1953); Dunsford, "The Establishment Syndrome and Religious Liberty," 2 Duq. L. Rev. 139, 203–12 (1964); Katz, "Freedom of Religion and State Neutrality," 20 U. Chi. L. Rev. 426, 428 (1953).

31. See Choper, supra, note 14, at 333–34 & no. 20.

32. Everson v. Board of Educ. 330 U.S. 1, 12 (1947).

33. School Dist. of Abington Twp. v. Schempp, 374 U.S. 203, 232 (1963) (Brennan, J., concurring).

34. See Kauper, "Church and State: Cooperative Separatism," 60 *Mich. L. Rev.* 1, 5–6, 9 (1961); Pfeffer, "Some Current Issues in Church and State," 13 *W. Res. L. Rev.* 9, 18 (1961).

35. Everson. v. Board of Educ. 330 U.S. 1, 65–66 app. (1947) (Rutledge, J., dissenting). (Memorial and Remonstrance Against Religious Assessments 3).

36. "An Act for Establishing Religious Freedom," 12 W. Hening, *Statutes at Large, Laws of Virginia* 84, 85 (Richmond 1823).

37. Everson v. Board of Educ., 330 U.S. 1, 16 (1947).

38. 463 U.S. 783 (1983).

39. Id. at 786–92.

40. 465 U.S. 668 (1984).

41. Id. at 681–82.

42. See text accompanying notes 93–95, infra.

43. But see Selective Service Draft Law Cases 245 U.S. 366, 389–90 (1918), and discussion at notes 89–104, infra.

44. But see Wisconsin v. Yoder, 406 U.S. 205 (1972), and discussion at note 88, infra.

45. See text accompanying notes 9–11, supra.

46. See, for example, Gillette v. United States, 401 U.S. 437, 461 n.23 (1971) (draft exemption); Arlans Dep't Store, Inc. v. Kentucky, 371 U.S. 218 (1962) (dismissing for want of a substantial federal question an appeal testing the constitutionality of a Sabbatarian exemption from a Sunday closing law); Zorach v. Clauson, 343 U.S. 306 (1952) (released time program).

47. See L. Tribe, *American Constitutional Law* Sect. 14–4, at 822–23 (1978).

48. 449 U.S. 39 (1980).

49. Id. at 42.

50. Id. at 41.

51. 393 U.S. 97 (1968).

52. Id. at 107–08.

53. See text following note 14, supra.

54. School Dist. of Abington Twp. v. Schempp, 374 U.S. 203, 306 (1963) (Goldberg, J., concurring).

55. See text following note 78.

56. See note 46 and accompanying text, supra.

57. 472 U.S. 38 (1985).

58. Id. at 56–60.

59. 472 U.S. 38 (1985).

60. Choper, "Religion in the Public Schools: A Proposed Constitutional Standard," 47 *Mill. L. Rev.* 329, 371 (1963).

61. See text at notes 10–11, supra.

62. Kurland, "Of Church and State and the Supreme Court," 29 *U. Chi.*

63. See Mitchell v. McCall, 273 Ala. 604, 143 So. 2d 629 (1962).

64. See Giannella, "Religious Liberty, Nonestablishment and Doctrinal Development" (pt. 2): "The Nonestablishment Principle," 81 *Harv. L. Rev.* 513,

522–26, 537–55, (1968); Van Alstyne, "Constitutional Separation of Church and State: The Quest for a Coherent Position," 57 *Am. Pol. Sci. Rev.*, 865, 881–82 (1963).

65. See, for example, Moore, "The Supreme Court and the Relationship Between the 'Establishment' and 'Free Exercise' Clauses," 42 *Tex. L. Rev.* 142, 196 (1963).

66. 374 U.S. 398 (1963). Reaffirmed in Thomas V. Review Bd. of the Indiana Security Div., 450 U.S. 707 (1981) and Hobbie v. Unemployment Appeals Comm'n. 10, S. Ct. 1046 (1987).

67. Id. at 406.

68. School Dist. of Abington Twp. v. Schempp, 374 U.S. 203, 247 (1963) (Brennan, J., concurring).

69. See, generally, Choper, supra, note 16, at 315–17.

70. Galanter, "Religious Freedom in the United States: A Turning Point?" 1966 *Wis. L. Rev.* 217.

71. Id. at 291.

72. See 374 U.S. at 400.

73. Id. at 406.

74. Galanter, supra, note 70, at 291.

75. School Dist. of Abington Twp. v. Schempp, 374 U.S. 203 (1963).

76. See text accompanying note 64, supra.

77. See Sec. XI, infra.

78. Arlans Dep't Store, Inc. v. Kentucky, 371 U.S. 218 (1962) (appeal dismissed for want of a substantial federal question), raised precisely this claim.

79. See text accompanying notes 54–55, supra.

80. Schwartz, "No imposition of religion: The Establishment Clause Value," 77 *Yale L.J.* 692 (1968).

81. See notes 34–36 and accompanying text, supra.

82. See Choper, supra, note 14, at 368–77.

83. For discussion of the most recent decisions on aid to parochial schools, see Choper. "The Establishment Clause and Aid to Parochial Schools—An Update," 75 *Calif. L. Rev.* 5 (1987).

84. Schwartz, supra, note 80 at 728.

85. Id.

86. See text accompanying notes 102–104, infra.

87. It is obviously impossible to gather precise information on the number of fraudulent claims for conscientious objector status, or on the number of such claims which ripened into true belief. It is interesting to note, however, that a number of handbooks published during the Vietnam War era recommended tactics for asserting questionable claims. One handbook, for example, suggested that "many who consider themselves to be 'selective objectors' find that they can qualify for CO status by taking what might be called an existential approach." CCCO, *Handbook for Conscientious Objectors* 4 (12th ed. 1972). It is also interesting to note that the percentage of registrants classified as conscientious objectors increased sharply in the late 1960s, a time of widespread political opposition to military service. See (1973) *U.S. Dir. Selective Serv. Semi-Ann. Rep.*, JULY 1-DEC 31., at 32.

88. 406 U.S. 205 (1972).

89. 401 U.S. 437 (1971).

90. Id. at 461 n.23.

91. Id. at 452 n.17.

92. Id. at 452.

93. Id. at 452–53.

94. Id. at 453.

95. Id.

96. See text following note 78, supra.

97. Selective Service Law of 1917, ch. 15, Sect. 4, 40 Stat. 78 (1917).

98. 50 U.S.C. 456 (J) (1976).

99. See Welsh v. United States, 398 U.S. 333 (1970); United States v. Seeger, 380 U.S. 163 (1965).

100. Welsh v. United States, 398 U.S. 333 (1970).

101. United States v. Seeger, 380 U.S. 163, 173 (1965).

102. See Welsh v. United States, 398 U.S. 333 (1970); United States v. Seeger, 380 U.S. 163 (1965). See also United States v. Ballard, 322 U.S. 78 (1944).

103. See note 87, supra.

104. See, generally, L. Festinger, *A Theory of Cognitive Dissonance* (1957); Festinger & Carlsmith, "Cognitive Consequences of Forced Compliance," 58 *J. Abnorm. Soc. Psych.* 203 (1959).

105. See text accompanying note 78, supra.

6 Seeking Tolerance: Do Courts Respect Religious Observance?

Nathan Lewin

It is an appropriate time to be discussing religion and state, not merely because it is the bicentennial of the Constitution but because of a circumstance that is not generally celebrated. Just as the State of Israel is in its fortieth year, it is the fortieth year of meaningful church and state litigation in the United States. It was in February 1947 that the Supreme Court decided the case of *Everson* v. *Board of Education*.[1] Everybody agrees that the *Everson* decision was the start of meaningful litigation in the United States over the establishment clause and the free exercise clause.

Everson was a school busing case. It resulted in an opinion written by Justice Hugo Black with very broad language about what the Constitution prohibits with regard to the establishment clause. Justice Black's language has been quoted by courts ever since, almost as if Hugo Black had himself written the words in the Constitution rather than those gentlemen whom we call "The Founding Fathers." Of course, Justice Black's sweeping language about "no aid of any kind to religion" is not in the Constitution. Indeed, the irony in the *Everson* case, as noted years later by Justice Robert Jackson, who turned many an elegant phrase, was that Hugo Black's opinion was like Byron's Julia. "Protesting he would ne'er consent, consented." After all the language about what the establishment clause prohibits, the *Everson* decision was that busing children to parochial school under the New Jersey statute was constitutional. Then there began enormous confusion and chaos over the meaning of the two religion clauses in the First Amendment. And I think Professor Choper is certainly correct in saying that that is where we are today.

As a practicing lawyer, I try to look not, as the historians do, at bygones and where things were, but at where we are today and what my clients, the people who come to me with problems in the area of religion, stand for and what their prospects are. And my thesis is that we are, in the United States, in an age of intolerance. The decisions of the courts and the positions taken by administrators in the United States manifest an insensitivity and an intolerance to religious minorities that I think are frightening. I think these are not within the spirit of the free exercise clause of the First Amendment. They are not within the intention of the establishment clause as it was first drafted or even as it has reasonably been construed by the courts over the years. I believe that the courts, in their responsibility to the U.S. public to be teachers of morality, as they were in the history of desegregation, are not carrying out their duty to that public to lead in the areas of religious tolerance.

I would like to discuss two cases that I did argue in the Supreme Court of the United States. My position today is that of a losing litigant in the Supreme Court. One involved the question of the constitutionality of a Connecticut law that provided an absolute right to anyone who observed the Sabbath on any day of the week not to work on that day. Connecticut had repealed its Sunday laws, so that places of business could be open seven days a week. Concerned over the fact that people might be required to work on their Sabbath, their day of rest, the Connecticut legislature put a provision into the law that said very specifically that nobody could be forced to work on a day that is his or her Sabbath. No exceptions were provided in the statute for extraordinary hardship cases.

The first case that came up in litigation involved the situation where there was no record of any difficulty on the part of the employer in accommodating the right of the Sabbath observer. In fact, it happened to be a Sunday observer—a Presbyterian who would not work on Sundays and was fired from a job as manager of the men and boys' clothing section of a department store.

The Connecticut Supreme Court found the law unconstitutional on the bizarre ground that the law used the word "Sabbath."[2] Under the establishment clause, said the Connecticut Supreme Court, that is an aid to religion. The Connecticut court said that what the legislature was doing was promoting Sabbath observance by using the word "Sabbath."

We took the case up to the Supreme Court. In a very surprising opinion, which has been roundly and deservedly criticized, the Supreme Court invalidated the Connecticut law.[3] It has been viewed by even very staunch proponents of the Establishment Clause as a bizarre decision. In a bizarre opinion by Chief Justice Warren Burger, the Supreme Court said that the statute was a violation of the establishment clause because it provided unyielding weight, absolute rights, to the Sabbath observer, and put the Sabbath observer in the driver's seat. The employer, it was said, had no alternative, even in cases where it was difficult to accommodate. But this was not a case where it had been difficult to accommodate. The statute was struck down simply because it was allegedly so overbroad.

The other case that I cite to you has gotten some notoriety here in Israel. It is the yarmulke case. It involves the right of an Air Force psychologist, employed at a military Air Force base, working generally in a hospital in uniform, to wear a yarmulke indoors. Out of doors, he could wear his Air Force cap. Indoors, he could not wear his Air Force cap under the Air Force regulations. So he took it off and wore a yarmulke. There was no problem with that for three years. There had similarly been no problems with others whom we called to testify in his case. The others had been in the military as doctors or in some other capacity. But the Air Force said, "We are not going to allow this," and it litigated the case all the way up to the Supreme Court. The Supreme Court decided by a five-to-four vote that, in fact, the military had no constitutional obligation to accommodate the religious requirements of the Air Force psychologist.[4] It sustained the constitutionality of the military prohibition. In fact, it is not an express prohibition against a yarmulke, but just an enumeration of what may or may not be worn. The Court sustained the constitutionality of the prohibition although the military had never come up with any rational reason, any military necessity, any justification for saying you could not wear a yarmulke other than the fact that it was not part of the uniform.

That decision generated four dissenting votes. There were strong dissenting opinions both in the Supreme Court and in the Court of Appeals. There was a moving and passionate dissent from the denial of a rehearing in banc in the Court of Appeals by Judge Kenneth Starr. Judge Ruth Ginsburg and Justice Scalia, who is presently on the Supreme Court but was then on the Court of Appeals, also dissented from the refusal to rehear that case, although they did not specifically express a view as to how they would decide the case if it were reheard.

To me, these two cases are illustrative of a trend of decisions in U.S. courts, including the Supreme Court. In the term before the yarmulke case there had been an issue over the right of a woman who, for religious reasons, did not want to allow her photograph to be taken for a driver's license in Nebraska. The Iowa courts had held that she had a constitutional right not to have her photograph taken, and to be given a driver's license even without the photograph. The Supreme Court split four-to-four on the constitutionality of the obligation that she have her photograph taken. That was an ominous sign about where a majority of the court might stand.[5]

There were other cases that might be mentioned that have been litigated in New York. For example, just recently there were two decisions involving the Satmar Hasidic community in New York. The first involved the right of the community to have separate male and female drivers on publicly funded buses for its male and female students. The bus drivers were paid by state funds. The question was whether it was constitutional to accommodate the Hasidic community's requirement of separation by gender.

A District Judge in New York had held that it is an impermissible encouragement of religion to permit such separation.[6] I must admit I just don't understand that at all. Maybe it can be explained by Professor Choper's rationale, but I cannot agree with his distinction between the draft exemption and the school exemption. *Wisconsin* v. *Yoder*,[7] he says, is fine. There is no encouragement to religion when the old order Amish are told that they need not attend formal school past the age of 14. But draft exemption is unconstitutional. Exempting one from the army is an encouragement to religion, but exempting one from school is not an encouragement to religion. What would the kids think? If our kids were exempted from school because of their religion, would that not be substantial encouragement in a certain sense? Maybe more so than the adult's exemption from the draft. And yet Professor Choper draws his line between draft exemption that aids religion and school exemption that does not aid religion. I don't see either one as being an aid to religion. Nor do I see the authorization to have male bus drivers for male students and female bus drivers for female students as an impermissible aid to religion.

Another recent case involved the Satmar Hasidic community. The Supreme Court held in one very destructive decision that providing public school teachers for remedial education on the premises of religious schools to teach kids who are behind in reading or in math is unconstitutional because, said the Supreme Court Justice Brennan, that aids religion.[8] As a result of that ruling, the New York City authorities arranged with a public school that was half empty for it to be leased to the Satmar Girls' Yeshiva. The girls were brought to the public school building and were going to be taught by public school teachers in that public school building. The Court of Appeals for the Second Circuit recently held that this was an impermissible encouragement to religion and couldn't be done if the girls were kept in a separate walled-off section of the public school building.[9] And recently, a New York group, largely endorsed by the American Jewish Congress (which has been behind a lot of these lawsuits), brought a lawsuit in Federal Court in New York challenging the entire program of providing aid to handicapped yeshiva kids in what are called "mobile instructional units." You can't teach them in the yeshiva, because the Supreme Court has said that the surroundings somehow are religiously inspirational. The public school teachers have been moved out into trailers standing in the street or into other buildings. But that program is now being challenged and attacked in a major lawsuit.

These are all indications of an unwillingness by courts and litigators to view our governmental system as subject to flexibility to accommodate religious minorities. And I view that as being very dangerous.

The paramount question is "why?" Why does this happen? What encourages courts to rule as they have and litigators to bring these suits which result in the denial of accommodations that seem so very reasonable? Whether it is Simcha Goldman with his yarmulke or Mr. Thornton who can't work on a Sunday, why are they being denied?

One factor is an ignorance within the U.S. system of what religion really is. In the U.S. tradition, religion encompasses what you believe, where you pray, or how you pray. Only belief and prayer. And I suspect that our courts, if it were put to them, would say, "You have an absolute right to believe in anything. There is no religious test for office in the United States, and nobody can be discriminated against on account of what he believes."

I suspect the courts might even go so far as to say, "You have an absolute right to pray any way you like." If Captain Goldman had been disciplined not because he was wearing a yarmulke but because he was saying prayers in Hebrew, a court would say, "No Air Force regulation can say you can't recite your prayers in Hebrew."

But it is difficult for the U.S. judicial system and our governmental system to appreciate that wearing this little thing on your head is part of a religion. To the average U.S. citizen in the Midwest, it doesn't sound right. It is bizarre. It is strange. And that's true, I think, across-the-board regarding religious practices. That's why we have problems in Sabbath observance. That's why we have problems in other areas, such as wearing beards. There is frequently litigation over the wearing of beards. A fellow who was in jail in a New York prison who claimed the right to wear an unkempt beard litigated it before a federal judge in New York. Experts testified on both sides. The federal judge found for him.[10] But that case is going to be appealed, and I am very concerned about what the Court of Appeals will do.

I think there is a fear in the United States of a multiplicity of sects. That was the constant refrain that I heard in the *Goldman* case, when I was up there before the Supreme Court. "What are we going to do with the Sikhs and the Hare Krishnas and the Rastafarians? How are we ever going to draw lines for you?" And you say to the courts, "Well, your job in constitutional law is to draw lines. That is what courts are for. You have to weigh the harm on one side and the strength of the interest on the other." Courts are paid to make these decisions.

Yet the courts are as afraid in the area of religion as I think they are in the area of foreign policy and war. Courts have been reluctant in the United States to get into questions of foreign policy or war powers, because it is outside of their ordinary jurisdiction. The same kind of concern affects courts with regard to religious questions and with distinguishing among religions.

There are many other cases that I could cite that present these problems. Let me mention a very few. There has been litigation that has been going on in New York over the constitutionality of an *eruv*.[11] You may say, why should an eruv, which is essentially an invisible barrier consisting of telephone poles and wires, present a problem. An eruv is a rabbinically sanctioned authorization to carry within a certain area on the Sabbath. The eruv is, in a certain sense, a theoretical fence. It is a fence that can be made up of telephone wires and other parts of the landscape that the ordinary person doesn't recognize. But the theoretical fence is there so that the Orthodox Jews within that area may carry things out on the Sabbath. A statement of governmental authority is also required. You have to go to the mayor of the city, to the local county administrator, and say "May we do this?" This is rabbinically required. That statement of government authority, plus the authorization to use the wires, is being challenged in very serious litigation. There was a suit brought in Federal Court in New Jersey recently. There was a suit brought in Belle Harbor, New York, in state court which has been appealed to a New York appellate court where the matter has been pending for more than a year. You may say to yourself, "What possible constitutional infirmity can there be in an eruv?" Yet even this very minor accommodation to religious practice is being challenged.

Or take the matter of the exemption of students in public schools from compulsory classes that offend their religious observance. There is a lot of talk in the newspapers in the States about a Tennessee case where a judge authorized students to be exempted from certain reading classes. I don't know where Jesse Choper comes out on that, but to me it is a clear situation where nobody is harmed. The student alone is exempted from the class. We are not changing the public school curriculum. We are just exempting the student when the class offends his religious practice or his religious beliefs.

The most extreme situation, and I trust this will come out right, appeared in the papers recently. There is a girl in a public school in California who says that dissecting a frog offends her religious beliefs. And the school administrators say, "You are going to have to dissect that frog, whether your religious beliefs are offended or not." In all these cases there is a pattern. What happens is that the initial request for religious exemption is approved by the person who is immediately involved with the administrative problem. When it rises to the next level, the administrators say, "Oh, no. There is a policy here and we are going to fight." This poor girl who doesn't want to dissect a frog is going to find herself in the middle of litigation over her constitutional right to go through a class without dissecting her frog.

To me, there is a very basic philosophical problem here. I may lose some friends when I say this, but there is a very basic philosophical problem here which is particular to religious minorities. They are being treated worse than other groups to whom there may be an obligation to adjust and right wrongs of the past. In a decision announced a little while ago, the Supreme Court said that it is proper for any employer to adopt a program of affirmative action in favor of women, even where there is no showing of past discrimination with regard to women.[12] That is constitutionally permissible—and legally permissible under the Federal Civil Rights Act. But if we try to enact a Connecticut statute to provide an affirmative action program or some means of overcoming disabilities which religious minorities have in private employment—and I can tell you that there are dozens or hundreds of disabilities and problems in private employment with religious minorities—it is forbidden. Time after time, people are prevented from being promoted, find that they can't observe their holidays, or suffer other discrimination on account of religion. But with regard to that, we are told there is an establishment clause and the establishment clause prohibits recognizing or righting that kind of a wrong. The effect of all this is that religion is put at a disadvantage.

My theory is that the First Amendment was designed to protect religious practice. The establishmentarianists—those who view the establishment clause as being the be-all and end-all of the First Amendment—are to my mind the ones who are responsible for the greatest harm to religious liberty in the United States. The primary test ought to be, "Does a law impede, interfere with, or hinder religious minorities?" That's what the First Amendment was designed to do. Madison said that the protection of the First Amendment is in the multiplicity of sects. The great thing about the United States is that you have multiple religious communities. They ought to be able to practice their religion if their practices don't harm someone else. Nobody is talking about snake handlers or other conduct that causes harm to someone else. But the primary constitutional obligation is to protect the religious minorities.

The theory of the First Amendment is to encourage private employers and private people to tolerate religious minorities. To the extent a law does that, it should be protected under the First Amendment. The actions that are prohibited under the establishment clause are those that place the power and prestige of government behind one particular religious faith or behind all religion.

I disagree with my friend, Jesse Choper. If Congress were to say—even if it were to have no actual impact—"We hereby recognize today that Protestantism is the church of the United States, but we are not going to implement that in any way," I would say that it is clearly unconstitutional. That's what violates the establishment clause: placing the power and prestige of government behind one religion. If they were to say it about Judaism, it would be equally unconstitutional. That's the difference between the United States and Israel. In Israel, if they say it about Judaism, it is not unconstitutional, because that is what a Jewish state is all about.

But in the United States it is the placing of the power and prestige of government behind any single faith that is forbidden. And that is essentially what the establishment clause prohibits.

NOTES

1. 330 U.S. 1 (1947).

2. Caldor Inc. v. Thornton, 191 Conn. 336, 464 A. 2d 785 (1983).

3. The Estate of Thornton v. Caldor Inc., 472 U.S. 703 (1985).

4. Goldman v. Weinberger, 106 S. Ct. 1310 (1986).

5. Jensen v. Quaring, 472 U.S. 478 (1985).

6. Bollenbach v. Board of Education of Monroe — Woodbury Central School District, 659 F. Supp. 1450 (S.D.N.Y. 1986).

7. 406 U.S. 205 (1972).

8. Aquilar v. Felton, 473 U.S. 402 (1985).

9. Parents' Ass'n of P.S. 16 v. Quinones, 803 F. 2d 1235 (2d Cir. 1986).

10. Fromer v. Scully, 649 F. Supp. 512 (S.D.N.Y. 1986), aff'd 817 F. 2d 227 (2d Cir. 1987).

11. See New York Times, July 14, 1985, p. 26.

12. Johnson v. Transportation Agency, Santa Clara County, Calif. No. 85–1129 S. Ct. March 25, 1987. (Slip Opinion).

Comment

THE KEY QUESTION: THE RELIGIOUS FREEDOM OF THE INDIVIDUAL

Shlomo Slonim

Ever since the issue of conducting prayers arose at the Constitutional Convention in 1787, the place of religion in matters constitutional has concerned Americans. At the Constitutional Convention, a particularly critical moment arrived when the large states and the smaller states were at loggerheads over the composition of the legislature and whether there should be equal representation for the states in the second house, ultimately to become the Senate. At that critical moment, Benjamin Franklin proposed that the delegates engage in prayer.[1] Whereupon, it is said, Alexander Hamilton argued, "he did not see the necessity of calling in *foreign aid!*"[2] That is the apocryphal explanation for the refusal to engage in prayer. Actually, the real reason, as explained in Farrand's *Records* of the Convention, is that there was no money to pay for a clergyman to lead the delegates in prayer. Ultimately, it was decided that a clergyman would be invited to deliver a sermon on July 4, America's national Independence Day and henceforth every morning thereafter.[3]

With regard to the Choper chapter, I think it is very salutary when we are offered, as in the present case, a thesis that attempts to bring order out of chaos in the decisions of the Supreme Court. In matters relating to religion it is very, very difficult to know which way the Court is going to jump—although from Dr. Lewin's chapter we learn that a certain sort of bias has recently crept into Supreme Court decisions. We can therefore be very grateful for the scheme or thesis that Professor Choper proposes, namely that only such a law which is directed to the subject of religion and which contains an element of coercion or persuasion, compromising or influencing religious beliefs, would be declared unconstitutional. On that basis he maintains that, for instance, aid to sectarian schools, to parochial schools, where this aid would be directed only to helping them with reference to their secular studies, would be validated.

On the other hand, he would also find a released time program, such as that which was under consideration by the Court in *Zorach* v. *Clauson*,[4] unconstitutional since it involves an element of coercion. Here I find some difficulty, not so much with the basic thesis that he is presenting, but with the application of his thesis to such a subject as released time. And, in fact, the Supreme Court itself made the distinction in *Zorach*. Where classes in religion take place within the premises of the public school building, there might possibly be some element of coercion or influence present. However, where children are given the opportunity of leaving school earlier and going off to classes that are held in a church school or in a synagogue school under a released time program, I find it difficult to accept that this involves an element of undue coercion. There might be some element of influence, but undue coercion I do not see here.

Likewise, I can certainly concur with the view espoused in both papers that the case of *Thornton* v. *Caldor*,[5] involving the Connecticut Sabbath accommodation law, was a very wrong decision. The Supreme Court, I submit, simply misread the issues in deciding the way that it did. The court failed to take into account the realities of the situation, which are of course fundamental to both religion clauses of the First Amendment. Dr. Lewin, I believe, justly points out the Court's error.

In questions of religion there is a need to reconcile the inherent tension that exists between the establishment clause, under which both Congress and the states are prohibited from establishing any religion, and the free exercise clause, which ensures the right of a person to practice his faith untramelled by legal restrictions. Now what is the basic element that underlies both parts of the religion clause? I believe it is the principle of religious freedom. It is the idea that a person should be totally free of any element of coercion, whether it is with regard to determining for him what sort of religion he should observe or how he should conduct his own religious observance. This is the fundamental principle that underlies, on the one hand, the establishment clause and, on the other hand, the prohibition contained in the free exercise clause which proscribes governmental interference in the practice of religion.

If it is acknowledged that the cause of religious freedom underlies both parts of the religion clause of the First Amendment, then I think what we have to always look at, first and foremost, is the question: "How does this affect the individual?" The aim of the religion clauses is to guarantee the individual's freedom of religion. And it is here that I think the Supreme Court failed badly with reference to freedom of religion in the case of the Connecticut Sabbath accommodation law. Here was a provision that said that although business enterprises are permitted to remain open seven days a week, 24 hours a day, an employee who observes a Sabbath is permitted to exempt himself from working on his Sabbath. He is at liberty to declare that this day is his Sabbath and he should not in any way be penalized for the fact that he has this religious scruple and is unable to engage in labor on the day prescribed by his religion as a day of rest. Yet the court turned around and declared that this was a law establishing religion. It was nothing of the sort. It was simply a case of looking at the individual and ensuring the free exercise of his rights under the First Amendment. Because the establishment clause is in a very real sense subordinate, as one might say, to the free exercise clause, and because both clauses are directed to ensuring that a person should have freedom of exercise of religion, without coercion in any way, the Court should have concentrated on the true focus of the provision, the individual, and should have concluded that the accommodation law was simply a valid instance of free exercise.

I am also led to disagree with Professor Choper's conclusion with regard to *Sherbert* v. *Verner*,[6] which was a case involving the payment of unemployment insurance to a woman who was a Seventh Day Adventist. Mrs. Sherbert went to look for a job, but the job she was offered entailed working on Saturday. Since she was a Seventh Day Adventist, she could not accept work on that day. When she came before the unemployment insurance board the board ruled that she was entitled to the unemployment insurance. Subsequently it came before one of the courts, an appeal court, and that court ruled that to pay Mrs. Sherbert the unemployment insurance because of the fact that she could not work on Saturday, would involve the state in the establishment of a religion, of a Seventh Day Adventist type of religion.

Again, I think that here the focus was entirely wrong, and in this case, I am happy to note, the Supreme Court did subsequently overrule that decision of the Court of Appeals. But Professor Choper maintains, in accordance with his thesis, that the Supreme Court's decision was wrong.

Once again I think the focus must essentially be on the individual, on the individual's right to the free exercise of religion. And in this case, I think it is a simple matter of adopting a commonsense approach to the problem. The state pays unemployment insurance in every case where a person is unable to find work, unless the reason why the person is unable to find work is because of some consideration that might be deemed frivolous, or not really weighty enough, or in some way is not really deemed acceptable by society generally.

Can one say that a religious scruple is a frivolous consideration? Of course not. The exception here was not a case of imposing any form of establishment at all. It was once again a simple case of freedom of exercise of religion. And I think that the commonsense approach would recognize that the exception of a religious consideration is simply one of many considerations that the state will acknowledge and recognize as valid. There is no room for viewing this as a case of imposing or instituting any sort of religion.

Fundamentally, in looking at the two religion clauses I think the approach should be to recognize that in essence the free exercise clause should justly be considered as the dominant element.[7] If this approach is adopted then, of course, those same clashes to which we have been referred regarding the establishment clause would not arise. There would simply be no inherent conflict between the establishment and free exercise clauses.

NOTES

1. Max Farrand, ed., *The Records of the Constitutional Convention*, 4 vols., rev. ed. (New Haven, CT: Yale University Press, 1937), Vol. 1, pp. 450–52.

2. Ibid., vol. 3, p. 472 (emphasis in original).

3. Ibid., vol. 1, p. 452; and vol. 3, pp. 499–500 and 531.

4. 343 U.S. 306 (1952).

5. 472 U.S. 703 (1985).

6. 374 U.S. 398 (1963).

7. See in this regard, Moore "The Supreme Court and the Relationship Between the 'Establishment' and 'Free Exercise' Clauses," 42 *Tex L. Rev.*, 142, 196 (1963).

V MINORITY RIGHTS UNDER THE CONSTITUTION: RACE

7 Affirmative Action: Is It Just? Does It Work?

Glenn C. Loury

INTRODUCTION

This chapter is about the ethical propriety and practical efficacy of a range of policy undertakings which, over the past two decades, have come to be referred to as "Affirmative Action." A good deal of public argument has been engendered by this policy, and a variety of justifications have been advanced in its support. Here I try to close a gap, as I see it, in this "literature of justification." After describing in broad terms the problem of group inequality in the United States and various efforts to deal with it, I shall turn to the task of setting out this argument. I then consider how it is that some forms of argument in support of affirmative action, quite different from that which I offer here, not only fail to support the practice, but even worse, have the effect of undermining the basis for political cooperation among different ethnic groups in the U.S. democracy. In the final sections of the chapter I shall take up the matter of the practical effect of the use of preferential treatment on those individuals intended to be the beneficiaries of it. I will argue that the use of group preferences can, under circumstances that I will detail in the sequel, produce results quite different from the egalitarian objectives which most often motivate their adoption.

It is important to emphasize that this chapter is neither a brief for, nor an argument against, the practice of affirmative action. Sadly, this issue has taken on such a highly symbolic character in U.S. political discourse that rational discussion of its foundation in a political philosophy, and of its effectiveness in application, have become very difficult. In certain quarters of public opinion support for affirmative action is a litmus test of political progressivity, while in others opposition to affirmative action is a necessary posture for those who would call themselves supporters of individual liberties.

I do not see the issue as being quite so clear-cut as this. This will become evident with my argument below. There I suggest that the specific historical conditions which have given rise to the current degree of inequality between ethnic groups in U.S. society must be taken into account in any consideration of the merits of preferential treatment. I maintain that it is insufficient, as a standard of justice, simply to require that state action be formulated with equal regard to the rights and dignity of every member of society, and without regard to race, when the formative social environments of current citizens have been engendered by a past in which no such proviso was adhered to.

Nevertheless, I also regard it a dangerous folly to suppose that, simply through the use of group preferences, one can adequately redress the consequences of this historic injustice. Group preferences constitute but one limited tool which may be used (either wisely or foolishly) in pursuit of racial justice. As I argue later in this chapter, it is quite possible that one will do serious harm to the very persons who have been most limited by the practice of past discrimination, if one is not careful about precisely how such efforts to restore the racial balance are implemented. This is an extremely complicated question of social policy requiring an elaborate analytic framework to evaluate the merits of any particular proposal for state action. It is to the development of such a framework that I hope to contribute with this chapter.

THE PROBLEM OF GROUP INEQUALITY IN THE UNITED STATES

In 1903 the noted black scholar W.E.B. DuBois wrote "the problem of the twentieth century is the problem of the color-line—the relation of the darker to the lighter races of men. . . . " Forty years later Gunnar Myrdal characterized the race problem in the United States as a great dilemma that, if not resolved, threatened the ultimate success of our democratic experiment. Though there may have been a degree of exaggeration in both of these statements, it cannot be denied that throughout the twentieth century the problem of race has been at the center of U.S. politics, and so it remains today.

The past 25 years have witnessed substantial progress on this problem, beyond which neither DuBois or Myrdal would have imagined. This transformation, in the spheres of law and politics and economics, represents a remarkable accomplishment, powerfully illustrating the vitality and virtue of our free institutions. In little more than a generation we have advanced from a circumstance in which the great majority of U.S. citizens were indifferent or actively hostile to blacks' quest for full citizenship rights, to one in which racial equality of opportunity is a value staunchly upheld by the law and universally embraced in our politics.

This achievement, attained with comparatively little violence, contrasts quite favorably with the experience of those many nations whose very survival is threatened by long-standing conflicts among ethnic and religious groups.

Nevertheless, racial division remains an important theme in U.S. public life. Today we are faced with what might be called a new American dilemma: the persistence of groups' economic disparity in the face of substantially equal legal rights and protections. The median family income of blacks has remained at roughly 55 percent of the median white family income over the last generation. Black children are nearly three times as likely as whites to be living in a family with income below the poverty line. The unemployment rate for adult black males is roughly twice that of whites, and among teenagers it is nearly three times as great. More than two-fifths of white men but fewer than one-third of black men are employed in white-collar jobs. An alarming proportion of young black men in the critical age range of 20 to 24 years old (in a recent study, 27 percent compared with 11 percent of whites) have dropped out of the economy, in the sense that they are not in school, nor working, nor looking for work.

Moreover, the past generation has seen the advent of what has come to be called the black underclass. This is a population of low-income blacks living in central city ghettos where conditions have probably worsened in the past 20 years. The social disorganization of these black communities has reached alarming proportions and has been the subject of widespread commentary in the press and in political circles. The problems of early unwed pregnancy, of protracted welfare dependency, of chronic unemployment, of poor academic performance and low rates of school completion, and of violent crime are all far greater in this central city black population than among blacks generally, or in the U.S. population at large.

For many observers of the U.S. political scene, the questions posed by this chapter—Is affirmative action just? Does affirmative action work?—would appear fatuous in the extreme. These observers would argue that the historical and moral imperative for preferential treatment is self-evident. They would ask: Must not those who value the pursuit of justice be intensely concerned about the remaining economic disparities between the races? They would assert: We should engage in affirmative action practices because the inequality which currently exists between racial groups is but the external manifestation of the ongoing oppression of individuals on the basis of their group identity.

The fact of contemporary *group* economic disparity is critical to the political support for, and the intellectual justifications of, the practice of affirmative action. And yet, this link between current racial disparities in economic standing on the one hand, and the practice of preferential treatment on the other, warrants critical examination. One well might ask: Why should the mere existence of *group* disparities evidence the oppressive treatment of individuals? There is little support in the historical record for the notion that, in the absence of oppression based on group membership, all socially relevant aggregates of persons would achieve roughly the same distribution of economic rewards.[1] Indeed, to hold the view that the races should have approximately equal economic achievements in the absence of any discrimination against individuals is in effect to deny the economic relevance of those historically determined and culturally reinforced beliefs, values, interests, and attitudes that in themselves constitute the defining features of distinct ethnicities. It is the case throughout history that distinct cultures have produced distinct patterns of interests and work among their adherents. And while this need not be an argument against egalitarianism (since distinct interest and different work, need not receive different remuneration), this observation does serve to shift our focus from disparities among groups per se, to disparities in the rewards for the diverse activities toward which various groups' members incline.

In fact, there is a subtle logical problem that haunts the idea of equality among groups. To the extent that the arguments for equal group results presuppose the continued existence of general inequality, they end up (merely) demanding an equality *between groups* of a given amount of inequality *within groups*. They leave us with the question: Why is inequality among individuals of the same group acceptable when inequality between the groups is not? Indeed, there is "group inequality" whenever there is inequality—one need only take those at the bottom to constitute a "group." This is precisely what a radical class analysis of society does. The unanswered question here is why the ethnic-racial-sexual identification of "group" should take precedence over all others. That is, while there undoubtedly remains substantial group inequality, and while there has undoubtedly been egregious discrimination against minority groups in the past, it does not follow from these facts alone that the current inequality is evidence of ongoing discrimination, nor is it obvious that the remedy for the current disparity should require differential treatment of individuals on the basis of their ethnic group membership.

It is, of course, possible to hold that the very existence of distinct beliefs, values, interests, and so on, in distinct groups is evidence of oppression. And it is surely true that one major consequence of domination is to alter the conception of self held by the dominated. Women are socialized into the acceptance as natural or desirable of roles that undermine their competitive position in the world of work. Minorities, so this argument goes, do not aspire to those professions in which there are presently few persons like themselves to serve as role models, to illustrate that the opportunity for success is really there. In this view

group disparities evidence oppression even when arising most immediately out of differences in "tastes" among persons, since those differences are themselves due to oppression. A focus on groups is justified
by the view that any economically relevant difference in the behavior
of groups' members is itself the legacy of unjust oppression.

But this argument, if valid, would prove too much. The differentiating
effect of oppression has sometimes worked to make a group of persons
more effective in economic competition.[2] Moreover, the differences of
belief and values among various groups sometimes reflect centuries of
historical development, in lands far removed from those which they
currently occupy. If group differences in beliefs and values bearing on
economic achievement are the fruit of oppression, then why not also
those group differences in cultural style so much celebrated by cultural
pluralists? If, to put the matter in simplistic but illuminating terms, poor
academic performance among black students reflects "oppression," why
then should not outstanding athletic performance stem from the same
source? We remain then with the questions: When does group inequality
constitute a moral problem? How should the history of group relations
figure in this judgment? What may appropriately be done by the state
to eliminate group differences?

In contemporary U.S. society such disparities are often taken to constitute a moral problem, and to occasion a public policy response. The
use of racial preferences in education, employment, or even politics is
a frequent policy response. This has been controversial; courts and philosophers have sought to define the circumstances under which such
preferences might legitimately be employed. Recently, both in the courts
and in public discourse, questions have been raised about the legitimacy
of government efforts on behalf of women, blacks and other racial minorities. Some of these questions strike deeply at the philosophical foundation of preferential policies.

This is not the place for a thorough review of all of the arguments
advanced in support of affirmative action. I will note however that there
has been a continual evolution in the structure of these arguments from
the early days of the civil rights movement. In the beginning, the "antidiscrimination principle," which became codified in many statutes and
court rulings in the 1950s and 1960s, simply asserted that the use by the
state (and under certain circumstances, by individuals in their private
transactions) of ascriptive personal characteristics as a basis for distinguishing among individuals is wrong. Race became a "suspect classification." Discrimination on the basis of race in the allocation of
opportunities, in employment, housing, credit, and the like, was seen
as stigmatizing the individuals involved, and as reinforcing private inclinations to make invidious distinctions based upon ascriptive characteristics like race. In his famous oration Dr. Martin Luther King, Jr., put

it well when he said: "I have a dream that my four little children will one day live in a nation where they will not be judged by the color of their skin, but by the content of their character."[3] It was not contemplated by civil rights leaders at this time that it might be desirable, in the interest of advancing the principle of antidiscrimination, for the state to make use of racial characteristics in order to bestow benefits upon minorities. Indeed, civil rights advocates in the legislature, when working for the passage of the Civil Rights Act of 1964, offered extensive assurances that they sought only to enforce on the private sector such restrictions in their business practices as were consistent with assuring color-blind hiring and promotion standards.[4] Throughout this early history of the civil rights revolution, the classical liberal principle of aversion to the use of racial (or religious or sexual) classification was adhered to by the advocates of change. And this antidiscrimination principle has a noble intellectual pedigree, harking back to the Enlightenment-era challenges to hereditary authority[5] and reflected in the "anonymity axiom" of modern social choice theory.[6]

Today, however, the antidiscrimination principle is no longer interpreted in such a straightforward manner. It is no longer the idea of color-blind practice that informs the policy prescriptions of antidiscrimination advocates, but rather a principle that is often described as "equality of life chances." Instead of ensuring that public and private practices are to the extent possible devoid of the use of racial identity as a factor in allocating opportunity, the current drift in public policy and related social philosophy is to involve the state actively in assuring that racial minorities, and especially blacks, have greater opportunity than would be the case without state intervention.[7] As a result, King's dream that race might one day become an insignificant category in U.S. civic life today seems naively utopian. It is no small irony that a mere 25 years after Dr. King's moving oration, the passionate evocation in public debate of his color-blind ideal is for many an indication of a *limited* commitment to the goal of racial justice.[8]

It is not hard to understand what has happened here. The experience of the early civil rights movement showed that limiting government action to the mere assurance that race *not* be a factor in public or private economic decisions is insufficient to cause a substantial reduction of economic inequality between the races. Such color-blind policy has, for example, practically no impact on the life chances of the ghetto poor. However, unlike the earlier mandate of color-blind practice, this more recent use of color-conscious state action rests on a rather less firm philosophical ground. The key point here is the distinction (if any) to be drawn between the equality of individual opportunity on the one hand, and the equality of group results, on the other. If one conceives of the fundamental ethical principle as the imperative to guarantee to all citizens equality of opportunity, then one can deduce the color-blind principle as an implication of this more fundamental premise. (It is obvious, so long as blacks and whites of similar socioeconomic backgrounds and abilities were treated differently, that violation of the color-blind principle would imply a violation of the principle of equality of opportunity.) But the implication does not run in the other direction: Adherence to the color-blind principle may not by itself be sufficient to ensure that the principle of equality of opportunity for all individuals be adhered to. On the other hand, if one believes that inequality of group results is prima facie evidence of inequality of individual opportunity, then only a policy that produces equal results can be judged consistent with the basic ethical imperative of equal opportunity. The question would then become: To what extent can the contemporary practice of affirmative action, which of necessity violates the color-blind principle, be justified in the interest of bringing about a greater equality of opportunity among individuals?

This is the question that contemporary arguments in support of affirmative action attempt to address. Yet, it is my judgment that this "literature of justification" has not been entirely successful. The arguments encountered in support of the practice of affirmative action in our ordinary political discourse seem to be more tortured and less compelling than those put forward on behalf of the color-blind principle.[9] The key court decisions supporting the practice of preferential treatment are, in the main, closely divided ones. In the philosophical literature arguments in support of affirmative action typically begin by demonstrating that "merit" is, by itself, an insufficient guide to the just allocation of opportunities, but too often end with a set of unsupported empirical claims regarding the benefits sure to flow from a more equal distribution of groups among positions.

The use of empirical evidence in support of arguments favoring affirmative action raises some thorny issues. One often encounters the following fallacious argument: "There exists substantial inequality between groups in the achievement of certain positions. Since there is no innate difference in the inherent capacity of members of different groups to perform various tasks, this inequality must be evidence of discrimination in access to those positions. Therefore the use by the state of color-conscious methods to rectify the inequality is justified as a remedy for the discrimination."

This argument fails because the inference of the existence of discrimination from the fact of differential group achievement is simply not valid. By saying this I do not question the premise of the argument that innate capacities for performance are distributed roughly equally among members of different groups. Yet, it can hardly be denied that the achievement of success in various lines of endeavor depends on more than the innate capacities of individuals, and in particular is dependent upon skills and experiences that persons may acquire during the course of life, and that may vary dramatically among the members of different ethnic groups. Thus, for example, a substantial underrepresentation of blacks among those receiving advanced degrees in science need not reflect either discrimination by institutions of higher education, or differences in the innate capacities of blacks to master scientific disciplines. Rather, this inequality might well be reflective of group differences in the quality of primary and secondary education, and/or cultural differences in attraction to and interest in the sciences as a field of study.

Thus, a rigorous argument in support of affirmative action must take some account of the process by which various skills are acquired, and cannot simply rest its case on the fact that groups differ in their unassisted rates of achievement. Nevertheless, the fact of substantial and ongoing differences in hiring rates, say for blacks and whites in a relatively unskilled occupation, cannot be ignored. Indeed, from the point of view of law enforcement, as opposed to philosophy, the observed rates of hiring of the members of different groups will be the primary evidence that one has to go on in determining whether or not a case for further investigation of an employer for violation of the anti-discrimination laws exists. Currently in the United States, Presidential Executive Order 11246 requires employers of any size contracting with the federal government to provide extensive information on their work force by race and sex, and to formulate numerical targets or guidelines for their hiring so as to bring the percentages of the various groups' members employed into line with their representation in the overall work force. This practice is often criticized by opponents of affirmative action for its violation of the color-blind hiring principle. And yet, bearing in mind the distinction between color-conscious state action the purpose of which is to prevent overt but undetectable private discrimination, on the one hand, and color-conscious state action aimed at increasing the representation of protected groups without any implication that their under-representation evidences illegal private behavior, a strong case for the practices mandated by E.O. 11246 can be made. Given that the federal government has laws prohibiting employers from discriminating against women or minorities in their hiring practices, and given that the resources for enforcing those laws are necessarily limited, some criteria must be used to select from among the countless employers those who warrant closer attention from the federal enforcement officials. It is crucial therefore that information on the hiring rates of various employers be available to enforcement officials so that they can make a judicious selection of targets for closer investigation.

It is possible to distinguish between two types of departures from the color-blind principle. One, which I might term "enforcement-oriented," takes race into account in order to ensure that agents in the private sector are making decisions without regard to race. As just discussed, this is entirely consistent with the principle of equality of individual opportunity. The second type of departure, call it "result-oriented," involves state intervention to alter the outcome of private actions that may be wholly unobjectionable, but that occur in the face of unacceptable de facto racial disparities. It is clear that the two types of policies cannot be rationalized in the same manner, and that a coherent theory of the practice of affirmative action must be able to distinguish between them. How, if at all, can the result-oriented use of racial categories by the state be justified?

A MINIMALIST'S ARGUMENT FOR DEPARTING FROM THE COLOR-BLIND STANDARD

In this section I shall attempt to defend a departure from the color-blind standard. My purpose will be, in the first instance, to establish that a plausible specification of how multi-ethnic societies actually function will lead to the conclusion that social justice is not consistent with a blanket prohibition on the use of group categories as a basis for state action. In making this argument I shall rely on an intellectual tradition long familiar to economics—one that justified departures from laissez faire when, due to some sort of market failure, the outcomes of private actions are socially undesirable. The market failure to which I refer, it will be seen, rests upon the very social behavior that induces there to exist, as a permanent structural matter, distinct racial and ethnic groups among which inequality might arise in the first place.[10]

This last point is worth expanding upon a bit. While affirmative action is concerned primarily with legal questions of individual rights, and with policy issues regarding the mitigation of group economic disparity, it is clear that the larger phenomenon of ethnic group differences occurs within a social and historical context. The very fact that there exist distinct ethnic groups in a society is a reflection of deep-seated behavioral patterns among the society's members regarding their social affiliations. In the absence of what might be termed "socially discriminatory" patterns of behavior, racial and cultural differences within a society would in due course be washed away by extensive intermingling. Thus, it is clear that, whatever one may mean by nondiscrimination, if one is to take as given the ongoing existence of distinct groups in a society, one does not mean to preclude all patterns of discriminatory association. Having recognized this, an interesting question then arises: How does the ongoing existence of social discrimination, given the fact of historic if not continuing economic discrimination, affect the way in which we should formulate policy to deal with such economic differences as may continue to exist between groups?

It can be accepted that families group themselves together into social clusters or local "communities," and that certain "local public goods" important to subsequent individual productivity are provided uniformly to young people of the same community. These "local public goods" may be very general in nature. One thinks naturally of public education, but also important might be peer influences shaping the development of personal character, contacts which generate information about the world of work, friendship networks that evolve among persons situated in the same or closely related "communities." One might even want to include here access to cultural resources—exposure to a system of values and attitudes promoting educational and/or economic achievements. What is critical is that these community "goods" (or, possibly, "bads") be provided *internal* to the social clusters in question, and that outsiders be excluded from the consumption of such goods. What I am calling here communities are to represent the private, voluntary associational behaviors common to all societies, in which persons choose their companions and affiliations, often on the basis of common ethnicity, religion, or economic class. Since access to these communities could depend on parents' social status, this provides another avenue by which parental background influences offspring's achievement—another source of social capital. Notice, though, that social capital resources may differ between economically equal families of different racial groups, if there is ongoing social discrimination, together with a history of economic discrimination. This will be a key point in what follows.

In order to pose the question most sharply, I assume that all individuals have identical preferences with respect to economic choices, and that an identical distribution of innate aptitudes characterizes each generation of majority and minority workers.[11] Thus, in the absence of any historical economic discrimination, and notwithstanding the tendency for persons to cluster socially, we should expect that the economic status of minority and majority group members would be equal, on average. However, I want to inquire in this idealized setup whether, given the fact of past economic discrimination, the competitive labor market would function so as eventually to eliminate any initial differences in the average status of the two groups which historical discrimination might have produced.

One can investigate this question by writing down a mathematical representation of this idealized world. I have done this in the previously published work cited in note 10, above. It can be shown that the results obtained depend upon whether only family income, or both family income and race, influence the set of social clusters—that is, communities—to which a family may belong. When persons in society discriminate in their choice of associates on the basis of economic class, but not ethnic group, one can show (with a few additional, technical assumptions) that equal opportunity as defined here always leads (eventually) to an equal distribution of outcomes between the groups. However, when there is social segregation in associational behavior along group as well as class lines, then it is not generally true that historically generated differences between the groups are attenuated in the face of racially neutral procedures. Examples may be constructed in which group inequality persists indefinitely, even though no underlying group differences in tastes or abilities exist.

This happens because, when there is some racial segregation among communities—that is, when race operates as a basis of social discrimination, though not economic discrimination—the process by which status is transferred across generations does not work in the same way for minority and majority families. *The inequality of family circumstance generated by historical economic discrimination is exacerbated by differential access to the benefits of those quasi-public resources available only in the affiliational clusters which I have called communities.* A kind of negative intra-group "externality" is exerted, through local public goods provision, by the (relatively more numerous) lower income minority families on higher income minority families of the same communities. (Or, if you prefer, a positive intra-group externality is exerted by the relatively more numerous higher income majority families on the lower income majority families of the same communities.)

The fundamental point here is that the creation of a skilled work force is a social process. The merit notion, that in a free society each individual will rise to the level justified by his or her competence, partially conflicts with the observation that no one travels that road entirely alone. Even if one neglects the transfers of monetary wealth within families, it remains the case that the economic achievements of an individual only partially reflect his or her innate productive capabilities. The fact that generations overlap, and that the prevailing social environment influences the development of individual intellectual skills, means that the present pattern of inequality among individuals and among groups will partly determine the extent of inequality which exists in the future. The social context within which individual maturation occurs strongly conditions what otherwise equally competent individuals can achieve. This implies that absolute equality of individual opportunity, where an individual's chance to succeed depends only on his or her innate capabilities, is an ideal that cannot be achieved.[12] What I have demonstrated in the work cited above is that the limited version of equal opportunity which is attainable, where one treats family and community background differences as given but assures that individuals are treated fairly once reaching the labor market, does not generally have the desirable property of eliminating historically generated economic differences between groups.

I'm suggesting that a satisfactory theory of racial inequality, which must underlie the formulation of an adequate justification for affirmative action, cannot be fashioned unless it explicitly takes into account the fact that some racial separation in social life is an equilibrium attribute of the system. The long-run existence within the same society of racially and culturally distinct groups of families points to a fairly deep-seated pattern of social behavior along group lines which may be expected to have economic consequences.

It is important to realize that this social segregation, in residential communities, in religious affiliations, in friendship networks, in fraternal organizations, in marital relations, and in the host of other important affiliations and associations to which people are attracted, and in which membership depends in part upon race and ethnicity, is the result of the choices of many autonomous individuals, and has effects that cannot be completely avoided by an individual's actions.[13] Membership in the various communities that make up the structure of our social life is not allocated according to market principles.

This discussion suggests that, as a general matter, we cannot expect laissez faire to produce equality of result between equally endowed social groups if these groups have experienced differential treatment in the past, and if among the channels through which parents pass on status to their children is included the social clustering of individuals along group-exclusive lines. On this argument, state action which is cognizant of groups is *legitimated* by the claim that, in its absence, the consequences of historical wrongs could be with us for the ages. It is *necessitated* by the fact that individuals, in the course of their private social intercourse, engage in racial distinctions that have material consequences. These distinctions are reflected in this model by what I referred to as the "choice of community"—with whom to spend one's time; in what neighborhoods to live; among which children to encourage one's offspring to play; to what set of clubs and friendship networks to belong; with what sort of person to encourage one's children to mate. Such decisions, in our law and in our ethics, lie beyond the reach of the anti-discrimination mandate. They are private matters which, though susceptible to influence and moral suasion about the tolerance of diversity and the like, are not thought to constitute the proper subject of judicial or legislative decree. Freedom to act on the prejudices and discriminations that induce each of us to seek our identities with and to make our lives among a specific, restricted set of our fellows, are for many if not most Americans, among those inalienable rights to life, liberty, and the pursuit of happiness enshrined in our Declaration of Independence.

One illustration of the argument advanced here to support affirmative action can be found in the practice of special outreach, advertising, and training efforts for prospective minority employees. There has been in the past 15 years, and in no small part due to federal affirmative action guidelines, a veritable revolution in the personnel practices of large employers. Today, in both the public and private sectors, the filling of a job opening takes place only after an objective and verifiably open search procedure has been undertaken, insuring that women and minority candidates have been given an ample opportunity to apply for the position to be filled. This effort to make special outreach, advertising, and even training resources available to women and minorities, and to ensure that they have an equal opportunity to compete for positions being filled, is sometimes referred to as "weak affirmative action," to distinguish it from the stronger practice of using quotas to guarantee the employment of protected groups.

Now there is a fair amount of evidence, both anecdotal and systematic, that word of mouth contacts and informal social networks play an important role in the distribution of information about employment. As such, membership in social networks rich with information about employment opportunities is an important economic asset. The effect of the practice of "weak affirmative action" is to redress such group inequality in access to job information which may have arisen from the historical fact that minorities had limited exposure to (and therefore knowledge about) a particular type of employment. It therefore helps to promote equal opportunity in a manner consistent with that suggested by the foregoing argument.

It is worth noting that this practice is seldom contested by political opponents of affirmative action. Indeed, it is often advanced by them as an example of what affirmative action was "originally intended" to achieve—namely, greater representation of qualified minority personnel without giving explicit racial preference at the point of an employment decision. And it is clear that these outreach efforts have been valuable and necessary, given the history of exclusion of women and minorities from various sectors of the society. They have served to make employers more conscious of what they are doing when recruiting and hiring workers, so that practices that inadvertently excluded minority candidates could be identified and corrected. And yet, this practice of weak affirmative action, far from being philosophically innocuous, raises all of the important questions that are engendered by the practice of other forms of affirmative action. For, by conceding the legitimacy of this weak form of affirmative action, one perforce acknowledges the inadequacy of a pure color-blind position. After all, a recruitment strategy based on race or sex necessarily confers some (modest) benefits on the targeted groups, and disadvantages on those groups not aggressively pursued in this manner.

There are two points I wish to stress about this "minimalist's" argument. First, it rests quite specifically on a conception of group differences in the transmission of status over time, and thus points to those state interventions which are intended to neutralize such disparities. That is, racial preference is not defended here in the abstract, as a generalized remedy for racial inequality, or repayment for past wrong. Rather, a specific mechanism that passes on from past to present to future the consequences of wrongful acts has been explicated. It is to neutralize that mechanism that "taking color into account" is legitimated. And, I would argue, any alternative justification for racial preference should be similarly grounded on an explicit delineation of the "fine structure" of social life that causes the need for such extraordinary state action to arise. The simple evocation of "two hundred years of slavery," or of "past discrimination against minorities and women" does not begin to meet this standard. For the question remains: What specifically have been the consequences of past deeds that require for their reversal the employment of racial classification? The attainment of equal educational opportunities through race-conscious public policy provides a good example. Racial criteria used in the siting or allocation of public housing units would be another. But those racial preferences which confer benefits upon minority group members who do not suffer background related impediments to their mobility (for example, minority business set asides) could only be rationalized in this way if it could be demonstrated that the recipients' connection to their less fortunate fellows was such as to ensure a sufficiently large beneficial spillover effect on the social mobility of the poor. This is a difficult empirical test for many current practices to meet.

Moreover, other remedies not dependent on race-conscious action, but intended severely to reduce the differential advantages due to poor social background for all citizens (such as early childhood education, employment programs for disadvantaged urban youth, or publicly financed assistance in the acquisition of higher education) might also be sufficient to avoid the perpetuation of past racial wrongs.[14] The greater the public provision of "social capital" to all citizens, the less important will be racial differences in private access to important social networks.[15] In other words, the type of argument which the late Justice William O. Douglas made in his *DeFunis* dissent, which acknowledges the legitimacy of taking social background into account when making admissions decisions at a public law school, but nonetheless rejects explicit racial considerations, well might suffice to meet the concerns raised here.

The second, perhaps more important, point is that, in addition to providing a rationale for extraordinary state action intended to limit the degree of group inequality, the underlying behavioral premises of this model suggest that there are limits on what one can hope to achieve through the use of racial classification by the state. The very argument

I offer here in defense of the practice of affirmative action also suggests that we ought not rely on that policy as the primary tool for reducing racial inequality. As noted above, our political and philosophical traditions are such that the reach of civil rights laws will be insufficient to eliminate all socially and economically relevant discriminatory behavior. That is, we are evidently not willing to undertake the degree of intrusion into the intimate associational choices of individuals that an equalizing redistribution of social capital would require.[16]

While we seek to maintain integration through race conscious allocation of public housing units, it is clear that such practice cannot prevent disgruntled residents from moving away when the racial composition of the neighborhood changes contrary to their liking. And while racial school assignments may be needed, it is also clear that busing for desegregation cannot prevent unhappy parents (those who can afford it!) from sending their children to private schools, or moving to another, more ethnically homogeneous district. How intrusive we choose to be in restricting such responses is ultimately a political question, though it would seem that elimination altogether of this kind of discrimination would not be a reasonable possibility in this society. Application of the nondiscrimination mandate has in practice been restricted to the domain of impersonal, public, and economic transactions (employment, credit, housing, voting rights) but has not been allowed to much interfere with social discrimination in personal, private, and intimately social intercourse.

We are, of course, intimately familiar with these socially discriminatory behaviors because we all engage in them daily. We choose our friends and neighbors, decide upon our business partners and professional associates, select the schools our children will attend, influence (to the extent we can) the prospective mates of our children, and of course choose our own mates. Moreover, for the great majority of us—black and white—race, ethnicity, and religion are factors in these discriminating judgements.

While all but the old style integrationists now celebrate the embrace of diversity implied by this new pluralism, advocates of equality are not always happy with its consequences. For there is an inevitable tension between the ideal of equality of opportunity for individuals and the fact of pluralistic organization along group lines. The fact is, as amply demonstrated in the preceding argument, that such social clustering has important economic consequences. A number of analysts of the black underclass have come recently to stress the debilitating consequences of the social isolation of inner-city communities—isolation from whites and from those black families that, in the post–1960s era of declining housing discrimination, have availed themselves of the opportunity to move out of traditionally black residential areas.[17]

Thus, the fact of social segregation suggests that state intervention along group lines will be necessary, but also limited in its effect. It is crucial to realize that what is involved here is in the main not a legal or even an attitudinal problem, but an inescapable social fact. If people are left with the liberty to choose their social environments, then their exercise of that liberty will inevitably produce a situation in which only mutually advantageous associations can be sustained. As a result, some persons will be deprived of the benefits of an association that, while desirable from their point of view, is perceived as undesirable from the point of view of the other. When the association at issue is that between an employer and an employee the antidiscrimination mandate of the Civil Rights Act of 1964 requires that race play no part in the calculation of mutual advantage. But when the association is that between two prospective neighbors, mates, business associates, or friends, no such statutory restraints apply. And, while preferential treatment may be able to mitigate some of the consequences of this behavior for inequality between groups, it cannot hope to reverse them all. For example, affirmative action has almost no impact on the life circumstances of the ghetto poor, even though they constitute what many would agree is the most profoundly troubling manifestation of contemporary racial inequality.

CARING ABOUT GROUP INEQUALITY FOR THE WRONG REASONS

In the preceding section I have offered an argument for departure from the color-blind standard. This argument turns on the observation that, in the absence of such a departure, the consequences of historic racial discrimination might be perpetuated across the generations. It is important to emphasize what this argument does not say. Specifically, I do not intend to suggest that the practice of preferential treatment involves no injustice to those who are not its beneficiaries. Indeed, I am prepared to concede that racial preference does violate some principles of justice. I want to suggest that, even if discrimination is no longer practiced, the failure to give racial preference may result in even worse injustices, which could persist into the indefinite future. In a sense then I am suggesting that we choose the lesser injustice, considered over an extended temporal dimension. That is why I refer to my argument as "minimalist." It is also why I am very concerned to examine the practical efficacy of specific modes of preferential treatment, as discussed in the next section.

Moreover, because the use of preferential treatment involves the denial of opportunities to nonfavored individuals on the basis of their group membership, it is extremely important from a political point of view (as distinct from a philosophical point of view) to show sensitivity to the rights and interests of those who are disadvantaged by the policy. As political theorists have long recognized, more is required in the achievement and maintenance of a just society than the writing of philosophical treatises or the establishment of a constitution upholding essential principles of liberty. It is also necessary to secure as a practical political matter the means through which such principles might be lived by and followed in the everyday life of the polity. In a pluralist society such as ours, where distinctions of race and religion are deep and widespread, this is not a trivial matter. And while I would venture at this historical juncture to assert that the practice of preferential treatment may be necessary to secure this desired end, I also believe that the maintenance of comity in the relations between groups in our society requires a certain degree of restraint in how it is that one argues for such practices.

Yet, there are certain features of our public discourse over the legitimacy of racial preference which undermine the maintenance of this kind of comity. For example, affirmative action represents for many not merely needed public action in the face of past wrong, but rather a just recompense for that wrong. The distinction is vital. For many, affirmative action finds its essential rationale in an interpretation of history— that is, in an ideology: that blacks have been so wronged by white Americans that justice now demands they receive special consideration, as a matter of right and as a group. This mode of argument contrasts sharply with the means-end calculus which I have offered above.

In fact, I would venture to say that this doctrine of collective benefit and collective harm—that is, all white males have gained from past discrimination, and all blacks have been disadvantaged by it—is both morally dubious and factually weak. It risks bestowing benefits on persons who were not necessarily harmed by past wrongful acts, while at the same time disadvantaging individuals who have not benefited from those acts. It permits the denial of opportunities for a legal education, say, to lower-class whites and their provision to upper-class blacks on the basis of nothing more than the color of a person's skin. (And, although this may sometimes be the consequence of any policy of preferential treatment, it is one thing for it to occur as an unintended and unfortunate side effect of a policy rationalized on other grounds, and quite another for it to be the objective of the policy, or to be defended as the rightful due to the middle-class black for the wrongs endured by his race.) One well might ask: On what factual or logical basis are all whites, no matter what their individual circumstances, assumed to be beneficiaries of some collective benefit associated with past discrimination? Similarly, what historical experience permits one to assert that all blacks, no matter how well-off they may be should be, treated as if they were "damaged goods?"

This doctrine of collective claims leads to such questions as this: Have white women as a collective been so advantaged by virtue of their race that, notwithstanding their presumed general sexual disadvantage, they still deserve to be passed over in employment or educational admissions decisions in favor of black men whose presumed collective sexual advantage is more than offset by racial disadvantage? There is something patently absurd about an attempt seriously to address such a question. Moreover, in a nation of immigrants, as we have been and shall for some time continue to be, the use of this generalized historic harm/advantage model creates indefensible distinctions, for example, between those new arrivals from South America on the one hand and the south of Europe on the other, that have no logical or historical basis.

The reparations argument, moreover, immediately raises this question: Why do the wrongs of this particular group and not those of others deserve recompense? This can be a poisonous question for the politics of a pluralistic democracy. There is, of course, a favored answer to this question: slavery. But this answer does not really satisfy anyone—black or white. For no amount of recounting the unique sufferings attendant upon the slave experience makes plain why a middle class black should be offered an educational opportunity denied a lower class white. It is manifestly the case that many U.S. citizens are descended from forebears who had, indeed, suffered discrimination and mistreatment at the hand of hostile majorities both here and in their native lands. Yet, and here is the crucial point, these Americans on the whole have no claim to the public acknowledgement and ratification of their past suffering as do blacks under affirmative action. The institution of this policy, rationalized with this specific reparations argument, therefore, implicitly confers special *public* status on the historic injustices faced by its beneficiary groups, and hence implicitly devalues the injustices endured by others.

The public character of this process of acknowledgement and ratification is central to my argument. We are a democratic, ethnically heterogeneous polity. Racial preferences become issues in local, state, and national elections; they are the topic of debate in corporate boardrooms and university faculty meetings; their adoption and maintenance requires public consensus, notwithstanding the role that judicial decree has played in their propagation. Therefore, the public consensus requisite to the broad use of such preferences results, de facto, in the complicity of every U.S. citizen in a symbolic recognition of extraordinary societal guilt and culpability regarding the plight of a particular group of citizens. Failure to embrace the consensus in favor of such practice invites charges of insensitivity to the wrongs of the past or, indeed, the accusation of racism.[18]

But perhaps most important, the public discourse around racial preferences inevitably leads to comparisons among the sufferings of different groups—an exercise in what one might call "comparative victimology." Was the anti-Asian sentiment in the western states culminating in the Japanese interments during World War II "worse" than the discrimination against blacks? Were the restrictions and attendant poverty faced by Irish immigrants to northeast cities a century ago "worse" than those confronting black migrants to those same cities some decades later? And ultimately, was the Holocaust a more profound evil than chattel slavery?

Such questions are, of course, unanswerable, if for no other reason than that they require us to compare degrees of suffering and extents of moral outrage as experienced internally, subjectively, privately, by different peoples. There is no neutral vantage, no Archimedian point from which to take up such a comparison. We cannot expect that the normal means of argument and persuasion will reconcile divergent perceptions among ethnic groups about the relative moral affront which history has forced upon them. We must not, therefore, permit such disputes to arise if we are to maintain an environment of comity among groups in this ethnically diverse society. Yet some critics of affirmative action can be heard to say "Our suffering has been as great;" and some defenders of racial quotas for blacks have become " . . . tired of hearing about the Holocaust."

These are enormously sensitive matters, going to the heart of how various groups in our society define their collective identities. James Baldwin, writing in the late 1960s on this subject, in the face of Jewish objections to the use of quotas in New York City, declared what many blacks believe: "One does not wish to be told by an American Jew that his suffering is as great as the American Negro's suffering. It isn't, and one knows it isn't from the very tone in which he assures you that it is." And when, in 1979, Jesse Jackson visited Yad Vashem, the Holocaust memorial in Jerusalem, he deeply offended many Jews with what he may have considered a conciliatory remark—that he now better understood "the persecution complex of many Jewish people that almost invariably makes them overreact to their own suffering, because it is so great." By forcing into the open such comparative judgments concerning what amount to sacred historical meanings for the respective groups, the public rationalization of racial preference as payment for the wrongs of the past has fostered deeper, less easily assuaged divisions than could ever have been produced by a "mere" conflict of material interests.

So the legitimation of racial preference is not simply a matter of whether *blacks* think our ancestors' brutalization under slavery exceeded—in its inhumanity, its scale, its violence—the evil of Hitler's ovens. By involving judgments arrived at through democratic process, racially preferential treatment expresses the collective priorities of the nation as a whole. The special place of blacks in the practice of affirmative action is, therefore, doomed to be controversial, and in the end—should it become a permanent institution and should its application continue to favor blacks of comfortable social backgrounds over whites of more modest circumstance—unacceptable to a majority of U.S. citizens.

Individual citizens—be they Catholics, Jews, Armenians, blacks, or other—will, of course, understand it as an important responsibility to ensure that their children are imbued with a keen sense of the wrongs done to their group in the past. It is important for many Americans to keep alive in the memory of successive generations what their ancestors endured; this is crucial to their knowing, fully, who they are. It is, however, another matter entirely when one group of citizens requires all others to share such a private understanding—when, as a matter of proper social etiquette, it is required that all others share a sense of guilt about the wrongs a particular group has endured.

There is something tenuous, and ultimately pathetic, about the position of blacks in this regard. Do not recoil here at the use of the word "pathetic"; that, after all, is what this is all about—evoking the pity and the guilt of whites. But, for that very reason, the practice is inconsistent with the goal of freedom and equality for blacks. One cannot be the equal of those whose pity or guilt you actively seek. By framing the matter thus, the petitioner gives to those being petitioned an awesome power. He who has the capacity to grant your freedom, evidently has the ability to take it away—one is therefore dependent upon his magnanimity.

How long can blacks continue to evoke the "slavery was terrible, and it was your fault" rhetoric, and still suppose that dignity and equality can be had thereby? Is it not fantastic to suppose that the oppressor, whom strident racial advocates take such joy in denouncing, would in the interest of decency, upon hearing the extent of his crimes, decide to grant the claimants their every demand? The direct sociological role of the slave experience in explaining the current problem seems to be quite limited. The evocation of slavery in our contemporary discourse has little to do with sociology or with historical causation. Its main effect is moral. It uses the slave experience in order to establish culpability.

Yet the question remains: Why should others—the vast majority of whom have ancestors who arrived here after the emancipation, or who fought against the institution of slavery, or who endured profound discriminations of their own—permit themselves to be morally blackmailed with such rhetoric? How long can the failures of the present among black Americans be excused, and explained, by reference to the wrongs of the past? Would not one expect that, in due course, nonblack U.S. citizens would become inured to the entreaties of the black who explains teenage motherhood, urban crime, and low SAT scores with the observation that blacks have been in bondage for four hundred years? When pummelled with this rhetoric nowadays, most whites sit in silence. Dare we ask: What does that silence mean? (And, indeed, what does the constant repetition of this litany do to blacks themselves?) Must not, after some point, there begin to be resentment, contempt, and disdain for a group of people which sees itself in such terms? Consider the contradictions: Blacks seek general recognition of their accomplishments in the past, and yet must insist upon the extent to which their ancestors were reduced to helplessness. Blacks must emphasize that they live in a nation which has never respected their humanity, yet expect that by doing so, their fellow countrymen will be moved to come to their assistance.

It seems clear that it is the crushing poverty in which a minority of the black U.S. population lives in the core central cities of our country that makes this mode of rhetoric possible. In view of the history of racial oppression under which we as a political community must labor, the ongoing fact of significant group economic disparity is bound to be attributed by those advocating the interest of the dispossessed to a failure to make good on the promise of the U.S. civic creed. As such, the most likely remedy to be sought is an extension of special privileges and considerations to the members of the disadvantaged group, as a way of compensating for the perceived role which the limitation of citizenship rights in the past has played in generating the current condition. Thus, as a matter of politics again, the continued existence of profound racial economic disparity, higher poverty and unemployment rates for blacks, growing welfare dependency, inner-city urban decay, and so on, provide a primary source of legitimation of affirmative action. Yet, as a matter of policy, as distinct from symbolism, there is simply no evidence that racial preference has played anything other than a marginal role in achieving this goal of overall group equality. There is no evidence that the minority set-asides for millionaire black businessmen have caused benefits to trickle-down to the poor blacks. The studies of the impact of Office of Federal Contract Compliance programs shows employment effects too small to impact meaningfully on the overall racial difference in unemployment rates. If one were to look at black economic progress since 1940 one would find that most of the gains occurred before the advent of affirmative action in the 1970s. Moreover, the progress in narrowing the black-white wage gap has been relatively greatest for the most highly educated blacks and those working in the most prestigious occupations.

The reason for this is straightforward—affirmative action cannot get at the deep effects of past discrimination as they are manifest in the lowest economic strata of the black community, namely poor skills, disrupted family life, communities in decline, and the poor quality of inner-city primary and secondary education. It is one thing to say that the past demands redress as I did suggest earlier and quite another to prescribe employment preferences useful only to persons not suffering the worse consequences of that past as the means of accomplishing that redress.

Yet this is precisely what many advocates of affirmative action have done. In the late 1960s a very powerful idea was born. This idea is the general presumption that, due to our history of social oppression, blacks' failure to reach parity in U.S. society derives *exclusively* from the effects of past and ongoing racism, and can only be remedied through state intervention. This notion serves to rationalize the embarrassing pathology of the ghetto, even as it legitimizes governmental transfers to the black middle class.

The reasoning that leads to this curious result takes several steps. First, the large and growing number of black poor directly attests to the existence and severity of racial inequality. This inequality, in turn, must necessarily be understood as deriving from discrimination. (The unpalatable alternative is that blacks are less effective competitors in the U.S. economy—a possibility that will not be taken seriously as long as its very contemplation is regarded as a racist act.) But discrimination is best remedied by ensuring equal results in those arenas where blacks and whites directly compete. The conclusion is that racial injustice is best ameliorated through adopting the goal of proportional representation of blacks in business, professional, and governmental employments. Thus, for example, the squalor and hopelessness of the Harlem ghetto comes to ensure the legitimacy of preferential treatment for medical school applicants who are black but live in, say, Scarsdale, New York.

The fallacies in this argument have already been touched upon earlier in this chapter, and in any event are manifestly evident. Nevertheless, the damaging political consequences of this line of reasoning warrant further comment. The growing black underclass has become a constant reminder to many Americans of an historical debt owed to the black community. Were it not for the continued presence of these worst-off of all Americans, blacks' ability to sustain public support for affirmative action, minority business set-asides and the like would be vastly reduced. The suffering of the poorest blacks creates, if you will, a fund of political capital upon which all members of the group can draw when pressing racially based claims. Yet, when this political capital is expended for benefits that can be appropriated only by those blacks who are already fairly well-off, it is fair to question whether the overall interests of the group have been advanced. One might imagine that reference to the conditions of the black poor in order to justify programs of benefit mainly to the black middle class would engender little sympathy among whites for the claims of either group.

UNINTENDED NEGATIVE CONSEQUENCES OF THE USE OF RACIAL PREFERENCE

In the final section of this chapter I would like to explore some of the deleterious side effects that can issue from the use of color-conscious methods of employment selection in the public or private sectors. There is the danger that reliance on affirmative action to achieve minority or female representation in highly prestigious positions can have a decidedly negative impact on the esteem of the groups, because it can lead to the general presumption that members of the beneficiary groups would not be able to qualify for such positions without the help of special preference. This presumption, when widely held, can diminish the objective effectiveness of the beneficiaries of preferential selection.

If, in an employment situation, it is known that racial classification is in use, so that differential selection criteria are employed for the hiring of different racial groups, and if it is known that the quality of performance on the job depends on how one does on the criteria of selection, then it is a rational statistical inference, absent further information, to impute a lower average quality of job performance to persons of the race that was preferentially favored in selection. Using racial classification in selection for employment creates objective incentives for customers, coworkers, and others to take race into account after the employment decision has been made. Selection by race makes race "informative" in the post-selection environment.

In what kind of environments is such an "informational externality" likely to be important? Precisely when it is difficult to obtain objective and accurate readings on a person's productivity, and when that unknown productivity is of significance to those sharing the employment environment with the preferentially selected employee. For example, in a "team production" situation (like a professional partnership, or among students forming study groups), where output is the result of the effort of several individuals though each individual's contribution cannot be separately identified, the willingness of workers to participate in "teams" containing those suspected of having been preferentially selected will be less than it would have been if the same criteria of selection had been used for all employees.[19]

Also, when the employment carries prestige and honor, because it represents an unusual accomplishment of which very few individuals are capable, (an appointment in a top university faculty, for example), the use of preferential selection will undermine the ability of those preferred to garner for themselves the honorary, as distinct from pecuniary, benefits associated with the employment. (And this is true even for individuals who do not themselves require the preference.) If, for example, Nobel prizes in physics were awarded with the idea in mind that each continent should be periodically represented, it would be widely suspected (by those insufficiently informed to make independent judgments in such matters, and that includes nearly everyone) that a physicist from Africa who won the award had not made as significant a contribution to the science as one from Europe, even if the objective scientific merit of the African's contribution were as great. If law review appointments at a prestigious law school were made to ensure appropriate group balance, it could become impossible for students belonging to the preferred groups to earn honor available to others, no matter how great their individual talents.

An interesting example of the phenomenon I am discussing here can be found in the U.S. military. Recently sociologist Charles Moskos published an article in *The Atlantic* describing the results of his investigation of the status of blacks in the U.S. Army.[20] He noted that roughly 7 percent of all army generals are now black, as are nearly 10 percent of the army's officer corps. Moskos reports that among the black officers he interviewed the view was widely held that in the army blacks "(s)till . . . have to be better qualified than whites in order to advance." That is, racial discrimination still exists there. One senior black officer was "worried about some of the younger guys. They don't understand that a black still has to do more than a white to get promoted . . . If they think equal effort will get equal reward, they've got a big surprise coming." Yet, despite this awareness of racial discrimination, these officers were dubious about the value of racially preferential treatment in the military. Black commanders tended to be tougher in their fitness evaluation of black subordinates than were white commanders of their white subordinates. Even those officers who thought affirmative action necessary in civilian life disapproved of its use in the military. According to Moskos, "They draw manifest self-esteem from the fact that they themselves have not been beneficiaries of such (preferential) treatment—rather the reverse. Black officers distrust black leaders in civilian life who would seek advancement through racial politics or as supplicants of benevolent whites."[21]

Further illustration of the kind of unintended consequence that should be taken much more seriously by proponents of affirmative action, combining both the "team production" and the "honor" effects, comes from the world of corporate management. Many of those charged with the responsibility of managing large companies in the U.S. economy today are quite concerned with the state of their minority hiring efforts. The advent of affirmative action masks some serious, continuing disparities in the rates at which blacks, Hispanics, and women are penetrating the very highest ranks of power and control within these institutions. While equal opportunity could be said to be working tolerably well at the entry and middle level positions, it has proven exceedingly difficult for these "newcomers" to advance to the upper echelons of their organizations. The problem is so widespread that a name has been invented for it— the "plateauing phenomenon."

Increasingly, able and ambitious young women and blacks talk of taking the entrepreneurial route to business success, feeling stymied by their inability to get on the "fast track" of rapid promotion to positions of genuine power within their companies. Wall Street brokerage and law firms, though increasing the number of young black associates in their ranks, still have very few black partners, and virtually no senior or managing partners.[22] Though many large companies now have their complement of minority vice-presidents and staff personnel (especially in the governmental relations and equal opportunity areas), they remain with very few minorities at the rank of senior vice-president or higher, and with a paucity of nonwhites in those authoritative line positions where the companies' profits, and future leaders, are made.

In addition, minority or female employees may be hired or promoted into jobs for which they are not ready; better qualified nonminority personnel may, from time to time, be passed over for promotion. Here too, nonfavored employees will often perceive that mistakes of this sort are being made, even when in fact they are not. Resentments and jealousies are likely to arise. Charges of "reverse discrimination" will, in all probability, be mumbled more or less quietly among white men who sense themselves disadvantaged. It only takes one or two "disasters," in terms of minority appointments that do not work out, to reinforce already existing prejudices and convince many in the organization that all minority managers are suspect. *The use of racial or sexual employment goals is therefore likely to alter the way in which minority or women managers are viewed by their white male subordinates and superiors.*

And even though most minority employees may measure up to, or even exceed, the standards of performance that others in the firm must meet, the presence of just a few who do not casts an aura of suspicion over the others.

Given that competition for advancement from the lower rungs of the corporate ladder is sure to be keen, there is a natural tendency for those not benefiting from the organization's equal opportunity goals to see the progress of minorities or women as due in great part to affirmative action. If, to illustrate, four white men and one woman are competing for a position which ultimately is awarded to the woman, all four male employees may harbor the suspicion that *they* were unfairly passed over in the interest of meeting diversity goals, when in fact this supposition must be false for at least three of them, who would not have been promoted in any case.[23] When, as happens in many companies, the attainment of equal opportunity goals is seen as something that occurs only at the expense of productivity—as a price to be paid for doing business in the inner city, or to "keep the feds off our backs"—then these suspicions are given tacit confirmation by the organization's very approach to the problem of diversity.

Thus, the use of racial classification can entail serious costs. It can, if not properly and carefully administered, create or promote a general perception that those minorities or women who benefit from the firm's interest in increasing diversity are somehow less qualified than others competing for the same positions. And this general perception, when widely held, whether well-founded or merely a reflection of prejudice, can work to limit the degree of success and long-term career prospects of minority and female managers. For it is plausible to hold that in such a managerial environment, the productivity of an individual is not merely determined by the individual's knowledge, business judgment, industry, or vision. It depends as well on the ability of the manager to induce the cooperation, motivation, trust, and confidence of those whom he or she must lead. It depends, in other words, on the extent to which the manager can command the *respect* of his or her colleagues and subordinates.

This observation illustrates the fact that general suspicion of the competence of minority or female managerial personnel can become a self-fulfilling prophecy. When the bottom-line performance of a manager depends on his or her ability to motivate others, and when those who are to be motivated begin with a lack of confidence in the ability of the manager, then even the most technically competent, hardworking individual may fail to induce top performance in his or her people. And the fact that top performance is not achieved only serves to confirm the belief of those who doubted the manager's competence in the first place.

This self-reinforcing cycle of negative expectations is likely to be a particularly significant problem in the higher-level and line, as distinct from lower-level and staff, positions in an organization. Here an individual's contribution to company profitability depends heavily upon leadership and interpersonal qualities, securing the confidence and trust of peers, and motivating subordinates to achieve up to their potential. Managerial performance at this level depends rather less on individual, technical skills. That is, whether or not one becomes really "good" at these jobs is determined, in part, by how "good" others believe one can be.

Another critical factor at this level of an organization is self-confidence. This too may be undermined by the use of racial classification. Most people in such a situation want to be reassured that their achievement has been earned, and is not based simply on the organizational requirement of diversity. A genuinely outstanding person, who rises quickly to the mid-level of an organization without ever knowing for sure whether or not this career advance would have taken place in the absence of affirmative action, may not approach the job with the same degree of self-assurance as otherwise would be the case.[24] And this absence of the full measure of confidence that the person's abilities would otherwise have produced can make the difference between success and failure in the upper managerial ranks.

All of these potentially detrimental effects which I associate with the use of preferential treatment of nonwhite and female employees within an enterprise are reinforced by the general discussion of racial and sexual inequality in our society. The constant attention to numerical imbalances in the number of blacks v. whites, or women v. men, who have achieved a particular rank in the corporate sector in addition to placing what may be entirely warranted pressure on individual companies, serves to remind people—black and white, male and female—of the fact that such preferences are a part of their work environment. In order to defend affirmative action in the political arena, its advocates often seem to argue that almost no blacks or women could reach the highest levels of achievement without the aid of special pressures. Yet, this tactic runs the risk of establishing the presumption that all blacks or women, whether directly or indirectly, are indebted to civil rights activity for their achievements. And this presumption may reinforce general suspicions about minority or female competence that already exist.

None of this should be construed as an expression of doubt about the desirability of vigorously promoting diversity in corporate management, or elsewhere in U.S. society. What seems crucial is that, in the light of the pitfalls discussed above, the process of achieving diversity be managed with care, mindful of the dangers inherent in the situation. What is involved with affirmative action is not simply the rights of individuals, as many lawyers are given to argue, but also the prudence of particular means used to advance their interests. The "plateau" phenomenon, where able young minority or female managers find themselves unable to advance to the top ranks of their companies, undoubtedly reflects factors beyond those I have discussed. But it is the consensus judgment of personnel managers with whom I have talked that these factors are involved in many cases. In particular, it seems quite probable that general distrust of the capabilities of minority and female managers will accompany and reinforce old-fashioned racist or sexist aversion to having "outsiders" join the "old boy's network" of those holding real power within the organization. Such suspicions can, where occasionally validated by experience, provide the perfect excuse for preexisting prejudices. These prejudices are not merely "bad" behaviors that should be sanctioned. They are a part of the environment in which these policies operate, and may determine their success or failure.

CONCLUSION

In this chapter I have suggested the need for a more rigorous justification than has been offered of the departure from the simple "color-blind" interpretation of the antidiscrimination principle which the contemporary practice of preferential treatment represents. I have sought to provide such a justification. My argument turns on the extent to which *social* discrimination among today's citizens can perpetuate indefinitely the group inequality engendered by *economic* discrimination that may have occurred in the past. Because the antidiscrimination principle does not extend into the most intimate of private, associational choices, it is compatible with the continued practice of racial discrimination in such choices. Yet this practice, together with a history of racial discrimination in the public sphere, can ensure that the consequences of past bigotry become a permanent part of the social landscape. To avoid this possibility, I argue, the use of group conscious public action is justified.

Yet, I have recognized that such preferential policies may not be the only, or the best, response to persistent group inequality. And I have suggested that some of the arguments used to justify racial preference seem likely to exacerbate, rather than diminish, the problems of racial conflict that continue to afflict our society. I have been particularly critical of the "reparations" argument, which justifies special treatment of today's blacks on the basis of the mistreatment of blacks in the past. I have noted that such public practice implicitly elevates the past suffering of blacks to a privileged position over the mistreatments endured by other ethnic U.S. citizens, and does so in a way likely to be particularly controversial. This problem seems particularly severe when the preferential practices in question benefit blacks of comfortable economic circumstance at the expense of ethnic whites who may be more poorly situated.

Finally, I have noted that, even where justified, the use of racial preference may not be wise. This is a prudential argument which is meant to have only restricted applicability. There are certain types of environments where the danger of the negative unintended consequences of racial preference that I identify seems particularly acute. In these environments I urge that much greater caution be employed when efforts to increase "out-group" participation are undertaken. For, under the conditions outlined, the use of differential standards for members of different groups can work to undermine the capacity of the intended beneficiaries to garner for themselves the full benefits of their achievements, and can even objectively impede their functioning.

The debate over affirmative action has been left too much to lawyers and philosophers, and has engaged too little the interests of economists, sociologists, political scientists, and psychologists. It is as if, for this policy unlike all others, we could determine a priori the wisdom of its application in all instances—as if its practice were either "right" or "wrong," never simply "prudent" or "unwise." If I accomplish anything here I hope it is to impress upon the reader the ambiguity and complexity of this issue, to make him or her see that there is in this area the opportunity to do much good, but also the risk of doing much harm. The impassioned pursuit of justice, untempered by respect for the reasoned evaluation of the consequences of our efforts, is not always an advance over indifference.

NOTES

I have benefited from the comments of my colleague Dennis Thompson on an earlier draft of this essay, and from reactions to my seminar presentations by colleagues at The Institute for Advanced Study in Princeton, and at the Hebrew University of Jerusalem. A closely related version of the arguments presented here has been published under the title "Why Should We Care About Group Inequality?" in *Social Philosophy and Policy*, Vol. 5, no. 1 (1987), pp. 249–71.

1. See, for example, Thomas Sowell, *The Economics and Politics of Race: An International Perspective* (New York: William Morrow and Co., 1983). Sowell chronicles numerous instances around the world in which group differences in economic status do not correspond to the presence or absence of oppression. Often, as with the Chinese in Southeast Asian countries, or Indians in East Africa, or Jews in Western Europe, those subject to oppression have done better economically than those in the role of oppressor.

2. Compare Sowell, *The Economics and Politics of Race*.

3. Martin Luther King, Jr., "I Have A Dream," speech reprinted in F. Broderick and A. Meier, *Negro Protest Thought in the Twentieth Century* (Indianapolis, IN: Bobbs-Merrill, 1965).

4. Hubert Humphrey's speech to the Senate, during the floor debate on the Civil Rights Act of 1964, is often cited in this regard.

5. See Michael Walzer, *Spheres of Justice* (New York: Basic Books, 1981), ch. 5.

6. See, for example, Amartya Sen, *Collective Choice and Social Welfare* (Amsterdam: North Holland Publishing Co., 1979), p. 68. The anonymity axiom requires social decision makers to be indifferent as between two distributions of economic advantage which differ only in terms of who gets what reward, but which have the same overall pattern of reward.

7. See, for discussion of this transformation, William Bennett and Terry Eastland, *Counting by Race* (Ithaca, NY: Cornell U. Press, 1976); and, with par-

ticular focus on the area of school desegregation, Raymond Wolters, *The Burden of Brown* (Knoxville, TN: U. Tennessee Press, 1984).

8. I intend here no implication that King himself would have opposed these developments. Rather, on the basis of such evidence as is available, it seems likely that he would have supported them. See, for example, the biography of David Garrow, *Bearing the Cross* (New York: Morrow, 1987).

9. I think here, for example, of Ronald Dworkin's essay "Defunis v. Sweat," in which he attempts, with uncharacteristic inelegance, to distinguish between *Defunis*, on the one hand, and *Sweat* v. *Painter* on the other. R. Dworkin, *Taking Rights Seriously* (Cambridge, MA: Harvard Univ. Press, 1977), ch. 9. For a critical analysis of Dworkin's argument see Michael Walzer, *Spheres of Justice* (New York: Basic Books, 1981), ch. 5.

10. Following argument draws on my previous work. See *Essays in the Theory of Income Distribution*, PhD. thesis, Dept. of Economics, M.I.T., 1976, ch. 1; "A Dynamic Theory of Racial Income Differences," in P. A. Wallace and A. LaMond (eds.), *Women, Minorities and Employment Discrimination* (Lexington, MA: Lexington Books, 1977); "Is Equal Opportunity Enough?" *Am. Econ. Rev. Proc.*, May 1981, pp. 122–26; and "Beyond Civil Rights," *The New Republic*, October 5, 1985.

11. In keeping with my earlier discussion, it would be possible to treat such differences in tastes that have economic consequences (e.g., occupational preferences, entrepreneurial inclinations) as a part of what is conveyed through parents' social capital.

12. That is, it cannot be achieved so long as we respect the rights of individuals to make associations of their choosing, especially within the family. See Fishkin, *Justice, Equal Opportunity and the Family*.

13. See, for example, Thomas Schelling, *Micromotives and Macrobehaviors* (New York: W. W. Norton, 1978), ch. 4, for an analysis of how even a very mild individual preference for association with one's own kind can lead, in the aggregate, to a highly segregated outcome. For instance, Schelling notes that if everyone would rather live in a neighborhood in which their group is in the majority, then only complete separation will satisfy the preferences of all members of both groups.

14. This, in essence, is what sociologist William Julius Wilson has been arguing with respect to the inner-city poor. He notes that the primary problems facing poor blacks derive from their economic plight, and afflict poor whites as well. Moreover, he argues that political support for dramatic efforts to reverse these problems will be more readily had if those efforts are couched in racially universal terms. See, generally, his *The Declining Significance of Race* (Chicago, IL: Univ. of Chicago Press, 1978), and more specifically his recent article, "Race-Specific Policies and the Truly Disadvantaged," *Yale Law and Policy Review*, Vol. II, no. 2 (Spring 1984): 272–90.

15. Of course, public decisions regarding the provision of such services will be influenced by many considerations other than racial inequality.

16. The Supreme Court decision in the Detroit cross-district busing case *Milliken* v. *Bradley* (418 U.S. 717, 1974), limiting the use of metropolitan busing to solve the "white flight" problem, gives a classic illustration of this point.

17. See the work of the sociologist William Julius Wilson, *The Truly Disadvan-*

taged: Essays on Inner-City Woes and Public Policy (Chicago, IL: University of Chicago Press, 1987).

18. I have made this argument in somewhat more detail in my essay "Behind the Black-Jewish Split," *Commentary*, January 1986.

19. Recently lawsuits have been brought by mid-level minority employees working in large bureaucracies, at IBM and the U.S. State Department, for example, alleging that they are not treated the same by supervisors and co-workers. Yet, if they were hired under different criteria than the coworkers, they in fact, on the average, are *not* the same! Differential treatment, though regrettable, should come therefore as no surprise.

20. Charles Moskos, "Success Story: Blacks in the Army," *The Atlantic Monthly*, May 1986, p. 64.

21. Indeed, in order to defend such programs in the private sector, it becomes necessary for advocates to argue that almost no blacks could reach the positions in question without special favors. When there is internal disagreement among black intellectuals, for example, about the merits of affirmative action, critics of the policy are attacked as being disingenuous, since (it is said) they clearly owe their own prominence to the very policy they criticize. (See, e.g. Cornel West, "Unmasking the Black Conservatives," *The Christian Century*, July 16–23, p. 645.)

22. Frank Raines, black partner in Lazard Frères, reported in an interview that there are only three black partners in Wall Street investment firms, two of whom handle public finance issues (local, black governments being primary among their clients).

23. Psychological "incentives" exist for people to use this excuse even when it is not true. This gives them a good rationale for their own failure. As one colleague cleverly observed, "Affirmative Action is a boon to mediocre whites— by giving them reason to think better of themselves than they otherwise could."

24. Moreover, if you push too fast, good people may fail and be marked for life by that failure. Consider the case of the graduate student who would have done just fine in a State U., but who ends up at the bottom of his class at Harvard.

8 Socio-Dynamic Equality: The Contribution of the Adversarial Process

Frances Raday

It has been argued that equality under the Fourteenth Amendment is an "empty idea."[1] It is none other than a "premise of rational thought,"[2] "an axiom of all rational ethics . . . implicit in the notion of a norm or law of action as such."[3] By this reasoning, it is wrong to think that, once a rule is applied in accordance with its own terms, equality has something additional to say about the scope of the rule—something that is not already inherent in the substantive terms of the rule itself. To say that a rule should be applied "equally" or "consistently" or "uniformly" means simply that the rule should be applied to the cases to which it applies."[4]

I shall argue that the notion of equality which has developed under the Fourteenth Amendment is not empty but, on the contrary, signalled a revolutionary shift of perception on the philosophical as well as the socio-legal level. It is at one and the same time the product and the generator of an unprecedented process of social introspection as to the nature of equality between human beings. I shall suggest that this is a process that has gone beyond recognition of the formal norm of uniform application of rules. It is a process in which the concept of human equality as a social axiom is being redefined.

It is true that initiation of this process cannot be attributed to the wording of the "equal protection" formula itself. The formula as such adds nothing to classical imperatives requiring equality before the law. In this respect the philological critics of equality analysis cannot be faulted.[5] Nevertheless use of the formula has helped to promote a shift of perception as regards the meaning of human equality and even if the word equality in its classical sense cannot explain this phenomenon, the shift of perception is no less real for all that. How can this apparent gap between the theoretical analysis of equal protection and the empirical evidence of its development be reconciled? I shall argue that the word equality is being used to describe an ethical predicate which is different from its classical counterpart and that the classical concept, based on an arithmetic formula, has been replaced by a different kind of equality principle.

This modern concept of human equality is socio-dynamic rather than static. It does not postulate a final static model of equality as a blueprint for social organization but rather provides tools for the constant correction of existing inequalities. It is concerned with the elimination of blatant forms of discrimination rather than with the description or construction of an ideally egalitarian society.[6] Socio-dynamic equality designates the need for an ongoing process of social introspection as regards existing inequality in the treatment of members of society. It is not mere sophistry to claim the greater feasibility of eliminating inequality than of implementing equality or even defining it. While the differences between human beings may arguably be regarded as ultimately voiding the mathematical concept of human equality of all logical content,[7] there is certainly consensus as to a model of equality between human beings for a wide range of purposes, even if not for all purposes, which can act as a measuring rod against which current social conventions may be tested. A great deal may be achieved in this way without ever reaching problematic marginal areas of definition.

It is in this process of social introspection that the role of the Supreme Court under the Fourteenth Amendment has been of central importance. While it can be convincingly argued that the Supreme Court has not in its judgments moved consistently toward an ideal of equality, and while it is incontrovertible that the Court's judgments have not achieved concrete results in the form of a meaningful redistribution of social goods, positions and power,[8] this chapter will suggest that the process before the Supreme Court has nevertheless served an invaluable function. First, I shall argue that the adversarial process in producing a dialectic between the victims of discrimination and its perpetrators has stimulated an unprecedented articulation of the worldview of the victim and has provided a stage for its public presentation. Articulation of the view of the victims of discrimination has an intrinsic value in the shifting of perceptions on race and sex inequalities, which will remain for some time to come a necessary part in the struggle to achieve concrete change. Second, I shall show that this process has produced a notion of socio-dynamic equality that enables legal systems to play a meaningful role in the elimination of discrimination.

Although unique in its form, the process of reexamining social inequality under the Fourteenth Amendment is of course closely interlinked with other social developments, political and intellectual. There are those who would argue indeed that the process is so closely interlinked with nineteenth century developments in political theory in Europe that there is nothing new and nothing creative in the concepts of equality developed under the Fourteenth Amendment. Marxist analysts who regard the capitalist class structure as the true basis for all forms of human inequality regard analysis of subgroup oppression resulting from sexism and racism as redundant or as a mere branch of Marxist thinking. In the context of Marxist analysis there can be no meaningful correction of such oppression without confronting the entire class structure, and indeed liberal reform of the symptoms of such oppression serve merely to "legitimise the reality and ideology of the class society."[9] However, there is considerable evidence for the view that, although our ability to recognize and analyze subgroup inequality on grounds of race and sex owes much to Marxist analysis, it relates to a phenomenon that is separate not only in its source but also in its solutions.[10] Racism and sexism are phenomena that exist in noncapitalist societies as well as capitalist societies, and they have characteristics that cannot be convincingly attributed to the general economic class structure. The pervasive quality of subgroup oppression and the effectiveness of the socialization of both victims and perpetrators to acceptance of subgroup stereotyping which justifies oppression are problems that have evaded solution, intellectual or empirical, in the movements of social egalitarianism. Hence the dialectic process under the fourteenth amendment has made a contribution that cannot be dismissed as a mere application of nineteenth century European political thought.

Both as regards Marxist economic analysis of economic inequality and as regards constitutional analysis of discrimination, the process of introspection as to the nature of human equality appears to belong to the larger pattern of transition from status determined by group birthright to the open society where rights are acquired by contract between individuals starting from a doctrinally equal bargaining position. The importance of the concept of human equality for the legitimization of a contractual basis of social organization is strikingly illustrated by the Rawlsian analysis of the hypothetical "original position": "Among the essential features of this situation is that no-one knows his place in society, his class position or social status, nor does anyone know his fortune in the distribution of natural assets and abilities, his intelligence, strength and the like . . . The principles of justice are chosen behind a veil of ignorance. This ensures that no-one is advantaged or disadvantaged in the choice of principles by the outcome of natural chance or the contingency of social circumstances."[11] There is clearly a connection between the demise of group birthright and the growth of opposition to group discrimination. The shift in perception regarding the right of members of subgroups to equal opportunity is perhaps a natural outcome of this fundamental change in sociopolitical organization. However it was not inevitable, and in this chapter I want to explore the special contribution of the methodology of the adversarial system under the Fourteenth Amendment to the process of redefining human equality.

In the first part of the chapter I shall argue, empirically, that the judicial process under the Fourteenth Amendment made an important historical contribution to transforming the legal concept of equality. In the second part I shall explore the methodological contribution made by the adversarial system. In the last part I shall illustrate the concept of dynamic equality developed through the litigatory process.

HISTORICAL TRANSFORMATION OF THE LEGAL CONCEPT OF EQUALITY

Historically, the Fourteenth Amendment heralded a change in legal application of the principle of equality. Prior to this century, the prevailing paradigm of equality in political and legal science was based on the Aristotelian definition of equality as a requirement of justice: things that are like should be treated alike, while things that are unlike should be treated differently in proportion to their unalikeness.[12] This formula did not, as a matter of historical fact, lead to social introspection as to the characteristics which qualify different human beings as being equal or unequal for the purposes of political and legal rights. It did not render unequal treatment of slaves suspect; in Aristotle's opinion slaves were naturally inferior, with less spirit, marked out for subjection from birth; like tame animals they were better off when ruled by their masters.[13] The Napoleonic Code ensconced the principles of equality, liberty, and fraternity and made a revolutionary contribution to the legal implementation of the concept of equality before the law but it did not lead to a wholesale reexamination of the meaning of human equality; thus, for instance, it remained natural and undisputed to apply its principles only to male citizens—the right to equality remained the preserve of those within the "fraternity" and thus excluded women. The American Declaration of Independence stated the principle that all men are created equal and yet the Constitution originally excluded slaves and women from the right of suffrage. Under these accepted norms of equality, the Supreme Court held, in the *Dred Scott* case, that members of the "negro African race" were "not intended to be included in the general words used in that memorable instrument"; "they had for more than a century before been regarded as beings of an inferior order and altogether unfit to associate with the white race, in either political or social relations."[14] The Fourteenth Amendment was adopted and ratified in order to reverse the *Dred Scott* decision. Had the Fourteenth Amendment been applied according to the prevailing historical pattern of Aristotelian equality, its historical importance would have been limited to the immediate social reform with which it was associated. It would have dissolved into history as a limited political constitutional measure that signalled the enfranchisement of black Americans in the way the Napoleonic Code enfranchised the third estate.

Empirically, the breaking away from the established historical pattern cannot be denied. In applying the equal protection formula, the Supreme Court undertook a process of probing the exclusion of members of stigmatized subgroups of society from the sphere of equality itself which went far beyond the amendment's immediate political objectives. In the application of the formula by the Supreme Court, there was a reexamination of the "all" in "all men are created equal." There was a widening of the sphere of equality. Disqualifications on grounds of race and subsequently sex were struck down. The shift of perception that took place with regard to race and sex subgroups was accompanied by a breakdown in assumptions regarding exclusion of other subgroups. Thus disqualification or exclusion of members of groups on grounds of religion, alienage, disability, age, or illegitimacy was opened to question. Classifications on the basis of stereotypes applied to an individual because of his/her membership of a stigmatized subgroup were probed to establish whether they were based on relevant differences or whether they were based on discriminatory stereotypes. Westen writes: "Without moral standards, equality remains meaningless, a formula that can have nothing to say about how we should act. With such standards, equality becomes superfluous, a formula that can do nothing but repeat what we already know."[15] The impact of the "equal protection" formula, however, belies the assertion that there was nothing to be discovered in the concept of equality that we did not already know.[16]

This historical change in the application of the predicate of equality reveals a change of conceptual paradigm. The legal developments cannot be ascribed to the concept of equality in its Aristotelian form. They did not result from a formula for the uniform application of rules nor from an arithmetic equation in which the definition of those who are alike for the purpose of being treated alike was based on unexamined a priori social consensus and classification. I shall suggest below that the more meaningful concept of human equality that has developed under the Fourteenth Amendment is a concept of socio-dynamic equality which acknowledges the historical perspective and the influence of past inequalities on present rights to equal treatment. While there is valid controversy as to the extent to which the Supreme Court has adopted and applied this dynamic concept of equality in the outcome of its decisions, there can be no question that in many landmark decisions, in important minority opinions and in all articulation of the claims of victims of discrimination, socio-dynamic equality has been a persistent theme. Whatever the current level of its application, this is a new concept of equality that, unlike its classical counterpart, provides a legal framework for social introspection and for shifts of perception. Furthermore, to the extent that change has indeed been wrought in social consciousness and in prohibition of discrimination, this has been achieved, not through an arithmetic formulation of static equality, but through the systematic elimination of historical inequalities.[17]

The concept of sociodynamic equality involves recognition of discrimination and its elimination. This may constitute merely a temporary measure required for making the necessary adjustment to the open society and to a world in which birthright is no longer determinative. Once the adjustment has been effected and individuals have been freed from the historic chains of their birthgroup, the concept of elimination of discrimination might become redundant. In this form, the process will wither away as its objectives are achieved. Alternately, socio-dynamic equality may constitute a perpetual process of introspection and never bring about a static state of equality. In this form, it might be regarded perhaps as an Animal Farm antidote.

METHODOLOGY OF THE ADVERSARIAL SYSTEM

I want to suggest that the reason why the judicial process under the Fourteenth Amendment succeeded in making such an important contribution to the historical transformation of the concept of equality is in large measure attributable to the nature of the adversarial system. On the one hand, under the adversarial system, the method of analyzing issues leads to a different kind of philosophical analysis from that which results from abstract philosophical thought. On the other hand, the adversarial system provides, for subgroups seeking social change, a political forum that is in some ways unique.

As regards the philosophical analysis of equality, there has been an unusual interaction of the judicial and the philosophical method. The transformation in historical concepts of equality, which has been partially described above and which will be further analyzed below, originated in legal thinking and often became the subject of philosophical debate only after the issue had been raised in the Supreme Court.[18] It seems probable that the reason why the process of adjudication has made such a special contribution to conceptualization of equality theory is that the adversarial system has attributes that have in this sphere supplemented preexisting philosophical tools of analysis. If the problem of analysis of equality as an arithmetic formula was the unsuitability of human beings as subjects for exact equations, the very essence of the adversarial system corrected this lack. The process of adjudication in the adversarial system is highly individualized, rooted in a specific environmental reality and involves dialectic reasoning. It is these attributes that have lent the process of adjudication a power of philosophical creativity in this field.

It is characteristic of the adversarial system to develop the law on the basis of individual cases. The result of this method of investigation is that the judge, faced with decisions on concrete cases, is firmly rooted in a specific environmental reality. The parties each present their perception of the factors that have contributed to the allegation of inequality in the specific case. The socio-historic sources of the specific alleged inequality are presented to the Court by the parties and form a part of the analysis of the relative present positions of the protagonists, affecting the way in which present facts are interpreted. Furthermore, since it is to this end that the arguments of the parties are directed, whatever the majority outcome of the decision, the formulation of issues is necessarily from a concrete individual standpoint.

It is this special attribute of concrete individuality in the adversarial system which has contributed a perspective of social realism to the traditional philosophical debate on equality. Thus equality in the Supreme Court falls within the parameters of concrete rather than abstract universality. "Concrete universality . . . implies an alternative conception of the nature of history itself. As against the view that historical events are exemplifications of fixed a priori essences, this view regards essences, as well as history itself, as constituted or created by the actions of individuals. Concrete universality conceives the present as the moment in which individuals create history through their interaction with each other and the objective world. It sees the past as the set of interactions which provides the circumstances for present action."[19] Hence the judge, rather than seeking to define an ultimate static model of social equality, is bound to take on the more limited immediate task of eliminating individual and concrete inequalities.

The dialectic of the adversarial system is a central factor in the Supreme Court's contribution to the shift of perspective as regards the right of members of subgroups to be included within the sphere of equality. This system creates a framework in which the worldview of those previously considered nonpersons is articulated and must be taken into account. The standing bestowed on the individual member of the subgroup before a forum empowered to grant a remedy for the social wrong he/she protests opens up an official avenue for the articulation of the subgroup worldview which has been systematically silenced through the process of objectification.[20] Brittan and Maynard describe the impact of objectification on the formation of ideas: "both racism and sexism belong to the same discursive universe. By this we mean that they are both constituted by the objectification process. . . . Those who are objectified come to see the world through males eyes. The male epistemological stance becomes everybody's stance. Women and other objectified groups define their own realities through the perspective of their oppressors."[21] The adversarial system has in this respect a unique contribution to make. This system, unlike the inquisitorial process for instance, requires that the protagonists themselves not only make the claim but also set the agenda and formulate the issues. This results in a combination of empowerment and responsibility for subgroups that stimulates them to develop an alternate epistemological stance. In the adversarial system, the universality of the epistemological stance of the dominating group is replaced by a polemic presentation of opposing stances.[22]

The public rhetorical value of the polemics of equality in the Supreme Court has undoubtedly been secured and enhanced by the political diversity of its justices. Where the victims' perception has not gained majority acceptance, it has nevertheless usually been documented and approved in important minority decisions. While there is an innate value in the very formulation and articulation of an alternative worldview, the preservation and publication of that view in decisions where it has not gained majority acceptance plays an invaluable educative role. The dissenting opinions of Justices Brennan and Marshall form an integral part of our understanding of dynamic equality even where they have not been the basis for the Supreme Court's majority findings.[23]

The importance of the Supreme Court as a political forum lies in the fact that progress can be made in small steps without formulation of universal solutions and without activating a lobby for reform within the institutions of established power. If the individual can establish a case and convince a limited number of persons who belong to the institutions of power, that is, a majority of the justices of the Supreme Court, then that individual can obtain redress. The power of the individual to achieve redress and affect indirectly other members of his/her subgroup frees the pioneers from the almost insuperable obstacle of achieving equalization through the power of political lobby.[24] The adversarial system, then, transfers initiative for instituting the equalization process away from the repositories of established power and relocates it in the individual. Of course, it is only the power to initiate the debate and not the power to implement change which is thus transferred. The decision-making power remains with the judges who are themselves imbued with the prevailing epistemological stance as members of the dominating group that enjoys the benefits of that stance. Hence the importance of the Supreme Court as a political forum is limited to the process of articulating inequality and the Court cannot be expected to be an organ for the revolutionary change of social norms.

There are those who argue that the provision of a judicial forum for the grievances of victims of oppression is a way of diffusing their political power rather than enhancing it. Thus Polan argues, "when oppressed individuals and groups believe that they can rely on the legal system to redress their grievances and remedy their subordinate status in society, there is a decreasing likelihood that they will seek more radical solutions to their situation."[25] Certainly there is much to be said for the view that the use of the Supreme Court as a forum without the creation of political organization aimed at changing social institutions might create illusions or myths of action, which would damage the effectiveness of social protest. However, as Polan herself admits, the Supreme Court provides an important political forum even if it should not be regarded as the exclusive one for oppressed groups.[26] The process of articulating rights before that forum has an important role to play in those political organizations which Polan regards as crucial in the struggle for political power. These organizations gain focus and reinforcement of values by this articulation of rights and they in turn empower plaintiffs to continue to pursue their judicial remedies. In other words the processes of political empowerment and articulation of rights appear to be symbiotic rather than mutually exclusive.

The Court can fulfill the role of political forum even if its decisions do not consistently promote equality for oppressed individuals and groups. Should the Court, however, become so consistently antithetical to the victim perspective that it chills the readiness of oppressed groups to have recourse to the Court, that would of course put an end to this role. Several recent decisions of the Supreme Court, released since the time of writing this article, have altered the nature and the burden of proof in discrimination litigation in a way which handicaps discrimination plaintiffs.[27] It remains to be seen whether this signalizes the end of the Court's historic role as a major forum for the equality dialectic.

SOCIO-DYNAMIC EQUALITY

To illustrate the way in which the common law adversarial system promotes a socio-dynamic rather than a static concept of equality, I shall analyze a number of cases. These cases all deal with the themes of suspect or quasi-suspect classification and affirmative action. They are not intended to present a total picture of the results of Supreme Court decision making. There are other cases and indeed, as will be evident, there are decisions and dicta within the chosen cases that reject the historical perspective, insisting on color blindness,[28] on protection of vested rights of majority group members,[29] and proof of intent on the part of the perpetrator of discrimination.[30] I have, rather, chosen these cases to illustrate the way in which the adversarial process has promoted a concept of socio-dynamic equality, which even if it is not the exclusively prevailing doctrine of the Supreme Court, has gained acceptance as an alternative concept of equality and has contributed to some major gains for members of discriminated against subgroups.

In *Loving* v. *Virginia*,[31] the Supreme Court was presented with a claim, made by a black woman and a white man who had been convicted of violating Virginia's ban on interracial marriages, and that the prohibition of interracial marriage in Virginia was unconstitutional. The state's defence was that the prohibition was equal treatment—its purpose was to preserve the racial integrity of its citizens and its miscegenation statute punishes the white and the black participants in an interracial marriage equally. Thus the prohibition restricted the freedom of whites to marry blacks in the very same way that it restricted the freedom of blacks to marry whites.

Applying the Aristotelian formula of equality to this case would leave us with two alternatives. Alternative One: If blacks and whites are entirely alike for the purposes of marriage, then since application of the rule is equal, punishing as it does both whites and blacks equally for interracial marriage, the rule is egalitarian.[32] Alternative Two: If blacks and whites are different for the purposes of marriage, then the rule will be just as it treats different cases differently. Aristotelian equality analysis does not lend us tools to solve a problem of which we are intuitively aware as members of the society which prohibited interracial marriage, the problem of the all pervasive treatment of blacks as inferior.[33]

The Supreme Court presented with the Virginia statute enacted in a specific historical context, and presented with dialectically opposed "equality" arguments, developed its own equality analysis under the Fourteenth Amendment. The Court held that it was the clear and present purpose of the Fourteenth Amendment to eliminate all official state sources of invidious racial discrimination and that racial classifications must hence be subjected to the most rigid scrutiny. This amounts to creation of a presumption that blacks and whites are equal for all purposes including marriage and, hence, can be regarded as application of Alternative One of the Aristotelian equality analysis. The Court then probed the apparently equal application of the rule and found that "the fact that Virginia prohibits only interracial marriages involving white persons demonstrates that the racial classifications must stand on their own justification as measures designed to maintain White Supremacy." Furthermore, the Court adds in a footnote, "we find the racial classifications in these statutes repugnant to the Fourteenth Amendment, even assuming an evenhanded state purpose to protect the "integrity" of all races."[34] This goes beyond a mathematical formulation of equality. It is an awareness of historical inequality that brings the Court to find the present application of the rule unequal and a discrimination against blacks rather than against mixed-race couples. I suggest that it is the same awareness which brings them to regard the concept of preserving racial integrity as repugnant. Neither of these conclusions can be justified on an arithmetic analysis of equality.

Thus I contend that the concept of equality which emerges from judicial analysis of suspect classification in *Loving* v. *Virginia* is one of elimination of past discrimination. The Court chooses an analysis that is not neutral as between the races but that specifically acknowledges, in its indication that the classification is designed to maintain white supremacy, past oppression of blacks by whites. The very use of the word "suspect" indicates a need for social introspection with regard to racial classifications that disadvantage those who were previously assumed to be inferior.[35] It is an acknowledgment of the need to discard habits of thought and stereotypes that have obstructed the recognition of the basic premise that members of stigmatized subgroups are "like" other members of society. It arises from the need to combat prejudice.[36] It is because the devaluation of these "others" is so pervasive and engrained that one must treat with suspicion apparently "rational" classifications based on an assumed difference between the "others" and the classifiers, where these classifications disadvantage those who are stigmatized and devalued.[37]

The Supreme Court's equality criterion may not tell us for all cases which resemblances between persons are relevant but it does tell us which are irrelevant. Westen argues that the trouble with arguing that race and color are simply irrelevant constitutionally to the way that people should be treated is "that race and color are sometimes relevant to the way people should be treated. They are relevant to public physicians in deciding whether to test for race specific diseases; . . . to Public Broadcasting Directors . . . in staging color-specific performances . . . ; to public employers . . . in implementing race-specific affirmative action programmes."[38] If a static view of equality is taken, this bankruptcy of concept has to be admitted but when the immediate past, from which the present emerged, is one in which the importance of skin color was that it entirely excluded those with black skins from the sphere of equality, the more important task of equality analysis is to adjust the starting point. By a process of elimination of historical inequality, one approaches ever closer to the ideal of human equality even if one does not have the formula for finally reaching all-embracing equality. The concept of suspect classification is an auxiliary tool that facilitates perception of inequality which might otherwise be obscured by prejudice.[39]

The second case analysis in this chapter is not of one case but of a series of cases—the affirmative action cases. The issue in all these cases has been the validity of preferences given to members of minority groups and women in affirmative action programs. Before analyzing the fascinating equality dialectic which was precipitated by these cases, I want to summarize on a simple factual level four landmark affirmative action programs challenged before the Supreme Court and the fate they met there. (1) The U.C. Davis Medical School Plan was designed to admit 16 minority students in each entering class of one hundred; minority students were admitted in a special admissions program and the grade point average required for preliminary eligibility for admission did not apply to them. The plan was held to be unconstitutional.[40] (2) The Kaiser–USWA Plan was designed to increase the number of black craftworkers in the Kaiser Aluminium Plant till their numbers became commensurate with the number of blacks in the local labor force. The plan reserved 50 percent of the positions in in-plant craft training programs for black employees, thus giving them preference over more senior, white employees. This plan was upheld under Title VII.[41] (3) The Jackson Board of Education–JEA (Jackson Education Association) Plan was designed to maintain the existing percentage of minority teachers employed by the board in economic layoffs. In order to achieve this goal, the plan provided for an exception to the basic criterion that teachers with the most seniority would be retained. The plan was held to be unconstitutional.[42] (4) The Santa Clara Transportation Agency Plan was designed to achieve a statistically measurable yearly improvement in hiring and promotion of minorities and women in job classifications where they are underrepresented. The plan provided that in making promotions to traditionally segregated jobs in which women have been significantly underrepresented, the agency may consider as one factor the sex of a qualified applicant. The plan was upheld under Title VII.[43]

I shall not attempt here to weave a detailed tapestry of the numerous issues raised in this series of cases, or of the variety of opinions of different judges, or of the same judges in different cases. I shall rather sketch in broad lines the dialectic of equality that emerges from the consideration of the issue of affirmative action in the Supreme Court. The issue of affirmative action involves a rather different polemic strategy than that in the preceding cases. Here the voice that has been heard is not that of the historically burdened groups claiming the right to equalization but that of the white/male group claiming that they have become the victims of unequal treatment. This polemic produced what appears to have been a novel philosophic puzzle, the puzzle of "reverse discrimination."[44]

In the *Bakke* case, the equality dialectic stimulated by the reverse discrimination issue produced two distinct schools of thought: According to one school of thought, racial classifications are always suspect, even where they purport to be beneficial to racial or ethnic minorities who have been subject to prejudice and discrimination. Hence, in order to justify an affirmative action program, the employer must show a compelling state interest. Thus equal protection is, at least initially, color-blind.

"The concepts of 'majority' and 'minority' necessarily reflect temporary arrangements and political judgments . . . the white majority itself is composed of various minority groups most of which can lay claim to a history of prior discrimination at the hands of the state and private individuals. . . . Not all of these groups can receive preferential treatment because then the only 'majority' left would be a minority of White Anglo-Saxon Protestants. There is no principled basis for deciding which groups would merit 'heightened judicial solicitude' and which would not." Since preferential treatment is suspect, it can only be justified if its use is "necessary" to achieve a governmental interest that is legitimate and substantial. "Remedying the effects of past societal discrimination" is "too amorphous" a concept of injury to vindicate "a governmental interest in preferring members of the injured groups at the expense of others. . . . the government has no compelling justification for inflicting such harm."[45]

According to the other school of thought, race classifications are not invariably "suspect"; they are suspect only when they are "drawn on the presumption that one race is inferior to another . . . even today officially sanctioned discrimination is not a thing of the past. Against this background, claims that law must be colorblind or that the datum of race is no longer relevant to public policy must be seen as an aspiration rather than a description of reality. . . . we cannot . . . let color blindness become myopia which masks the reality that many "created equal" have been treated within our life times as inferior both by the law and by their fellow citizens."[46] Where the race classification purports to be benign to the stigmatized racial group, it is enough to show an important rather than a compelling government objective to justify use of the classification. An articulated purpose of remedying "past societal discrimination" is sufficiently important to justify the use of race-conscious admissions programs.[47]

In the most recent of the affirmative action cases, *Johnson* v. *Santa Clara Transportation*, Justice Stevens summarizes the history of the dialectic in the Supreme Court on the issue of affirmative action, before *Bakke* and after. He describes a transition from the initial position that the prohibition of discrimination was intended "to eliminate all practices which operate to disadvantage the employment opportunities of any group protected by Title VII including Caucasians" to the present position that "the statute does not absolutely prohibit preferential hiring in favor of minorities; it was merely intended to protect historically disadvantaged groups against discrimination and not to hamper managerial efforts to benefit members of disadvantaged groups that are consistent with that paramount purpose." He regards this as the "authoritative construction" and, in adhering to it, he joins the majority of the Court.[48] However, the dialectic does not end here. The dissenting minority remains convinced that "The Court today completes the process of converting [Title VII] from a guarantee that race and sex will not be the basis for employment determinations, to a guarantee that it often will."[49]

The adversarial process opened the way for those who regarded themselves as victims of affirmative action programs to articulate their grievance and produced a rich philosophical dialectic as to the egalitarianism of measures introduced to adjust or correct inequality.

Dworkin devotes a chapter of his book, *Taking Rights Seriously*, to analysis of "Reverse Discrimination." He points out that the *DeFunis* case "split those political action groups that have traditionally supported liberal causes." Dworkin describes the core of the moral argument that split the liberals as follows. "[E]ven if reverse discrimination does benefit minorities and does reduce prejudice in the long run, it is nevertheless wrong because distinctions of race are inherently unjust. They are unjust because they violate the rights of individual members of groups not so favoured, who may thereby lose a place as DeFunis did."[50] Justifying affirmative action, Dworkin distinguishes it from racial classifications used for segregation. He argues that the entitlement to equality is not a "right to equal treatment" but rather the "right to be treated as an equal."[51] In this case, disadvantage resulting to DeFunis does not give him grounds for complaint provided it improves the general welfare. Although DeFunis is not receiving equal treatment, he is being treated as an equal. The general welfare is improved by affirmative action in a way which it is not improved by segregation. Segregation can serve only utilitarian objectives, while the "arguments for a discrimination programme in favor of blacks are both utilitarian and ideal. . . . The ideal arguments do not rely on preferences at all, but on the independent argument that a more equal society is a better society even if its citizens prefer inequality."[52]

Unfortunately it seems to me that this analysis does not resolve the dichotomy. The question whether a society is indeed more equal where it refuses to allow race to be used as a disadvantaging classification, whatever the race, or where it allows "discrimination programmes" in favor of the disadvantaged, cannot be resolved unless one chooses between the two alternate concepts of equality discussed in this chapter. If one chooses arithmetic equality, then it seems clear that the "more equal" society will be that in which race is not permitted as a relevant classification, irrespective of which race. As a static equation, once it has been determined that black = white then it follows that white = black. It is only if one chooses the socio-dynamic concept of equality, equalization, that it can be asserted that a society that reduces the residual inequality of those historically deprived of equality is a "more equal society."[53]

Owen Fiss, analyzing the interpretation of the equal protection formula, considers that an antidiscrimination formula has been developed which rests on illusions of blindness to irrelevant characteristics, value-neutrality, and objectivity. This form of antidiscrimination is deficient in his view because it will not allow us to uphold preferential treatment for blacks and reject it for whites even though we perceive it as a measure of desirable reform. He suggests a shift from classification to class and the reinterpretation of the equal protection clause as providing protection for "specially disadvantaged groups."[54] He writes: "Equality is a relativistic idea. The concern should be with those laws or practices that particularly hurt a disadvantaged group."[55] Two kinds of justification are offered for this interpretation of equality. The first is a theory of compensation: "..blacks as a group were put in that position by others and the redistributive measures are owed to the group as a form of compensation. The debt would be viewed as owed by society. . . . " The second is a political theory: "[T]he elimination of caste might be justified as a means for (a) preserving social peace; (b) maintaining the community as a community, that is as a cohesive whole; or (c) permitting the fullest development of the individual members of the subordinated group . . . "[56]

While the group-disadvantaging principle would conform to a socio-dynamic concept of equality, Fiss does not justify it in terms of equality. He justifies affirmative action in welfare or political terms. I suggest that, at least at its core, affirmative action can be regarded as a principle of equality. Affirmative action, narrowly defined, is no more than the process of equalizing. Just as there are good socio-historic grounds for "suspecting" racial classifications which limit the freedom or opportunities of blacks or women, there are similar grounds for suspecting that underrepresentation of blacks or women in educational institutions or job classifications is lingering evidence of discrimination. Thus one can justify as a socio-dynamic equalization measure that form of affirmative action which says that wherever whites and blacks or men and women are qualified for an opportunity of which they have been deprived, historically by formal edict and presently by statistical evidence, continuing refusal to give the "deprived" group member the opportunity should be suspect.[57] Measures that attempt to obviate the grounds for suspicion, by injecting race or sex as a criterion which has to be positively taken into account, are socio-dynamic equalization measures.

The socio-dynamic equalizing role of affirmative action is not problematic at the group level. The whole of white/male society can be regarded as compensating the whole of black/female society for the injury which the former caused the latter.[58] Since the compensation is an aggregate compensation and the group inequality inherited from past denial of personhood is not contested, the process of compensation can be justified even on a test of Aristotelian equality.[59]

However, as regards the application of affirmative action at the individual level, it has been suggested, and indeed the entire polemic of reverse discrimination in the Supreme Court demonstrates, that the white/male may be regarded as a new victim of inequality. Thus, the argument is put, "Generally, when one employs a remedial principle as a device for compensation for damages sustained, the compensated party is the one who has been injured, and he who compensates is he who has caused the injury. . . . [In the case of] preferential treatment in hiring, there is no reason to assume that the specific black candidate who is preferred over non-blacks who are equally or better qualified than he for the position was himself discriminated against in the past as to such employment. Moreover, the one who truly pays the price of 'compensating' the black candidate for employment is not the employer who has previously discriminated against blacks, but rather the non-black candidate who is forced to be rejected in favour of the black."[60]

Various constructions have been applied to avoid the victim dilemma: the concept that the "new victim" is not subject to a specific disability but only to a "diffuse burden" or the requirement that the plaintiff must show that there has been discrimination not by society at large but by the employer and this has resulted in identified race-based injuries to individuals held entitled to the preference.[61] These tactics, however, scarcely solve the "victim" dilemma. The first, the concept of a diffuse burden on the victim is a mere question of degree. The second, a test of prior discrimination by the administrator of the affirmative action plan, may identify an oppressor and a victim but these are not the very same persons who are to pay the price and gain the benefit of the affirmative action. Thus, by this analysis, we are still confronted with a possibly undeserving beneficiary and a clearly innocent "victim."

Although the Supreme Court may not yet have succeeded in resolving the issue, the cases themselves tell us a number of stories about "victims" that may be suggestive of other ways of looking at the problem. Perhaps instead of searching for attributable blame and diffuse remedial burdens, we could retrace our steps and ask ourselves whether the affirmative action in each case is truly reverse discrimination, creating a new victim of inequality, or whether it is a measure of socio-dynamic equalization and hence only disappoints expectations that were themselves based on inequality. For this enquiry there are different kinds of stories.

The first story is one in which the minority candidate or the woman is not anonymous and the criteria for acceptance to the job or admission to the educational institution are not mechanical. This is, in fact, the story in the *Johnson* case, where pursuant to the affirmative action plan, Diane Joyce was appointed to a position as road dispatcher, which was one of 238 positions held by men. She was appointed in preference to Paul Johnson, although they were both qualified by experience for the job and Johnson scored marginally higher than Joyce in interview. Justice Brennan, giving the opinion of the Court, pointed out: "there is rarely a single, 'best qualified' person for a job. An effective personnel system will bring . . . several fully qualified candidates who each may possess different attributes which recommend them for selection. . . . final determinations as to which candidate is 'best qualified' are at best subjective."[62]

If we admit the pervasiveness of objectification and devaluation of members of burdened groups on grounds of their group membership, then we can deduce that, unless we adjust it, the subgroup membership will act as a negative factor against the individual. We can assume that in the interviewing, the fact that Joyce was a woman counted against her, whether at a conscious or unconscious level. (Can any human being pretend to be capable of judging as if "it" were in Rawl's original position?) An appropriate way to rebut the resulting assumption of discrimination is by admitting qualified group members until their numbers are indicative of the demise of unequal treatment. Articulated denial of discrimination alone will not suffice to rebut the assumption, both on grounds of the profit to be gained by denial and because prejudice is not necessarily consciously recognized by the holder. Here the affirmative action program is no more than an equalization technique and the concept of a "victim" is an illusion.

Under conditions of arithmetic equality, without socio-dynamic equalization by affirmative action, in a world which is barely emerging from a history of subgroup inequality to the point of loss of personhood, the white/male would have been able to make a strong probabilistic prediction that he would be preferred over any equal black/female. This expectation would be based on the reality of inequality. Affirmative action frustrates this prediction. In this sense it disappoints the expectations of the white/male. However, it does not produce a symmetrically reverse discrimination. The white/male is not suffering from imposition of an unequal burden but only from the adjustment of his erstwhile unequal advantage. Affirmative action will, in this story, be operative only until such time as the justifiable suspicion that the black/female is not really in the running, in spite of equal formal qualifications, has been dispelled.

The second story is that of an admissions or appointments system which uses in its qualification requirements a points system in which members of subgroups have not had the opportunity to gather the points. This is the story of *Wygant*. The affirmative action plan was intended to maintain the proportion of minority teachers in the schools when carrying out layoffs. The criterion for staying in the job was seniority; the minority teachers had lower levels of seniority than white teachers.

Here, where there is an apparently neutral criterion for allocating jobs, it is less easy to talk of equalizing in each individual case, of merely

countering latent or hidden discrimination. Even in this context, however, it is possible to seek out the historical source of inequality and to
ask whether minority teachers actually had less opportunity than the
white teachers to acquire seniority, to gather the points. This way of
looking at the problem presents possibilities for discovering equalization
rather than reverse discrimination in an application of affirmative action
measures to adjust the lack of seniority.[63] If we apply a test of socio-
dynamic equalization, it is not enough to ask, as did Justice O'Connor
in *Wygant*, whether the present numbers of black teachers employed by
the board tally with numbers of qualified teachers in the job market. In
order to determine whether the black teachers had a real opportunity
to accumulate seniority points, one has to ask whether they were admitted, freely and in numbers appropriate to the pool of qualified potential applicants, to universities or teachers' training courses at the time
when the senior whites were training to be teachers, and whether the
intake of black teachers by the board corresponded at that determinative
time with the number of black teacher graduates. If the minority teachers
can show a discrepancy in training opportunities or employment opportunities at the time when the Jackson Board teachers began to acquire
seniority, they will have made out a case of unequal opportunity in
acquiring seniority and of entitlement to application of an equalizing
procedure. The white teachers will not be victims of unequal treatment
but, as in the first story, the holders of disappointed expectations that
were themselves based on inequality.

The third story is the story of an anonymous admissions system that
uses apparently neutral criteria. This is basically the story of *Bakke*. Although there was an interview procedure involved in the Davis Medical School admissions process, there was also a mechanical cutoff
undergraduate grade point average, which the minority students did
not have to meet under the affirmative action plan. This feature of the
plan has received little attention. However, it is instructive to note that
it was not a feature of the Harvard plan, which was approved by the
majority of the Court while the Davis plan was rejected. The distinction which the Court drew between the Davis and the Harvard plans
was that while in the former, race was the only characteristic for eligibility, in the latter, it was only one of a variety of diverse characteristics to be taken into consideration.[64] While this articulated distinction
has rightly been criticized as unconvincing, the absence of disparate
application of a neutral cutoff grade may, as I shall illustrate, contribute to an understanding of the differing intuitions that the Court had
as to the two plans.

The differing application of anonymous neutral criteria is the most
difficult of the stories to explain in terms of equalization. Here we need
not be on guard against suspected discriminatory motive in the people
making the admissions decision. And, if we want to show that minorities

were disadvantaged on grounds of race in gathering the points for eligibility, we are faced with the incontrovertible fact that the minority students were given the formal opportunity to gather points, since they had already acquired the basic qualifications, they had completed undergraduate school. However, even in this story there are ways of perceiving affirmative action as equalization, and not as compensatory inequality the cost of which is imposed on innocent victims, but these ways are more amorphous.

Here the claim of adjusting inequality would rest on a history of societal discrimination that has produced both cultural bias and psychological disadvantage that handicap members of subgroups in taking full advantage of newly opened opportunities for education. If the adverse temporary impact of societal discrimination could be quantified in the way that the statistical impact of exclusion from specific social institutions can be quantified as regards their impact on the individual, affirmative action could perhaps be as easily perceived as equalization in this story as in the others. However, we do not have these means of quantification at our disposal and hence a perception of affirmative action in applying anonymous neutral criteria as equalization at the individual level depends on a preparedness to assume that every member of a subgroup bears some historic handicap and that, whatever the level of his/her achievements, these achievements have been gained from a disadvantaged starting point and are lower than they would otherwise have been. It is the difficulty of quantifying the impact of past societal discrimination on current achievement which makes it impossible to prove the case for equalization. As such, this is the story which has drawn the strongest opposition to affirmative action and which feeds the perception that affirmative action creates innocent victims. It is this story which leads to warnings of the dangers of perpetuating the stigmatization of the subgroup. A case for equalization may be conceptualized in this story too but, without more exact means of measurement, it is realized at the cost of making problematic assumptions.

Where the parameters of affirmative action as equalization can be accurately established, within these parameters the problems of affirmative action as reverse discrimination recede. Beyond these limits, affirmative action becomes a welfare or political project. As such it may be justified, but on grounds other than "equalization," at the individual as well as the group level.[65] It may be argued that, in view of the difficulties of accurately setting the parameters of the equalization process or in view of the narrowness of those parameters once established, this distinction between equalization and compensation is mere sophistry. However I think that a perception that the kernel of affirmative action is equality and not compensatory inequality increases our understanding of the issues. The dialectic of equality in the Supreme Court has sharpened our awareness of these issues and the ongoing differences in the thinking of the Court as to the parameters of affirmative action demonstrate that the process of defining the new equality has not been completed. An arithmetic equality analysis cannot resolve the issue of reverse discrimination and its use will always necessitate the finding of other justifications for affirmative action. A dynamic socio-historical version of equality as equalization allows for narrowly defined affirmative action programs within the context of equality analysis. This does not preempt further arguments in favor of welfare or compensatory affirmative action but allows us to recognize that, at its core, affirmative action is not reverse discrimination.

The seeds of a meaningful concept of equality—the concept of socio-dynamic equality—have been sown in the adversarial process under the Fourteenth Amendment. Socio-dynamic equality is indeed equality in all its phases—looking to the past, it requires elimination of inequality; in the present, it seeks to identify and adjust the lingering impact of inequality; and, for the future, it holds out a vision of human equality, which, even if it cannot be ultimately and comprehensively defined, can be perpetually sought and approached.

NOTES

1. Westen, "The Empty Idea of Equality," 95 *Harvard L. Rev.* 537 (1982).

2. Freund, "The Philosophy of Equality," 1979 *Wash.U.L.Q.*, 11,14.

3. Ginsberg, *On Justice in Society* (1965) 80. Browne, "The Presumption of Equality," 53 *Australasian J. Phil.* (1975): 46,51.

4. Westen, p. 551.

5. See Westen, "The Meaning of Equality in Law, Science, Math and Morals: a Reply," 81 *Michigan L. Rev.*, 604, 606–612.

6. Evidence of this conceptualization of the modern idiom of equality is to be found in the formulation of the various U.N. Conventions "for the Elimination of All Forms of Discrimination"—on grounds of race, 1965, and against women, 1980.

7. See Westen.

8. See Freeman, "Anti-Discrimination Law—a Critical Review," in Kairy, ed., *The Politics of Law* (New York: Pantheon Books, 1982).

9. Freeman, pp. 97, 110.

10. Brittan and Maynard, *Sexism, Racism and Oppression* (Oxford, England: Blackwell, 1984).

11. Rawls, *The Theory of Justice*, (Cambridge, MA: Harvard University Press, 1971), p. 12.

12. Aristotle, *Nichomachean Ethics*, Ostwald trans. (Indianapolis: Babbs-Merrill, 1962), p. 118, para. 1131a-b.

13. Gould and Wartotsley, *Women and Philosophy* (New York: Putnam, 1976), p. 159; Aristotle, "Politica" in *Works of Aristotle*, Jowett trans., vol. 10, book 1 (Oxford: Clarendon, 1921), para. 1254b, 1255 a-b.

14. Dred Scott v. Sandford, 19 How 393, 15 L.ed. 691, 701.

15. Westen, "The Empty Idea of Equality," pp. 547, 565.

16. For further debate on this issue, see Chemerinsky, "In Defence of Equality: A Reply to Professor Westen," 81 *Michigan L. Rev.* 575 (1983); Westen, "The Meaning of Equality in Law, Science and Morals: A Reply," pp. 604, 634.

17. See Wechsler, "Toward Neutral Principles of Constitutional Law," 73 *Harvard L. Rev.* 1, (1959).

18. An outstanding example is the issue of affirmative action. It was only after the Supreme Court considered the issue of affirmative action in the case of DeFunis v. Odegaard, 416 U.S. 312 (1974), that the first major philosophical analysis of the issue appeared: Nigel, Scanlon, et al., *Equality and Preferential Treatment* (Princeton, NJ: Princeton University Press, 1977).

19. Gould, "The Woman Question: Philosophy of Liberation and the Liberation of Philosophy," in *Women and Philosophy—Toward a Theory of Liberation,* Gould & Wartofsky, eds., (New York: Putnam, 1976), p. 27.

20. Kuper, *Race, Class and Power* (London: Duckworth, 1974), pp. 13–14. MacKinnon, "Feminism, Marxism, Method and the State: An Agenda for Theory" in Keohane et al., eds., *Feminist Theory* (Brighton, England: Harvester Press, 1982), pp. 23–24.

21. Brittan and Maynard, *Sexism, Racism and Oppression* (Oxford, England: Blackwell, 1984), pp. 203—04.

22. See Chemerinsky, "In Defense of Equality: A Reply to Professor Westen," 81 *Michigan L. Rev.* 575, 591 (1983) on equality as a "rhetorically necessary concept."

23. Compare Freeman, 98: "modern American law has adopted what I have called the perpetrator perspective. It purports to be a stance of society as a whole, or of a disinterested third party gaze looking down on the problem of discrimination, and it simply does not care about results."

24. See Brittan and Maynard, *Sexism, Racism and Oppression* (Oxford, England: Blackwell, 1984), 71–112.

25. Polan, "Toward a Theory of Law and Patriarchy," in Kairy ed., *The Politics of Law* (New York: Pantheon Books, 1982), pp. 294, 300.

26. Ibid., 300–01.

27. See, for instance, *City of Richmond* v. *J. A. Croson Company,* 1989 U.S. Lexis 579, 57 U.S.L.W. 4132; *Price Waterhouse* v. *Hopkins,* 1989 U.S. Lexis 2230; 57 U.S.L.W. 4469.

28. See below, Justice Powell in *University of California Regents* v. *Bakke,* 438 U.S. 265 (1978).

29. See below, *Wygant* v. *Jackson Board of Education,* S. Ct. No. 84–1340, 54 U.S. Law Week 4480 (1986).

30. Washington v. Davis, 426 U.S. 229 (1976); and compare Griggs v. Duke Power, 401 U.S. 424 (1971).

31. 338 U.S. 1, 87 S.Ct. 1817, 18 L.Ed.2d. 1010 (1967).

32. This was indeed the basis of the decision in Pace v. Alabama, 106 U.S. 583 (1883).

33. In this vein, Westen analyzes the case of Sweatt v. Painter, 339 U.S. 629 (1950) and argues that the appellant's challenge of the constitutionality of a state statute that barred blacks from attending the state's all white law school, where

alternative education at an all black law school was provided, posed a question that equality cannot answer: Westen, p. 566.

34. See Note 4 regarding the judgment.

35. Nevertheless, in Korematsu v. United States, 323 U.S. 214 (1944), the original test was formulated neutrally: " . . . legal restrictions which curtail the civil rights of a single racial group are immediately suspect." The neutrality of the phrase "a single racial group" combined with the clearly partisan nature of the word "suspect" indicates an ambivalence which, as I shall show below in discussing the affirmative action cases, has accompanied application of the doctrine ever since.

36. "Prejudice is a misjudgment of the members of a supposed human group: it is socially oriented action. One may misjudge the speed of an approaching car, but one is anxious to correct the error. Prejudice is a misjudgment which one defends." Simpson and Yinger, *Race Discrimination*, p. 21.

37. See Ely, "The Constitutionality of Reverse Racial Discrimination," 41 *U.Chi.L.Rev.* 723 (1974), "When the group that controls the decision making process classifies so as to advantage a minority and disadvantage itself, the reasons for being unusually suspicious are . . . lacking."

38. Westen, p. 566.

39. See Hart, *Concept of Law*, p. 155.

40. University of California Regents v. Bakke 438 U.S. 265, 98 S.Ct. 2733, 57 L.Ed.2d.750 (1978).

41. United Steelworkers v. Weber 443 U.S. 193 (1979).

42. Wygant v. Jackson Board of Education, S.Ct. No.84–1340. Decided May 19, 1986, 54 *U.S. Law Week* 4480.

43. Johnson v. Transportation Agency, Santa Clara County, Calif., No.85–1129 S.Ct. March 25, 1987 (Slip opinion).

44. See Note 18.

45. Justice Powell. At pp. 307–309. Similarly, Justice Stevens, Justice Stewart, Chief Justice Burger, Justice Rehnquist. A majority of the Court hence found the Davis plan created reverse discrimination against the petitioner. Justice Powell did not, however, exclude all uses of racial classification in university admissions. He considered the "Harvard plan" legitimate in that it only included race as one of a large variety of criteria used to diversify the student body.

46. Justice Brennan. At p. 327. Justices White, Marshall, Blackmun, JJ. concurred.

47. Justice Brennan. At p. 362. Similarly Justices White, Blackmun, Marshall. Re sex-conscious affirmative action see similarly majority opinion in Johnson v. Transportation Agency Santa Clara County, note 43 at p.80.

48. Justices Brennan, Marshall, Blackmun, Powell JJ., note 43, at pp. 14–15. This was also, it should be remembered, the position taken by the 5 to 2 majority in United Steelworkers v. Weber.

49. Justice Scalia, Chief Justice Rehnquist, Justice White, note 43 at p. 21.

50. Dworkin, *Taking Rights Seriously* (Cambridge, MA: Harvard Univ. Press, 1977), p. 224.

51. At p. 227.

52. At p. 239.

53. See Rosenfeld, "Affirmative Action, Justice and Equalities: A Philosophical and Constitutional Appraisal," 14 *Ohio State L. J.* 846, 904 (1985).

54. Owen Fiss, "Groups and the Equal Protection Clause," 5 *Philosophy & Public Affairs* 147–156 (1975–76).

55. At p. 157.

56. At p. 151. See also Rosenfeld, pp. 909–13.

57. Compare Friedman, "Redefining Equality, Discrimination and Affirmative Action under Title VII: the Access Principle," 65 *Texas L. Rev.* 41, 51, 67.

58. See Owen Fiss, p. 150.

59. See Aristotle, *The Nichomachean Ethics,* Vol IX Book V, chapter 4, on "rectificatory justice," pp. 120–23, paras. 1132a-b.

60. Goldstein, "Reverse Discrimination—Reflections of a Jurist," 15 *Israel Yearbook on Human Rights* 28, 36–37, (1985).

61. See Powell and O'Connor JJ. in Wygant v. Jackson Bd of Education, 54 U.S.L.W. 4480 at 4481, 4484–86.

62. Slip Opinion Supreme Court No. 85–1129, 13.

63. Justice O'Connor points out: "It is agreed that [an affirmative action] plan need not be limited to the remedying of specific instances of identified discrimination for it to be deemed sufficiently narrowly tailored." Wygant v. Jackson Bd. of Education, note 61 at 4485.

64. Per Justice Powell in Bakke. At pp. 321–24.

65. See above for discussion of the grounds for affirmative action given by Owen Fiss. The maxi-min principle of Rawls, justifying inequalities where this improves the position of the worst-off members of society, can also be used to justify this redistributive policy between groups. See Rosenfeld, pp.913–21 for an attempt to explain why the white/male victims should agree in a social contract to bear the cost of compensation.

Comment

THE IMPACT OF THE SUPREME COURT

Malcolm Feeley

The Raday and Loury chapters reflect contrasting philosophies. Professor Raday celebrates judicial activism and sees judge-made law as an important source of social progress. In contrast, Professor Loury implicitly celebrates the market and is skeptical of the ability of the government, including the courts, to serve as an instrument of positive social change.

According to Raday, Fourteenth Amendment jurisprudence has been an inspiration for people around the world. In its creative and expansive development of the Fourteenth Amendment, the U.S. Supreme Court has set an example for other courts and has provided inspiration for potential litigants. As such, it has helped contribute to egalitarian legal policies throughout the world.

Although I share her enthusiasm, I believe that Raday has overstated the importance of the Supreme Court both in the United States and abroad. One might imagine that the quest for equality and social justice was an invention of the Supreme Court that brought justice and equality to U.S. citizens and later exported its arguments to heighten the consciousness of the rest of the world. This prominence of the role of law and courts is clearly a lawyer's eyeview—and a common lawyer's eye, at that—of social and governmental processes. As such, it overstates the importance of courts and ignores other forms of politics. And in the situations she alludes to, it neglects the historical context. For in fact, the quest for equality in Europe has much more to do with the legacy of the political ferment of 1848 than the rulings of the U.S. Supreme Court. Indeed, the social democratic revolution in Europe was under way long before the Supreme Court realized that the Fourteenth Amendment could be used for something other than to protect property interests.

It is instructive to recall that most of the evidence relied on by then lawyer Louis Brandeis in his famous brief in *Muller* v. *Oregon* (1908) came from Europe. At that time virtually every Western industrialized country but the United States had health and safety regulations placing limits on the numbers of hours people could work. Brandeis was simply asking the Supreme Court to uphold a modest version of a set of policies that were already well entrenched throughout much of Europe. One could go on to cite similar laws with respect to race and sex discrimination, where many countries had earlier adopted policies through legislation that only came later via court-initiated action in the United States. In short, I am not convinced that the Supreme Court is as influential as Professor Raday thinks it is.

I have a related set of comments about another facet of the U.S. legal process that is celebrated in this chapter. Professor Raday attributes much of the success and influence of the U.S. Supreme Court to the adversary system, a system which she admires a great deal. She believes that the adversary system coupled with an activist judiciary allows individuals a forum for pursuing their causes when other avenues are not available to them. This ignores the larger context in which legal and political struggles take place in the United States. Most landmark Supreme Court decisions are the result of sustained activity by coalitions pursuing change on many fronts. While it is certainly true that some important Supreme Court cases have arisen independently of these movements, I suspect that almost all of them have taken place in the context of this broader effort for change. Furthermore, those rulings of the Court which have wider implications are likely to have an impact only if they have broad political support (Scheingold 1973, Horowitz 1977). To celebrate the adversary system because it is a forum for redress of grievance that allows the lonely individual to take a case to the Supreme Court is to fall prey to a type of Horatio Alger myth. While there is a grain of truth in this version of litigation, it dramatically overstates the importance of individuals, ignores the social context in which change takes place, and fails to recognize that almost all social change litigation emerges as an organized effort by interest groups that takes place simultaneously on many levels and in many places (Olson 1984, Sorauf 1976).

Professor Loury's chapter is an eloquent conservative statement extolling the virtues of the market and warning against the evils of government intrusiveness and judicial interference with the pursuit of private preferences. As such, it stands in sharp contrast to the chapter by Professor Raday which extols the virtues of activist courts questing for communal justice. Where she sees courts as engines of progress and instruments of the community, Loury sees them as meddlesome and intrusive institutions that can easily undermine integrity and honor in the name of equality.

Loury argues against affirmative action, which he defines as a selection policy that modifies a pure merit system to give preference to candidates because of race or gender. It is contrasted to a pure merit-based selection process that is color- or sex-blind.

In developing his case against preferential treatment, he points to what he believes is a serious omission in the consideration of proponents of affirmative action. He argues that they tend to think of affirmative action as if it were a single great leap forward, a single distinct act to help people who because of sex or color have been disadvantaged. In contrast, he argues that affirmative action must be understood as a process, a series of decisions each with lingering implications and consequences. Propelling people into positions on bases other than merit, he argues, has a host of lingering consequences, consequences that tend to undermine the very aspirations that drive the desire for affirmative action. Initial selection, he argues, is simply the first and easiest of a series of actions that ultimately corrupt relations among coworkers and frustrate organizational integrity. Affirmative action, he maintains, robs people of their dignity, has lasting corrosive consequences in relationships among coworkers and continues to affect the quality of institutional life, either because affirmative action is pursued in promotion to the detriment of organizational effectiveness or it is not, and the result is bitterness and resentment of those with reduced chances of promotion. In either case, he argues, individual honor and organizational integrity suffer.

Despite his sweeping indictment of race-conscious policies, I wonder if Professor Loury would really want to abandon all of them. To remove all race-conscious selection policies, as he seems to want to, could easily lead to an individual-based discrimination approach in which only those who could prove they, individually, were discriminated against, could receive redress. This approach to combating discrimination has proven ineffective, and if we returned to it, it would undermine the ability of the courts—and other institutions—to deal effectively with discrimination. The history of injunctive relief and remedial orders since *Brown* v. *Board of Education* (1954) has been to broaden relief in order to combat structural discrimination and massive resistance. This has led away from exclusive reliance on individual-based claims and emphasis upon relief to group-based claims. But with this transformation came remedial orders that were not strictly limited to providing redress only to those who were individually victims of discrimination.

If we take Loury's arguments at face value, he would oppose race-conscious remedial orders as well as affirmative action. Thus, in the name of honor and integrity, discrimination could be perpetuated. This is certainly not what Professor Loury would want.

If I were to develop a thesis, it would require modification of the radical individualist premises upon which his argument is constructed. It would emphasize notions of community and the ideal of shared aspirations. But in the process of justifying race conscious remedial orders after findings of discrimination, my argument would also justify affirmative action more generally.

If Loury cannot justify race in any conscious policies, how then would he construct an effective judicial strategy of ridding organizations of their legacy of discrimination? But if he begins to accept remedial race-conscious policies, can he distinguish them from affirmative action more generally?

REFERENCES

Cases

Brown v. Board of Education, 347 U.S. 484 (1954)
Muller v. Oregon, 208 U.S. 412 (1908)
Regents of the University of California v. Bakke, 438 U.S. 265 (1978)
Swann v. Charlotte–Mecklenburg Board of Education, 403 U.S. 12 (1971)

Books and Articles

Becker, Theodore and Feeley, Malcolm M. *The Impact of Supreme Court Decisions* (New York: Oxford University Press, 1969).
Bell, Derrick. "Foreword: The Civil Rights Chronicles," *Harvard Law Review* 98 (December 1985): 4–83.
Bumiller, Kristen. *The Civil Rights Society* (Baltimore, MD: Johns Hopkins University Press, 1988).
Edelman, Murray. *Political Language: Words That Succeed and Policies That Fail* (New York: Academic Press, 1977).
Freeman, Alan. "Legitimizing Discrimination through Anti-Discrimination Law: A Critical Review of Supreme Court Doctrine," *Minnesota Law Review* 62 (1978): 1049–1119.
Horowitz, Donald L. *Courts and Social Policy* (Washington, D.C.: Brookings Institute, 1977).
Olson, Susan. *Clients and Lawyers: Securing the Rights of Disabled Persons* (Westport, CT: Greenwood Press, 1984).
Scheingold, Stuart. *The Politics of Rights* (New Haven, CT: Yale University Press, 1973).
Sorauf, Frank. *The Wall of Separation: The Constitutional Politics of Church and State* (Princeton, NJ: Princeton University Press, 1976).

VI MINORITY RIGHTS UNDER THE CONSTITUTION: GENDER

9 Reconstitutions: History, Gender, and the Fourteenth Amendment

Norma Basch

At first glance, the constitutional bases of social change for women appear to be clustered in the civil rights legislation and Supreme Court decisions of the last two decades. For the long balance of its existence, the United States Constitution seems to have meted out justice to women as women with either harsh indifference or paternalistic zeal. Gender barely figures in the vast historical landscape of the Constitution, and in those few instances where it does, it is with dismal consequences for the legal status of women.

There is much to support this view. The original language of the Constitution could be strikingly neutral with respect to gender precisely because the states would continue to regulate both domestic relations and political and civil rights. To be sure, the persistence of terms such as *person* in this eighteenth-century document suggests that the Founding Fathers left the door open for persons, in all their legal and political manifestations, to encompass females. If they did so consciously, however, they were secure in the knowledge that the states were closing the door by employing the term *males* in their own statutes and constitutions. Federalism, then, helps to account for the Constitution's silence on gender. Only when the Reconstruction amendments reshaped relations between the citizen, the state, and the federal government and delineated distinctions between male citizens and female citizens, did gender work its way into the formal language of the Constitution.[1]

In post–Civil War tests of the status of women under the Fourteenth Amendment, the Supreme Court endowed antebellum state restrictions with a new constitutional legitimacy to which it added a gloss in the early twentieth century in the course of validating protective labor legislation for women only.[2] Even the luster of the Nineteenth Amendment dimmed in the 1920s when the Court drew on it to invalidate the minimum wage legislation for women that reformers had envisioned and promoted as a corollary of maximum hours legislation.[3] Divided between advocating equality or protection for women, the women's movement declined and ceased to serve as a catalyst for constitutional change.[4] Subsequently neither depression nor war created a climate conducive to revamping the constitutional status of women, and women lacked the organizational structures and coherent goals with which to mount a campaign for reform.

Considering the sparse and dreary role of gender in much of the evolution of the Constitution, it is not at all surprising that scholars have riveted their attention on the last two decades. Dramatic innovations came in the wake of the civil rights legislation and renewed feminist agitation of the 1960s, and in a spate of Supreme Court decisions in the 1970s and 1980s.[5] Once again race and gender intertwined in altering the contours of the Constitution, but this time with salient legal results for both blacks and women. Notwithstanding the defeat of the Equal Rights Amendment, and as a result of concentrated efforts by the Women's Rights Project of the American Civil Liberties Union, women went further toward achieving legal equality with men in the last two decades than in the preceding 180 years of constitutional development.[6]

The recent spurt of legal change, in turn, rekindled conflict over special versus equal status for women and renewed tensions in the women's movement between what can be termed separatist and assimilationist goals. Conservative doubts about the desirability of setting out equality with men as a legal goal were first exploited with devastating effectiveness by Phyllis Schlafly in the anti-ERA campaign, spelled out in visions of an Amazonian republic with unisex toilets, and reinforced with such slogans as "You can't fool Mother Nature."[7] But doubts also were embedded in the dilemma of transposing forming legal equality with men into equitable results for women. They began to take shape in feminist critiques of "legal liberalism" and expanded into an indictment of the entire androcentric, rights-oriented legal tradition. In one wing of the women's movement demands for gender neutrality in law in the 1970s gave way to a rejection of neutrality itself in the 1980s, a development that marks the emergence of a new feminist jurisprudence.[8]

Identifying itself with "relational feminism" and paralleling feminist scholarship in a host of other disciplines, the new jurisprudence takes its cues from Carol Gilligan's *In a Different Voice*.[9] If, as Gilligan asserts, an ethos of care informs the moral decision of girls in contrast to the abstract, rules-based approach of boys—if women really speak

in a different voice—then advocates of the new jurisprudence are determined to draw on that voice to create a care-based model of justice
as an alternative to a rights-based one. Thus the new jurisprudence
rejects the degradations of a male-dominated past and puts its intellect and imagination into the construction of a female-defined future.
Yet relying as it does on fixed and binary oppositions between man
and woman, individualism and relatedness, rights and responsibilities, competition and cooperation, power and love, and numerous
other antinomies, it is by its very nature ahistorical.[10] And in celebrating what it deems to be the feminine side of those oppositions, it assumes a stance that is by implication separate from and antithetical to
the concept of constitutionalism as a series of incremental and historically related changes occurring within a framework of competing
powers and individual rights.

These binary divisions have a ring of authenticity that helps to explain
the extraordinary impress of Gilligan's work. Who can deny that Mother
Nature, for example, and the Founding Fathers conjure up two distinct
figurative worlds? Clearly concepts of masculine and feminine permeate
and bifurcate all aspects of culture, and the legal culture is no exception.
Indeed, the collective identity of the women's movement rests on and
derives its integrity from the perception of that bifurcation. Our very
presence here today on a panel that places the constitutional treatment
of gender under the accepted rubric of minority rights attests to the
enduring legal otherness of women. Inasmuch as women do not constitute a numerical minority, they qualify as a minority only in the secondary meaning of the term: a group that is different from the larger
group of which it is a part.

The conflation of women's rights with minority rights points up the
comparative newness of gender as an analytical category and suggests
the need for greater precision in incorporating the status of women into
constitutional discourse. Because gender is a neutral term encompassing
men and women both, it has the potential to be a sophisticated tool for
relating legal concepts about women to legal concepts about men and
to the mainstream of constitutional development. As a historian, what
is at issue for me on this panel is the complex relation between the
changing social construction of gender and the legal and constitutional
order. I am convinced that gender, in that complex, evolving, historical
sense, remains one of the most intriguing and least explored categories
in U.S. constitutional scholarship. My reservations about the new "relational" jurisprudence, then, emanate not from its critiques of the contemporary legal order but from the separatist and ahistorical terms in
which they are framed.

My intent is not to debunk the bleakness of the image we have of
women in the life of the Constitution; rather it is to underscore its lack

of historical texture and particularity. We have scarcely identified and connected the bare bones of a women's legal history, much less mounted lucid discourse over its larger political and social ramifications. While feminist scholars have been disinclined to trace the byways of a constitutional tradition that proffered women little, more traditional scholars have ignored women altogether. Our understanding of gender in the Constitution is impoverished not only by the historical vacuum in which contemporary discourse flourishes but also by the extent to which discourse on gender has remained segregated from the constitutional mainstream. The history of the very real but changing legal marginality of women has occupied a marginal place in constitutional scholarship that differs sharply from the place accorded to race.

Consider the consequences. Trends in constitutional scholarship radiate outward into casebooks, textbooks, and legal primers, and ultimately shape the public perception of the Constitution. Most U.S. freshmen begin college with a dim recollection of *Plessy* v. *Ferguson*, and there is every chance that those who do not will be introduced to the case before they graduate. In contrast, *Minor* v. *Happersett* is unlikely to appear anywhere in the curriculum. Consequently students come away with a sense that race has been and continues to be a constitutional issue but develop no corresponding sense of gender. Admittedly *Minor* did not dominate the headlines of the day, but neither did *Plessy*.[11] Contemporaries evinced far greater interest in the Civil Rights Cases of the preceding decade. Scholars and jurists elevated *Plessy* to the status of a major landmark retrospectively as their awareness of its significance intensified. And if Justice John Marshall Harlan's dissent speaks presciently to us across the gulf of time, haunting us with the possibilities in the road not taken, so too does the brief filed by Francis Minor on behalf of his disfranchised wife.[12]

I draw on this case to suggest that history is an integral part of the Constitution not only as a formal requirement of Anglo-American reliance on precedent but also as a dynamic component in collective memory and public perception. I draw on it in an effort to move beyond a simple legal calculus of gains and losses that has telescoped the constitutional history of women into a tidy little stack of losses. And I draw on it to explore the possibilities of connecting gender to the constitutional past and, frankly, to promote integrating the connections into the mainstream of constitutional consciousness.

On October 15, 1872, Virginia Minor, identified in the plaintiff's brief as a "tax-paying, law-abiding citizen" of St. Louis County, Missouri, and the United States, appeared before Reese Happersett, an election registrar in the county. She requested that the oath to support the Constitution of the United States and the State of Missouri be administered to her so that she might vote in the presidential election of 1872. Happersett refused to place her name on the list of registered voters because "she was not a male citizen, but a woman."[13] That distinction between male as citizen and woman as other went to the heart of the suit. In a sense, the suit represented an effort to use the Constitution and its post–Civil War reforms to obliterate one of the oldest distinctions in Western political theory and jurisprudence, one that Francis Minor would argue was contrary to the very principles of republican government.

With her husband as coplaintiff and counsel, Virginia Minor sued Reese Happersett in the Circuit Court of St. Louis County, maintaining that the provisions of the state constitution which limited the franchise to males were in conflict with the original provisions of the federal Constitution and the recently ratified Fourteenth Amendment. Ironically, she was prevented from suing for her political independence independently because Missouri still required that a married woman be joined by her husband in a civil suit. Virginia Minor lost her suit in the circuit court, appealed her case to the Missouri Supreme Court and lost, and appealed it to the United States Supreme Court where she lost yet again in a unanimous decision.

What more is there to say? That the very presence of her case on the Supreme Court docket in the October term of 1874 constitutes a turning point in the role of gender in the Constitution. The historical dimensions of *Minor* are misconstrued from the start if we conceive of it only as relegating women to second-class citizenship; women were second-class citizens both before and after the decision. What the case did was to draw the inferiority of their status out of the grooves of common law assumptions and state provisions and thrust it into the maelstrom of constitutional conflict. The demands for woman suffrage did not die when the decision was rendered; they acquired a contentious national life.

The power of the Court to bring exposure to submerged demands was noted recently by Justice William Brennan, who refuses to delegate the reading of certiorari petitions to clerks because he views the selection of cases as the Court's single most important task.[14] But there can be no cases, no docket, and of course no Constitution without people. It is flesh-and-blood men and women who convert demands into formal tests and press the Supreme Court and the lower courts for "reconstitutions."[15] At certain junctures, the issues people choose to place before the Court for reconstitution and the willingness of the Court to hear them are as revealing as the resolutions themselves. Given the indeterminate language of the Fourteenth Amendment, the determination of a small but militant group of woman suffragists to test its boundaries, and the defiant campaign these former abolitionists had waged against its ratification, *Minor* represents just such a juncture.[16]

It is for precisely this reason that the Minor case invites speculation about the motives of the members of the Court. That ways to delay and even to avoid hearing a case were available to the post–Civil War Court is exemplified by Justice Ward Hunt's disposition of the case of Susan B. Anthony. Hunt, who had presided over the Federal Circuit Court in New York where Anthony was prosecuted for voting in the election of 1872, had personally crushed Anthony's effort to bring her case up to the Supreme Court on appeal. Insisting that there was no question of fact in the case but only one of law, he removed the issues from the consideration of the jury and ordered a verdict of guilty.[17] Here was a procedure one critic found "contrary to all rules of law, and so subversive of the system of jury trials in criminal cases, that it should not be allowed to pass without an emphatic protest on the part of every public journal that values our liberties."[18] The Grant administration put the finishing touches on the Anthony affair by failing to prosecute Anthony for not paying her fine and by pardoning the three Rochester registrars who had also been indicted and tried for violating the federal election statute.[19] The outcry from legal formalists and friends of woman suffrage over procedural irregularities and the sheer political volatility of the case may have pointed to the need for a clear and authoritative judicial resolution.

Other considerations undoubtedly influenced the Court. Although the prospect of woman suffrage met with savage derision in the press, it was now a viable reality. Women were already voting in the Wyoming and Utah territories and even serving on juries in Wyoming.[20] Elsewhere hundreds of women tested the Fourteenth Amendment by voting illegally while others demonstrated against its alleged limits by casting symbolic ballots in bogus elections organized adjacent to official polling places.[21] If the Court deemed it advisable to interpret the citizenship of women in light of the Fourteenth Amendment, the Minor case presented them with a good opportunity to do so. Furthermore, the Fifteenth Amendment seemed to take the steam out of Francis Minor's arguments.

Of even greater interest, however, are the motives of the litigants who sought a hearing for their demands in the Supreme Court. Virginia Minor and Susan B. Anthony along with the battery of able attorneys representing them may have hoped for a broad reading of the Fourteenth Amendment, but in the context of prior decisions, they surely must have anticipated the likelihood of legal defeat.[22] As woman suffragists and activists in the radical wing of the women's movement, they presumably saw some political advantage in working out their claims through the legal process.

Anthony pressed her claim as an eloquent martyr so as to prod the conscience of the nation. She painstakingly staged her test as a legal melodrama taking the form of a federal criminal prosecution. By casting herself as a modern Joan of Arc confronting the full force and fury of the United States government, she evoked so much sympathy and press coverage that one journalist estimated it would be hard to find a jury in the state of New York that would convict her.[23] Her counsel, Henry R. Selden, underscored the criminal nature of the case:

If the advocates of female suffrage had been allowed to choose the point of attack to be made upon their position, they could not have chosen it more favorably for themselves; and I am disposed to thank those who have been instrumental in this proceeding for presenting it in the form of a "criminal prosecution."[24]

Of course, the advocates of female suffrage had chosen the point of attack; Anthony had cajoled the Rochester registrars into enrolling her and 14 other women and guaranteed that she would provide them with counsel if they were criminally prosecuted.[25]

The Minor's campaign was less dramatic but no less well planned, and from a constitutional perspective, it provided a clearer and broader challenge. Even if Anthony had succeeded in appealing her case to the Supreme Court, it hinged on the claim that she voted in good conscience and without criminal intent and not exclusively on the inherent constitutionality of woman suffrage. The Minors confronted the Fourteenth Amendment head-on in a test of the relations between female citizenship, state suffrage provisions, and the federal Constitution.

Francis Minor alluded to the transforming potential in such a test in a letter published in January of 1870 in which he announced Virginia Minor's intention to initiate the action in the election of 1872. He reasoned that their test would place the cause of woman suffrage "upon higher ground than ever before" because it would rest on citizenship secured by the United States government. Anticipating the distinctions made by the Court between citizenship and suffrage, he outlined his determination to argue that states may impose only those qualifications for suffrage that all citizens may attain sooner or later. Moving beyond demeaning common law classifications that lumped women together with children, he asserted that "to say one-half the citizens possess all the qualifications but shall never vote" was the essence of "despotism."[26]

It seems evident that the Minors hoped to take advantage of the re-forming spirit of Reconstruction to begin to reshape legal attitudes and constructs and thereby legitimate a role for women in politics. As for effecting woman suffrage by judicial fiat, the state of Missouri did not take the challenge seriously enough to file a brief, leaving Happersett with a defense consisting of a three-sentence demurrer.[27] Portions of the Minors' brief, moreover, indicate they had few illusions about the outcome. Comparing slavery with the disenfranchisement of women, Francis Minor argued that just as the one injustice to which men had been inured had been obliterated over time, so too would the other.

Men accept it as a matter of fact, and take for granted it must be right. So in the days of African slavery, thousands believed it to be right—even a Divine institution. But this belief has passed away; and, in like manner, this doctrine of the right of the States to exercise unlimited and absolute control over the elective franchise of citizens of the United States, must and will give way to a truer and better understanding of the subject.

The plaintiff's case is simply one of the means by which this end will ultimately be reached.[28]

The Minors launched their case to promote "a truer and better understanding of the subject." The promotion of such an understanding through a hearing before the Supreme Court did not depend on hope alone but on an innovative reading of the text of the Constitution. By invoking for women as a class specific rights derived from and defined by the Constitution, the Minors endowed the role of gender in constitutional discourse with a rhetorical coherence that transcended almost one hundred years of silence on the subject. In this ultimate constitutional forum, they expressed their disagreement about one thing, woman suffrage, by agreeing on everything else—the only way in which disagreement can enter into formal constitutional dialogue.[29] Rearranging and reinterpreting the inherited terms at hand, they forged an argument for reconstitution.

The Minors built their case on the original silences and neutral language in the Constitution, on provisions in the Bill of Rights, and even on the Thirteenth Amendment. The Fourteenth Amendment, the historical catalyst for the case, emerged as supportive of but not essential to their primary argument. Francis Minor's application of "the doctrine of original intent" proposed that women were empowered to vote in *federal* elections from the inception of the Constitution. The Missouri "bar of perpetual disfranchisement," and that of other states as well, were the result of a monumental misreading of the original text. The fact that the women of New Jersey had voted in the early republic when the Founding Fathers were alive and well became proof of the founders' intent. Not only did he argue that further enabling legislation was unnecessary but he asserted that the disfranchisement of qualified female voters was a bill of attainder, an infringement on freedom of speech, a form of involuntary servitude, and in a prescient interpretation of the phrase, a violation of due process.[30] The Fourteenth Amendment, then, merely obliterated any remaining doubts on the subject.

Minor's emphasis on pre–Civil War constitutional provisions allowed him to thread his argument through the new provisions for *males* in the Fourteenth and Fifteenth Amendments. Thus he interpreted that section of the Fourteenth Amendment which reduced congressional representation in states denying "the right to vote" to males to be a special security for the black population, a provision which, by the terms of the Ninth Amendment, in no way denied other rights retained by the people.[31] As for the Fifteenth Amendment, ostensibly the most formidable legal obstacle in his path, it was not in his path at all. It had no bearing on the case for it was prohibitory and confirmed a right already expressed in the Fourteenth Amendment.[32]

The brief concluded that "the great principle of fundamental right" for which Virginia Minor was suing, embraced "the rights of millions of others, who are thus represented through her." As Minor put it, the suit rested on "those principles upon which, as upon a rock, our government is founded," for that government which disfranchises one-half of its citizens cannot be a republican one.[33]

It was a brilliant argument, a dazzling reconstitution of law as it ought to be, and a trenchant indictment of the way it was. In a unanimous decision, the Court saw it otherwise. Its opinion found that woman suffrage was neither intended in the original Constitution nor guaranteed by the privileges and immunities of the Fourteenth Amendment. Responding to the characterization of the disfranchisement of women as antirepublican, the opinion declared that inasmuch as all states except for New Jersey had limited the franchise to males at the time of ratification, it was too late now to contend that such a government was not republican. The opinion noted that if the law was wrong, it ought to be changed, but it was not within the power of the Court to change it.[34] It would take almost half a century and a constitutional amendment to effect the change.

The Minor case, however, represents more than an unsuccessful test of woman suffrage under the Fourteenth Amendment. It demonstrates the readiness of dissident groups in general and nineteenth-century feminists in particular to frame their demands as if they were constitutional rights, or to put it another way, to envision the changes that they sought as reconstitutions. From Reconstruction onward, the challenges that were audaciously mounted and tenaciously sustained by such groups often shaped the constitutional bases of social and political change far more than judicial or legislative initiatives. It was not until the advent of Reconstruction that gender could become the focal point of formal constitutional controversy, but once it did, the controversy could not be eradicated by a single stroke of the Supreme Court. Rather it intensified, raising vexing questions not only about the status of women but about U.S. political values.

Viewed as a form of political agitation, then, the Minors' challenge provides insights to the relation between the social construction of gender in Victorian America and the legal and constitutional order, and perhaps nowhere more than in their insistence on the legitimacy of a political role for women in a republic. Chief Justice Morrison R. Waite's opinion positively bristled at their contention that the prevailing constitutional understanding about women was fundamentally unrepublican. If eighteenth-century synonyms for republican had grown murky in the aggressively competitive commercialism of the 1870s, antonyms retained their clarity. To be unrepublican was to be despotic, selfish, uncaring, and bereft of virtue. Yet the bourgeois culture of the nineteenth century attached the caring, cooperative virtues of the republic ever more firmly to the moral superiority of its women and not to the political capacity of its men.

This disjunction of politics and morals in the nineteenth century had profound consequences for women. Both women and men believed that women spoke "in a different voice," to use Carol Gilligan's popular phrase. As historians have noted, it was a voice that afforded women considerable dignity in the domestic sphere and sufficient authority in the public sphere to participate in community reforms and quasi-political activities. But it was a voice without terms for expressing the autonomous female self. The assertion of the female self as a discrete, independent, political being became a subversive form of selfishness, and the moral superiority of women served, in the end, to buttress their legal and political inferiority.

To be sure, advocates of woman suffrage insisted that women would purify politics, but invariably they faced the counterclaim that politics would contaminate women.[35] Only by appropriating the rights-oriented, masculine voice of the constitutional order, as the Minors did, was it possible to challenge directly the exclusion of women from politics. Conversely the masculine voice of the dominant culture gave men no compass for affirming cooperative values. Thus gender both informed and obfuscated the disjunction of politics and morals in the nineteenth century.

The small capsule of history presented here may lend itself to alternative interpretations, but at the very least it suggests the promise of gender as an analytical tool in constitutional discourse. To view the opposition of masculine and feminine as contextually defined and in flux invites new readings of the constitutional past and new strategies for shaping the future. To perpetuate the assumptions and disjunctions of a bifurcated Victorian world in the name of promoting cooperative values for the end of the twentieth century seems ill-advised and futile. Such reconstitutions would seem to require more androgynous terms.

NOTES

1. Section 2 of the Fourteenth Amendment refers to "male inhabitants" and "male citizens," and Section 1 of the Fifteenth Amendment prohibits the denial of a citizen's right to vote "on account of race, color, or previous condition of servitude," but it does not include sex; on Reconstruction and the Constitution, see Harold M. Hyman, *A More Perfect Union: The Impact of the Civil War and Reconstruction on the Constitution* (New York: Knopf, 1973).

2. Bradwell v. Illinois, 83 U.S. 130 (1873); Minor v. Happersett, 88 U.S. 162 (1875); Muller v. Oregon, 208 U.S. 412 (1908).

3. Adkins v. Children's Hospital, 261 U.S. 525 (1923).

4. On protection as a divisive issue in organized feminism, see Sybil Lipshultz, "Workers, Wives, and Mothers: The Problem of Minimum Wage Laws for Women in Early Twentieth-Century America," Ph.D. diss., University of Pennsylvania, 1986; Susan D. Becker, *The Origins of the Equal Rights Amendment: American Feminism between The Wars* (Westport, CT: Greenwood Press, 1981).

5. See, for example, Nancy Erickson, "Equality Between the Sexes in the 1980s," *Cleveland State Law Review* 28 (1979): 591–610.

6. Joan Hoff-Wilson, ed., *Rights of Passage: The Past and Future of Era* (Bloomington: Indiana University Press), pp. xiv–xv.

7. Edith Mayo and Jerry K. Frye, "The ERA: Postmortem of a Failure in Political Communication," in ibid., pp. 85–86.

8. For a perceptive overview of the new feminist jurisprudence that likens its relationship to more traditional legal concepts as that of a web to a ladder, see Kenneth L. Karst, "Woman's Constitution," *Duke Law Journal* (1984): 447–508; see also, for example, Catherine A. MacKinnon, *Feminism Unmodified: Discourses on Life and Law* (Cambridge, MA: Harvard University Press, 1987); Christine A. Littleton, "In Search of a Feminist Jurisprudence," *Harvard Women's Law Journal* 10 (1987): 1–7; and "Papers From the 1986 Feminism and Legal Theory Conference," *Wisconsin Women's Law Journal* 3 (1987).

9. Carol Gilligan, *In a Different Voice: Psychological Theory and Women's Development* (Cambridge, MA: Harvard University Press, 1982).

10. Joan W. Scott, "Gender: A Useful Category of Historical Analysis," *The American Historical Review* 91 (1986): 1053–75. Scott's analysis of gender as a historical tool and her critique of Gilligan comprise the starting point for this essay.

11. Michael Kammen, *A Machine That Would Go of Itself: The Constitution in American Culture* (New York: Knopf, 1986), p. 28.

12. Plessy v. Ferguson, 163 U.S. 537, 557–562 (1896).

13. "Argument and Brief," Minor v. Happersett, *Landmark Briefs and Arguments of the Supreme Court of the United States*, eds. Philip B. Kurland and Gerhard Casper (Arlington, VA: University Publishers of America, 1975), 7: 209–50, citation on p. 214; hereinafter referred to as "Argument and Brief." For a similar version of the facts in the case on the state level, see Minor v. Happersett, 53 Missouri 58 (1873).

14. Interview, National Public Radio, aired February 1987.

15. For the concept of reconstitutions in law, I have relied on James Boyd White, *When Words Lose Their Meaning: Constitutions and Reconstitutions of Language, Character, and Community* (Chicago: University of Chicago Press, 1984).

16. Ellen Carol DuBois, *Feminism and Suffrage: The Emergence of an Independent Women's Movement in America* (Ithaca, NY: Cornell University Press, 1978).

17. *An Account of the Proceedings of the Trial of Susan B. Anthony on the Charge of Illegal Voting* (Rochester, NY: Daily Democrat and Chronicle, 1874), pp. 78–82; hereinafter referred to as *Trial of Susan B. Anthony*.

18. John Hooker, "Judge Hunt, and The Right of Trial by Jury," in ibid., p. 206.

19. Elizabeth Cady Stanton, Susan B. Anthony, Matilda Joslyn Gage, and Ida Husted Harper eds., *History of Woman Suffrage*, 6 vols. (Rochester and New York: 1881–1922), 2: 949.

20. Women on juries in Wyoming provoked considerable attention. See, for example, *Albany Law Journal* 1 (1870): 197, 210, 313; "The Woman Suffrage Movement in Wyoming," *Galaxy* 8 (June 1872): 755–60.

21. Tests in the District of Columbia included Spencer v. Board of Registration, Webster v. Superintendents of Election, cited in *Albany Law Journal* 4 (1871): 281–82; for other tests, see Stanton et al., *History of Woman Suffrage* 2: 586–600.

22. In particular, Bradwell v. Illinois. Susan B. Anthony, however, wrote to Francis Minor for his opinion on the effect of the Bradwell case, and he responded that the opinions were not necessarily conclusive on the issue of suffrage. Nancy T. Gilliam, "A Professional Pioneer: Myra Bradwell's Fight to Practice Law," *Law and History Review* 5 (1987): 130.

23. New York *Sun*, January 4, 1873, cited in Stanton et al., *History of Woman Suffrage*, 2: 937–38.

24. *Trial of Susan B. Anthony*, p. 17.

25. Stanton et al., *History of Woman Suffrage*, 2: 628.

26. "Letter from Francis Minor," *The Revolution* 5, January 20, 1870, pp. 38–39. The legal tack announced in this journal of the National Woman Suffrage Association, which was edited by Elizabeth Cady Stanton and Susan B. Anthony, was introduced as a resolution at the Missouri National Woman Suffrage Association of which Virginia Minor was president. Aside from the criminal nature of the Anthony case, the argument made by Anthony's counsel, Henry R. Selden and by Anthony herself followed the same basic contours.

27. "Argument and Brief," pp. 216–17.

28. Ibid., p. 220.

29. White, *When Words Lose Their Meaning*, p. 246.

30. "Argument and Brief," pp. 222, 224, 227, 235, 244–48.

31. Ibid., p. 215.

32. Ibid., pp. 235–37.

33. Ibid., p. 250.

34. Minor v. Happersett, 88 U.S. 162, 167, 170, 178.

35. See, for example, *The Nation* 3, December 20, 1866, pp. 498–99; ibid. 5, November 1867, pp. 416–17; and ibid. 18, May 1874, pp. 311–13.

10 Employment of the Constitution to Advance the Equal Status of Men and Women

Ruth Bader Ginsburg

I am pleased to be part of this program, all the more so because the topic assigned to me occupied a major part of my time from 1970 to 1980. In those years, I directed the Women's Rights Project of the American Civil Liberties Union, and I participated as counsel in several sex discrimination cases ultimately heard and decided by the Supreme Court.[1] I also spoke at many places advocating the addition of an "equal rights amendment" to the U.S. Constitution.[2]

Women played no part in the Constitution, as originally conceived. There were no founding mothers at the Constitutional Convention, and the Founding Fathers had decided views about women's place in society. Thomas Jefferson, principal author of the Declaration of Independence, stated the prevailing hope: "[O]ur good ladies . . . are contented to soothe and calm the minds of their husbands returning ruffled from political debate."[3] John Adams, despite the imprecations of his extraordinary wife, Abigail, had this to say about those who counted among "We the People" in his home state of Massachusetts: "[I]t is dangerous to open [the subject of] alter[ing] the qualifications of voters; there will be no end of it. New claims will arise; women will demand the vote, lads from twelve to twenty-one will think their rights are not enough attended to, and every man who has not a farthing will demand an equal voice with any other in all acts of state. It tends to confound and destroy all distinctions, and prostrate all ranks to the common level."[4]

As Adams's statement indicates, "We the People," left out the majority of the adult population: slaves, debtors, paupers, Indians, and women. The Constitution, as framed in 1787, was intended to be an instrument of government by and for white propertied adult males— people free from dependence on others, and therefore not susceptible to influence or control by masters, overlords, or superiors.

The equal status of men and women before the law thus was not an issue in 1787, nor did it figure as a featured topic in celebrations of the Constitution's centennial one hundred years ago. In 1887, women were still 33 years away from securing the right to vote. And the Fourteenth Amendment, added to the Constitution in 1868, did not inspire feminists of that day. Rather, it alarmed them; for it added to the Constitution for the very first time the word "male," and linked that word to the word "citizens."[5] The suggestion seemed to be that, even if women were citizens too, they were (like children) something less than full citizens.[6] My remarks center on why talk of "Gender Equality and the Constitution" came alive in the 1970s.

To set the stage, I will recall a scene in a Florida county courtroom in 1957, just 30 years ago. Gwendolyn Hoyt stood trial there for murdering her husband; the instrument of destruction, a baseball bat. Florida, in those ancient days, did not put women on the jury rolls unless they volunteered for service by registering with the county clerk. Few women volunteered, so the county list of eligible jurors included only 220 women alongside over 9000 men. The jury drawn for Ms. Hoyt's case was all male. (She believed that female jurors might have better understood— and explained to the others—her plea, akin to temporary insanity, that her philandering husband had abused, degraded, and humiliated her to the breaking point.) The all-male jury convicted Ms. Hoyt, not of manslaughter, the lesser of the homicide charges against her, but of the graver offense of second degree murder, and she eventually appealed to the United States Supreme Court.

Ms. Hoyt urged before the High Court that Florida's volunteers-only system for women violated the Fourteenth Amendment's commands that no state "shall deprive any person of . . . liberty . . . without due process of law," or "deny to any person . . . the equal protection of the laws." Not so, a unanimous Supreme Court, then headed by Chief Justice Earl Warren, replied in 1961 in *Hoyt* v. *Florida*;[7] it was not unreasonable, the justices held, for a state to require men but not women to serve on juries, for society "still regarded [women] as the center of home and family life."[8] If anything, most women—even if not Ms. Hoyt—were in fact favored by Florida's system, the Court supposed. Women were off the starting list, but they could put themselves on later for the asking. This was not the sort of "invidious discrimination" that judges believed they could (or should) strike down under the banner of the Fourteenth Amendment.

The 1961 *Hoyt* decision was faithful to a century's precedent; it continued an unbroken line of Supreme Court judgments signalling the same clear message: Except for the Nineteenth Amendment—which, in 1920, granted women the right to vote—the Constitution remained an empty cupboard for sex equality claims.[9] Women and men seeking to share equally in the opportunities and responsibilities of life in the United States would have to look beyond the Constitution and outside the courtroom for legal assistance.

The 1961 Supreme Court was not oblivious to developments in society; it did see that change was in the wind. Acknowledging the trend of the times, the opinion in the *Hoyt* case notes the "enlightened emancipation of women from the restrictions and protections of bygone years."[10] But the Warren Court, so often labeled "liberal," "activist," or "interventionist," was content to remain passive in this domain. It simply held the baseline set by the Supreme Court in the 1870s,[11] at the turn of the century,[12] and in the 1940s.[13] That baseline reflected the prevailing "separate-spheres" mentality, or breadwinner-homemaker dichotomy: It was man's lot, because of his nature, to be breadwinner, head of household, representative of the family outside the home; and it was woman's lot, because of her nature, to bear and raise children, and keep the home in order.

Against this background, the Supreme Court's position on gender-based classifications in the 1970s stands out in bold relief. At odds with its "conservative" reputation, the Burger Court's performance was comparatively unrestrained in this area. Beginning in 1971, the Court declared law after law, both federal and state, unconstitutional, for discriminating impermissibly on the basis of sex.[14] In 1974, to cite one of several 1970s examples, a Louisiana jury selection system virtually identical to the Florida system unanimously upheld in 1961 in the *Hoyt* case encountered a different fate: The high court declared the system unconstitutional, voting 8–1.[15]

What happened in the intervening years—the years from 1961 to 1971—that might explain this remarkable switch in the direction of the Supreme Court's judgments? The change in the justices' responses reflected movement occurring in society at large during the same period. Rapid growth in women's employment outside the home, attended and stimulated by a revived feminist movement, changing patterns of marriage and reproduction, longer lifespans, even inflation—all were implicated in a social dynamic that yielded this new reality: in the 1970s, for the first time in our nation's history, the "average" woman in the United States was experiencing most of her adult years in a household not dominated by childcare requirements. Columbia economics professor Eli Ginzberg has called this development "the single most outstanding phenomenon" of the era in which we are living.[16] Few lives have been unaffected by the profound change wrought in the latter decades of the twentieth century in demands on, and opportunities for, women.

What were the interrelations between the realignment in society and in constitutional doctrine? Was evolving constitutional doctrine one of the agents of change? Or were the justices simply trailing—merely responding to the new social reality, a world in which the notion of women "at the center of home and family life" was shared with—or giving way to—other perceptions, for example, the notion captured in a slogan popular in the 1970s: "A woman's place is in the House—and in the Senate"?

Dramatic descriptions of the role the Supreme Court plays in the process of social change feature periods of national crisis. Two "models" or styles of Court participation are delineated in vivid descriptions of the extremes. In one model, the Court aggressively seizes the lead rein of social progress, as some believe the Court did when it mandated the desegregation of public school systems beginning with the decision in *Brown* v. *Board of Education*[17] in 1954. At the opposite extreme, the Court in the early part of the twentieth century found—or thrust—itself into the vanguard of *resistance* to change, striking down as unconstitutional laws embodying a new philosophy of economic regulation at odds with the nineteenth century's laissez-faire approach.[18] During both these periods of confrontation and turbulence, the Supreme Court was the object of intense public outcries, and its precarious position in our constitutional system was exposed.

The framers of the Constitution allowed great authority as final arbiter of the Constitution's meaning to rest in the Court's hands; but they armed the Court with no swords to carry out its pronouncements. President Andrew Jackson, according to an often-told legend, said of a Supreme Court decision he did not like: The Chief Justice has made his decision, now let him enforce it. With prestige to persuade, but not physical power to enforce, and with a will for self-preservation, the Court generally follows, it does not lead, changes taking place elsewhere in society. But without taking giant strides and thereby risking a backlash, the court, through constitutional adjudication, can moderately accelerate the *pace* of change. In the gender-equality area, the Court functioned in that fashion; it played a vital role, although generally not an extravagant or divisive one.[19] As we consider the employment of the Constitution as a brake on, or accelerator of, political and social change, some worthwhile insights may be gained by examining the temperate brand of constitutional interpretation indicated in the Supreme Court's post–1970 gender-equality decisions.

I should qualify or clarify at this point that I do not here address among the gender-equality decisions *Roe* v. *Wade*,[20] the Supreme Court's pathbreaking 1973 abortion decision. A woman's ability to control whether and when she will have children no doubt bears vitally on her life's choices. But the Supreme Court rested its *Roe* v. *Wade* decision on a personal privacy or autonomy analysis pinned to the Fourteenth Amendment's due process clause, and not essentially to an equal rights or sex discrimination rationale. Most important for its bearing on the main theme of this chapter, the *Roe* v. *Wade* decision, in contrast to the gender-equality decisions, is not fairly described as "moderate."[21]

In 1973, when *Roe* v. *Wade* was issued, abortion law was in a state of change across the nation. There was a distinct trend in state legislatures "toward liberalization of abortion statutes."[22] The movement for abortion reform in legislative arenas ran parallel to another law revision effort then underway in the states—the change from fault to no-fault divorce, a reform that swept through the states inside of a decade.

The *Roe* decision and its companion, *Doe* v. *Bolton*,[23] were stunning in this sense: They called into question the constitutionality of the criminal abortion statutes of every state, even those with the least restrictive provisions (New York, Washington, Alaska, Hawaii). Around those extraordinary decisions, a well-organized and vocal right-to-life movement rallied and succeeded, for a considerable time, in turning the legislative tide in the opposite direction.

Professor Paul Freund once compared the *Roe* v. *Wade* decision to the response of the small boy asked if he knew how to spell banana. Yes, the child said, except I don't know when to stop. The Court might have stopped at invalidating the Texas law challenged in *Roe*; it was the most extreme law in the nation, allowing abortion only when medically necessary to save the pregnant woman's life. Had the Supreme Court simply ruled that extreme law impermissible, as an unreasonable accommodation of the competing interests, and said no more, the legislative trend might have continued in the reform direction in which it was moving in the early 1970s, and the animus against the Supreme Court, brought on by the actual *Roe* decision, might have been avoided or muted.[24]

I return now to my main theme. In contrast to the Court's initial, 1973, abortion decisions, which became and remain a storm center, the Court's gender-classification decisions, striking out sex-based differentiations in state and federal legislation, were unsensational and provoked no large controversy. But the Supreme Court needed education before it was equipped to make the gender-equality decisions of the 1970s. And the justices gained that education, publicly from the press and the briefs filed in Court; privately, I suspect, from the aspirations of women, particularly the daughters, in their own families and communities.

As I said at the outset,[25] the Court in 1961 in Ms. Hoyt's case was unwilling to participate at all in reformulating or adjusting the concept of equal protection of the laws, as that idea relates to the roles and responsibilities of men and women. In part, the Court stood pat in *Hoyt* because it was unable to view the differential treatment of men and women in the jury selection context as a *burden* on the exercise of women's rights. To turn in a new direction, the Court first had to comprehend that legislation apparently designed to benefit or protect women could often, perversely, have the opposite effect. This was of critical importance, for most laws that drew an explicit line between men and women did so, ostensibly, to shield or favor the fairer, but weaker, dependent-prone sex. Laws prescribing the maximum number of hours or time of day women could work, or the minimum wages they could receive; laws barring females from "hazardous" or "inappropriate" occupations (lawyering in the nineteenth century, bartending in the twentieth); remnants of the common-law regime which denied married women rights to hold and manage property, to sue or be sued, or to get credit from financial institutions (thus protecting them from their own folly or misjudgment)—all these prescriptions and proscriptions were premised on the baseline assumption or belief that women could not fend for themselves; they needed a big brother's assistance.[26] Until the Supreme Court perceived that women were unfairly constrained and pigeonholed by laws of this kind—laws of the breadwinning male/homemaking female mold—the justices could not be expected to grapple with the formulation of constitutional doctrine capable of curtailing that injustice.

In retrospect, it is not difficult to discern the burdensome nature of legislation that confined women to a sphere separate from the one occupied by men. By enshrining and promoting the woman's "natural" role as homemaker, and correspondingly emphasizing the man's role as provider, the state impeded both men and women from pursuit of the very opportunities that would have enabled them to break away from familiar stereotypes. Thus, for example, excluding otherwise qualified men from attending a nursing school tends, as the Supreme Court held in 1982,[27] to "perpetuate the stereotyped view of nursing as an exclusively woman's job";[28] instead of advancing women's welfare, this occupational reservation may help to keep wages low in the nursing profession. Similarly, providing Social Security spousal (derivative) benefits to wives and widows automatically, but to husbands and widowers, if at all, only on actual proof of "dependency,"[29] diminishes the worth of a woman's gainful employment, and can reinforce other disincentives to her work outside the family's home.

The changes in women's work and days, visible throughout the society by the 1970s, at last exposed to noticing judges the insidious and self-fulfilling potential of legislation once facilely accepted as benign. Alteration and expansion of women's pursuits insistently called into question the once largely unchallenged assumption of women's "natural" dependence on men, and their lack of fitness for men's occupations. As women in ever-increasing numbers began to pursue economic opportunities outside the home, it became ever harder to sustain the notion that their roles as wife and mother needed a panoply of special, sex-specific guards, lest the very fabric of society disintegrate. And once the protective labels were stripped away from traditional legal restrictions and classifications governing women, the pervasive discriminatory effects of those gross rankings stood out more clearly; most laws governing women *only* (or men *only*) could now be seen by people in the mainstream as hindering, not preserving, achievement of a genuinely natural division or sharing of labor between the sexes.

Thus, a more responsive Supreme Court was ready to hear Lt. Sharron Frontiero's plea in 1973. Sharron Frontiero, an Air Force officer, sought housing and medical benefits covering her student husband. Male officers, she observed, were automatically granted such benefits for their wives; female officers, on the other hand, could gain the same family benefits only upon proof that their husbands were dependent upon them for support. The Court, in the 8–1 *Frontiero* v. *Richardson* judgment,[30] grasped this simple inequity: the law's presumption that wives are dependent upon husbands, but not vice versa, netted Sharron Frontiero less pay. Such laws did women no favors; in the attention-attracting words Justice Brennan quoted, writing for the plurality, "in practical effect, [the laws in question] put women, not on a pedestal, but in a cage."[31]

Comprehending the discriminatory potential of this genre of legislation, the Supreme Court, by the mid–1970s, acknowledged that it had begun—and would continue—to scrutinize such schemes carefully. The Court would not sustain differential treatment of men and women that was merely *rationally* related to some *permissible* government objective; the Court would instead strike out any gender classification absent a *substantial* relationship to an *important* objective.[32]

These word changes in the Supreme Court's formulation of doctrine— from "rational" to "substantial," and from "permissible" to "important"—may seem trivial, the kind of fine distinction only a lawyer could love. But judicial application of a closer look test in gender-based classification cases has real significance. I will illustrate the point by referring to a key case in the evolution of the Supreme Court's current approach.

When Paula Polatschek Wiesenfeld died in childbirth in 1972, her husband, Stephen Wiesenfeld, applied for Social Security benefits for himself and their infant son. He discovered that the Social Security Act awarded so-called child-in-care benefits only to mothers, not to fathers. Stephen Wiesenfeld challenged this gender-based distinction, and ultimately won a unanimous judgment in the Supreme Court.[33] In defense of the sex line, the government argued, first, that the distinction between widowed mothers and widowed fathers was entirely rational—that, in fact, widows, *as a class*, were more in need of financial assistance than were widowers. True "in general," the Court replied, but defenses of sex stereotyping in laws as accurately reflecting the situation of the *average* woman or the *average* man were no longer good enough. The Court looked more closely at a U.S. society changing from old ways to new. That society included many widows who had not been dependent on their husbands' earnings, and some fathers like Stephen Wiesenfeld prepared to care personally for their children. Using sex as an administratively convenient shorthand to substitute for financial need or willingness to bring up a baby, while not irrational, failed to survive the Court's more exacting mode of review.

The government sounded another theme in the *Wiesenfeld* case, however, one with a modern ring. The challenged distinction, it claimed, was not an instance of "romantic paternalism," the sort of "favor" that in fact operated to keep women in their place; on the contrary, the government urged, the mother's benefit could be viewed as a kind of affirmative action—it served to compensate women for the economic discrimination they still routinely encountered. This claim, too, withered under careful inspection. As Justice Stevens, remarked, concurring in a follow-up Social Security case:

It [is] clear that . . . Congress simply assumed that all widows should be regarded as "dependents" in some general sense. . . . Habit, rather than analysis or reflection, made it seem appropriate to equate the terms "widow" and "dependent surviving spouse."

This old "habit," or traditional way of thinking about women, the Supreme Court has indicated, is no longer acceptable to explain or excuse a gender-based legal classification attacked as unconstitutional.

The High Court in *Wiesenfeld* and a number of cases thereafter took a genuinely intermediate position. It did not utterly condemn the legislature's product. In essence, the Court instructed Congress and state legislatures: Rethink and reanalyze your position on these questions. Should you determine that compensatory legislation is in fact warranted, because of the persistence of economic discrimination against women, we have left you a corridor in which to move. But your classifications must be refined, tied to an income test, for example, and not grossly drawn solely by reference to sex. The ball, one might say, was tossed gently back into the legislators' court, where the political forces at work as a result of the new social dynamic could operate, relieved of the baggage of traditional sex-role stereotypes. The Supreme Court wrote moderately, it imposed no specific philosophy on the public, but by forcing legislative reexamination of the question, it helped ensure that the sometimes glacial pace of legal change would be speeded up.

The framework evolving at the time of the *Wiesenfeld* case persists to this day; it has enabled the Supreme Court effectively to break the hold of the breadwinner-homemaker dichotomy by impelling equalization of the treatment of men and women with regard to social insurance and welfare benefits,[35] workers' compensation,[36] the right to spousal support after divorce,[37] the right to parental support[38]—even the right to purchase alcoholic beverages.[39]

As society changed and evolved with respect to the roles of men and women, so too did the force of the grandly general clause of the Constitution that inhibits government from "deny[ing] to any person . . . the equal protection of the laws."[40] As the stereotypes were successfully assaulted in the world outside the Court, the laws founded upon those stereotypes were sent back to the legislators for reconsideration, so that they would be revised to "catch up with a changed world."[41] And as the statute books were cleared of laws based on archaic and out-of-date generalizations, the generalizations were weakened still further; just as laws based on the assumption of female dependency once reinforced that dependency, nowadays laws founded upon ideals of equal dignity and opportunity advance shared participation by members of both sexes in our nation's economic and social life.

Engineers might call this a "positive feedback" process, with the Court functioning as an amplifier—responding to, and accelerating, the equalizing process. The analogy is apt, although I do not want to leave the impression that the judiciary has proceeded securely on course without missteps, detours, inconsistencies, and the like. Occasional fog is inevitable when the law is adjusting to a large social change. Registration for the military draft,[42] and statutory rape,[43] to take two 1980s examples, proved perplexing for the justices.[44] And no bold line divides justifiable and genuinely helpful "affirmative action"[45] from action that reinforces the harmful notion that women need a boost or preference, because they cannot make it on their own.[46] A court too sure of itself on these matters may, in its zeal, find itself out on a doctrinal limb—which, experience teaches, can be sawed off from behind.

James Madison once wrote that in the republic the U.S. Constitution serves, "the people are the only legitimate fountain of power";[47] federal judges at all levels, while freed from direct popular control, ignore Madison's maxim at their peril. At the same time, our constitutional scheme has endured because it is flexible enough to enable the system to adapt to ever-changing circumstances and conditions. Women are today unquestionably part of "We the People." Indeed, a prime part of the history of the Constitution is the story of the ways constitutional rights and protections came to be extended to once excluded groups, including women. Through a combination of change in society's practices, constitutional amendment, and judicial interpretation, a system of participatory democracy has evolved in which we take just pride. It has not been a simple process, but neither is the goal of the U.S. constitutional order a simple one. I hope these remarks have stimulated some thoughts on one of the interplays among the people, the political branches, and the courts that has kept the "more perfect Union" ordained by the Constitution alive and vibrant over these last two hundred years.

NOTES

1. See Ginsburg, "Women's Right to Full Participation in Shaping Society's Course: An Evolving Constitutional Precept," in *Toward the Second Decade: The Impact of the Women's Movement on American Institutions,* Justice & Pore eds. (Westport, CT: 1981), p. 171.

2. See Ginsburg, "Sexual Equality under the Fourteenth and Equal Rights Amendments," 1979 *Wash. U. L. Q.* 161.

3. Letter to Nathaniel Burwell, March 14, 1818, in *The Writings of Thomas Jefferson* vol. 10, P. L. Ford ed. (New York: Putnam, 1892–99), p. 104–06.

4. Letter to James Sullivan, in *The Works of John Adams*, vol. 9, C. F. Adams ed. (Boston: Little, Brown, 1850–56), pp. 375–78.

5. U.S. Const. amend. XIV, §2. This section provides for reduction in the number of representatives when the state denies "male citizens" the right to vote. The intent was to assure grant of the franchise to black men.

6. See Minor v. Happersett, 88 U.S. (21 Wall.) 162 (1874) (women qualify as persons and citizens within the Fourteenth Amendment's compass, so too do children; but status as a person and citizen does not carry with it the right to vote).

7. 368 U.S. 57 (1961).

8. Id. at 62.

9. See Fay v. New York, 332 U.S. 261, 290 (1947) ("changing view of the rights and responsibilities of women . . . has progressed in all phases of [public] life, . . . but has achieved constitutional compulsion on the states in only one particular—the grant of the franchise by the Nineteenth Amendment").

10. 368 U.S. at 61–62.

11. Bradwell v. Illinois, 83 U.S. (16 Wall.) 130 (1873) (rejecting woman's claim of constitutional right to be admitted to state bar if, apart from her sex, she possesses necessary qualifications).

12. Muller v. Oregon, 208 U.S. 412 (1908) (upholding state law restricting hours women permitted to work).

13. Goesaert v. Cleary, 335 U.S. 464, 467 (1948) (upholding state law precluding women, other than wives and daughters of bar owners, from tending bar).

14. See Williams, Sex Discrimination: "Closing the Law's Gender Gap," in *The Burger Years: Rights and Wrongs in the Supreme Court 1969–1986*, Herman Schwartz, ed. (New York: Viking, 1987), pp. 109, 123. ("In the seventeen years during which Warren Burger was chief justice, equal protection doctrine in sex discrimination cases underwent a modest revolution"); Ginsburg, "The Burger Court's Grapplings with Sex Discrimination," in *The Burger Court: The Counter-Revolution That Wasn't*, V. Blasi, ed. (New Haven, CT: Yale University Press, 1983), p. 132.

15. Taylor v. Louisiana, 419 U.S. 522 (1975); see Duren v. Missouri, 439 U.S.

357 (1979) (holding unconstitutional state statute allowing "any woman" to opt out of jury duty).

16. Quoted in Briggs, "How You Going to Get 'Em Back in the Kitchen? (You Aren't)," *Forbes*, Nov. 15, 1977, pp. 177–78.

17. 347 U.S. 483 (1954).

18. See, for example, Lochner v. New York, 198 U.S. 45 (1905) (state maximum hours regulation for bakery employees, covering men and women alike, held unconstitutional).

19. See Ginsburg, supra note 14.

20. 410 U.S. 113 (1973).

21. See, for example, Ely, "The Wages of Crying Wolf: A Comment on Roe v. Wade," 82 *Yale L. J.* 920 (1973); Ginsburg, "Some Thoughts on Autonomy and Equality in Relation to Roe v. Wade," 63 *N.C.L. Rev.* 375 (1985).

22. Roe v. Wade, 410 U.S. at 140.

23. 410 U.S. 179 (1973).

24. See Freund, "Storms Over the Supreme Court," 69 *A.B.A.J.* 1474, 1480 (1983) (adopted from inaugural Harold Leventhal Lecture at Columbia Law School); Ginsburg, supra note 21, 63 *N.C.L. Rev.*, pp. 379–83.

25. See supra, text at notes 7–13.

26. See Ginsburg, "Gender and the Constitution," 44 *U. Cin. L. Rev.* (1975): 1, 2–7.

27. Mississippi University for Women v. Hogan, 458 U.S. 718 (1982).

28. Id. at 729.

29. See Califano v. Goldfarb, 430 U.S. 199 (1977).

30. Frontiero v. Richardson, 411 U.S. 677 (1973). The turning point case preceded *Frontiero* by several months. In Reed v. Reed, 404 U.S. 71 (1971), a unanimous Court held in a brief opinion that it was unconstitutional for a state to accord men an automatic preference over women for estate administration purposes.

31. Id. at 684.

32. See Craig v. Boren, 429 U.S. 190, 197 (1976); see also Mississippi University for Women v. Hogan, 458 U.S., p. 724.

33. Weinberger v. Wiesenfeld, 420 U.S. 636 (1975).

34. Califano v. Goldfarb, 430 U.S., p. 222.

35. See Califano v. Westcott, 443 U.S. 76 (1979) (aid to families with dependent children).

36. Wengler v. Druggists Mutual Insurance Co., 446 U.S. 142 (1980).

37. Orr v. Orr, 440 U.S. 268 (1979). See also Kirchberg v. Feenstra, 450 U.S. 455 (1981) (holding unconstitutional Louisiana's former "head and master" rule under which husband had unilateral right to dispose of jointly owned property without his wife's consent).

38. Stanton v. Stanton, 421 U.S. 7 (1975).

39. Craig v. Boren, 429 U.S. 190 (1976) (boys must be permitted to buy 3.2 percent beer at the same age as girls).

40. The equal protection clause of the Fourteenth Amendment applies by its terms only to actions by states. However, the Supreme Court has declared an equality guarantee of the same quality implicit in the due process clause of the

Fifth Amendment, which controls actions by the federal government. See, for example, Weinberger v. Wiesenfeld, 420 U.S. 636, 638 n.2 (1975).

41. Williams, supra note 14, p. 123.

42. Rostker v. Goldberg, 453 U.S. 57 (1981) (upholding as constitutional military draft registration limited to males).

43. Michael M. v. Superior Court, 450 U.S. 464 (1981) (upholding state statutory rape law penalizing males but not females).

44. The Court has also wavered in dealing with claims of unwed fathers to full parental status, see Williams, supra note 14, pp. 120–21, and with classifications based explicitly on pregnancy. See id. p. 115.

45. See Johnson v. Transportation Agency, Santa Clara County, No. 85–1129 (U.S. March 25, 1987) (upholding as moderate and flexible a plan to effect a gradual increase in representation of minorities and women in skilled craft worker job classifications).

46. Compare Kahn v. Shevin, 416 U.S. 351 (1974) (upholding state property tax advantage reserved for widows); Associated General Contractors of California, Inc. v. County of San Francisco, No. 85–2420 (9th Cir. Mar. 23, 1987) (upholding provisions of ordinance that (1) reserved 2 percent of city's purchasing dollars for women-owned businesses, and (2) granted such businesses a 5 percent bidding preference).

47. *The Federalist* No. 49, at 339 (J. Madison), J. Cooke, ed. (Middletown, CT: Wesleyan Univ. Press, 1961).

VII INDIVIDUAL LIBERTIES AND THE RIGHTS OF PRIVACY

11 James Madison's "Triumph": The Fourteenth Amendment

Wallace Mendelson

> We need to be rid of the illusion that personal power can be benevolently exercised.
>
> Thurman Arnold

> Democracy is a device that insures we shall be governed no better than we deserve.
>
> George Bernard Shaw

Unlike such towering figures as Jefferson and Brandeis, James Madison (in 1787) had little confidence in state ability to manage even local affairs. Of course many in the Constitutional Convention feared parochial intrusion upon national interests. But, sharing that concern, Madison seems to have been peculiarly fearful of "aggressions of interested [state] majorities on the rights of [local] minorities and of individuals."[1] Hence his persistent struggle in and out of the convention for a congressional veto to check the states. Because the veto was rejected, Madison found the Constitution "materially defective."[2] In his view it would not "prevent the local mischiefs which everywhere excite disgusts against state government."[3]

Obviously the "father of the Constitution" had more confidence in congressional, than in state legislative, majorities. He explained why in his famous *Federalist* essays numbered 10 and 51. The diffusion of constitutional power and the vast expanse of the nation with its multiplicity of regional, economic, religious, and other interests were the true safeguards. Faction would resist faction; ambition would weigh against ambition. The hopes and fears of each subgroup would check and balance those of all the others. Government could act only after political compromise had found the common denominator of a host of mutually suspicious minorities. In the extended, pluralistic republic of the United States this could not be an easy, overnight venture. No program that had survived the give and take necessary to attain support by a concurrent majority of our incredibly varied factional interests could depart substantially from the nation's moral center of gravity. No governmental system could be expected to achieve more. In short, as Madison saw it, majority rule—given a vast empire of diffused sociopolitical power— was the most reliable security against governmental inhumanity.

Even the largest of our states is much smaller than the nation in size and in the number and variety of its competing factions. There, in Madison's view, lay the risk. For the "smaller the society, the fewer probably will be the distinct parties and interests composing it . . . and . . . the more easily will they concert and execute their plans of oppression."[4] By failing to adopt the congressional veto, Madison thought, we laid ourselves open to many of the troubles we had experienced under the Articles of Confederation.

It is not easy to understand what in U.S. experience justified, for example, the Brandeis idea that the states—acting as "experimental laboratories"—could lead us to the promised land.[5] Before Brandeis left the bench there was ample justification for the view that:

> In state government are to be found in their most extreme and vicious forms all the worst evils of misrule in the country. Venality, open domination and manipulation by vested interests, unspeakable callousness in the care of the sick, aged, and unfortunate, criminal negligence in law enforcement, crass deprivation of primary constitutional rights, obfuscation, obsolescence, obstructionism, incompetence, and even outright dictatorship are widespread characteristics.[6]

In 1955 the Final Report of the United States Commission on Intergovernmental Relations found "a very real and pressing need for the States to improve their constitutions . . . to make sure that they provide for [instead of impeding] vigorous and responsible government. . . ." A dozen years later a careful scholar observed: "In the course of two centuries, few observers have pointed with pride to American state governments."[7]

Madison seems to have been right. We had not fully learned the lessons of the confederation era. If one concentrates on what the Supreme Court does as distinct from what it says, one must conclude that it too finds the original Constitution "materially defective" for

want of adequate restraints upon the states. Obviously our judges
have tried to make good this defect by imaginative application of the
second sentence of the Fourteenth Amendment.[8] In effect that provision has become a substitute for what Madison wanted in the congressional veto: not merely a legal, but a political or policy curb upon state
"indiscretion" in local matters. Whom do we fool by pretending the
second sentence of Amendment Fourteen is nothing more than a rule
of positive law? Functionally it often resembles a standardless grant
of legislative power to judges. For it can not rationally *as a law* be
said both to permit and forbid racial segregation;[9] to permit and forbid
poll taxes;[10] to incorporate and not incorporate laissez faire;[11] to impose
and not impose the fair-value doctrine;[12] to permit and to outlaw
gender discrimination;[13] to allow and to not allow compulsory flag sa-
lutes;[14] to incorporate yet not incorporate most of the Bill of Rights;[15]
to prescribe both an abortion code and a code of criminal case procedure;[16] to protect trial by jury though not by the traditional jury of
12, and not by the ancient unanimity requirement.[17] Perhaps strangest of all, some claims deemed so "fundamental" as to be protected
by the Fourteenth Amendment are nevertheless not basic enough
to merit "retrospective" application.[18] Obviously many of these
were policy choices uninhibited by anything that can properly
be called law or principle. Whom did the Supreme Court *mean* to
fool when it held, for example, in *Griswold*[19] that recreational sex is
protected by positive law in an eighteenth century Bill of Rights
allegedly made applicable to the states by a fair-hearing provision in
a Reconstruction amendment? Apparently the Court did not fool itself! Its subsequent privacy cases, for example, *Roe* v. *Wade*, eschew
the *Griswold* incorporation-penumbra ploy in favor of a candid return
to substantive due process—the very thing *Griswold* tried so hard
to camouflage (obviously because of its then virtually universal ill
repute).

Madison's proposed congressional veto and an "activist" Fourteenth
Amendment have much in common. Each contemplates a political, or
policy, check—unlimited in scope—against state "provincialism." Yet
they differ in a way that surely would trouble Madison. He was after
all a deep-dyed Republican. For him the appeal of the congressional
veto is obvious—reflecting as it does the safeguards stressed in his *Federalist* essays numbered 10 and 15. That he would leave the final resolution of public policy issues to the least accountable branch of
government is at best dubious:

In the State Constitutions & indeed in the Federal one also, no provision is
made for the case of a disagreement in expounding them; & as the courts are
generally the last in making ye decision, it *results* to them by refusing or not
refusing to execute a law, to stamp it with its *final character*. This makes the

Judiciary Dept. paramount in fact to the Legislature, which was never intended and can never be proper.[20]

For a time (before the fact) Madison, like Jefferson, accepted judicial review. Both had second thoughts when they saw what it meant in practice.[21] What Madison really wanted was not judicial review, but a congressional veto to check the states, and a council of revision to check Congress (and its veto). Yet the council check was to be provisional only. Congress was to have the last word.[22]

For the same reasons that Madison wanted congressional power to protect civil liberty from state abuse, he looked also to Congress—rather than a judicially enforceable Bill of Rights—to safeguard civil liberty at the national level:

> I have never thought the omission [of a bill of rights from the original Constitution] a material defect, nor been anxious to supply it even by *subsequent* amendment, for any other reason than that it is anxiously desired by others . . .
>
> I have not viewed it in an important light . . .
>
> 4. because experience proves the inefficiency of a bill of rights on those occasions when its control is most needed. Repeated violations of these parchment barriers have been committed by overbearing majorities in every State. In Virginia I have seen the bill of rights violated in every instance where it has been opposed to a popular current. . . .[23]

It was only political expediency that led Madison in the first Congress to support what he called the "nauseous project of amendments" after the Bill of Rights idea had been deliberately dropped in the Constitutional Convention.[24] In his personal view the only use of a formal declaration was that "the political truths declared in that solemn manner acquire by degrees the character of fundamental maxims of free government, and as they become incorporated with the national sentiment, counteract the impulses of interest and passion."[25] How far this is from judicial review! And how close to Learned Hand's thought that the Bill of Rights is not law, but a moral admonition.[26]

Madison was unenthusiastic about the Bill-of-Rights-Judicial-Review approach because he foresaw a far more reliable, and far more sophisticated, shield for civil liberty: the structure and process of politics, given the conditions described in his Federalist essays. It comes then to this: "[T]he father of the Constitution" was indeed a republican. For him "the people themselves" are "the best keepers of their own liberties"[27] from whatever threat, be it a wayward state or a national faction. What even Madison did not anticipate was that some of the Supreme Court's worst self-inflicted wounds sprang from interpretation of the Bill of Rights, for example, *Dred Scott*,[28] *Adair* v.

United States,[29] *Adkins* v. *Children's Hospital*,[30] and the two child labor cases.[31]

We cannot know whether Madison's congressional veto would have been better than the Fourteenth Amendment judicial veto as a remedy against state indiscretion. We do, however, know something about the relative effectiveness of Congress and the Supreme Court vis-à-vis civil liberty at the national level. Despite our myriad, rival factions and our nationwide, sociopolitical check and balance system, there have been congressional lapses. The Sedition Act of 1789, the Espionage Act of 1917, the Smith Act of 1940 come to mind. But such measures, having survived trial by factionalism in a supercharged setting, inevitably reflect feelings so deep and widespread as to defy judicial veto (as Madison foresaw). In nearly two hundred years the Supreme Court has upheld Bill of Rights claims against Congress in pitifully few cases. It did not find a congressional violation of the First Amendment until 1965 toward the end of the Warren era![32] In contrast, the national political system in or out of Congress has crushed—as Madison anticipated—endless proposals reflecting every form of bigotry, intolerance, and demagoguery.

Have we so soon forgotten Professor (later Judge) Edgerton's conclusion in a 1937 study of all relevant cases?

In one who identifies the country with the well-to-do minority of its population, enthusiasm for judicial review over Congress is as logical as enthusiasm can be. It is hard to see why, apart from convention, one who does not make that identification should share that enthusiasm. . . . I wonder what cases [are] so valuable as to outweigh the *Dred Scott* case, which helped to entrench slavery; the *Civil Rights* and related cases, which protected the oppression of Negroes; the employers' liability and workmen's compensation cases, which denied relief to injured workmen; the child labor and minimum wage cases, which protected the hiring of women and children at starvation wages; the income tax cases, which prevented the shifting of tax burdens from the poor to the rich; and the many minor instances in which the Court's review has done harm to the common man.[33]

In 1943 Henry Commager reached essentially the same conclusion in his once famous study of *Majority Rule and Minority Rights*:

[The record] discloses not a single case, in a century and a half, where the Supreme Court has protected freedom of speech, press, assembly, or petition against congressional attack. It reveals no instance (with the possible exception of the dubious Wong Wing case) where the court has intervened on behalf of the underprivileged—the Negro, the alien, women, children, workers, tenant-farmers. It reveals, on the contrary, that the court has effectively intervened again and again to defeat congressional efforts to free slaves, guarantee civil rights to Negroes, to protect workingmen, outlaw child labor, assist hard-pressed farmers, and to democratize the tax system. *From this analysis the Congress, and not the courts, emerges as the instrument for the realization of the guarantees of the bill of rights* (emphasis added).[34]

Similarly in 1954 John Frank's "Review and Basic Liberties" concluded:

If the test of the value of judicial review to the preservation of basic liberties were to be rested on actual invalidations [of acts of Congress], the balance is against judicial review. . . . the actual overt exercise of judicial review of acts of Congress has been of almost negligible good to civil liberties, and has probably harmed those liberties more than it has helped them.[35]

In 1965, after Earl Warren had been Chief Justice for some 12 years, Leonard Levy reviewed all of the post-Commager Supreme Court decisions protecting civil liberty vis-à-vis acts of Congress. He concluded that "Taken as a group the cases are of greater symbolic than practical importance. None received much attention from the press or Congress; most were unnoticed. . . . Nothing that has happened since 1943 has impaired whatever validity Commager's principles or theoretical argument possessed, and events have merely modified, but scarcely impaired, his argument [against judicial review] based on history."[36]

The Edgerton-Commager-Frank-Levy findings support Madison's view that—at the national level—judicially enforceable "parchment barriers" would do little for civil liberty. So too, history seems to have vindicated Madison's prediction that state government—given its narrow political base—would be a threat to local minorities, a threat that had to be neutralized by national supervision. We got that supervision, as it turned out, not as Madison wished, but by judicial "interpretation" of the Fourteenth Amendment. We got it with a vengeance in the dismal days of laissez-faire, and again during the Warren enlightenment. The difficulty is that Warrenism had very limited popular (as distinct from columnist and campus) support. Indeed by the time Earl Warren left the bench, the Supreme Court had reached its nadir in public esteem.[37] Apparently it had been giving (imposing) more than was widely wanted—more than its platonic fictions could support. If the legislation of our 50 states is a key to what U.S. citizens find acceptable, *Roe* v. *Wade*, for example, was plainly inappropriate. Indeed as late as January 14, 1985—more than a decade after *Roe*—a *Newsweek* Poll (by Gallup) indicated 58 percent support for a ban on all abortions save in the case of rape, incest, or danger to the mother's life. This suggests an ancient problem: Is it to be "slip-shod" government by the governed, or something "better" by an elite? I leave that dilemma for others. My concern is make-believe in high places, be it in the Supreme Court or in the White House.

It was held in 1905 that a fair hearing provision in a Reconstruction amendment protected "privacy" with respect to hours of labor, while in 1973 it protected "privacy" with respect to abortion. The opinions in these cases and in *Griswold* are classic examples of Plato's insight that even allwise philosopher kings cannot rule unless they camouflage their raw power with "noble fictions." The fiction in *Lochner, Griswold,* and *Roe* is that the outcome was ordained not by a few mere men, but by law—not by a divided Court, but by the written Constitution. The fiction, of course, is calculated to hide the implacable moral difference between obedience to law and subservience to a cabal of fellow mortals. The ultimate collapse of the "nine old men" may be another facet of history's hint that no fiction, however noble, can forever cloak the philosopher-king with moral responsibility. Soon or late, it seems, his nakedness appears; and then we must begin again the unending struggle for law— *for government by something more respectable than the will of those who for the moment hold high office.*

Old-fashioned liberals are not the only ones troubled by fairy-tale jurisprudence as in *Griswold*. The most dynamic movement in our law schools today is led by avant-garde liberals of the ME-NOW generation whose formative years coincided with the enlightenment that Earl Warren inspired. Bemused by his sense of "fairness," these so-called "non-interpretists" are far too sophisticated to accept his simple-minded methodology. What they want is Warren Court activism without Warren Court mythology. They want, for example, contraception and abortion "privacy," but not the pretense that it derives from interpretation of the Constitution. As one of their gifted leaders puts it; they reject the Supreme Court's

resort to bad legislative history and strained reading of the constitutional language to support results that would be better justified by explication of contemporary moral and political ideals not drawn from the constitutional text.[38]

In short they want honesty on the bench. They want Warrenite lawmaking by judges, but they want it openly and candidly supported on public policy—not fairy-tale—grounds. Like Madison, they want a *national* veto to keep the states in line. Like him, they want it to be *legislative* in nature. Yet, unlike Madison, they want it in judicial hands. The reason is obvious. They want something better than they have reason to expect from state legislatures—given conventional morality and conventional wisdom. The rub is that selecting something better entails what Learned Hand called "the appraisal and balancing of human values which there are no scales to weigh. . . . The difficulty does not come from ignorance, but from the absence of any standard, for values are incommensurable."[39] Subjective preference then—what

Holmes called "can't helps"—become crucial. Thus not long ago "liberty of contract" outlawed minimum-wage, but not maximum hour, laws for women.[40] Now a woman's abortion "privacy" is absolute against her husband, yet qualified vis-à-vis the state.[41] Only one judge was on the majority side in both *Miranda*[42] and (eight days later) *Schmerber*.[43] Thus he alone on the bench found them compatible—the one permitting *forceful* extraction of a man's blood to incriminate him; the other outlawing unwarned custodial confession *no matter how voluntary in fact.* In *Plyler v. Doe*, according to Professor Tushnet,

Justice Brennan's opinion [is] analytically indefensible. It jams together doctrines that other cases carefully held [apart]. But its very awkwardness reveals much about what Justice Brennan was really doing: not writing a carefully crafted opinion, [but] building a coalition. [According to this view, Justices Brennan and Marshall were prepared to invalidate the statute because it] embodies a dreadfully unwise social policy. [The problem was how] to get three more votes. [Justice Brennan knew that Justice Blackmun] thinks that its not a nice thing to penalize kids for their parents' actions, [so he stressed the] analogy to illegitimacy. [He knew that] Justice Powell knows, from Virginia's experience during the period of massive resistance to desegregation, the severity of the social costs of wholesale denials of education, [so he stressed that the case] involves absolute deprivations of education, [And because] Justice Stevens has this bizarre attraction to the idea that equal protection cases involving state regulation affecting aliens are rather like preemption cases, [he stressed] the primary responsibility of the national government for regulating aliens.[44]

Such cases and the contradictory decisions mentioned above suggest that in Fourteenth Amendment litigation Supreme Court judges (despite their "reasoned explanations") are as unprincipled as more orthodox lawmakers—and no more immune than others from error and the corrupting effect of raw power. Yet they alone among those who govern in the United States are neither politically nor judicially accountable for their edicts.

To achieve its goals, noninterpretism would have judges look for guidance beyond the Constitution, for after all it was produced by people long since "dead and gone." Moreover, we cannot rely upon the political processes to bring it up to date by legislation and constitutional amendment, for those processes, it is said, are untrustworthy, prone as they are to compromise and accommodation—to say nothing of muddleheadedness and corruption.[45] *The ultimate goal is a new morality.* This cannot be achieved by our elected representatives because they are not sensitive to "opportunities for moral reevaluation and possible moral growth." Judges—free of voter pressure—are better able "to keep faith with the notion of moral [progress; to eschew] the sediment of old moralities [in favor of] emergent principles."[46] Of course not all non-interpretists fully agree with this formulation by one of their most inspired leaders. What is beyond doubt, however, is their broad agreement that neither conventional morality, the mandates of the Constitution, nor our political processes will achieve their utopia. Marked in their formative years by the Warren Court romance, they seem utterly blind to the risk that other judges in other times may (as in the past) come up with less congenial "emergent" values. The real problem is not that the Constitution and the founders' meanings are unclear. It is rather that what the Founding Fathers wrote—highlighted by what they did not write—is all too clear. They simply did not mean or write many things some think they should have written. They did not, for example, outlaw capital punishment, nor restraints upon abortion, nor did they forbid wage and hour laws. Recognizing, however, that we might want such things, they gave us legislative and amending procedures for achieving them. The catch is that voters and legislators are not adequately informed (according to Justice Marshall)[47] and not sufficiently free of conventional morality (according to Professor Perry, et al.).[48] Indeed the major premise of judicial activism is that the United States's political processes are for the birds—as Chief Justice Warren intimated over and over again in his *Memoirs*.[49]

Unlike Madison, some of our "best and brightest" seem to have forgotten at what cost Western civilization learned its basic precepts: consent of the governed, diffusion of power, and rule of law. These after all are the essence of the Constitution—the foundation of the structure and processes of U.S. government. Indeed there is very little else in the Constitution. For the founders knew the futility of trying to act as a legislature for future generations. Accordingly, they left virtually all substantive policy matters (even capital punishment and abortion) for popular resolution from time to time via constitutionally prescribed procedures. Unlike the founders, impatient activists of whatever vintage insist upon constitutionalizing *their* substantive moral values as in *Lochner* and *Roe* v. *Wade*.

CONCLUSION

For good or bad our practice implements Madison's insight that the states individually are not to be trusted with the management even of essentially local affairs.[50] Rejection of his remedy—a congressional veto—left a vacuum that judges fill under the guise of Fourteenth Amendment adjudication. Though they pretend otherwise, in fact their "judgments" in most crucial cases are ad hoc legislation. This violates a basic principle of what Madison called republicanism, and what old-fashioned liberals think of as democracy.

From the time of *Plessy*, Fourteenth Amendment jurisprudence has been a less than objective exercise in "civic virtue," as dissenting judges have suggested over and over again. If, as some insist, the Supreme Court is the keeper of our morality, two of its longest-lived precepts "legitimated" apartheid for blacks and something akin to that for women.[51] Moreover—Plato notwithstanding—fiat camouflaged by fiction is hardly the ultimate in morality. Why, for example, in *Griswold* did the Court not say simply that a ban on contraceptives is bad social policy for such and such reasons, and therefore would not be enforced? No doubt the Court thought such candor would have been fatal to its pretension—which presumably is what President Johnson thought with respect to Tonkin Bay, what President Nixon thought with respect to Cambodia and Watergate, and what President Reagan thought with respect to Iran and Nicaragua. If, as some political scientists insist, the Supreme Court is essentially a political agency, it would be naive to expect it to tell the whole truth and nothing but the truth. For politics after all is concerned with who gets what—we do not expect it to be neutral, objective, cerebral, or principled. As Martin Shapiro observed years ago: "Suicide is no more moral in political than in personal life. It would be fantastic indeed if [a politically oriented] Supreme Court, in the name of sound scholarship, were to disavow publicly the myth [of law] on which its power rests."[52]

NOTES

1. M. Farrand, *The Records of the Federal Convention of 1787*, vol. 1, pp. 164ff. See also notes 2, 3 and 22, below. For a detailed account of Madison's efforts on behalf of a congressional veto see C. F. Hobson, "The Negative of State laws: James Madison, the Constitution, and the Crisis of Republican Government." *William and Mary Quarterly*, vol. 36 (1979), p. 215.

2. Letter to Thomas Jefferson, October 24, 1787, pp. 207, 209 et seq., *The Papers of James Madison*, vol. 10, R. A. Rutland, Ed. (1977).

The Supremacy Clause of the Constitution's Article VI cures the defect with respect to state measures that impinge upon national interests as, for example, in McCulloch v. Maryland, 4 Wheaton 316 (1819). Save some quite limited provisions in Article 1, Sec. 10 and Article IV, nothing in the unamended Constitution deals with what for Madison was a prime concern: state intrusions upon the "rights of [local] minorities."

3. Letter to Thomas Jefferson, Sept. 6, 1787, Rutland, pp. 163–64; Farrand, p. 164ff. See also note 2, above.

4. *The Federalist*, No. 10.

5. See the Brandeis dissent in New State Ice Co. v. Liebman, 285 U.S. 262 (1932). For a more realistic view of "states rights" see the Cardozo opinion in Steward Machine Co. v. Davis, 301 U.S. 548 (1937).

6. R. S. Allen, *Our Sovereign State* (New York: Vanguard, 1947), p. vii.

7. J. W. Fesler, Ed. *The 50 States and Their Local Governments* (New York: Knopf, 1967), p. 29.

8. "No State shall make or enforce any law which shall abridge the privileges or immunities of citizens of the United States; nor shall any State deprive any person of life, liberty, or property, without due process of law; nor deny to any person within its jurisdiction the equal protection of the laws."

9. *Ex parte Virginia*, 100 U.S. 339 (1879); Plessy v. Ferguson, 163 U.S. 537 (1896); Brown v. Board of Education, 347 U.S. 483 (1954).

10. Breedlove v. Suttles, 302 U.S. 277 (1937); Harper v. Virginia Board of Electors, 383 U.S. 663 (1966).

11. Lochner v. New York, 198 U.S. 45 (1905); Ferguson v. Skrupa, 372 U.S. 726 (1963).

12. Smyth v. Ames, 169 U.S. 466 (1898); FPC v. Natural Gas Pipeline Co., 315 U.S. 575 (1942).

13. Groesaert v. Cleary, 335 U.S. 464 (1948); Craig v. Boren, 429 U.S. 190 (1976).

14. Minersville School District v. Gobitis, 310 U.S. 586 (1940); Board of Education v. Barnette, 319 U.S. 624 (1943).

15. Duncan v. Louisiana, 391 U.S. 145 (1968); Wolf v. Colorado, 338 U.S. 25 (1949).

16. Roe v. Wade, 410 U.S. 113 (1973); H. J. Friendly, "The Bill of Rights as a Code of Criminal Procedure," 53 *California Law Review* 929 (1965).

17. Duncan v. Louisiana, 391 U.S. 145 (1948); Williams v. Florida, 399 U.S. 78 (1970); Apodaca v. Oregon, 406 U.S. 404 (1972).

18. Linkletter v. Walker, 381 U.S. 618 (1965).

19. Griswold v. Connecticut, 381 U.S. 479 (1965).

20. Letter to Brown, October, 1788, in *The Writings of James Madison*, vol. 5, G. Hunt Ed. (New York: Putnam, 1904), p. 294. This problem seems also to have troubled the Warren Court for it said in Miranda v. Arizona, 384 U.S. 436 (1966):

Our decision in no way creates a constitutional straitjacket which will handicap sound efforts at reform, nor is it intended to have this effect. We encourage Congress and the States to continue their laudable search for increasingly effective ways of protecting the rights of the individual while promoting efficient enforcement of our criminal laws. However, unless we are shown other procedures which are at least as effective in apprising accused persons of their right of silence and in assuring a continuous opportunity to exercise it, the following safeguards must be observed.

A few days later, *Katzenbach v. Morgan*, 384 U.S. 611 (1966)—though enigmatic— invited congressional, as distinct from judicial, review in at least some Fourteenth Amendment contexts. This was a small step back to a major purpose plainly revealed in the amendment's Section 5, namely, to give Congress full enforcing power. For years following the *Dred Scott* disaster—to say nothing of the fugitive slave cases—the Supreme Court was widely deemed an enemy of freedom. What followed was, in Professor Robert McCloskey's words, the judicial ice age. It is revealing that Amendment Fourteen begins by repudiating *Dred Scott*, and ends by looking not to the judiciary but to Congress *as had Madison* for protection against state violation of minority rights. Congress tried diligently in the Civil Rights Acts of 1866, 1870, 1871, 1875 and a number of amendments thereto. Its efforts were largely nullified by judges. See, for example, the *Civil Rights Cases*,

109 U.S. 3 (1883). An overall view will be found in Gressman, "The Unhappy History of Civil Rights Legislation," 50 *Michigan Law Review* 1321 (1952).

21. As to Jefferson, see W. Mendelson, "Jefferson on Judicial Review: Consistency Through Change," 29 *University of Chicago Law Review* 327 (1962).

22. See Resolve No. 8 of the Virginia Plan in M. Farrand, *The Records of the Federal Convention of 1787*, vol. 1, (New Haven, CT: Yale University Press, 1966), p. 21. See also Letter to George Washington, April 16, 1787, in *The Papers of James Madison*, vol. 9, R. A. Rutland, ed. (University of Chicago Press, 1975), p. 384.

23. Letter to Thomas Jefferson, October 17, 1788 in *The Papers of James Madison*, vol. 11, R. A. Rutland, Ed. (University of Chicago Press, 1977), p. 397.

24. See L. Levy, *Constitutional Opinions*, (Oxford University Press, 1985), p. 121.

25. See note 23, above.

26. *The Spirit of Liberty*, 3rd ed. (University of Chicago Press, 1960), pp. 177–78.

27. *National Gazette*, Dec. 20, 1792.

28. Dred Scott v. Sandford, 19 How. 393 (1857).

29. 208 U.S. 161 (1908).

30. 261 U.S. 525 (1923).

31. Bailey v. Drexel Furniture Co., 259 U.S. 20 (1922); Hammer v. Dagenhart, 247 U.S. 251 (1918).

32. Lamont v. Postmaster General, 381 U.S. 301 (1965).

33. "The Incidence of Judicial Control Over Congress," 22 *Cornell Law Quarterly* 299 (1937).

34. H. S. Commager, *Majority Rule and Minority Rights* (New York: Oxford University Press, 1943), p. 55.

35. In E. Cahn, Ed., *Supreme Court and Supreme Law* (Westport, CT: Greenwood, 1968), p. 109.

36. L. Levy, *Judgments: Essays on American Constitutional History* (Chicago: Quadrangle, 1972), p. 41.

37. See, for example, Gallup Survey, *New York Times*, June 15, 1969, Sec. 1, p. 43.

38. T. Grey, "Do We Have an Unwritten Constitution?," 27 *Stanford Law Review* 703 (1975). See also P. Brest, "The Misconceived Quest for the Original Understanding," 60 *Boston University Law Review* 204 (1980); M. Perry, *The Constitution, The Courts, and Human Rights* (New Haven, CT: Yale University Press, 1982).

39. Hand, p. 161.

40. Muller v. Oregon, 208 U.S. 412 (1908); Adkins v. Children's Hospital, 261 U.S. 525 (1923).

41. Planned Parenthood v. Danforth, 428 U.S. 52 (1976); Roe v. Wade, 410 U.S. 113 (1973).

42. Miranda v. Arizona, 384 U.S. 436 (1966).

43. Schmerber v. California, 384 U.S. 757 (1966).

44. See notes 9–19, above.

45. Michael Perry, *The Constitution, the Courts and Human Rights*, (New Haven, CT: Yale University Press, 1982), pp. 99, 102; Alexander Bickel, *The Least Dan-*

gerous Branch, (Yale University Press, 1980), pp. 25–26; Richard Parker, "The Past of Constitutional Theory—And Its Future," 42 *Ohio State Law Journal* 259 (1981).

46. Perry, pp. 99–111.

47. Gregg v. Georgia, 428 U.S. 153, 232 (1976).

48. See notes 37 and 49.

49. See *The Memoirs of Earl Warren* (Garden City, NY: Doubleday, 1977), pp. 53, 174, 262, 335, 337.

50. Unlike Jefferson's Kentucky Resolutions, Madison's Virginia Resolutions contemplated, not that an individual state, but all states acting together, could "interpose" (not nullify). Thus Madison satisfied his *Federalist*, No. 10 safety-in-numbers principle. See I. Brant, *James Madison: Father of the Constitution*, (Indianapolis, IN: Bobbs-Merrill, 1950), pp. 461ff.

51. In a famous article published at the end of the Warren era we were told the justices' approach to women's rights has been characterized, since the 1870s, by two prominent features: "a vague but strong substantive belief in women's 'separate place,' and an extra-ordinary methodological casualness in reviewing state legislation based on such stereotypical views of women." Brown, Emerson, Falk & Freedman, "The Equal Rights Amendment: A Constitutional Basis for Equal Rights for Women," 80 *Yale L. J.* (1971): 871, 875–76.

52. *Law and Politics in the Supreme Court* (New York: Free Press, 1964), p. 27.

12 The Right to Privacy and Legitimate Constitutional Change

Walter F. Murphy

INTRODUCTION

The idea of "privacy" is, as Richard A. Posner has said, "richly ambiguous and highly charged."[1] It includes but goes beyond solitude: A private person need not be a recluse. One can have privacy in one's self, one's family, and in one's associations. The right's basic function is to allow people to control who knows certain things about their inner selves and with whom they share, on a mutually consenting basis, certain intimate relations.[2] At bottom, it is a moral notion, resting on a belief that human beings are entitled to a significant measure of autonomy and dignity and thus must enjoy almost total sovereignty over a portion of their lives. The citizen—not government, not the state, not society—determines with whom he or she shall be on intimate terms. The "concept of privacy embodies the 'moral fact that a person belongs to himself and not others and not to society as a whole.' "[3] The notion is thus closely connected with the even more basic concept of "personhood," a view of each human being as a distinct moral entity, entitled to equal respect and value as every other human.[4]

As moral postulates about human nature and the purposes of society, privacy, and personhood—their scope and even their status as values—are subjects of sharp dispute. In the United States, criticism of an extensive right to privacy has come from the feminist left,[5] Reagan's right,[6] and, insofar as it is derived from judicial interpretation of the Constitution, even from the libertarian center.[7]

Neither the American constitutional document of 1787 nor the Bill of Rights explicitly mentions such a right. If, however, one believes, as the framers at Philadelphia apparently did, that enumerating powers itself limits government, the document implies a right of privacy against the nation. Moreover, one can perceive in several provisions of the Bill of Rights protections of specific aspects of privacy, such as religious freedom, the prohibition against quartering of troops in civilian homes in peacetime, and the ban against unreasonable searches and seizures.[8] In addition, the imperative mood of the Ninth Amendment,[9] commanding interpreters not to restrict rights to those listed in the document, makes omission of a specific listing of privacy less than fatal.

Still, in the United States a constitutional status for a right to privacy must be justified by interpretation. If one takes the Ninth Amendment seriously, this legal genealogy does not disparage the right; but it does make it more controversial than it would be had the document explicitly acknowledged its importance. And, although privacy has long roots in Anglo-American jurisprudence, its status as a constitutional right is recent, growing out of litigation involving specific clauses, especially the prohibition of unreasonable searches and seizures[10] and the application of the Bill of Rights to the states via the Fourteenth Amendment.

My purpose in this chapter is not to analyze privacy as an abstract concept, or to reconstruct its development as a constitutional right, or to pick apart the Court's—or Congress's—interpretations of such a right. Others have attacked those objectives with greater skill than I could bring to bear.[11]

My purpose, rather, is to use the right to privacy as an instrument to help deepen understanding of the nature of constitutions and constitutional change. I begin with a brief summary of what the U.S. Supreme Court has said about the right, then move to more theoretical concerns about the nature of constitutions and the American Constitution, in particular, in order to address problems of privacy, constitutional interpretation, and legitimate constitutional change. I argue that a meaningful concept of protected privacy is embedded in the American "constitution," and that it would not be legitimate, even by formal amendment, to remove that notion from the "constitution." The nub of my thesis is that:

1. The nature of the American Constitution requires recognition of a thick and powerful right to be let alone, a right that runs against both state and federal governments. I do not claim that current constitutional law marks the proper boundaries of that right. Indeed, I think that the Court has construed the right too widely in cases involving abortion[12] and too narrowly in cases involving sexual relations conducted in private between consenting adults.[13] My point only is that a version of the right that is both muscular and capacious is essential to constitutional systems like that of the United States.

2. Constitutions continually change, develop, and/or regress, and they do so by a variety of means. Nevertheless, there are real, if imprecise, limits on legitimate constitutional change. And a right to privacy sets one of these limits.

READING PRIVACY INTO THE CANON

As often happens in U.S. constitutional interpretation, the first ringing defense of a general constitutional right to privacy came in a dissenting opinion. A federal court had convicted Roy Olmstead for violating the prohibition laws, hardly an unusual occurrence for the time.[14] What made his case notable was that the government had gathered much of its evidence through wiretaps, and Olmstead charged that this practice violated the Fifth Amendment's ban on compulsory self-incrimination and the Fourth's prohibition against unreasonable searches and seizures. The Supreme Court divided 5–4 against him.

Louis D. Brandeis wrote a dissenting opinion in which Oliver Wendell Holmes and Harlan F. Stone partly joined (Pierce Butler dissented separately), defending a broad right of privacy:

The makers of our Constitution undertook to secure conditions favorable to the pursuit of happiness. They recognized the significance of man's spiritual nature, of his feelings and of his intellect. . . . They conferred against the Government, the right to be let alone—the most comprehensive of rights and the right most valued by civilized men. To protect that right, every unjustifiable intrusion by the Government upon the privacy of the individual, whatever the means employed, must be deemed a violation of the Fourth Amendment. And the use, as evidence in a criminal proceeding, of facts ascertained by such intrusion must be deemed a violation of the Fifth.[15]

Brandeis's happy phrase "the right to be let alone" became a battle cry in the struggle for recognition of a constitutional right to privacy. But it was Holmes, in his own brief dissent, who offered what was to become the interpretive talisman—the possible location of such a right in the "penumbra" of specific constitutional clauses.

The Court eventually overturned *Olmstead*,[16] but more important for a general right to privacy were cases beyond the Fourth Amendment, such as *Public Utilities Commission* v. *Pollack* (1952), challenging the constitutionality of a public bus company's bombarding its riders with radio programs that included commercial advertising. Seven of the eight justices participating in the decision found no constitutional flaw. Only William O. Douglas dissented, and he both echoed Brandeis and adumbrated what was to come:

The case comes down to the meaning of "liberty" as used in the Fifth Amendment. Liberty in the constitutional sense must mean more than freedom from unlawful governmental restraint; it must include privacy as well, if it is to be a repository of freedom. The right to be let alone is the beginning of all freedom. . . .
The right of privacy should include the right to pick and choose from com-

peting entertainments, competing propaganda, competing political philosophies. If people are let alone in those choices, the right of privacy will pay
dividends in character and integrity. The strength of our system is in the dignity,
the resourcefulness, and the independence of our people. . . . The right of privacy, today violated, is a powerful deterrent to any one who would control
men's minds.[17]

A decade later, in *Poe* v. *Ullman*, a physician and two married couples
attacked a Connecticut statute that made it a crime to use or abet the
use of contraceptives. The Court dismissed the suit because the justices
saw no real danger of prosecution.[18] Justices Potter Stewart, John Marshall Harlan, and Douglas charged that the Court was merely evading
a difficult question. The latter two, in separate opinions, also addressed
the merits.

Once again Douglas's view of privacy was generous. He began by
shoring up the right's weakness as unlisted, noting that, while he believed "due process" embraced the first eight amendments, "I do not
think it is restricted and confined to them."[19] Furthermore, he repeated
his claim in *Pollack* that "liberty" included a right to "privacy" (Douglas's
quotes) and continued:

[T]o say that a legislature may do anything not within a specific guarantee of
the Constitution may be as crippling to a free society as to allow it to override
specific guarantees so long as what it does fails to shock the sensibilities of a
majority of the Court.

He concluded that it would be necessary for police to penetrate the
marital bedroom to enforce the statute, an act that would constitute "an
invasion of the privacy that is implicit in a free society."[20] Cryptically,
he described the derivation of this "implied" right: "This notion of privacy is not drawn from the blue. It emanates from the totality of the
constitutional scheme under which we live."[21]

Harlan's dissent also stressed privacy, but it was the more specific
right to privacy of the home and family, rather than a general right to
be let alone. He located the sources for these rights in due process and
liberty in themselves, rather than as shorthand for specific clauses of
the Bill of Rights.

Almost the same case returned to the Court three years later, after
Connecticut prosecuted two people for instructing married couples
about contraception. This time Douglas's argument gathered a majority
of votes, and Chief Justice Warren assigned him the task of writing the
opinion of the Court.

After some hesitant beginnings,[22] Douglas utilized his own previous
work and that of Prof. William M. Beaney.[23] First, the justice dismissed
the objection that the constitutional document did not mention a general

right to privacy, cataloguing a series of other rights, such as freedom of association, that were also unlisted but constitutionally protected. Then, more positively:

[S]pecific guarantees in the Bill of Rights have penumbras, formed by emanations from those guarantees that help give them life and substance. Various guarantees create zones of privacy. The right of association contained in the penumbra of the First Amendment is one. . . . The Third Amendment in its prohibition against the quartering of soldiers "in any house" in time of peace without the consent of the owner is another facet of that privacy. The Fourth Amendment explicitly affirms the "right of the people to be secure in their persons, houses, papers, and effects against unreasonable searches and seizures." The Fifth Amendment in its Self-Incrimination Clause enables the citizen to create a zone of privacy which government may not force him to surrender to his detriment. The Ninth Amendment provides: "The enumeration in the Constitution, of certain rights, shall not be construed to deny or disparage others retained by the people."[24]

Seven years later, the Court again used *Griswold's* reasoning when, in *Eisenstadt* v. *Baird*, it invalidated a state law against distributing information about birth control to *unmarried* people. For the majority, Justice William J. Brennan wrote:

If the right of privacy means anything, it is the right of the *individual*, married or single, to be free from unwarranted governmental intrusion into matters so fundamentally affecting a person as the decision whether to bear or beget a child.[25]

The following year, *Roe* v. *Wade* twisted this thread into a cord:

The right of privacy, whether it be found in the Fourteenth Amendment's concept of personal liberty and restrictions upon state action, as we feel it is, or, as the District Court determined, in the Ninth Amendment's reservation of rights to the people, is broad enough to encompass a woman's decision whether or not to terminate her pregnancy.[26]

Despite decisions broadening a woman's right to abortion, since *Roe* the Court has not been consistently protective of a general right to privacy. *Paul* v. *Davis* (1976)[27] turned a blind eye toward defensible concepts of liberty and personhood. There, police had circulated a flyer to local merchants with names, descriptions, and photographs of shoplifters "known to be active in this criminal field." Included in this rogues' gallery was Edward Charles Davis, III, who had never been convicted of a criminal offense. He sued for damages in a federal district court and eventually lost. Speaking for a five-judge majority, William H. Rehnquist found that Davis had not suffered injury to any constitutionally protected right to privacy or reputation.

Earlier, without opinion, the Court had affirmed a ruling of a special three-judge district court upholding the constitutionality of Virginia's statute punishing homosexual acts, even between consenting adults committed in private homes.[28] Then in 1986 *Bowers* v. *Hardwick* retreated further from both *Griswold* and *Eisenstadt*—and logically from *Roe* v. *Wade*. Police had arrested Michael Hardwick for allegedly violating Georgia's anti-sodomy statute[29] in his own home with a consenting male adult, but the prosecutor dropped the charges. Hardwick then asked a federal district court to enjoin the state from enforcing the statute. The judge dismissed the suit, but the court of appeals reversed. The Supreme Court divided 5–4, with the majority agreeing with the trial judge.

For the Court, Byron White limited the issue to sodomy between homosexuals, a right which he asserted had no support "in the text of the Constitution," and was neither " 'deeply rooted in this Nation's history and tradition,' " nor " 'implicit in the concept of ordered liberty.' " For the dissenters, Harry A. Blackmun pointed out that Georgia's statute affected not only homosexual but also heterosexual relations, even between married couples. "[T]his case," he emphasized, is about " 'the most comprehensive of rights and the right most valued by civilized men,' namely, 'the right to be let alone.' "

LEGITIMATE CONSTITUTIONAL CHANGE

Knowing what the Supreme Court has said about a putative right is important but not sufficient. As Felix Frankfurter once asserted, the touchstone of constitutionality is the Constitution and not what the justices have said about it. Thus to debate the validity, reach, and vulnerability to legitimate change of a right to privacy, one must look at the nature of constitutions in general and the U.S. Constitution in particular.

In such an analysis, three questions are paramount: First, what is the constitution's authority? Whom and to what extent does it bind? Is it in fact, as well as in claim, "the supreme law of the land"? If so, supreme for whom?

Second, what are the constitution's functions? Is it, for instance, supposed to act merely as a charter for government? If it so operates, does it also play other roles? What more? To "constitute" a people as well as map a government? To serve as a storehouse for public values and societal aspirations?

Third, what does the term "the constitution" comprise? Only the document as amended? That document minus some parts, such as, in the U.S. case, the Preamble and the Ninth Amendment, whose terms prove so nettlesome to naive legal positivists? Does the term include more than the amended document? Intentions and understandings of framers and/or ratifiers? Other documents? Ancient practices? Interpretations? Political theories?

I have tried elsewhere[30] to explain and justify my responses to these sorts of questions. Because of a lack of space, I shall here only summarize my arguments at places where they are relevant to a discussion of the right to privacy and constitutional change. For purposes of this chapter, I assume that the U.S. Constitution does bind officials as well as citizens, though that assumption may sometimes be counterfactual.

I am also assuming that, like most modern constitutions, the U.S. Constitution is constantly developing. The meaning of what Ronald Dworkin[31] calls the Constitution's conceptions may remain more or less constant, but the content and import of concepts change as problems change. What I do not assume—indeed what I dispute—is that those concepts function as blank checks. These concepts constrain not only interpretation but also amendments.

Paths to Change

One might look on usage, interpretation, and formal amendment as forming a hierarchy of legitimate constitutional change. Each is a process rather than a single event, normally involving increasingly conscious efforts at change and increasingly wider arenas in which the processes occur. Still, each is inherently creative; and it can be very difficult to tell, except in the most mechanical sense, when we move from one of these processes to the other. Officials who begin or continue a usage may well have thought out the implications of their actions (that is, interpreted the constitution), just as those who continue an interpretation may unthinkingly accept it as a usage. And there can be little doubt that some interpretations have generated more far-reaching effects than have some amendments.

Yet it is defensible to argue that some changes that could be effected via the amending processes are not validly open either to any one set of public officials or even to the electorate.[32] As an example, one might cite the U.S. Supreme Court's draining the Fourteenth Amendment's "privileges or immunities" clause of significance in the Slaughter-House Cases (1873).[33] Such a drastic alteration of the constitutional text cried out for revision by reamendment, assuming the deed could be done at all.

Limitations on Constitutional Change

Whatever the limits on legitimate constitutional change by usage or interpretation, can citizens and/or government officials, assuming they follow the procedures set forth in the constitutional document,[34] amend a constitution[35] in any way they see fit? If the answer is yes, then U.S.

citizens could legitimately eliminate the equal protection clause and remove any trace of an "equal protection component" from the due process
clauses of the Fifth and Fourteenth Amendments and authorize discrimination, racial and otherwise, at the discretion of state and federal officials; repeal the Thirteenth Amendment and legalize slavery; and repeal
the First Amendment and legitimize a state religion as well as political
censorship. In sum, an affirmative answer means the processes of Article
V validate U.S. citizens's progressing or regressing to any sort of society
they might wish.[36]

There are two usual reactions (or a two-part response) to such conclusions: (1) None of these horribles would ever become a reality. The
American people have learned from their not always happy history. (2)
And, if they did so behave, they, as sovereigns, would be within their
rights. I share the hope transmitted in the first response; still, the gravity
of such reconstitutions, if not their imminence, raises questions not only
about their wisdom but more fundamentally about their validity. At very
least, I would deny that the people could effect these changes through
the Constitution that we know.

PRIVACY AND ENTRENCHMENT

My argument that a robust right to privacy—and certain other rights
as well, such as to equal treatment by government—is embedded in and
absolutely essential to the U.S. Constitution (indeed, to any constitutional democracy) is based on the Constitution's functions and content
and on the notion of what "to amend" means.

Constitutional Functions

Looked at narrowly, a constitution forms a charter for government.
It sets out rules for the ways in which a government will operate: who
its officials are; how they are to be chosen and for what terms; how
power is to be divided among them; and what rights, if any, are reserved
to citizens. To some extent, all constitutions insofar as they are not
shams[37] fulfill this role, though they may do so more or less well. Their
capacity to control reality will depend in large part on their authority.

But a constitution may perform other, broader functions as well. "To
constitute" means to compose or make up; and a thing's "constitution"
refers to the way in which it is composed or made up. Thus a constitution
purporting to speak in the name of a people could define the sort of
people its subjects/authors are and would like to become—not only their
governmental structures and procedures, but also their goals, ideals,
and the moral standards by which they want to judge their own community and others to judge it.

Following Sotirios A. Barber and Gary Jacobsohn,[38] I argue that the U.S. Constitution[39] functions as a binding statement of a people's aspirations for themselves and their nation. "The aspirational tone of the Constitution," Barber writes, "is unmistakable in the Preamble."[40] That preface sets out the republic's purposes, not only to achieve more perfect union, national defense, the general welfare, and domestic tranquility but also to "establish justice" and "secure the blessings of liberty to ourselves and our posterity." Moreover, the Preamble proclaims a "CONSTITUTION for the United States of America," not simply for the *government* of the United States. The Constitution, Justice Brennan has said, "embodies the aspiration to social justice, brotherhood, and human dignity that brought this nation into being."[41]

The substantive and procedural articles[42] that follow the Preamble define some objectives more specifically and prescribe how society's goals are to be achieved. That the United States has often fallen short, sometimes far short, of those ideals does not mean that they have not been or will not continue to be important sources of political energy.

The argument from function to inclusion of a right to privacy is straightforward, resting on Brandeis's reasoning in *Olmstead* and Douglas's in *Pollack* and *Poe*: The notion of a people as free and autonomous as they can be in an interdependent world is and has been among the values, goals, and aspirations of U.S. society. Furthermore, it is anchored in the constitutional text by such phrases as "the blessings of liberty" and the specific clauses Douglas listed in *Griswold*. Privacy is, as Brandeis said, "the right to be let alone" and, as Douglas added, "the beginning of all freedom."

Constitutional Content

Any judgment about what a constitution includes must be based on something akin to H.L.A. Hart's "rules of recognition"[43] to define what is canonical. I have not formulated a complete set of such rules, but certainly one criterion would be performance of a foundational function. That is, it would have to play a significant role in forming or reforming a people into a nation. A second, alternative, standard would be functioning as a lens without which the basic constitutional document(s) could not be intelligibly read—in short, infusing the document(s) with coherent and consistent meaning.

The Declaration. By the first standard, paragraph 2 of the Declaration of Independence must be included in the canon. It called the American nation into being, explicitly committing the new republic to notions of freedom, natural rights, equality, and government by consent:

We hold these truths to be self-evident, that all men are created equal; that they are endowed by their Creator with certain unalienable Rights, that among these are Life, Liberty and the pursuit of Happiness. That to secure these rights, Governments are instituted among men, deriving their just powers from the consent of the governed. That whenever any Form of Government becomes destructive of these ends, it is the Right of the People to alter or abolish it. . . .

John Adams jealously dismissed the Declaration as not containing a single idea "but what had been hackneyed in Congress for two years before."[44] And Jefferson acknowledged he had tried "[n]ot to find new principles . . . but to place before mankind the common sense of the subject. . . ."[45] But commonplace or no in the colonies, such a claim was radical in the larger world of 1776. And it was precisely its radicalness in the world and its commonness in the colonies that attest to the distinctive political character the American people stamped on their republic, establishing, as Lincoln said, "a standard maxim for free society, which should be familiar to all, and revered by all; constantly looked to, constantly labored for, and even though never perfectly attained, constantly approximated, and thereby constantly spreading and deepening its influence. . . ."[46]

That the constitutional document of 1787 and the ensuing Bill of Rights omitted any reference to the Declaration is, I submit, irrelevant. The Declaration formed us as a people committed to a particular view of the human person and the purposes of government. To escape such clear, radical, and general philosophical principles the country would need explicitly to reject them.[47] As Carl Lotus Becker phrased it, "In the Declaration, the foundation of the United States is indissolubly associated with a theory of politics, a philosophy of human rights which is valid, if at all, not for Americans only, but for all men."[48] Justice Brennan has echoed this theme: "The Declaration of Independence, the Constitution and the Bill of Rights solemnly committed the United States to be a country where the dignity and rights of all persons were equal before all authority."[49]

Proving the existence of a political creed is difficult if not impossible. Still, it is hardly a novel observation that paragraph 2 of the Declaration, along with the less widely read constitutional document of 1787 as amended, forms the basis of a civil religion. The United States, G. K. Chesterton once wrote,

has a creed . . . set forth with dogmatic and theological lucidity in the Declaration of Independence; perhaps the only piece of practical politics that is also theoretical politics and also great literature. It enunciates that all men are equal in their claim to justice, that governments exist to give them that justice, and that their authority is for that reason just. . . . The point is that there is a creed, if not about divine, at least about human things.[50]

Equality of human dignity and worth, natural rights of individuals, the purpose of government to protect these rights, the necessity of government by consent, and the right of the people to revolution if government fails in its duty—are all basic building blocks of a coherent if not completely internally consistent political theory. And the course of U.S. constitutional development has run toward greater acceptance of the notion of equal dignity and worth, as the Thirteenth and Fourteenth Amendments emphatically attest, and the Fifteenth, Nineteenth, Twenty-third, and Twenty-fourth Amendments repeat. Recognizing the Thirteenth Amendment and the equal protection and privileges or immunities clauses of the Fourteenth as writing the second paragraph of the Declaration into positive law against state governments is, I believe, the best reading of the American "constitution."[51]

Political Theories. Indirectly the second paragraph of the Declaration committed the republic to constitutionalism and, to a lesser extent, to democracy. More directly, the second rule of recognition would identify theories of representational democracy and constitutionalism as part of the larger constitution.

Representational democracy is the more familiar set of normative concepts: It goes beyond "government by consent" to argue that the people should in fact rule through their elected agents. "The claim is most persuasively put," Michael Walzer says, "not in terms of what the people know, but in terms of who they are. They are the subjects of the law, and if the law is to bind them as free men and women, they must also be its makers."[52] Democratic theory looks to protect individual rights in the belief that the people as rulers will not oppress themselves. The "mass of citizens," Jefferson once claimed, "are the safest depository for their own rights." Free, open processes of speech, writing, association, and voting are thus essential elements of this theory. Without these, the people cannot, in fact, choose.

The essence of constitutionalism is that citizens bring rights with them into society. Its "core objective," Carl J. Friedrich asserted, is

that of safeguarding each member of the political community as a political person, possessing a sphere of genuine autonomy. The constitution is meant to protect the *self* in its dignity and worth. . . . The prime function of a constitutional order has been and is being accomplished by means of a system of regularized restraints imposed upon those who exercise political power.[53]

Where democratic theory sees free and open political processes as legitimizing public policy, constitutionalism—much more pessimistic about human nature—imposes substantive standards, most especially the preservation of individual rights, as determinative of the legitimacy of public policy. As Jefferson, who embraced both theories, stated: "An elective despotism was not the government we fought for.... "[54] Thus constitutionalism would uphold individual rights against a freely elected legislature no less than against a military dictator.

The two theories coexist in tension, but without variants of each the American constitutional document of 1787 as amended would be a political version of a seed catalogue, a mere listing of authorities and rights, informed by no general concepts, organized by no architectonic scheme,[55] linked only by consecutively numbered articles and clauses. It would, in sum, be intellectually incoherent and its claim to be "the supreme law of the land" a farce.[56]

Without a theory of representative democracy, one could not read the document(s) as an effort to establish a polity based not only on consent but also on representation of the people through elected officials. It is patently true that U.S. political arrangements do not construct a "pure" representative democracy.[57] Nevertheless, not even the most avid defender of any other political theory—and I confess I am more a constitutionalist than a democrat—could sensibly deny that the document of 1787 carried out a large, though tempered, element of democratic theory and that many amendments have more fully embodied democratic theory.

A similar argument holds for constitutionalism. It was present in the document of 1787 and the Bill of Rights in even larger doses than was democratic theory; and, while some specific devices the framers foresaw as limiting government have weakened or vanished, the power of constitutionalism itself has increased.

Despite important differences about who[58] shall determine what rights are fundamental and what criteria make such decisions legitimate, both theories start from similar beliefs about the value of human rights. For constitutionalism, privacy is quintessential. As Douglas, Brennan, and Blackmun have explained, without controlling a core of physical and psychological space, without being able to share some aspects of our lives *only* with those whom we choose, we would be unable to define ourselves, to develop our talents and personalities, or to live with dignity or any autonomy. To the extent that we cannot refresh ourselves with occasional solitude, enjoy the quiet necessary for thought and reflection, or choose those with whom we share our most intimate associations, we live less than fully human lives.

The essence of totalitarianism, the antithesis of constitutionalism, lies in its effort to enable the state to control all aspects of its people's lives. It prescribes an ugly and pervasive form of rape. Any meaningful theory of constitutionalism demands a wide ambit for a right to privacy.

At first glance, however, democratic theory might seem to leave protection of privacy completely to the people's freely chosen representatives. A pure representative democracy, lacking any institutional checks on representatives other than the political processes themselves, might impose on itself a form of democratic totalitarianism by using free, open processes to abolish, on an evenhanded basis, privacy in all phases of life.

On the contrary, I would argue, such a result would be a perversion of democratic theory. For a strong and extensive right to privacy is also essential to a functioning democracy. A political system that rests on free and open debate, association, and political choice also needs a wide scope for privacy. One reason some of the men at Philadelphia gave for opposing democracy was its vulnerability to corruption. Voting in those days was oral and public. As Gouverneur Morris reportedly explained,

If the suffrage were open to all *freemen*—the government would indubitably be an aristocracy. . . . It would put into the power of opulent men whose business created numerous dependents to rule at elections. Hence so soon as we erected large manufactories and our towns became more populous—wealthy merchants and manufacturers would elect the house of representatives. This was an aristocracy. This could be avoided by confining the suffrage to *free holders* [of landed property].[59]

When Morris's predictions materialized and city bosses developed the capacity to march hordes of newly arrived immigrants from polling place to polling place to vote often, electoral privacy—achieved through the secret ballot—became an attractive remedy against corruption.

Moreover, to the extent that intelligent electoral choice requires discussion, it requires discussion with those whom we trust, not merely with those who thrust themselves—or whom government thrusts—upon us. Thus we need to control selection of the people to whom we bare our political concerns. So, too, intelligent choice requires some physical and psychological space in which to think, free from the bombardment of others' words.

But more than open debate and a secret ballot are necessary for electoral processes to be truly free. There is also a need, as recent history sadly testifies, for freedom from sanctions, social as well as legal, for espousing unpopular views or supporting unpopular candidates. After black people operating through the NAACP succeeded in persuading courts to strike down government-imposed segregation,[60] most southern states in the 1950s and 1960s tried to stifle further black gains by requiring the association to turn over to the states its membership lists. The plan was to publish the names and allow private white citizens to levy economic sanctions on these "agitators."

Invalidating Alabama's attempt, the U.S. Supreme Court held that "It is beyond debate that freedom to engage in association for the advancement of beliefs and ideas [a right not enumerated in the constitutional document of 1787 or subsequent amendments] is an inseparable aspect of the 'liberty' assured by the Due Process Clause of the Fourteenth Amendment, which embraces freedom of speech."[61] The Court continued:

It is hardly a novel perception that compelled disclosure of affiliation with groups engaged in advocacy may constitute as effective a restraint on freedom of association as the [other, directly repressive] forms of governmental action. ... *This Court has recognized the vital relationship between freedom to associate and privacy in one's associations....* Inviolability of privacy in group association may in many circumstances be indispensable to preservation of freedom of association, particularly where a group espouses dissident beliefs.[62]

The point is not that the Supreme Court has formulated ruling law or found ultimate truth, only that the justices, on this and similar occasions,[63] have properly identified a tight linkage between a robust right to privacy and representative democracy. To eliminate or even drastically weaken this "vital relationship" would hack at democracy's foundations almost as savagely as would political censorship.

The Meaning of "Amend"

"To amend" means to modify or rephrase, so as to add or subtract. Its root is the Latin *emendare*, to correct. The plain words of Article V provide substantive, not merely procedural, limitations on constitutional change, for that article speaks of "Amendments," not of creations of a new constitution. Most simply, given the commitment of the American Constitution, broadly defined to include the document of 1787 as amended plus the Declaration as well as democratic and constitutional theory, removing or severely restricting the "right to be let alone" would so fundamentally change the system as to remake rather than modify or correct it. Such a change would mean that the United States had become a different polity, its people would be re-constituted, re-formed rather than reformed. As I explain below, I do not deny the possibility or even the potential validity of such a transformation, only that, to use Harris's terminology, the constitution does not authorize it from "the inside."[64] Article V establishes procedures for modifications. For legitimation of wholesale revision, we have to look elsewhere.

To American ears, accustomed to crude forms of legal positivism, the idea of an unconstitutional part of a constitution seems strange, even absurd. But it seems a logical possibility if one accepts the notion that a constitution does more than order public offices, includes more than a single amended document, and contains a hierarchy of principles. All constitutional clauses are not equal. Surely no intelligent U.S. citizen would equate his or her right to a trial by jury in a civil suit where 20 dollars was at issue with the right to freedom of religion or to equal protection of the laws. The Federal Constitutional Court of West Germany stated the matter succinctly:

That a constitutional provision itself may be null and void, is not conceptually impossible just because it is part of the constitution. There are constitutional principles that are so fundamental and to such an extent an expression of a law that precedes even the constitution that they also bind the framer of the constitution, and other constitutional provisions that do not rank so high may be null and void, because they contravene these principles.[65]

Summary

My argument has been unusual, but it is, I hope, clear: A constitution can—and the U.S. Constitution does—perform functions other than to establish governmental processes. Among those functions in the American case is to set out the nation's goals, to specify the kind of people we are and want to become. A constitution may include more than the document so labelled. And "the American constitution" includes, at least, the second paragraph of the Declaration of Independence and democratic and constitutional theory. These sources deeply entrench individual liberty and thus a zone of privacy in the "constitution." Moreover, there are limits to changes that a system can effect through amendment under this or any other "real" constitution. A change so fundamental as to destroy a central value of the "constitution" would be radical in the true sense of the word, going to the root of the nation's reason for being. Such a change would make the United States a different nation, its people a different people.

LEGITIMATE RADICAL CHANGE

Any normative theory that would attempt to bind a nation in perpetuity would be worthy of King Canute's curia. Thus I do not deny that a nation can escape from even the most fundamental tenets of its constitution; I do deny that it can do so within the terms of its constitution (assuming that its constitution is not a sham). I do not claim that a constitution, defined narrowly or broadly, may not run for only a set span of years,[66] merely that, as long as it is in force, neither its public officials nor its people can validly violate its fundamental principles.

What about radical change then? Is it possible for a people to abandon constitutional democracy or one of its essential elements?[67] As a matter of sheer power, the answer, of course, must be yes: A people can reform themselves. If one believes in government by consent, one must also believe the people may, as a matter of right, change their political system.[68] And while I would argue that some form of constitutional democracy is most likely to secure justice, I would not claim either that there is no room for debate on this issue or that specific circumstances might not occur that would modify my reasoning. My point remains simply that one may not validly use a constitution to justify radical changes in that constitution's basic values and underlying principles. Even if the new framers did not admit their attempt to form a new people—to create a new polity—their product's authority would derive from the people's acceptance, not from the old constitution.

In the United States, the engine for such a change might be a constitutional convention called by Congress under Article V. But insofar as such a convention asserted authority under Article V, its authority to try to re-form the American people would be severely limited. Its product, even if ratified by conventions chosen in the states, would not, solely because of these conventions' pedigree, be morally or legally binding either on private citizens or governmental agencies, including but not restricted to courts.

I speak of authority here, not power. Backed by governmental force, an amendment could effect radical changes and receive popular acceptance. I would argue, however, that if such an amendment does become operational, it is because the people have to that extent re-formed themselves, as to a great extent Americans did in 1787–88. The authority of the Constitution of 1787 flows from the American people as they formed themselves under the Declaration of Independence, not from their consent to the Articles of Confederation.[69]

If my argument is valid, it follows that the U.S. system cannot, without re-forming (as distinguished from reforming) its people, relax its requirements that government, even government by the people, respect the right to privacy. The system can, however, enhance that right. But even here there are limits, for drawing precise boundaries around a right to privacy raises complex problems of more than one person's or group's rights. One need look no further than to the issue of abortion to find grim evidence of this unhappy fact.

PRACTICAL CONSEQUENCES

What practical course is open to governmental agencies and private citizens if such a radical change as elimination or severe reduction of the right to be let alone were to become operational?

First, if the change were effected on its own merits as a radical re-forming of the people, then it would open the whole question of consent. Certainly by the theories underlying the old constitution, individuals would have the moral and legal right to exit, though the new regime, depending on how authoritarian it was, might deny such a right.

What about the states? Harris argues[70] that the new constitution should be valid, as Article VII specifies, only among those states that ratify. For two reasons, I am less sure: (1) Invoking Article VII implies that the radical change derives some legitimacy from the old constitution, and that I deny; (2) I am not certain—I am not prepared to deny it but neither am I prepared to affirm it—that gradual changes over the last two centuries, the Civil War, and the implications of the Fourteenth Amendment, have not deprived states of the status they held in 1787 as primary political entities.

Second, if the change were effected under the guise of a mere amendment rather than a re-formation, then individual citizens would face the age-old dilemma of what to do about unjust laws. Silent acquiescence might be the most prudent course, though the gallant might well fight to restore the old order, either peacefully or even through revolution. The less quietistic and less gallant might choose exit.

Public officials would face similar difficulties. Democracy and constitutionalism might pull in different directions. If the new system accepted political freedom, that is, allowed free and open debate, campaigns, and elections, and did not take away participational rights even from insular minorities, democratic theory would face a severe crisis. Where the political processes are open, a democratic theorist should find heavy obligation to obey. Still, because without a real measure of privacy democracy is likely to degenerate into oligarchy or even into a form of totalitarianism, thoughtful representative democrats might understand that to destroy privacy is to debilitate democracy. They might, then, accord the new system something less than full acceptance, even if it were the people's choice.

Constitutionalism would be less ambivalent. Although prudence might dictate extreme caution, constitutional theory would not easily admit[71] a moral or legal obligation to obey any system that violated constitutionalism's norms. Thus it would most probably justify a public official's refusing to enforce the new order.

Would such resistance be effective? There can be no abstract answer beyond "it depends." Were an official or set of officials in a respected institution—the President or the Supreme Court, for instance—to declare the "amendment" unconstitutional and refuse to enforce it, we might see change. Public officials can act as republican schoolmasters.[72] They can also whistle in the dark.

NOTES

I am indebted to Professor M. Stanley Kelley, Jr., of Princeton University for carefully reading the manuscript and to Bernard Roberts of the Princeton class of 1988 and Suzette M. Hemberger, then a graduate student at Princeton, for research assistance. The Center of International Studies of Princeton supported the research on which this chapter is based.

1. Richard A. Posner, *The Economics of Justice* (Cambridge, MA: Harvard University Press, 1981), p. 231. W. A. Parent has described current scholarship

on the right to privacy as being in a state of "hopeless disarray." "Recent Work on the Concept of Privacy," 20 *Am. Phil. Q.* 341 (1983). See also Paul A. Freund, "Privacy: One Concept of Many?" in J. Roland Pennock and John W. Chapman, eds., *Privacy* (New York: Atherton, 1971), pp. 182ff.

2. See especially Stanley I. Benn, "Privacy, Freedom, and Respect for Persons," in Pennock and Chapman; Joel Feinberg, "Autonomy, Sovereignty, and Privacy: Moral Ideals in the Constitution?" 58 *Notre Dame L. Rev.* 445 (1983); Kenneth L. Karst, "Freedom of Intimate Association," 89 *Yale L. J.* 624 (1980); and Jeffrey H. Reiman, "Privacy, Intimacy, and Personhood," 6 *Phil. & Pub. Affrs.* 26 (1976).

3. Justice John Paul Stevens, concur. in Thornburgh v. Am. Coll., 476 U.S. 747, 777n. (1986); the internal quotation is from Charles Fried's work.

4. Evidence from cultural anthropology indicates that even primitive societies recognize and accomodate demands to be let alone. Barrington Moore, Jr., *Privacy: Studies in Social and Cultural History* (Armonk, NY: Sharpe, 1984), especially ch. 1. See also Alan F. Westin, *Privacy and Freedom* (New York: Atheneum, 1967).

5. See, for example, Catherine A. MacKinnon, "Pornography, Civil Rights, and Free Speech," 20 *Harv. Civ. Rts.–Civ. Libs. L. Rev.* 1 (1985).

6. Robert H. Bork, *The Tempting of America* (New York: The Free Press, 1989), *passim*. Richard A. Posner, *The Economics of Justice*, chs. 9–11, drains the right of any moral content.

7. See, for example, Justice Hugo L. Black's dis. op. in Griswold v. Connecticut, 381 U.S. 479 (1965).

8. Ibid., Douglas's opinion for the Court.

9. "The enumeration in the Constitution, of certain rights, shall not be construed to deny or disparage others retained by the people."

10. See especially Boyd v. United States, 116 U.S. 616 (1886); Weeks v. United States, 232 U.S., 383 (1914); and Mapp v. Ohio, 367 U.S. 643 (1961).

11. For example: Edward J. Bloustein, "Privacy as an Aspect of Human Dignity," 39 *N. Y. U. L. Rev.* 962 (1964); J. Braxton Craven, Jr., "The Right to be Let Alone," 1976 *Duke L. J.* 699; Charles Fried, "Privacy," 77 *Yale L. J.* 475 (1968); Fried, "Privacy: Economics and Ethics," 12 *Ga. L. Rev.* 423 (1978); Hyman Gross, "The Concept of Privacy," 42 *N. Y. U. L. Rev.* 34 (1967); Gerald Gunther, *Constitutional Law*, 11th ed. (Mineola, N.Y.: Foundation Press, 1985), ch. 8, §3, and ch. 9, §4; Louis Henkin, "Privacy and Autonomy," 74 *Colum. L. Rev.* 1410 (1974); Karst, "Freedom of Intimate Association"; Jacob W. Landynski, *Search and Seizure and the Supreme Court* (Baltimore, MD: Johns Hopkins University Press, 1966); Louis Lusky, "Invasion of Privacy: A Clarification of Concepts," 72 *Colum. L. Rev.* 693 (1972); Arthur R. Miller, *The Assault on Privacy: Computers, Data Banks, and Dossiers* (Ann Arbor: University of Michigan Press, 1971); Walter F. Murphy, James E. Fleming, and William F. Harris, II, *American Constitutional Interpretation* (Mineola, N.Y.: Foundation Press, 1986), ch. 17; David M. O'Brien, *Privacy, Law and Public Policy* (New York: Praeger, 1979); W. A. Parent, "Privacy, Morality, and the Law," 12 *Phil. & Pub. Affrs.* 269 (1983); Pennock and Chapman, *Privacy*; Posner, *Economics of Justice*, chs. 9–11; C. Herman Pritchett, *Constitutional Civil Liberties* (Englewood Cliffs, NJ: Prentice-Hall, 1985), ch. 12; William L. Prosser, "Privacy," 48 *Calif. L. Rev.* 383 (1960); James Rachels, "Why Privacy Is Important," 4 *Phil. & Pub. Affrs.* 323 (1975); David A. J. Richards, "Sexual Autonomy and the Consti-

tutional Right to Privacy," 30 *Hastings L. J.* 957 (1979); Thomas Scanlon, "Thomson on Privacy," 4 *Phil. & Pub. Affrs.* 315 (1975); Rogers M. Smith, "The Constitution and Autonomy," 60 *Tex. L. Rev.* 175 (1982); Symposium on the Economics of Privacy, 9 *J. of Legal Stud.* (December, 1980); Judith Jarvis Thomson, "The Right to Privacy," 4 *Phil. & Pub. Affrs.* 295 (1975); Laurence H. Tribe, *American Constitutional Law*, 2d ed. (Mineola, NY: Foundation Press, 1987), chs. 11, 15; Westin, *Privacy and Freedom.*

12. See, for example, Roe v. Wade, 410 U.S. 113 (1973); Akron v. Akron Center, 462 U.S. 416 (1983); and Thornburgh v. Am. Coll., 476 U.S. 747 (1986). I agree with the views of Chief Justice Declan Walsh, at least as Justice C. Bradley Walker has reported them. *The Vicar of Christ* (New York: Macmillan, 1979), ch. 9.

13. Doe v. Commonwealth's Attorney, 425 U.S. 901 (1976), and Bowers v. Hardwick, 478 U.S. 186.

14. Olmstead v. United States, 277 U.S. 438 (1928). See Murphy, *Wiretapping on Trial* (New York: Random House, 1965).

15. Olmstead v. United States, at 478. Brandeis's writing such a panegyric is hardly surprising. Thirty-eight years earlier, he and Samuel D. Warren had coauthored the most famous U.S. commentary on the right: "The Right to Privacy," 4 *Harv. L. Rev.* 193 (1890).

16. Katz v. United States, 389 U.S. 347 (1967).

17. 343 U.S. 451, 467, 469 (dis. op.).

18. 367 U.S. 497 (1961).

19. At 517 (dis. op.).

20. Ibid., at 518.

21. Ibid., at 520.

22. See Bernard Schwartz, *The Unpublished Opinions of the Warren Court* (New York: Oxford University Press, 1985), ch. 7.

23. Beaney had written: "Virtually all enumerated rights in the Constitution can be described as contributing to the right of privacy, if by the term is meant the integrity and freedom of the individual person and personality." "The Constitutional Right to Privacy," 1962 *Sup. Ct. Rev.* 212, 214.

24. Griswold v. Connecticut, at 484 (1965). In his concurring opinion, Goldberg also utilized the Ninth Amendment, not as a source of substantive rights, but as a means of interpreting such explicitly protected rights as "liberty." As one would expect, Hugo Black dissented vigorously against judicial use of a clause so open-ended as the Ninth Amendment.

25. 405 U.S. 438, 453 (italics in original).

26. Roe v. Wade, at 153. Immediately preceding this statement, the Court said:

The Constitution does not explicitly mention any right of privacy. In a line of decisions, however, going back perhaps as far as Union Pacific Railroad v. Botsford (1891), the Court has recognized that a right of personal privacy, or a guarantee of certain areas or zones of privacy, does exist under the Constitution. In varying contexts, the Court or individual Justices have, indeed, found at least the roots of that right in the First Amendment, in the Fourth and Fifth Amendments, in the penumbras of the Bill of Rights, or in the concept of liberty guaranteed by the first section of the Fourteenth Amendment (Ibid., at 152).

27. 424 U.S. 693.

28. Doe v. Commonwealth's Attorney.

29. Sec. 16–6–2 of the *Georgia Code* defines sodomy as engagement in "any sexual act involving the sex organs of one person and the mouth or anus of another. . . ."

30. Walter F. Murphy, *What Is the Constitution?* in T. Bonazzi, ed., *La Constituzione Statunitense e il Significato Odierno* (Bologna: Il Mulino, 1990); and "The Nature of the American Constitution," the James Lecturer, Dept. of Political Science, University of Illinois, 1989.

31. Ronald Dworkin, *Taking Rights Seriously* (Cambridge, MA: Harvard University Press, 1977), ch. 5.

32. Article V specifies at least four different ways of amending the Constitution.

33. 16 Wall. 36, especially Swayne's dis. op. See my argument in "*Slaughter-House, Civil Rights*, and Limits on Constitutional Change," 32 *Am. J. of Jurispr.* 1 (1988).

34. See generally: Lester B. Orfield, *The Amending of the Federal Constitution* (Chicago: Callaghan, 1942); Edward S. Corwin, "The Constitutional Law of Constitutional Amendment," 26 *Notre Dame Lawyer* 185 (1951); C. Herman Pritchett, *Constitutional Law of the Federal System* (Englewood Cliffs, NJ: Prentice-Hall, 1984), ch. 2; John R. Vile, "Limitations on the Constitutional Amending Process," 2 *Con. Comm.* 373 (1985); Vile, "Judicial Review of the Amending Process: The Dellinger-Tribe Debate," 3 *J. of L. & Pols.* 21 (1986); and that debate: Walter Dellinger, "The Legitimacy of Constitutional Change," 97 *Harv. L. Rev.* 386 (1983); Laurence H. Tribe, "A Constitution We Are Amending," 97 ibid. 433; and Dellinger, "A Rejoinder," 97 ibid. 446. See also some of the more important judicial decisions: National Prohibition Cases, 253 U.S. 350 (1920), and Leser v. Garnett, 258 U.S. 130 (1922), both sustaining constitutional amendments against claims that their substance violated the basic constitutional compact, and Coleman v. Miller, 307 U.S. 433 (1939), holding that the question of when an amendment has been duly ratified is not justiciable.

35. With as much merciful concern for the reader as prudential concern for my own ego, I shall not discuss in this chapter the very real problem of usage's and/or interpretation's slowly but effectively eroding a constitution's fundamental principles.

36. Wendell Wilkie made such an argument before the U.S. Supreme Court in Schneiderman v. United States, 320 U.S. 118 (1943), but the justices dodged the issue. See Sanford v. Levinson, *Constitutional Faith* (Princeton, NJ: Princeton University Press, 1988), p. 138.

37. One should distinguish between a state that has a "real" constitution and a state that has a real constitution that incorporates constitutionalism. See below for comments about this political theory. For a fuller discussion, see especially John E. Finn, "Can the Constitution Govern?" unpublished Ph.D. diss., Princeton University, 1986, ch. 1.

38. Barber, *On What the Constitution Means* (Baltimore, MD: Johns Hopkins University Press, 1984); Jacobsohn, *The Supreme Court and the Decline of Constitutional Aspiration* (Totowa, NJ: Rowman & Littlefield, 1986). For a different perspective, see Lief H. Carter, *Contemporary Constitutional Lawmaking* (New York: Pergamon Press, 1985), ch. 5, especially pp. 112ff.

39. For a discussion of the "paradox" in the U.S. Constitution's "constituting" a people, see ibid., ch. 3.

40. Supra note 38 p. 34.

41. "The Constitution of the United States: Contemporary Ratification," address at Georgetown University, October 12, 1985, p. 1.

42. John Hart Ely, *Democracy and Distrust* (Cambridge, MA: Harvard University Press, 1980) bolsters a claim to the Constitution's basically acting as no more than a charter for government with the fact that the document's terms are largely procedural. But distinctions between procedure and substance are easily exaggerated. See Laurence H. Tribe, *Constitutional Choices* (Cambridge, MA: Harvard University Press, 1985), ch. 2; and Harry V. Jaffa, "The Constitution: An Application of Natural Law," *The Center Mag.* (July/Aug. 1986): 41ff.

43. H.L.A. Hart, *The Concept of Law* (Oxford: Oxford University Press, 1961), especially ch. 6.

44. Quoted in Carl Lotus Becker, *The Declaration of Independence* (New York: Vintage, 1958), pp. 24–25 (first published 1922).

45. Ibid., p. 225.

46. Speech at Springfield, June 26, 1857; Roy P. Basler, ed., *The Collected Works of Abraham Lincoln*, vol. III (New Brunswick, NJ: Rutgers University Press, 1953), p. 406. For a convincing argument about the relationship between the Declaration and the larger constitution, see Dennis J. Mahoney, "The Declaration of Independence as a Constitutional Document," in Leonard W. Levy and Dennis J. Mahoney, eds., *The Framing and Ratification of the Constitution* (New York: Macmillan, 1987). For analyses of Lincoln's view of the constitutional status of the Declaration see: Harry V. Jaffa, *The Crisis of the House Divided* (Chicago: University of Chicago Press, 1982), ch. 14; and Gary Jacobsohn "Abraham Lincoln 'On This Question of Judicial Authority': The Theory of Constitutional Aspiration," 36 *West. Pol. Q.* 52 (1983).

47. I would also argue that, insofar as provisions of the constitutional document of 1787 legitimized slavery, those provisions were unconstitutional, which is not to say that as prudential matter any branch of the federal government should have so declared. Slavery was no doubt the price of union. Even before the Civil War, however, many people, including Salmon Portland Chase and John Quincy Adams, attacked the constitutionality of slavery. For the most systematic argument along these lines, see Lysander Spooner, *The Unconstitutionality of Slavery* (New York: Burt Franklin [no date]) (1st pub. 1860).

48. Becker, *The Declaration of Independence*, p. 225.

49. "The Constitution of the United States," see note 41, at 1.

50. G. K. Chesterton, *What I Saw in America* (New York: Dodd, Mead, 1923), p. 7. Compare Samuel P. Huntington: "the Declaration and the Constitution constitute the holy scripture of the American civil religion." *American Politics: The Promise of Disharmony* (Cambridge: The Belknap Press, 1981), p. 159.

51. See Jacobus tenBroek, *Equal Under Law* (London: Collier-Macmillan, 1951). Many of the proponents of the two amendments defended them precisely as fulfilling the Declaration's principles. That point supports but hardly proves my argument.

52. Michael Walzer, "Philosophy and Democracy," 9 *Pol. Th.* 379, 383 (1981).

53. Carl J. Friedrich, *Transcendent Justice* (Durham, NC: Duke University Press, 1964), pp. 16–17.

54. Thomas Jefferson, "Notes on Virginia," (1784); Andrew A. Lipscomb, ed., *The Writings of Thomas Jefferson*, vol. II (Washington, DC: The Thomas Jefferson Memorial Association, 1903), p. 163.

55. I do not argue, though I think it correct, that such theories in fact, if not consciously, informed the drafting and ratification of most parts of the document and its amendments. My argument is only that without such theories the resulting document is unintelligible. Thus, whatever the intentions of various generations of "founders," we need these theories to make sense of what the Constitution is and what it is supposed to do.

56. For a discussion of the philosophic as well as practical implications of the document's claim to be "supreme law," see Barber, *On What the Constitution Means*, especially ch. 3.

57. See, for example, the requirements of: equal representation of states in the Senate; each state's having at least one representative in the House; staggered elections; the Electoral College to choose a president and the House's doing so, with each state having one vote, in case the Electoral College does not produce a majority for one candidate.

58. See Walter F. Murphy, "Who Shall Interpret the Constitution?" 48 *Rev. of Pols.* 401 (1986); and Murphy, Fleming, and Harris, *American Constitutional Interpretation*, chs. 6–7.

59. James McHenry's "Notes," Max Farrand, ed., *The Records of the Federal Convention of 1787*, vol. II (New Haven, CT: Yale University Press, 1966) (Reissue of 1987, James T. Hutson, ed.), pp. 209–10 (italics in original). McHenry added: "Mr. Maddison [sic] supported similar sentiments." Morris's objections came straight from Blackstone. See Forrest McDonald, *Novus Ordo Seclorum* (Lawrence: University of Kansas Press, 1985), pp. 26n and 239.

60. See espec. Brown v. Board, 347 U.S. 483 (1954).

61. NAACP v. Alabama, 357 U.S. 449, 460 (1958).

62. Ibid., at 462 (italics added).

63. Compare Talley v. California, 362 U.S. 60 (1960), striking down an ordinance requiring political handbills to give the names and addresses of the persons who prepared, distributed, or sponsored them. Buckley v. Valeo, 424 U.S. 1 (1976), upheld a requirement that contributors to political campaigns identify themselves; but the Court added it would look into any specific case where it seemed that publicizing a list of contributors might inhibit political activity. The justices fulfilled this promise in Brown v. Socialist Workers Party, 459 U.S. 87 (1982), where they invalidated, as applied to a left-wing party that advocated abolition of capitalism, an Ohio statute requiring political parties to disclose the names of their contributors and also those to whom the party distributed funds:

The First Amendment prohibits a State from compelling disclosures by a minor party that will subject those persons identified to the reasonable probability of threats, harassments, or reprisals. Such disclosures would infringe the First Amendment rights of the party and its members and supporters. In light of the substantial evidence of past and present hostility from private persons and Government officials against the SWP, Ohio's campaign disclosure requirements cannot be constitutionally applied to the Ohio SWP. (101–02)

64. William F. Harris, II, "Reconstitutive Words," paper delivered at the Annual Meeting of the APSA (1983).

65. The Southwest Case, 1 BVerfGE 14 (1951); reprinted in W. F. Murphy and J. Tanenhaus, *Comparative Constitutional Law* (New York: St. Martin's, 1977), pp. 208ff. For a general examination of the concept of a hierarchy of values in constitutional interpretation see Walter F. Murphy, "An Ordering of Constitutional Values," 53 *So. Cal. L. Rev.*, 703 (1980).

66. The Preamble and Article 146 of the Basic Law of West Germany look toward reunification and so provide for the Basic Law's extinction.

67. As I read him, Michael Walzer, "Philosophy and Democracy," answers "no" where democratic theory is concerned, but there are serious problems in such a claim.

68. The issue of consent raises a problem that has run below the surface of this and most other work on constitutional theory, whether standards for moral judgment—and constitutional theory is, at bottom, a concern for moral theory—are "relative/conventualist" or "objective/realistic." Does the fact that the people can consent to whatever they wish mean that their choice becomes the standard for judging either the rightness or wrongness of subsequent decisions? Democratic theory tends to answer "yes." Constitutionalism cannot give an unmodified affirmative response, but, as a child of liberalism, it has severe difficulties with the relationship of consent to political right and wrong.

As I shall try to explain and defend at another time, I do not believe that moral standards can, in the final analysis, be relative. Thus between positivism and natural law, I readily choose the latter. The issues here, however, are complex; and I prefer to discuss them when I can do so at length.

69. See Articles, Art. XIII: "The Articles of this confederation shall be inviolably observed by every state, and the union shall be perpetual; nor shall any alteration at any time hereafter be made in any of them; unless such alteration be agreed to in a congress of the United States, and be afterwards confirmed by the legislatures of every state." Congress's call for a convention, Farrand, *The Records*, vol. III, pp. 13–14, bypassed the state legislatures, as did the process of ratification. Moreover, the new constitution provided it would come into effect when nine states ratified, thus potentially denying as many as four states their continuance in a "perpetual" union. Time and again the Anti-Federalists hammered at these points. See, generally, Herbert Storing, ed., *The Complete Anti-Federalist* (Chicago: University of Chicago Press, 1981).

70. Harris, "Reconstitutive Words."

71. See the reference to the problem of consent and legitimacy, above in note 68, a problem to which constitutional theory is not immune.

72. See Ralph Lerner, "The Supreme Court as Republican Schoolmaster," 1967 *Sup. Ct. Rev.* 127.

Comment

LIMITS TO CONSTITUTIONAL INTERPRETATION

Jacob W. Landynski

While the topic at hand is privacy, it is fortunate that neither chapter deals with the content of this newly discovered right, but rather with whether there is constitutional justification for it.

It is a measure of the contemporary revolution in constitutional law that as recently as 20 years ago, the term "interpretivism" was unknown in the legal literature. And privacy was not an independent constitutional variable but was rather a descriptive term for specific constitutional rights, principally the Fourth Amendment's freedoms against unreasonable searches.

Professor Mendelson's chapter is the kind we have come to expect of him: concise, lucid, pungent, and of course, irreverent. I find his argument an original and entirely convincing account, at least with regard to judicial interpretation of the Fourteenth Amendment serving as a substitute for the congressional veto on state legislation that Madison failed to get. I am in agreement with much else that he says. He demonstrates very well how the constitutional theories advocated by such as Holmes and Brandeis to limit judicial power have been rejected in favor of the very methods of interpretation which, under other names and in other times, were employed to staunch the flow of progressive measures.

While Wallace Mendelson is an interpretivist, a vigorous opponent of the use of judicial power to impose idealistic visions on the country in the form of binding constitutional law, Walter Murphy rises to the challenge of defending the noninterpretivist approach.

Now I know that this is not the way Professor Murphy has described his method. Perhaps it is more accurate to say that he would extend the boundaries of the Constitution beyond its formal text to include much not normally considered part of the basic document, and thus transform noninterpretive into interpretive rights.

Among other things, he would include the Declaration of Independence and the Preamble in the constitutional canon. And, as he has made plain, he takes seriously the idea of the Ninth Amendment as a source of constitutional rights.

I find his work richly textured and filled with analytical insights. But I don't think the theory is sturdy enough to sustain the burden he places on it. I shall deal with specifics rather than with the theory as a whole. Let us begin with the Declaration of Independence. Is it part of the constitutional canon? Should it be?

I thought I had heard the Declaration used before in the way that Professor Murphy would use it, but couldn't recall where. Professor Mendelson's chapter jogged my memory. Of course, it was invoked as part of the U.S. Constitution by Justice Bradley in his Slaughter-House dissent[1]—the dissent which, together with Justice Field's in the same case, paved the way for a half-century of constitutional laissez-faire.

This is merely another way of saying that the verbal formulations of the Declaration allow one to arrive at numerous and contradictory results. And how much do we gain by inserting the Preamble into the constitutional canon? The most promising phrase in the Preamble would seem to be to "establish justice." It is not easy to reconcile this ideal with the claims of "the common defense," another one of the goals mentioned there. We all know that the trampling of civil liberties in U.S. history has never been as blatant as in time of war or emergency, real or imagined. In fact, however, the words to "establish justice" do not refer to a value at all, but rather to nothing more than the establishment of a system of courts, as provided for in Article Three of the Constitution.

That is not an original insight. Such was the interpretation placed on the phrase in the first important Supreme Court case, *Chisholm* v. *Georgia*[2], by the second most important framer, James Wilson, as well as the first chief justice, John Jay.

As for the Ninth Amendment, it is no more a source of individual rights than the Tenth of its own force is a source of state power. Each of these amendments was written for a similar reason—as a reassurance. In the case of the Ninth, it was to counteract the argument of Hamilton in *Federalist* No. 84, and of James Wilson in Pennsylvania, that inclusion of a Bill of Rights in the Constitution would be dangerous, because the list of rights must inevitably be a short one and might be construed as negating any rights not listed.

Even if, for the sake of argument, it is conceded that the Ninth was intended to be a reservoir of rights, I assume that this meant rights well-known and recognized at the time. There is simply no evidence that it was envisioned as an empty vessel to be filled in the distant future with whatever rights might be deemed necessary to comport with judicial conceptions of human dignity. No wonder the Supreme Court ignored its existence for one and three-quarter centuries, and has not to this day employed the amendment alone to invalidate a single piece of legislation. It was indeed invoked in *Griswold* v. *Connecticut*[3], but only tangentially, in conjunction with a host of other constitutional provisions.

As for Brandeis' eloquent dissertation on the "right to be let alone" in *Olmstead*[4], he clearly referred to constitutionally articulated rights. After all, Brandeis was the justice who had coined the term "super-legislature"[5] to describe the Court's substantive due process role. He even questioned whether the court was justified in incorporating First Amendment rights of speech and press into the Fourteenth, because they were substantive rather than procedural in character, though he deferred to precedent.[6] And Holmes used the term "penumbra"[7] in referring to the Fourth and Fifth Amendments purely as a rhetorical device in the *Olmstead* case. These amendments had been employed in tandem to offer protection against unreasonable searches ever since the *Boyd* case[8] in 1886. The Fourth was the source of the right and the Fifth was used to justify the exclusionary rule. Holmes merely introduced *penumbra* to describe a long-standing constitutional practice of uniting the Fourth and Fifth Amendments in defense of the right against unreasonable searches by precluding judicial consideration of evidence illegally obtained.

In addition, let us not confuse implied rights with penumbral rights. Take freedom of association[9], which is also discussed in Murphy's chapter. It might not be listed in the Constitution, but I think it is clearly implied in every single right of the First Amendment to the extent that it does not even need to be stated. In fact, it is a precondition for the enjoyment of those rights. Of what value, for instance, is freedom of speech if one may not associate with others for the purpose of propagating one's views? That is a very different thing from a penumbral right, as Justice Black indicated in his *Griswold* dissent.[10]

I also have difficulty with Murphy's jurisprudence of original ideals. Economic egalitarianism, for example, is not an original value in either the Constitution, the Bill of Rights, or the Fourteenth Amendment. On the contrary, anyone familiar with early American history and especially with the writings of the framers, knows very well that redistribution of wealth was one of the things most feared by them. They were, indeed, obsessed by this fear, Jefferson no less than Madison, and Madison no less than Hamilton. As for Jonathan Bingham, "the Madison of the first section of the Fourteenth Amendment,"[11] as Justice Black accurately described him, he epitomized social Darwinism in his economic views. Why not enshrine their economic ideals and declare the New Deal unconstitutional?[12]

In order to preserve original constitutional ideals, Professor Murphy would place strong limits on the power to amend the Constitution. A plain reading of the text of the Constitution does not seem to justify such limits, because only two restrictions on the power to amend were inserted: one concerned slavery, and the other equal representation of states in the Senate. The *Federalist*'s authoritative discussion on the subject of constitutional amendment contemplates no limitations beyond the two specified.[13]

Let us also consider Jefferson's views. He did not attend the convention, but he might as well have, because he was Madison's mentor and to all intents and purposes a powerful presence in Philadelphia. I had often wondered how Jefferson, a man of great intelligence, could have supported the states' rights position of strict interpretation contended for in such cases as *McCulloch* v. *Maryland*.[14]

Some years ago, when reading him carefully, I discovered why. Because, unlike John Marshall, he did not regard the Constitution as one that should serve through the ages but rather as a document for that generation alone. Jefferson advocated the calling of a new constitutional convention periodically, authorized not simply to tinker, but to restructure the entire Constitution, if deemed necessary.[15] I don't say that Jefferson's was the accepted view. (Madison, of course, disagreed in *Federalist* No. 49). But his was an influential voice at the time, and it never occurred to Jefferson that there were limits on the amending power in the Constitution.

In fact, given the restrictions Murphy has placed on the amending power, I suggest—and not irreverently—that in the light of the framers' economic ideals, so very different from ours, one would be justified in viewing the progressive income tax, authorized by the Sixteenth Amendment, as violating the restrictions on constitutional amendment which he wishes to impose on the polity.

NOTES

1. The Slaughter-House cases, 16 Wall. 36, 115–16 (1873) (dissent).
2. 2 Dall. 419 (1793).
3. 381 U.S. 479 (1965).
4. Olmstead v. United States, 277 U.S. 438, 478 (1928) (dissent).
5. Jay Burns Baking Co. v. Bryant, 264 U.S. 504, 534 (1924) (dissent).
6. Whitney v. California, 274 U.S. 357, 373 (1927) (dissent).
7. Olmstead v. United States, 277 U.S. 438, 469 (1928) (dissent).
8. Boyd v. United States, 116 U.S. 616 (1896).
9. NAACP v. Alabama, 357 U.S. 449 (1958).
10. Griswold v. Connecticut, 381 U.S. 479, 507 (1965) (dissent).
11. Adamson v. California, 332 U.S. 46, 74 (1947) (dissent).
12. Compare Richard A. Epstein, *Takings: Private Property and the Power of Eminent Domain* (Cambridge, MA: Harvard, 1985).
13. See *Federalist* Nos. 43 and 85.
14. 4 Wheat. 316 (1819).
15. See, for example, Merrill D. Peterson (ed.), *The Portable Jefferson* (New York: Penguin, 1980), pp. 559–60.

VIII REFORMING THE CONSTITUTIONAL SYSTEM

13 The Case for Reform

James L. Sundquist

I was on one of those radio call-in programs in Seattle, Washington, a while ago, talking about why I thought the U.S. Constitution needs to be revised, and the first caller asked, "Is this a nice, proper way to greet the Constitution on its 200th birthday—to rip it to pieces and try to replace it with something entirely different?" I quickly assured him that nothing that drastic ever would—or ever could—happen in America, and nobody was seriously proposing anything more than minor, incremental changes in our ancient document.

But the most serious and responsible criticism of the Constitution heard at any time in our two centuries of life under it is being voiced this year. A group called the Committee on the Constitutional System has just issued a series of recommendations—most of which surely fall into the minor and incremental category—and the coincidence that this is our bicentennial year with all kinds of national conferences and local meetings being organized, means that the proposals are bound to be widely discussed. I say coincidence because the group was formed six years ago without any particular awareness that the bicentennial was coming up and, on the basis of meeting twice a year, has simply taken that long to make up its collective mind.

What gave rise to this unprecedented organized movement for constitutional reform was a commencement address by Douglas Dillon, the former cabinet member and a Republican, and a journal article by Lloyd Cutler, the then White House counsel and a Democrat, both raising fundamental questions as to whether the structure of our government created in the eighteenth century embodying those unique inventions—separation of powers and checks and balances—was really suitable for the rest of the twentieth century, let alone the twenty-first. These gentlemen attracted some attention in the press, and Charles Hardin, a political scientist who had been raising that question for quite a few decades and acting as a one-man committee of correspondence among his academic colleagues, decided the time had come to call a meeting. The CCS was formed, and Cutler and Dillon became the bipartisan cochairmen—joined later by a current senator, Nancy Kassebaum, Republican of Kansas. Leadership of this caliber attracted a response from other elder statesmen—people who had labored to make our government work and concluded, on the basis of their experience, that there just had to be a better system somehow, or somewhere. And many, of course, looked enviously at Britain and Canada and the other parliamentary systems of the world—where governments were *not* divided into branches that were forever quarreling with one another and flying off in different directions. The common theme of those who formed the CCS, and those who have joined it, is the old complaint that the separation of powers and checks and balances have given us a government prone to excessive conflict, stalemate, deadlock, indecisiveness—a government that lacks the unity to adopt and carry out decisive policies.

Before the CCS, constitutional reform was mainly the province of academics. But now practical people are actively involved, and people with records as leaders, such as—and I'll have to do some more name-dropping to make my point—former senior chairmen of congressional committees like Senator Fulbright of Foreign Relations, Representative Bolling of House Rules, Reuss of the Joint Economic Committee and House Banking, and John Rhodes, former Republican leader of the House; a half-dozen former cabinet members beside Dillon, the most active of whom has been Robert McNamara of Defense; a score of sub-cabinet members and White House advisers, a former CIA director, a former comptroller general, some long-time Washington journalists, and assorted academics, including university presidents and deans—the best-known of whom is James MacGregor Burns.

You may be asking, how can a group like that be so naive as to think the U.S. Constitution *can* be changed—given the amendment process that requires something close to unanimity before anything can be done? The answer is, they're not, of course. But it is a measure of their earnestness that they think it would be irresponsible not to begin the long course of public discussion that has to precede action. And many of them have a foreboding that one more constitutional crisis—and we're in our latest one right now, as we talk here—and the whole system may collapse. Then there will be a public outcry for some kind of change—and it will be well that somebody has done his homework as to just what changes might be feasible and might work. So for now, it's an academic exercise, mostly. But then, this is an academic conference, so we can consider ourselves in order here at least.

Those who question the constitutional structure are asked, in effect, who do you think you are to reject, and overturn, the wisdom of the Founding Fathers? The best answer to that is that the founders themselves, almost as soon as they began to run their new government, rejected the basic principle of the model that they had written into the Constitution. They overturned their own wisdom.

Those of you who have read the proceedings of the 1787 convention, as recorded by Madison and others, and the *Federalist* papers, know that the framers' model was a government *without* political parties. Only the most rudimentary forms of today's parties then existed in the states, or anywhere else, but insofar as the framers referred to these grouping at all, they condemned them. They rarely termed them parties, but factions or cabals, and they were blamed for the "corruption" and "intrigue" that the delegates saw in the legislatures of the new states as well in legislative bodies elsewhere.

It was to prevent the control of the entire government by any one individual or group—and for group, read faction or cabal or party—that the separation of powers doctrine was embraced and the checks and balances devised. A House of Representatives might be seized by a transient popular majority but the Senate would be a stable body of distinguished elders with long overlapping terms who would rise above factionalism, and the president—with his veto—would be the very embodiment of the nonpartisan ideal. That is why the framers rejected popular election of the president, or even his election by the Congress, and conceived the electoral college as a nonpartisan apparatus—like the search committee a corporation or university or city council sets up to select a new chief executive—but made up of men who did not know one another, would not be in communication with one another, and hence—as Madison put it at the Convention—"there would be little opportunity for cabal, or corruption."

No more powerful diatribe against political parties has ever been penned than the *Federalist*, particularly Madison's No. 10. He speaks of the "violence of faction," of the instability, unsteadiness, confusion, oppression, and "schemes of injustice" that flow from "that dangerous vice," those "sinister combinations"—factions and factionalism.

But before George Washington's first term was up, what became the Federalist and Republican parties were taking form, and they developed so quickly that in his celebrated farewell address, Washington felt constrained to warn his countrymen "in the most solemn manner against the baneful effects of the spirit of party generally"—the "worst enemy" of democratic governments everywhere, leading to "riots and insurrections," "corruption," and all the rest. Ironically, each year a senator and representative arise in their respective chambers on Washington's Birthday to solemnly intone those words to their colleagues, who have all been elected on party tickets, have organized their respective chambers through party caucuses and party-line votes, and have entrusted the conduct of legislative business to party organizations and leaders.

By 1800, two national parties were in full-fledged operation, with candidates for president and vice-president. The electoral college had been converted from a search committee with the gravest of responsibilities to a rubber stamp, its members pledged to the parties' nominees. "The election of a President of the United States is no longer that process which the Constitution contemplated," one of the framers, Rufus King of New York, remarked in an 1816 Senate debate. Parties, James Madison acknowledged in his retirement years, are "a natural offspring of Freedom." By that time, of course, Madison had been elected and reelected president as a party nominee.

Why then are parties natural? Yet, they must be, because they have appeared in every democratic country of the world, without exception. They are natural because people who share a common background or philosophy or approach to government, or all of these, want control of government in order to enact their policies and their programs, and a political organization is the obvious, indeed unavoidable, means to that end. When the organization or party wins an election, it does what it promised—or tries to, anyway—and then takes responsibility, at the next election, for the results.

In other words, it does what, in the United States, the Constitution was explicitly designed to prevent. This violation of the spirit and philosophy of the document begins with the framers themselves—save only Washington, who was consistent to the end—and it has continued ever since. No party ever said, "We only want the presidency," or the Senate, or the House. They say, give us *total* responsibility. In the 1984 election, Ronald Reagan's Republicans said, give us control of the House and Senate, as well as the presidency, so we can enact our program. And so did Walter Mondale's Democrats.

In other words, our country's political leadership, of every party, for two centuries, has organized and utilized political parties not to support the constitutional system—but to overcome it. And the discipline of political science has been overwhelmingly in favor of their doing exactly that. In fact, the organized discipline went more or less officially on record to that effect in 1950, with the famous report of its Committee on Political Parties. Political science textbooks call parties the tie that binds, the glue that cements, the web or the bridge that unites the disparate organs of the government to make the constitutional structure work.

And there is every evidence that the people have accepted that idea too. Rarely, until 30 years ago, did they fail to elect each four years a president and Congress of the same party. In the nineteenth century, that was largely an artifact of the election process—parties printed the ballots and the voter selected the ballot of his choice, which was a party slate. But even after the secret ballot was invented and ticket splitting was made not only possible but easy, the overwhelming majority of voters continued to vote a party ticket, and one party or the other, at each presidential election, was given control of both elective branches of the government. In this century, the Republicans had complete control in the 1900s and 1920s, and the Democrats, with one two-year hiatus, from 1933 to 1953.

In 1956, however, the country passed through a momentous transition—the historic importance of which has simply not been understood in America—a transition from a system of single-party government nearly all the time to one of divided government most of the time. In that year, for the first time in more than seven decades, the people denied to a newly elected president a Congress controlled by his own party, and they repeated that decision in four of the next seven presidential elections. As in 1956, in 1968, 1972, 1980, and 1984, they placed Republican presidents in the White House but sent Democratic majorities to the House of Representatives, and in the first three of those elections to the Senate as well. Neither party was given full responsibility, with corresponding accountability.

Does this mean, then, that the people, beginning at mid-century, came to reject the concept of responsible party government that, until then, they appeared to have accepted? By no means.

I won't go through the mathematics here, but it is demonstrable by both polls and election returns that most people still vote straight tickets for president, Senate, and House. It is the minority—never more than 20 percent and in most elections, many fewer than that—whose ticket splitting between a Republican for president and a Democrat, or maybe two, for Congress gives us our divided governments. A very small minority is getting what it wants, and denying responsible party government to the country.

The constitutional reformers, in the CCS and elsewhere, are those who accept the views of the framers after those gentlemen had changed their minds—that is, their views after they had entered the government and tried to make it work, rather than when they designed it—the belief that political parties are natural and necessary, both as the glue that holds the government together and gives it the unity to act, and as the means by which the people can hold someone accountable through the electoral process. So there is much talk, in the reform literature, of the need to strengthen our notoriously weak political parties.

But the prior problem, and an overriding one, is this new phenomenon of divided government. By definition, if two parties split the control of government, neither is responsible, and nobody can be held accountable—for each can point the finger at the other when things go wrong.

In most countries, coalition governments that try to combine the major right-wing and left-wing parties are adopted rarely, either accidentally, as in Israel today, or in response to the deepest crisis, for it is the business of the major parties to discredit and defeat each other, and they can lay aside their normal partisanship only under extraordinary circumstances and for short periods. Yet in the United States, such governments are now routine. And they have been marked, as one would expect, by confusion and conflict in foreign policy and ineffectiveness in grappling with domestic problems—of which our inability to come to grips with our horrendous budget deficits is the outstanding current illustration.

But when we ask, how could we change our Constitution, or our political practices, to make divided government less likely, we have to come to the frustrating conclusion that, as a practical matter, nothing of significance can be done.

Two approaches are possible. Since divided government is the result of ticket splitting, the simplest remedy would be simply to prohibit it— go back, in effect, to the nineteenth century when the ballots were designed in such a way that people were compelled to vote the straight ticket of one or another party, and divided government was therefore a rarity. Voters could be required to choose between party slates, or "team tickets," consisting of a party's candidates for national office (presidency, vice-presidency, Senate, and House). That would virtually assure the president's party control of the House, and usually of the Senate also. A second approach would be to award the party that won the presidency enough bonus seats in the Congress to assure a majority of both houses.

These two proposals however, illustrate the practical problems that constitutional reformers face. Because the amendment process requires extraordinary majorities—two-thirds of the House and Senate and three-fourths of the states, it demands, in effect, bipartisan agreement. Therefore, both parties would have to see benefit in the change. But since redistribution of power always creates both winners and losers, one party is bound to lose. In the current case, it would be the Democrats, for either of the reforms—had it been in effect—would have given the Republicans control of the Congress during much or all of the time that they have held the presidency. You can argue that that would have benefited the Democrats over the long run, because if the Republicans had had to take responsibility for everything that happened during their presidencies, instead of having a Democratic Congress to blame, they would have been discredited and turned out of the White House more often. But politicians do not take that long a view. The Democrats in the Congress would never take a second look at any scheme that would convert their majorities into minorities every time their candidate for president was beaten.

So the CCS has defined what it considers one of the grave weaknesses in the U.S. constitutional system, without being able to offer an effective remedy. We simply have to hope that the continuing political realignment will somehow translate Republican strength at the presidential level into *party* strength—so that when people vote Republican for president they will support the party's candidates for Congress as well. Unfortunately, the signs do not appear even to point clearly in that direction. If recent and current trends are all interpreted as favorably as possible from the Republican standpoint, it will still be well into the twenty-first century before the Republicans can conceivably gain control of the House of Representatives—barring, of course, some catastrophic national misfortune that could unmistakably be blamed on the Democrats as a party.

But, given the cyclical nature of politics, a Democrat will one day reside in the White House—if not after 1988, surely in the 1990s. We will then again have one-party control of both the presidency and the Congress, and the unity and effectiveness of the government will depend—as they always have—on the strength and cohesion of the governing party, as the glue, the tie, the web, the bridge. And here the outlook is, for once, favorable. One reason is the much greater internal homogeneity today of each of the two major parties. The second is the series of historic reforms of Congress enacted since the 1960s.

The growing homogeneity is the consequence of the party realignment that began in the 1930s and has been working its way, gradually but inexorably, through the political system. Simply put, the minority wings that were once strong enough to disrupt the internal unity of the two parties have been dying out. First to fade were the liberal Republicans— the G.O.P. wing that goes back to Theodore Roosevelt and Bob La Follette and has been led in recent years by such men as Governors Nelson Rockefeller and George Romney, and Senator Jacob Javits—who as recently as 20 years ago were powerful enough to seriously contest for the presidential nomination but are now an ineffectual remnant, as John Anderson's 1980 campaign so sadly revealed. Their counterparts, the conservative Democrats, have been vanishing as well, although more slowly. Since the New Deal era, their wing of the party has been virtually confined to the South, and now its base there is being steadily eroded as conservatives find their natural political home in the burgeoning Republican party.

So the Republicans have become a solidly right-of-center party—very much in Ronald Reagan's image—and the Democrats, a liberal-to-moderate party that is not quite of one mind but far more cohesive ideologically than it was 30, or 20, or even 10 years ago.

Meanwhile, the historic congressional reforms have brought the dissenters among the Democratic majorities under a remarkable—by past standards—degree of party discipline.

Any article on strengthening political parties written before the 1960s would have opened and closed with a call for destruction of the seniority system in the Congress, and that has now been accomplished on the Democratic side. As long as seniority was automatically honored, any Democrat, no matter how out of step with the majority of the party in the Congress, could acquire all the plenary power of a committee chairmanship through mere longevity. Through that device, some of the Senate and House committees most crucial to the enactment of the Democratic party's program were turned over to the conservative Democrats who voted regularly not with their own party but with the Republicans. Supporters of the party program outside the Congress found the seniority system intolerable, and those inside grew increasingly restive. Finally, the revolution occurred. Liberals in the House organized, and forced through the party caucus a series of rules changes that not only scrapped seniority but reduced the arbitrary power of committee chairmen. The revolt was solidified in 1975 when three chairmen were deposed by the caucus, and that body has continued to exercise its disciplinary power. This year, it voted to remove Les Aspin of Wisconsin from the chairmanship of the House Armed Services committee and reversed itself only after Aspin humbly promised to accept the guidance of the caucus on major questions of military policy.

That event illuminated another major change in the House: the caucus has been revitalized as a means of building policy consensus. For 40 years, until the 1970s, the caucus had been moribund, meeting only at the outset of each congress to nominate the party's candidates for speaker and other House offices. But the liberals won a demand for regular monthly party caucuses, with provision for additional meetings whenever 50 members petitioned for them. The caucus did prove to be an effective consensus-building mechanism, particularly in the long and acrimonious debate over the Vietnam War. Since then, the caucus has expressed itself on a wide range of measures, including the issues of defense policy that led to Les Aspin's pledge of conformity.

The arbitrary power of committee chairmen has been effectively curtailed in the Senate as well. Within the committee structures in both houses, democratic norms prevail.

Finally, the new Democratic party rule that guarantees seats in the quadrennial presidential nominating convention to 80 percent of the party's members of Congress may prove to be an important move in the direction of greater party cohesion. While most of the members will no doubt be guided by the sentiment of their states' voters, as expressed in primaries and caucuses, and while they are unlikely to vote as a bloc in any case, their influence will be enhanced. In a close convention contest, a determined network of House and Senate leaders could conceivably be decisive in selection of a nominee who would be experienced in dealing with the Congress, as opposed to an outsider like Jimmy

Carter—whose misfortunes in his relationships with the legislators and the rest of the party establishment gave rise to the rules revision.

So advocates of responsible party government may yet to expect to see, whenever the next Democratic president is elected, a close approximation to their model. Given reasonable luck in the nominating process, today's more homogeneous Democratic party should be able to attain a degree of cohesion under presidential leadership that observers of the party system have not seen—except for the honeymoon years of Lyndon Johnson—in half a century.

The most important reform that the Committee on the Constitutional System was able to agree upon—and the reason they could agree on this one is that it has some degree of feasibility—is lengthening of the terms of members of the House and Senate. The Committee proposes a four-year term for House members and eight-year terms for senators, with the entire House and half the Senate chosen in each presidential election. The midterm election, such as the one held last November, would disappear.

This, of course, has no direct bearing on the central problem I have been talking about, but is being recommended to resolve another problem—which is, that our midterm congressional election simply comes too soon. No other major democracy in the world gives its elected legislature only a two-year life. The result, for us, is that House members are constantly campaigning, unless they happen to come from absolutely safe seats, and at any given time one-third of the senators—except the few who have announced their retirement—are also running frantically for reelection.

The current House was elected last November, sworn in in January, and by February its members were already making the rounds of the political action committees (PACs) starting to raise money for next year's campaign—and making the inevitable promises that the PACs demand in return for their cash. Members who expect tough challenges are dashing home almost every weekend, and next year it will be *every* weekend. The senators up for reelection in 1988 have been heavily engaged in money raising for a year or two already. Senators, with their six-year terms, have a saying that in the first two years you can be a statesman, in the second two you're a politician, and in the last two you're a demagogue. By that token, House members are demagogues all of the time.

Defenders of the two-year term say that short tenure keeps the representatives close to the people, and that is a fundamental principle of democracy. It is, of course, but how close is close enough? Last fall, the representatives went through an intensive period of closeness, listening to constituents constantly for two solid months, expounding their views, and asking for a mandate. Should not the winners, who received their mandate, have a breathing spell to do what they promised to do before they must again be back in the intimacy with their constituents of the campaign period? It is not as though they are ever completely out of touch—not with the telephone, and the daily mail, and the media, and the public opinion polls. But if they had more time before they had to face the voters, House members would have a chance, like senators, to be statesmen for a while, and do the difficult, unpopular things that sometimes have to be done—such as, in our current situation, to raise taxes, which a majority of the members of both the House and the Senate will admit privately is absolutely necessary to reduce the dreadful budgetary deficit.

A four-year term, with all the members elected in the presidential year, would eliminate the midterm election for the House. To eliminate it for the Senate as well would require either lengthening the term of senators to eight years or reducing it to four. As between those two, what would be more acceptable to senators seems clear enough. The immediate reaction of most U.S. citizens is that eight years is far too long for any elective office, and it is likely that any amendment seriously considered would be limited to the four-year House term. That would, of course, negate the fundamental purpose, as I see it, because there would still be a midterm election to distract the Senate, and the president and his whole administration, if not the House. Moreover, substituting an eight-year term for one of six years would affect the composition of the Senate hardly at all. Very few senators are retired by the voters after only one term, and to give those few an extra two years would make no appreciable difference in the character of that body.

Lengthened terms would give members that necessary breathing spell between elections. It would also lead—or should lead—to a somewhat more orderly legislative process. Now, every piece of legislation must be considered and enacted within the two-year span, or it dies and must be considered afresh from the beginning when the next Congress meets. This results each two years in a great traffic jam as the Congress rushes to adjournment. Good bills are lost altogether for want of time, and other measures are passed in an unseemly rush, with members not able to keep up with everything that is going on. A more leisurely four-year process would lead to some additional procrastination, no doubt—applying Parkinson's law—but it would surely also result in a better considered and better drafted legislative product.

The Committee also recommends a reduction in the two-thirds vote of the Senate that is now required for the approval of treaties. U.S. citizens of my post–World War I generation were brought up to believe that one of the great tragedies of history was the failure of the United States to join the organization that the world had created as its hope for preventing World War II—the League of Nations. That was a flagrant case of minority rule in our country. Our president, Woodrow Wilson, had taken the lead in designing the League; the country from every evidence—in those days before public opinion polls—was for it; and 58 percent of the Senate voted for it. But that was less than 66 2/3 percent, and so it lost.

A recalcitrant minority can still defeat any constructive international agreement that a large majority of the country may be ready and eager to accept. Right now, for instance, you can be sure that our arms control negotiators are looking over their shoulders and saying to each other, "It's no use agreeing to anything that Senator Jesse Helms will not accept." So the irreconcilable minority that has made up its mind in advance that almost any agreement short of unilateral disarmament by the Soviet Union is unacceptable is the unseen negotiator at the conference table. It sets the outer limits of what the majority can commit the country to. It is ironic that it only takes a simple majority of the Congress to declare war but a two-thirds majority is required in the Senate to make peace, or to take steps to avert war.

The Committee recommends that treaties be approved by an absolute majority of both houses, which has the additional advantage of admitting the House into the approval process.

Finally, the Committee has recommended for further discussion a proposal that would adapt to the U.S. system one of the central features of parliamentary government. That is a provision for special elections that could be invoked whenever—for whatever reason—the government has lost its ability to lead and govern. We are so heavily dependent on presidential leadership that one flinches in contemplating all the things that can happen to an individual human being. We do have a safeguard now, in the Twenty-fifth Amendment, when a president becomes physically disabled, as Woodrow Wilson was during the final 18 months of his term in office. Even that requires a kind of palace coup, with the Cabinet—consisting entirely of the president's own appointees—taking the initiative, and one wonders whether that would have happened even in Wilson's case. And there is also the impeachment process, if the president can be convicted of high crimes and misdemeanors. Impeachment has been carried all the way to a trial only once, when President Andrew Johnson was acquitted by a single vote back in 1868. And it was carried, in the case of Richard Nixon, to the point where it forced a president to resign for the first time in history. But if a president is neither physically incapacitated nor guilty of an indictable crime or some other abuse of power so gross that even his own party is compelled to repudiate him, there is no safeguard whatever in the U.S. system. A president can turn out to be weak, or stubborn, or erratic, or he can develop aberrations under the pressures of his office—have a mental or emotional, as distinct from a physical, breakdown—as has happened to top executives in many other organizations, public and private, and nothing can be done about it.

Or the government can be in a state of collapse even if a president is strong and healthy, if he finds himself in a state of hopeless deadlock with the Congress—which is always on the verge of happening, and has indeed happened at least two or three times, depending on one's definition, in these recent years of Republican presidents confronting Democratic congresses. In such cases, as in the cases of presidential failure, the United States is in bondage to the calendar. Everybody in office, all the parties to the deadlock, the president and the legislators alike, hang on to their offices as a kind of property right until that November date in the year divisible by four rolls around. We can be without an effective government in a time of crisis; we can be impotent to deal with a collapse of the economy (as we were during the administration of a narrow-visioned president in the early years of the Great Depression) or we could be losing a war, and there is no way to bring fresh leadership to the pinnacle of government, as Winston Churchill was brought in to supplant Neville Chamberlain after Narvik. If a Narvik happened to us, we would just go on losing.

There is a belief in the country that the midterm election—which we abolished a few minutes ago—is the U.S. solution to the problem of government failure. But that is clearly a myth, because the midterm election does not include the presidency. The people can send a message to the president, as they often do, by voting for the opposition candidates for House and Senate. But strengthening the opposition does not re-constitute the government or break a deadlock, quite the opposite. All it can do is intensify an existing deadlock, if one exists, or create one, if it doesn't.

Just how can a remedy for this endemic weakness be fitted into the U.S. system? The Committee makes no recommendation on this issue—beyond recommending that it be discussed—partly because of doubts that any so drastic a change is really necessary but partly because of the technical difficulty of designing the solution. My own reflection has led to the conclusion that a system for special elections to install fresh leadership is needed when the government has clearly and palpably failed; that it needs to be written in such a way that it will not be invoked casually, for reasons of petty, partisan advantage, and that the best means to that end is to require that all elected officeholders—every member of the House and Senate as well as the president—vacate their seats; that, with this proviso, the special election be called either by the president or a constitutional majority of either house, which would enable either side in a deadlocked government to take the initiative to put the case before the people to decide; and that, after the ordeal of a special election, the newly elected officeholders begin new complete terms—adjusted to the nearest January, so that we could return at the next election to the November date that the voters have been so long accustomed to.

All of these issues will be considered by a Senate subcommittee this Spring, and there is the possibility that a House committee or subcommittee will also hold hearings. All over the United States groups are holding meetings and conferences on the Constitution this year, and Chief Justice Rehnquist, whose voice is of great influence on this matter, has said that the bicentennial should be the occasion not merely to celebrate the Constitution but to consider its adequacy for the next century. But it is hard to visualize that any of these measures—save perhaps the four-year term for House members—will achieve the degree of consensus necessary to become part of the Constitution.

Action on the two central problems of our constitutional structure that I have been discussing—divided government, and the lack of a mechanism for reconstituting a failed government—will not occur until the country lives through a crisis in which the government collapses utterly, over a sustained period. It would be better, of course, to repair the structure before it does collapse. The necessity to experience governmental failure of crisis proportions, in order to prepare for it, is not a happy prospect. But today has enough pressing problems, without worrying about tomorrow's, is the way of politicians, and of people generally. That nothing happens short of crisis has been the case with all fundamental constitutional reform, in every country and throughout history.

14 Obstacles on the Road to Reform

Theodore J. Lowi

Four questions will govern this inquiry into constitutional reform:

1. Does history demonstrate a capacity to reform the Constitution in a timely and appropriate way?
2. Have social, economic, and political changes in our time rendered the Constitution inadequate and in need of reform?
3. If yes, what reforms are now timely and appropriate?
4. Do Americans understand the functions and limits of the Constitution well enough to make the appropriate changes and stop there?

CONSTITUTIONAL REFORM

What Does History Demonstrate?

The Constitution has been formally amended 26 times since 1789. Review of these amendments will not only answer the first question about reformability but will reveal some important insights about constitutionalism itself.

The first ten amendments were all ratified the same year, 1791. These amendments can be considered part of the completion of the original Constitution, because they were promised during the ratification debates themselves. Nevertheless, they can tell us a lot about the character of the Constitution as well as the appropriateness of the amending process.

As shown on Table 14.1, the purpose of the ten amendments, called the Bill of Rights, was basically structural: *To give each of the three branches clearer and more restricted boundaries.* The First Amendment, for example, clarified the jurisdiction of Congress. Although the powers of Congress under Article I, Sec. 8, would not have justified laws regulating reli-

Table 14.1
The Bill of Rights: Completing the Construction of the National Government

Amendment	Purpose
I	**Limits on Congress:** Congress is not to make any law establishing a religion or abridging speech, press, assembly, or petition freedoms.
II, III, IV	**Limits on Executive:** The executive branch is not to infringe on the right of people to keep arms (II), is not to arbitrarily take houses for a militia (III), and is not to engage in the search or seizure of evidence without a court warrant swearing to belief in the probable existence of a crime (IV).
V, VI, VII, VIII	**Limits on Courts:** The courts are not to hold trials for serious offenses without provision for a grand jury (V), a petit (trial) jury (VII), a speedy trial (VI), presentation of charges, confrontation of hostile witnesses (VI), immunity from testimony against oneself (VI), and immunity from trial more than once for the same offense (V). Neither bail nor punishment can be excessive (VIII), and no property can be taken without just compensation (V).
IX, X	**Limits on National Government:** All rights not enumerated are reserved to the states or the people.

gion, speech and the like, the First Amendment made this limitation explicit: "Congress shall make no law...." The Second, Third and Fourth Amendments did similar things to the executive branch. Specification of the limitations contained in these three amendments was considered important at that time because of the abuses of executive power Americans had endured under British rule.

The Fifth, Sixth, Seventh and Eighth Amendments contain some of the most important safeguards for individual citizens against the arbitrary exercise of government power. Nevertheless, this was to be accomplished by structural change, by defining the judicial branch more concretely and clearly than had been accomplished in Article III of the original document. Pursuing chronological order for the moment, two amendments were adopted during the dozen years following the Bill of Rights—the Eleventh in 1794 and Twelfth in 1803. Considering this the decade of state building, two amendments are by anybody's reckoning a relatively small amount of fine tuning during such a sensitive period in the life of any "new nation." And 62 years and a civil war were to pass before the next amendment. This may, to some, already be indicative of lack of timeliness in U.S. constitutional reform, but that question

Table 14.2
Expanding the Constitution to Expand the Electorate

	Amendment and Purpose	Year Proposed	Year Adopted
XV	Extended voting rights to all races	1869	1870
XIX	Extended voting rights to women	1919	1920
XXIII	Extended voting rights to residents of the District of Columbia	1960	1961
XXIV	Extended voting rights to all classes by abolition of poll taxes	1962	1964
XXVI	Extended voting rights to citizens aged 18 and over	1971	1971*

*The Twenty-sixth Amendment holds the record for speed of adoption. It was proposed on April 23, 1971, and adopted on July 5, 1971. The only other adoption time that comes close is the prohibition repealer (XXI), proposed February 20, 1933, and adopted December 5, 1933.

will have to be deferred until we have had a chance to explore the character and purpose of all the amendments—which will require categorization by subject matter out of chronological order.

Table 14.2 shows that five of the 16 amendments adopted since 1791 are directly concerned with expansion of the electorate. Occasional efforts to expand the electorate were made necessary by the fact that the founders were unable to establish in Philadelphia a national electorate with uniform voting qualifications. Stalemated on that issue, the delegates decided to evade it by providing in the final draft of Article I, Section 2, that eligibility vote in a national election would be the same as "The Qualification Requisite for Elector of the most numerous branch of the state Legislature." Article I, Section 4, added that Congress could alter state regulations as to the "Times, Places and Manner of holding elections for Senators and Representatives." But this meant that any *expansion* of the American electorate would almost certainly require a constitutional amendment. That does not mean that such amendments would pass simply because they were proposed; not does it mean that amendments to the Constitution would be restricted to the electoral arena. Nevertheless, five of the 16 were in this area.

Table 14.3 demonstrates that six more of the 16 amendments adopted since 1791 were also electoral in nature, although not concerned directly with voting rights and the expansion of the electorate. Rather, these six amendments are concerned with the elective offices themselves or with the relationship between elective offices and the electorate.

Table 14.4 shows that three of the 16 amendments adopted in 1791 sought to expand or to delimit the powers of the national state governments themselves. The Fourteenth Amendment is included as a fourth

Table 14.3
Amending the Constitution to Change the Relationship between Elected Officers and the Electorate

	Amendment and Purpose	Year Proposed	Year Adopted
XII	Separate ballot for vice-president in the Electoral College	1803	1804
XIV	(Part 1) Provided a national definition of citizenship*	1866	1868
XVII	Provided direct election of senators	1912	1913
XX	Eliminated "lame duck" session of Congress	1932	1933
XXII	Limited presidential term	1947	1951
XXV	Provided presidential succession in case of disability	1965	1967

*In defining citizenship, the Fourteenth Amendment actually provided the constitutional basis for expanding the electorate to include all races, women, and residents of the District of Columbia. Only the "eighteen-year-olds' amendment" should have been necessary, since it changed the definition of citizenship. The fact that additional amendments were required following the Fourteenth suggests that voting is not considered an inherent right of U.S. citizenship. Instead it is viewed as a privilege.

Table 14.4
Amending the Constitution to Expand or Limit the Power of Government

	Amendment and Purpose	Year Proposed	Year Adopted
XI	Limited jurisdiction of federal courts over suits involving the states	1794	1798
XIII	Eliminated slavery and eliminated the right of states to allow property in persons	1865*	1865
XIV	(Part 2) Applied due process of Bill of Rights to the states	1866	1868
XVI	Established national power to tax incomes	1909	1913

*The Thirteenth Amendment was proposed January 31, 1865, and adopted less than a year later, on December 18, 1865.

item on this table as well as in Table 14.3 because this amendment seeks not only to define citizenship but *seems* to define citizenship in such a way as to incorporate all the rights of the Bill of Rights, regardless of the state in which the citizen resides. This became a hotly disputed issue almost immediately after its adoption in 1868. More will be said about this below.

Two amendments, the Eighteenth and Twenty-first, are missing from these tables, and their absence points to the meaning of the rest. The Eighteenth Amendment is the only instance in which the country tried to *legislate* by constitutional amendment. In other words, this is the only amendment of all the 26 which was designed to deal directly with some substantive social problem and to determine either how it was to be treated or what the outcome was to be. Moreover, this was the only amendment ever to have been repealed—in 1933, by the Twenty-first Amendment. Two other amendments—the Thirteenth, which abolished slavery, and the Sixteenth, which established the power to levy an income tax—can be said to have had the effect of legislation. However, the purpose of the Thirteenth was to restrict the power of the states, by forever forbidding them from treating any human being as property. As for the Sixteenth, it is certainly true that income tax legislation followed immediately; nevertheless, the amendment concerns itself strictly with establishing the power of Congress to enact such legislation. Not only did the legislation come afterwards; if later on a majority in Congress had wanted to abolish the income tax, they could also have done this by legislation, rather than having to go through the arduous business of adopting another constitutional amendment repealing the power itself.

All of this points to the principle underlying the 24 existing amendments, as these are categorized in Tables 14.1–14.4: All of these amendments are concerned with the *structure or composition of the government*. If a constitution is, by definition, the "makeup or composition of a thing," our Constitution is a precise illustration thereof, because this has been the consistent criterion in the history of the amending process. Even those who would have preferred more changes in the Constitution would have to agree that there is great wisdom in this criterion. If the purpose of the Constitution is to establish a *framework within which* government and politics can take place, then the Constitution ought to enable legislation to take place rather than to set forth the legislation as part of the structure itself.

But if the criterion of concern for the framework is wise, have the particular amendments been appropriate? I personally think the answer to this is strongly affirmative, because all of the adjustments embodied in the 24 amendments have been oriented either toward the powers and limits of government itself or toward representation. For U.S. citizens this is precisely why there had to be structure and why it had to be embodied in a written document. The Constitution has meant a balancing of power and limitations to U.S. citizens, and this is accomplished by the three structural principles embodied in the amendments as categorized in Tables 14.1–14.4; by jurisdiction (clearer lines of authority between branches and between the nation and its states); by juxtaposition (checks and balances); and by representation (who votes and the relationship between the voters and those they elect).

The question of timeliness is a more difficult one because so much of the answer lies in the eyes of the beholder. A comparison of changes in the federal constitution to changes in the constitutions of the states would suggest that the answer to the question of timeliness at the federal level would be distinctly in the negative. Between 1789 and 1980, 9100 proposals were officially made to amend the U.S. Constitution. Of these, Congress officially adopted only 29, and 26 of these were eventually ratified by the states, with only 16 since 1791—two of which cancelled each other out. In contrast, the states, as of 1981, had actually approved, ratified, and added to their respective constitutions 4988 amendments (heaven only knows how many amendments were offered). This turns out to be an average of nearly one hundred constitutional amendments per state. And, as Sundquist puts it, "Given that the states were then, on the average, only 139 years old, that represents a frequency of constitutional change more than five times that of the national government.[1] Quite clearly, at the federal level, the old Calvinist doctrine seems to hold very well, "Many are called but few are chosen."

Some will respond to the argument that direct and official constitutional amendment did not have to be timely in any sense of statistical frequency because of the Supreme Court and its ability to adjust the Constitution through judicial review. However, despite its reputation, the Supreme Court engaged in surprisingly little judicial review during more than the first century after the founding. In the first place, Congress gave the Courts little of a constitutional nature to review, because Congress rarely took actions that even remotely put to the test a strict construction of the national powers, despite the invitation by Chief Justice Marshall to treat the "necessary and proper" clause of Article I, Section 8 as an "elastic clause."[2] As constitutional scholar Herman Pritchett put it,

It was not until the adoption of the Interstate Commerce Act in 1887 that the federal government really entered the domestic regulatory field. Consequently, during the first century of the nation's history the Commerce clause problems which the Supreme Court was asked to decide grew for the most part out of *state* regulation challenged as infringing the constitutionallity protected but largely unexercised power of Congress. . . . [3]

And even here, the Court was consistent in maintaining an original intent position that the national government and the states were to be fairly independent and distinct from one another. For example, in what is probably the most important of all the interstate commerce cases, Chief Justice Marshall argued that the states may not take any actions that infringed on the power of Congress to regulate commerce—even where Congress was not choosing to be active.[4] At the same time, the Supreme Court held in another case that the Bill of Rights does not extend as a set of protections of citizens against the bad or harmful actions of the state governments. In other words, the Bill of Rights was adopted strictly to protect citizens against the actions of the national government, thus confirming the most strict idea of federalism, that citizenship was in fact quite distinctly dual.[5]

But even after judicial review with constitutional implications became more frequent, it was nevertheless far more limited than was commonly assumed. It was largely confined to litigation arising out of the Fourteenth Amendment, which affected in fairly marginal, albeit poignant, ways the relationship between citizens and the powers of the state governments, and depended upon the question of how much of the Bill of Rights was "incorporated" by the Fourteenth Amendment—in other words, to what extent was *Barron* v. *Baltimore* actually reversed by the Fourteenth Amendment. There was in fact a great flurry of activity in the 1930s during which the Supreme Court attempted to hold back changes in the Constitution that seemed timely and appropriate to meet the urgencies of the Depression. But this flurry of judicial review with constitutional implications did not last very long, and the Supreme Court reversed its position by 1937. In 1936, Justice Brandeis articulated a set of standards to define and delimit the conditions under which the Court would actually confront constitutional questions at all. And, as one can see, these are deliberately designed to avoid wherever possible such a confrontation. Brandeis provided four such guidelines: (1) The Court will not take on a question of constitutional law in advance of the clear necessity of deciding it; and the Court will not decide questions of a constitutional nature unless they are unavoidable in reaching a decision. (2) The Court will not formulate a constitutional rule broader than is absolutely required by the facts to which it is to be applied in the specific case. (3) The Court will not pass upon a constitutional question, even when it has been presented directly to them in litigation, if there is also present some other ground upon which the case may be decided. (4) When the constitutionality of an act of Congress is put before the Court, "it is a cardinal principle" that the Court will give the statute a construction that renders it constitutional if it possibly can.[6]

When we confront the relative infrequency of constitutional change, and lacking an absolute standard of appropriateness or of timeliness, the only answer seems to be a rhetorical question, How often does a constitution *need* to be changed? If a constitution is to concern itself with structure and framework, it should be relatively resistant to change. Granted, a constitution must be capable of being changed; but it must also be immune to changes that merely meet the convenience or policy goals of a momentary majority. But rather than try to go further in answering these questions for the past, let us use the problem as presented here as a context for dealing with these questions of the present and the future: Have there been changes in U.S. society, economy, or politics in our time that have rendered the Constitution inadequate and therefore in need of reform to get us into the future?

IS THE CONSTITUTION ONCE AGAIN OUTDATED?

Constitutional historians point to 1937 as the beginning of the First Constitutional Revolution, implying that the Constitution was in fact adjusted sufficiently at that time to meet the exigencies of the Depression. How? Not by positive amendment or by a positive rendering by judicial review of a change that would be the functional equivalent of an amendment, but by virtually the reverse: The Supreme Court all but tendered its resignation. Beginning with the great NLRB case of 1937, the Supreme Court said in effect that it would no longer bother to review acts of Congress that extended the power of the national government and increased the power and the discretion of the president to implement these large programs.[7] Now the question arises as to whether conditions in U.S. society during the past 50 years have rendered the 1937 Constitution obsolete.

Of the many changes one can identify in the past 50 years, I have chosen three that seem to me to be of greatest salience to the problem at hand. This is far from an exhaustive listing, but it will suffice for the purposes at hand. They will be identified here and taken up each in its turn:

1. The nationalization of economic and civic values;

2. The rise of the democratically elected chief executive;

3. The transformation of the theory of representation.

The Nationalization of Values

The national government's intervention into the economy that became sustained and systematic only after the 1930s had the unintended effect of nationalizing the focus and the attention of U.S. citizens. Until that time, most of the fundamental governing in the United States was done by the states, as intended by the Constitution. All the property laws, all the family, morality and sexual behavior laws, all the laws concerning education and the professions, all the laws concerning crime (except in the federal territories)—in sum, nearly all the laws in virtually all of the areas of fundamental importance to U.S. citizens were made by the state legislatures and implemented by state executive agencies and the state courts. This fundamental fact about federalism actually parochialized U.S. civic values. U.S. citizens were always active in politics; this was something Alexis de Tocqueville recognized as extremely significant about U.S. democracy as early as the 1830s. However, it would have been a waste of time for U.S. citizens to concern themselves very much about the national government. When there were important political issues to debate and to struggle over, the place to go was the state legislature or, in some instances, city hall; but certainly not Washington, DC. The expansion of the national government eventually penetrated into the localities, and this gave U.S. citizens, *for the first time in our history*, a common political experience no matter what part of the country they lived in.

One can argue that this was fed by, perhaps even created by, World War II, except that we had had wars before in which virtually the total population was mobilized. The post–World War II period was different because this time we could not so fully demobilize back into our prewar parochialism. To the national economic focus coming out of the 1930s was added still other nationalizations. Two of the most important, of course, were the civil rights revolution and the welfare revolution. In other words, U.S. blacks were not going to be willing to return to the *status quo* ante. And as the social security system of the 1930s became the welfare system of the 1950s, where representatives of national programs were actually involved in decisions regarding the eligibility of dependent persons for federal assistance (decisions that were always considered the domain of local welfare agencies and churches), there was not going to be any return to the autonomous authority of local leaders.

Thus, it would be a profound misrepresentation of history to suggest that the nationalization of American values was caused by the emergence of the "mass media." In the first place, there were "mass media" before the electronic media of radio and television came along. Second, as suggested here, the focus and attention of all U.S. citizens were being pushed and pulled toward a common national viewpoint well before radio and television became the ubiquitous force we recognize today. It is certainly true that the electronic media have fed and reinforced the nationalization of civic values. But the nationalization of U.S. government and its programs was going to accomplish that nationalization of values with or without the help of the media. If one example can demonstrate the sequence of events, it would be the history of the Washington bureau of the *New York Times*. When Arthur Krock was assigned by the *New York Times* in 1932 to go to Washington to reorganize the Washington bureau, Krock did so only with reluctance, preferring to remain in New York. When he turned his job over to James Reston in 1953, his twenty-four–man bureau was the elite corps not only of the *New York Times* but of U.S. journalism. Like the national government itself, the Washington bureau of the *New York Times* emerged out of World War II as a much larger and much more important institution, and, like the national government, it did not demobilize in the postwar period.

The nationalization of civic values would quickly implicate the Constitution, producing what has been called the Second Constitutional Revolution beginning in the late 1950s. This revolution concentrated largely on the Fourteenth Amendment and the expansion of those parts of the Bill of Rights that the Fourteenth Amendment incorporated as safeguards against state action. Table 14.5 is a liberal translation of this revolution from Henry Abraham's masterful *Freedom and the Courts*. Note well on Table 14.5 that, except for the First Amendment, the process of expanding the Fourteenth Amendment to incorporate the Bill of Rights really didn't begin until 1961, although the trigger for it was probably *Brown* v. *Board* in 1954.[8] However, the nationalization of civic values that produced the Second Constitutional Revolution was much broader than that. The demands of nationalized civic values created whole new problems of governing, and the pressure was intense on the national government to reach areas of local conduct hitherto untouched by national government, and in some instances untouched by any government at all. The nationalization of civic values went beyond the Supreme Court's efforts to remove constitutional barriers from the national government and to place certain constitutional barriers on the state governments. The nationalization of values has begun to exert constant pressure on the national government to *become a positive state*. That is to say, such are the pressures that come from national expectations that the national government can no longer wait for things to happen to react to them; it must constantly take initiatives to prevent bad things, to reduce risks, and to create an environment whereby groups of citizens can exert virtual rights to certain kinds of government services and certain kinds of out-

Table 14.5
Incorporation of the Bill of Rights into the Fourteenth Amendment

Not "Incorporated" Until	A Selection of (Provisions and Amendments)	Key Case
1925	Freedom of speech (I)	Gitlow v. New York
1931	Freedom of press (I)	Near v. Minnesota
1939	Freedom of assembly (I)	Hague v. CIO
1961	Freedom from warrantless search and seizure (IV) ("exclusionary rule")	Mapp v. Ohio
1963	Right to counsel in any criminal trial (VI)	Gideon v. Wainwright
1964	Right against self-incrimination and forced confessions (V)	Malloy v. Hogan Escobedo v. Illinois
1966	Right to counsel and to remain silent (VI)	Miranda v. Arizona
1969	Right against double jeopardy (V)	Benton v. Maryland
1973	"Right of privacy" (III, IV and V)	Roe v. Wade Doe v. Bolton

comes from government programs. This is a type of pressure for which an eighteenth century constitution would certainly be found ill equipped.

The Plebiscitary Presidency

Growth of the national government and the positive state was accomplished largely through the mechanism of delegation of the powers of policymaking from Congress to the executive branch, culminating in the chief executive. Each delegation of power from Congress to the president was a delegation of responsibility. And as the civic values of U.S. citizens were nationalizing, they came into focus not merely on the national government in Washington but directly, self-consciously and concentratedly on the president. One can almost state as a modern variant of the Malthusian principle that as presidential powers went up at an arithmetic rate, expectations as to the use of those powers went up at a geometric rate.

As these expectations intensified and concentrated themselves more and more directly upon the presidency, it was no longer possible for presidents to rely exclusively on their political party as their popular base. And it was no longer possible for presidents to share their powers and their celebrity with appointed associates. Even before the end of the domestic New Deal in the 1930s, President Roosevelt was already beginning to abandon his political party and to appeal directly to the masses for support. Roosevelt tried in 1938 in vain to remake the Democratic party as a programmatic, basically social democratic party. His failure to purge the party of the conservative opposition within it led him increasingly to the use of mass politics techniques, including his ingenious use of the available electronic medium, radio.

By the end of the Eisenhower administration, the national political parties had lost their grip on the presidential nominating process; and when political parties lose their grip on nominations, they lose their grip on their share of governing. By the end of the nineteenth century, it was quite clear that there was a new popular base of presidential power, the mass base. In other words, at the national level party democracy had been displaced in large part by mass democracy.[9] This shift toward mass democracy is as important for twentieth century U.S. government as the rise of party democracy was for nineteenth century government. We can call this a constitutional change in itself, or we can call it a gigantic political change with constitutional implications.

Transformation of the Theory of Representation

The original American theory of representation was articulated best by James Madison, beginning with the following passage:

... Take in a greater variety of parties and interests [and] you make it less probable that a majority of the whole will have a common motive to invade the rights of other citizens ... [Hence the advantage] enjoyed by a large over a small republic.[10]

According to this view, a good constitution encourages multitudes of interests so that no single interest can ever tyrannize over the others. The basic assumption, so well expressed by Madison, is that competition among interests will produce balance, with all the interests regulating each other. Consent is the result, but it is no mere summation of all the individual interests in society. Instead, it is something people grant independently of their specific interests as a means of maintaining the right to pursue them. *Group interests* are contrary to the *public interest*. Thus, according to Madison, "Regulation of these various interfering interests forms the principal task of modern legislation."[11]

It was on this basis that Madison and his colleagues preferred a republic to a democracy. To them, a republic was "a government in which a scheme of representation takes place," and they believed that it would help control the effects of interests ("the mischiefs of faction") without suppressing any of them. Interests would have to go through a representative assembly and be publicized as well as balanced against all other interest. Competition would give representatives an opportunity to make decisions independent of all interests. This arrangement would tend to produce a government "more consonant to the public good than if pronounced by the people themselves," but only because it would provide a good method of regulating interests.[12]

If the Madisonian theory of representation required that interests be regulated, the new theory emerging in recent decades holds that interests must be accommodated. According to the old theory, all interests were averse to the public interest. That is why they needed regulating. According to the new theory, no interest is averse to the public interest unless it is involved in a violation of law. The new theory thus gives all legal interests approximately equal status. No moral ordering among them is possible. The only choice among them is to be made through a process by which interests with the best organization and resources win out over the others.

A system of representation with consent based on accommodation of interests is a goal far more difficult to achieve than the same under the old theory. The new theory of consent requires detailed information about interests before policies are made. It also requires detailed information afterward to determine whether a sufficient number of claims have been accommodated.

Judging from their behavior, most politicians seem to accept the new theory. They spend an enormous amount of time and money trying to gain the opinions of individuals as well as the demands of organized interest groups. And political leaders in the United States prefer to operate on this theory of representation even when they can get what they want without it. Yet, the new theory, which amounts to "government by accommodation to all those who have an interest" requires political knowledge on a scale almost beyond belief. It also requires governmental satisfaction of demands on a scale beyond conceivable capacity. And the distance between what government can produce and what people expect is filled by deceit. In the 1960s and 1970s, people began to call this deceit the "credibility gap."[13]

It should be patently clear at this point that the three changes in society, economy and polity identified here are of such a degree and scale as to render the Constitution, by whatever interpretation, inadequate to the future and in need of some kind of reform. What kind of reform?

WHAT REFORMS ARE APPROPRIATE?

To agree, as I do, with Sundquist and other prominent reformers that the Constitution is in need of reform is only the bare beginning. Disagreements emerge almost immediately thereafter, because there are fundamental differences among us on what the problems are for which constitutional reforms are necessary. Since Sundquist speaks well for himself in his accompanying paper and in his other publications,[14] I will only review his positions very scantily, mainly in order to highlight my own. This is not the place to debate and to justify each point. Although there may be some points of diametric disagreement among us, for the most part the disagreements are more matters of priority.

As I understand Sundquist and his associates, the main problems for which constitutional reform is a solution are as follows. This will not be an exhaustive listing, but it will serve the purpose without doing an injustice to Sundquist, because they are not here to be criticized but only to help define my own. I take Sundquist's list of problems needing constitutional reform from the opening chapter of his book, first because these set the framework for virtually all of the chapters following that first chapter, and second, because "questions such as these" are the ones he most intensely shares with the important organization set up in 1983, the Committee on the Constitutional System, composed of very prominent Democrats and Republicans dedicated to reform along these lines.

1. Ineffective, unresponsible and nonaccountable government, resulting largely from split party control of the "three centers of decision making." ("Would an electoral system that encouraged unified party control of the three centers of decision making—Presidency, Senate, and House make for more effective, responsible and accountable government?")

2. Inability to confront and resolve crucial issues. ("Would longer terms for the president or for legislators . . . enable leaders to rise to a higher level of statesmanship in confronting crucial issues, permit the resolution of issues that now go unresolved . . . , and permit greater deliberation and care in the legislative process?")

3. Governmental immobility. ("Can a better solution be devised to deal with the immobility of government brought about by leadership failure, or deadlock and quarreling between the president and Congress . . . ?")

4. Lack of continuity between legislators and administrators. ("Can harmonious collaboration between executive and legislative branches be induced by formal interlocking of the branches or strengthening the political parties that are the web that binds administrators and legislators to the common purpose?")

5. Breakdown of the constitutional system of checks and balances. ("Should any of the constitutional checks and balances, by which the executive and legislative branches are enabled to thwart each other, be modified to permit one or the other branch to prevail more readily and thus facilitate decisions?")

6. Lack of integration and effectiveness in foreign policy. ("The country's foreign affairs . . . offer innumerable examples of ineffective policy, brought about by

the inability of leaders to harmonize all of the institutional elements that, under the Constitution, must act in concert before any decisive policy can be carried out.")[15]

For me, the problems needing constitutional attention occur *prior* to government decision and government action. Although I sympathize with the need for governmental decisiveness, a prior question must be asked about the purpose for which this decisiveness is to be used. There is no basis for a general assumption that an integrated, active, decisive, vigorous and effective government would want to do good things. Before that point can be reached, it seems to me that we need to confront the governmental institutions themselves and how they relate to their respective constituencies and to social forces at large. For my money, the national government is too closely, too intimately, too directly associated with masses and with groups. As the power of the national government increased drastically decade by decade after the 1930s, there was an insufficient development of intermediate institutions and buffers to keep these newly empowered governmental institutions from being too vulnerable to immediate demands. The so-called new theory of representation is in reality a rationalization for power relationships that are self-defeating and counterproductive; the government emerging out of the new theory of representation is under so much pressure to respond immediately to demands and to produce benefits, or to create the appearance of producing benefits, that the government is incapable of transcending specific demands and has no sound basis for balancing (i.e., regulating) interests. The resulting policy decisions are not only highly specific to the demands originally made but are in severe violation of the rule of law, however that might be defined.

It would misrepresent my analysis to say simply that we should go back to Madison. What we do need to do is to go forward following Madisonian guidelines. The two interrelated goals would be to restore republicanism and put groups and masses back in their proper place, within a structure where it would be extremely difficult for groups to make their claims on government directly and without need of balancing against other claims.

How is the Constitution to be reformed toward these goals? First and foremost, it is absolutely essential to parliamentarize the presidency. This does not require anything so drastic as a British type of parliamentary system. There is no need to abolish the separation of powers, but there is need to move somewhat in a parliamentary direction. The main point is to find some means of freeing the presidency from the mass constituency it has developed during the past 50 years and to make Congress the constituency of the presidency to the fullest extent possible. The mass popular base could remain, but it must be counterbalanced or buffered with the intermediate constituency of the representative institution. As an institution with a single elected chief, the executive branch can never be a representative institution but can only be a democratic institution in the simplest most rudimentary sense of the occasional plebiscite. In all other respects, the executive branch is not a representative institution but an institution that can be made vulnerable to varieties of interests. That is, to repeat, not representativeness but mere vulnerability.

The gains from parliamentarizing the presidency would be numerous and profound. In brief, we could gain most of the virtues of a parliamentary system without losing the virtues of the independently elected president. But rather than spell out the reasoning back of that proposition, on the assumption that most readers would be able to work that out for themselves, let me spend the remaining available space speculating on how this might be done by simple and practicable constitutional reform.

The ideal way to parliamentarize the presidency without destroying the virtues of its vigor and independence would be the establishment of a multiparty system. I agree wholeheartedly with the constitutional reformers and with many others who argue that we need to restore strong parties and party government. But I am not sympathetic with their faith in the two-party system. The two-party system is dying all over the world; its inappropriateness to modern, positive government explains why it has declined. But modern governments need parties just as much as older democratic governments did; the problem is finding a party system that is compatible with modern government. Since our present U.S. two-party system, what is left of it, is a mere artifact of all of the state laws biased in its favor, then we could have our multi-party system very quickly by adopting a constitutional amendment that removed from the states the power to pass laws that are deliberately biased against the emergence of new political parties. A multiparty system would immediately parliamentarize the presidency with no further amending activity. The problem of "divided government" that Sundquist and others lament would disappear almost immediately. Parliamentarization would be all the more certain to happen if the existing method of presidential election through the electoral college were left as is in the Constitution. Here is the reason why: Assume a third party large enough to elect a few electors in the presidential election. This would render almost certain in a close election that neither of the major candidates would receive an absolute majority in the electoral college. This means that the actual election would then take place in the House of Representatives, with each state getting one vote. Assume also that this third party is successful enough to elect a few members of Congress, just enough to be certain that this third party could determine the unit vote of at least one state of the House. If this occurred on a regular basis over an eight- or 12-year period, all presidential candidates would have to conduct their strategies as though the final election would take place in the House of Representatives. This would mean that the November election would be more like a nominating process, with the final election taking place in the House. It is in this sense that Congress could become the primary constituency of the presidency.[16]

Parliamentarization to a more modest degree could be obtained by more modest means. One way is to amend the Constitution to permit members of Congress to hold posts simultaneously in the president's cabinet. This would produce a great deal of continuity and collaboration between the two branches and would be all the more important if the present trend continues whereby the Democrats control Congress and the Republicans control the White House. But some parliamentarization could take place without any constitutional amendment at all by expanding on a principle proposed by Ronald Reagan when he was an unsuccessful candidate for the presidential nomination in 1976. Reagan announced that if he received the nomination for president he would choose Senator Schweiker of Pennsylvania as his vice-presidential running mate. Moreover, he proposed to the Republican convention a motion to adopt as a rule that all candidates for the nomination announce in advance their choice of vice-presidential nomination. Although this failed of adoption on a roll call vote (in fact it was the major test of strength between Reagan and Ford prior to the actual balloting for the nomination), it provides the basis for an important reform that should be studied with great care. My proposal is that each and every candidate for the presidential nomination announce well in advance the list of the eight or 12 or more persons who would be in that candidate's "cabinet" if elected president. (No harm would be done if the names of certain prominent persons appeared on the list of more than one candidate). This would be immensely helpful during the campaign, but most importantly, it would identify the persons who would be sharing the responsibilities of office with the president, and it would give the voters a much better sense of what that president's administration would be like. It is very sad and indicative that we refer to each presidency as "the administration" as though that were a collective reality, when in fact there is no collectivity at all. The most difficult and impractical part of this suggestion is not the putting together of such a list, but in fact brainwashing presidential candidates to get them to reduce their lust for the celebrity of the office and to be willing to share power in order to buffer themselves from the overwhelming and impossible responsibilities inherent in the presidential office.

Parliamentarization of some sort is also the proper direction of reform for what ails the conduct of U.S. foreign policy. Without getting into particular directions, right or left, we can agree with Sundquist et al. that the conduct of foreign policy ought to be integrated so that U.S. citizens can speak with a single voice. There is a dangerous confusion as long as the world's preeminent power must tolerate many agencies with traditional or legal rights to have their own foreign policy. Another danger we can agree on without getting into right or left is that there is too much pressure on the president to produce results. "What have you done for us lately" is a question a mass constituency asks in the foreign as well as the domestic arena. This sort of pressure goads presidents into the short circuiting of foreign policy institutions, leading each recent president into a debilitating scandal. The regularity of this outcome means that there has to be some institutional reason why the Tower Commission found that the foreign policymaking institutions are sound but that President Reagan did not use them. Mass expectations in foreign policy have made the president and diplomacy natural enemies. Any reform that can take this sort of pressure off the White House is to be desired on the right as well as the left. Parliamentarization would help here most of all.

For example, that was the point and purpose of "bipartisanship" in foreign policy. This method was adopted in fact during the very sensitive early cold war period when Congress and the president were under split party control. Bipartisanship was badly wounded by the duplicity of the Gulf of Tonkin resolution—which also wounded president/Congress cooperation in general. Bipartisanship and president/Congress cooperation in foreign policy were fairly well put to rest at Watergate.

Can parliamentarization in foreign policy be imposed by constitutional reform? Since the inherent and unavoidable power of the president in foreign affairs cannot really be abolished (but only hampered) by constitutional amendment, the only alternative is to alter the context in which those powers are used, so that presidents will choose to use their imperial power differently and will be rewarded, electorally and otherwise, for patience, negotiations, diplomacy and the search for ambiguous outcomes in foreign policy rather than for impatience, go-it-alone unilateralism, and unambiguous victories over adversaries. Parliamentarization has to be one answer and here is where we can best see the virtues of combining parliamentary constituency with presidential independence. Rather than following the British in this case, we would be taking a leaf from the French Fifth Republic constitution. Presidential independence combined with a parliamentary constituency.

Meanwhile, can anything be done to keep the spirit but improve on the structure of the War Powers Resolution as an aspect of parliamentarization? This law is certainly unworkable as it is. It and CIA oversight have probably contributed more than anything else to pushing the president to more and more secrecy rather than to cooperation with Congress. One alternative to the authoritative command to cooperate would be the constitutional revision of the impeachment provisions to make impeachment more like a vote of confidence. At the moment, impeachment is comparable to having only an atom bomb for dealing with minor skirmishes. There has to be some sanction other than conviction and removal of office. There also has to be some alternative to the provision for the calling of an immediate general election in the event of a no confidence vote—which would make us truly parliamentary rather than putting us on the road toward a small amount of parliamentarization. The vote of confidence power in Congress would, almost by definition, make Congress more of a presidential constituency.

Such frequent reference to the goal of making Congress the presidential constituency arises first out of recognition that Congress is the best possible solution to the unbearable pressure on the president of the mass constituency that exists today. It also arises out of recognition that once Congress gave up so many of its powers to the president by successive acts of delegation in hundreds of highly discretionary policies, the United States was irrevocably on the road to presidential government and could never come anywhere near to regaining for Congress its position as a coequal branch, let alone the supreme source of law. Parliamentarization would be Congress's as well as the president's salvation. And if the political parties remain weak, constitutional provision fostering parliamentarization could become all the more important.

Moreover, the whole Congress need not be involved in each instance of parliamentarization. Congress already has experience with the use of standing committees in special assignments as the sentinel of Congress at large in the "oversight process." Something more creative along those lines would contribute to added parliamentarization. For example, Congress could by constitutional amendment create a U.S. version of the *Conseil d'état* for foreign policy. This would in effect be a constitutional Fourth Branch with powers, including executive privilege, to put Congress as well as the executive branch under its oversight powers to protect and defend existing institutional arrangements for foreign policymaking. A similar or the same institution could be used to replace the "independent counsel" that is now under serious constitutional jeopardy. This would not duplicate the Supreme Court but could easily grow into a keeper of the administrative conscience, dealing with many questions the Court now deals with yet is unequipped to handle adequately, while at the same time dealing with many questions which the Supreme Court would consider purely political and beyond its jurisdiction. A Conseil d'état would not, strictly speaking, be a direct contribution to parliamentarization. However, as the supreme administrative court, it would be in a position to police and defend any and all procedures whose main purpose is to systematize president/congressional cooperation. For example, such an institution would be infinitely superior to the present combination of the Budget and Impoundment Act plus the Gramm-Rudman Act efforts to have an integrated budget and to stay within some preconceived budgetary limits. The present arrangements are completely self-defeating, even where they are not unconstitutional. A Conseil d'état could supervise an orderly budget process without displacing presidential or congressional participation.

Finally, there is one constitutional reform that would help parliamentarize the House of Representatives. Ironic as it may sound at first blush, constitutional reform would be aimed at giving more members of the House a real constituency rather than the artificial ones they are given by the present geographic districts. One approach would be take all cities or metropolitan areas which warrant more than, say, three members of the House and to provide for their election at large, by methods of proportional representation or otherwise. This would give each such representative a perspective large enough to enable them to transcend the most particularized interests in artificially drawn urban districts without duplicating the statewide constituencies of senators. At present, by virtue of campaign financing, the decline of parties and the rise of PACs, members of the House have become ruthless entrepreneurs. A constitutionally prescribed metropolitan constituency cannot make any human being more honest and less ruthless, but it can alter their perspectives and their reward structures.

DARE WE RISK CONSTITUTIONAL REFORM?

The final question was posed in a relatively snobbish way: "Do Americans understand the functions and limits of the Constitution well enough to make the appropriate changes and stop there?" Snobbish or not, the signs indicate a negative answer. If anything is clear from the past it is that constitutional reform works when it concentrates on structures—the composition of powers and functions. But there has been a tendency to disregard this pattern in present decades; the efforts to reform have concentrated on substantive goals. Even when the wording is structural, the legislative purpose is not far behind.

Take for example the foremost recent constitutional reform movements: The Equal Rights Amendment, the School Prayer Amendment, the Right to Life Amendment, and the Balanced Budget Amendment.

The Equal Rights Amendment and the Balanced Budget Amendment come closest to the fore to following the criterion of reform implicit in the past constitutional amendments. ERA provided simply that sex or gender could not be used as a criterion of discrimination in the law. This follows the proscriptions of race and religion in past constitutional amendments by defining one more characteristic as an unreasonable basis of distinction. The Balanced Budget Amendment also comes close to the traditional criterion by taking away from Congress the power to produce large and consistent deficits. This amendment is unwise for other reasons—particularly that it could be violated with impunity—but it nevertheless upholds the primal criterion of structural reform.

The other two amendment proposals come closer to violating the traditional criterion. On the face of it, both of these amendments uphold the criterion by simply attempting to restore to the states two powers taken away from the states by Supreme Court interpretation. However, although on the face of it they are both structural in nature, both are also more substantive than any major constitutional amendment since prohibition. And even if these two are not ultimately ratified—and signs are that the passion for their approval has been cooling—they do, in my opinion, set the tone for what is likely to happen in the years to come if constitutional reform becomes fashionable. From the left as well as from the right, there is likely to be an increasing effort to imbed in the Constitution a particular, substantive notion of rights or a particular, substantive notion of goals.

This new fashion of substantive constitutionality has been engendered in part by the "public interest" movement of the left and its stress on collective rights to clean air, beautiful environment, and so on. And there is also a "public interest" conservatism as well. But this tendency toward substantive constitutionality is also, and in greater part, the result of presidential appeals, particularly the stress of recent presidents on the constitutionality of something that they want to do. Each president has been, in effect, his own constitutional interpreter and has made it a practice of asserting an interpretation of the Constitution giving himself the power to take one kind of action or another in foreign policy and in domestic actions related to the conduct of foreign policy. It should be conceded that presidents have the right to interpret the Constitution, but the practice has been to deal with the Constitution as though it were a game of touch-base-and-go—that is to say, "discovering" that there is constitutional authority for some desirable action and then moving ahead to take that action without fear of opposition or reprisal.

But I think it has been shown here that the Constitution is much more than a game of touch-base-and-go. If the Constitution is primarily concerned with the composition of the regime, then the question is not one of mere constitutionality but of the nature of the Constitution itself. The main problem with focusing on mere constitutionality is that it has led both parties—Democratic and Republican, liberal and conservative—to excesses. Each party has a stake in expanding presidential power when it is in power, and those interpretations do not pass away when the opposition party takes the White House. At present it is the Republican party that is writing the theology of expanded presidential and executive power; and when they leave office the right-wing intellectuals are likely to start singing a different tune. But the Democratic party, even though it is now expressing some reservations, will gladly accept right-wing support of executive power if they should win next time. Both sides are obviously and patently wrong. And neither side can be entrusted with constitutional reform precisely because they have a stake in the outcome. The only alternative is to transcend partisanship by sticking strictly and rigidly to the criterion of structure and composition. This is the only way to avoid excess.

To me, therefore, the problem is self-government—I should emphasize *self*-government. To me this means proportionality of power, and this can be subdivided into two parts: (1) not to use power in excess; and (2) to provide citizens with advance knowledge of how power will be used against them. The first counsels avoidance of violence to people and institutions; the second counsels rule of law.

Democracies, especially mass democracies, are most likely to be prone to excess—and there is ample evidence of this today. Two examples will suffice. On the domestic side, there is the consistent and unresponsive deficit. A deficit can be a very effective and positive technique of fiscal policy. But when deficits mount each year without regard to patterns in the economy, it is not then an example of fiscal policy but an example of the inability of democratic governments to govern themselves. It is an example of excess, the lack of proportionality of power. The example of excess on the foreign policy side would be the American stress on a unilateral definition of national security and an unambiguous commitment to results—in brief an antagonism to diplomacy.

There is an equal likelihood that democracies will be impatient with rule of law. This is true first because rule of law places a kind of absolute limit even on popular government action. Mass democracies will never be patient with a legislature that insists upon stating clearly the nature and direction of actions, and stating clearly the nature and character of individual defense against those actions, clearly and in advance of taking those actions. That's what rule of law is all about, and its very definition suggests how impatient the popular majorities are with it. Rule of law will be bashed secondly because it stresses an individual and procedural definition of rights rather than a positive, substantive, collective definition of rights.

These two concerns for the proportionality of power take us right back to the beginning question of what a constitution is for—to put certain things above and beyond the convenience of temporary majorities and popular sentiments. That is precisely why good constitutional reform will almost always be unsuccessful and successful constitutional reform will almost always be bad.

NOTES

1. James Sundquist, *Constitutional Reform and Effective Government* (Washington: Brookings Institution, 1986), p. 243.

2. McCulloch v. Maryland, 4 Wheat. 316 (1819).

3. Herman Pritchett, *The American Constitution* (New York: McGraw Hill, 1977), pp. 180–81.

4. Gibbons v. Ogden, 9 Wheat. 1 (1824).

5. Barron v. Baltimore, 7 Pet. 243 (1833).

6. These are a moderate translation of the set of principles for review worked out by Justice Brandeis in a concurring opinion in Ashwander v. Tennessee Valley Authority, 297 US 288 (1936). See also Pritchett, *The American Constitution*, pp. 136–37.

7. National Labor Relations Board v. Jones & Laughlin Corporation, 301 US 1 (1937).

8. Henry Abraham, *Freedom and the Court* 3d ed. (New York: Oxford University Press, 1977), especially Chapter III.

9. This process is spelled out in greater detail in my book *The Personal President—Power Invested, Promise Unfulfilled* (Ithaca, NY: Cornell University Press, 1985).

10. *The Federalist* #10.

11. *The Federalist* #10.

12. *The Federalist* #10.

13. Portions of this section were taken from Lowi, *Incomplete Conquest: Governing America* 2d ed. (Holt, Rinehart & Winston, 1981), pp. 130–31. See also Lowi, *The End of Liberalism* 2d ed. (New York: W. W. Norton, 1979).

14. In addition to the chapter in this volume, see James Sundquist, *Constitutional Reform and Effective Government*.

15. Sundquist, *Constitutional Reform and Effective Government*, p. 8. The last proposition and passage are not part of Sundquist's enumeration of the problems the book was organized to deal with. However, I am sure Sundquist would agree that this is another problem that rates with the others as far as he is concerned.

16. For more details on this scenario, see Lowi, *The Personal President*, chapter 7.

Comments _____

THE UNDESIRABILITY OF REFORM

Daniel J. Elazar

It is not surprising to see my old friend Jim Sundquist advocate far-reaching changes in the U.S. Constitution designed to introduce what is in effect responsible government in a parliamentary system. It is somewhat ironic, however, to learn of such a suggestion in light of the Israeli experience. Parliamentary democracy in Israel has led to precisely that kind of "deadlock of democracy" that our colleague and Sundquist's ally in his quest for reform, James Macgregor Burns, has ascribed to the constitutional system of the United States. It is also noteworthy that the latest election for the mother of parliaments, whose system has surely influenced the American reformers' quest for reform, was marked by a struggle in a three-way race between the Conservatives, Labour and the Social Democratic alliance, with none receiving an absolute majority of the popular vote. (In Britain, the so-called reformers are demanding proportional representation to solve this problem, paying no attention of course to situations like that which exist in Israel precisely because of proportional representation.)

This could lead us to the simple conclusion that since no constitutional system works perfectly, the grass always seems greener in the neighbor's garden. Thus in Israel there are also a number of reform efforts underway, most of which are designed to institute just the kind of system of checks and balances that Sundquist and his colleagues want to change in the United States. But there is something far more problematic about Sundquist's proposals. Here I do not refer to the misreading of U.S. history and the words of the Founding Fathers. While Madison and his colleagues clearly did warn of the evils of faction, it was not because they did not expect faction to exist. Madison points out quite clearly in *Federalist* No. 10 that it is impossible to conceive of any polity without factions, but only because by warning of the evils would it be possible to control the excesses of partisanship, not the fact of it. George Washington reiterates this in his farewell address, much of which is a paraphrase of the *Federalist Papers*, skillfully developed by his trusted confidant, Alexander Hamilton. There Washington makes the point I have just made in so many words. Nor am I referring to the fact that the proposed "reforms" come 20 years after the controversy over excessive use of presidential power in Vietnam, 15 years after Watergate and in the immediate aftermath of Irangate, three cases which have convinced the American people that it is a darned good thing to have a separation of powers that really works and that whatever is lost in terms of smooth governmental decision making is more than recouped in the insistence on truly responsible government, the kind that our founders saw separation of powers bringing. In this connection, divided government, even when further divided by different parties controlling the White House and the Congress, is deemed by virtually all U.S. citizens to be a great blessing.

The real problem is that these reforms are being proposed and touted almost exclusively by members of the Washington establishment, by those members of the club, so to speak, who have been frustrated in their attempts to secure enactment and implementation of their programs over years of faithful, dedicated and often brilliant public service. Jim Sundquist is one of those dedicated and highly successful public servants. It does not denigrate their contribution to steering the ship of state to suggest that here they have let their Establishment side run away with itself a bit. For while the inspiration for the reforms they propose historically has come from Anglophile political scientists and public servants, going back to the days of Woodrow Wilson and A. Lawrence Lowell, the end result in a democratic age is a Jacobin agenda for reform, one that would create a situation in which Robert Michel's iron law of oligarchy would be able to work its way essentially unimpeded so that the Washington Establishment would indeed become the governors of the country, restrained only by periodic elections. I would not want to suggest that the reforms are proposed for other than the best of democratic motives. I know the men involved too well for that. But we all know what is paved with good intentions. Precisely because the measures proposed by our friends and colleagues are tried and true in other parts of the world, we can evaluate the results. For those who seek Jacobin democracy whereby members of the club cannot only tell us what is good for us but govern us according to what they believe, then the proposals have merit. For those of us who believe in the democratic republicanism of the Founding Fathers of the United States, who see in checks and balances and the separation of powers not a country frustrated, but the first democratic country ever to become a world power while actually strengthening its democracy, which even in an age of cynicism and doubt retains a much higher level of citizen confidence in its institutions than any other country including Britain, where public confidence is extremely low according to the latest Roper poll just completed, then we are not persuaded.

At the very least, Ted Lowi is right. Virtually all Americans have far less confidence in their present ability to achieve workable reforms than they have confidence that the present system has been and can continue to be workable.

"DON'T MESS WITH THE CONSTITUTION"

Robert A. Goldwin

"Reforming the American constitutional system" is an old American political tradition. The first such reform effort occurred in 1789, in the first session of the first Congress, under the leadership of James Madison, the first framer of the Constitution. His list of reform proposals was debated and revised and reduced to 17 articles to be added to the Constitution, of which 12 passed the Congress to be submitted to the states. Of those 12 articles, 10 were ratified and became, in the eyes of many, the most important part of the Constitution, the Bill of Rights.

Madison's original intention was to interweave the new articles into the body of the Constitution in such a way that we would be unable to distinguish the additions from the original, but his interweaving proposal was defeated.

When it was decided to append the new articles at the end of the Constitution, a heading was composed which is now usually printed before the amendments, although the heading itself is not properly part of the Constitution, it never having been ratified by the states. It reads as follows: "Articles in addition to, and amendment of, the Constitution of the United States of America, proposed by Congress, and ratified by the legislatures of the several states" and so on.

If we consider the distinction it makes, between articles that amend (that is, alter or change) and articles that add to without amending or altering anything, we realize that all of the first group of articles passed and ratified, the justly famous Bill of Rights, *added to* the Constitution but *did not amend* it. Those articles that would have amended the original constitutional text in one way or another were either not passed in 1789 by Congress, or, if passed, were not ratified by the states.

If we look at amendments adopted since then we see that many of the most important ones are additions that change nothing in the text; for example, the Nineteenth Amendment provides that the right to vote "shall not be denied ... on account of sex." It added something but changed nothing in the text because the Constitution never included any barriers to voting on account of sex. Only a few amendments do change the original text; for example the Fourteenth Amendment, Article 2, eliminates the distinction between "free persons" and "other persons" (that is, slaves), changing the census provisions of the original Constitution and thus eradicating the infamous "three-fifths clause."

Most of the so-called amendments add to but do not alter the constitutional text. And whether the new article is an amendment or addition, it rarely has had the effect of changing the structure of the government.

The inclination and aspiration to reform the constitutional system by amending the Constitution have been very strong from the beginning, but the success rate has been very low. Through September 1986, 10,124 constitutional amendments have been introduced in the Congress; of these, just 33 were adopted by Congress and only 26 were ratified—or a success rate of one-fourth of 1 percent. In contrast, James Madison's success rate was 59 percent.

The prudent rule seems to be, if you are not James Madison, and if you are interested in results, don't mess with the Constitution. Despite this evidence of experience, the current list of proposed amendments with serious proponents includes the Equal Rights amendment, restriction of abortion, permitting prayer in the schools, prohibition of forced busing for racial balance, compulsory balancing of the budget, and many others.

For my part, I oppose them all. There are many things that can be improved in the governing of the United States, but amending the Constitution is not the best remedy. My reason can be illustrated by the reformer's humorous story about senators who say that in their first two years they can be statesmen, in the second two years politicians, and in the third two years demagogues.

What does taking that formulation seriously say to us? It expresses a contempt for democratic politics. That is, the closer these elected officials come to having to face their electorate, the less their dedication to the public good, as if statesmanship is possible only when they don't have to be accountable to the people who elected them. I think this distaste for democratic politics has much to do with the calls for structural reform, both by politicians and academic reformers, because the advocates of such positions, in my opinion, disapprove of entanglement in the very untidy political system that this Constitution establishes, and that, in one way or another, every democratic constitution establishes. Politicians and political scientists who don't like democratic politics are not likely to be the wisest political instructors.

If there are abuses, and there are many in the U.S. political process, then let us deal with them directly. There are many effective ways to correct campaign fund-raising abuses, for instance, without amending the Constitution.

In addition, of course, as the statistics show, amendments rarely succeed. There is not a sufficient constituency for the kinds of amendments that reformers typically propose to get through Congress and to be ratified in three-fourths of the state legislatures.

But in order not to be completely negative, I do have advice to those who, nevertheless, want to push forward constitutional amendments. Because of the difficulty of getting them ratified, and because of the difficulty of finding a constituency, my AEI colleague, the economist Herbert Stein, has suggested an amendment that would combine two powerful constituencies. He proposes an amendment to require the children in public schools to pray for a balanced budget. That one I would support, as unlikely to do any significant harm. All the rest I oppose.

IX THE IMPACT OF THE CONSTITUTION ABROAD: THE VIEW FROM ISRAEL

15 Judicial Perspectives: The View from Israel

Aaron Barak

In all important respects, there are major differences between the United States and Israel: size, history, population, national experience— everything differs. Closer to our topic, the United States is a federal system. We are a unitary system. The United States has a presidential system of government. We have a parliamentary system of government. The United States has a written constitution and judicial review of legislation. We have no written constitution and we have almost no judicial review. The United States has a Bill of Rights embodying several human rights. We have no bill of rights, as such. Is there any sense, then, in talking about the impact of the United States constitution on Israeli law? The answer is yes and no. Yes, because of the common experiences we share. No, because of the differences that set us apart. What I would like to do in this chapter is to try to draw the line and demonstrate.

As our experience in law shows, law is not just statutes and precedents. Constitutional law is not just the text of a written constitution. The text of the Constitution, like the text of a statute, is only the tip of the iceberg. When we use the text, we find ourselves relying upon a broad foundation: the basic concepts of law and society, the notions of a judiciary and its role in society, the aspirations of the nation and its goals and traditions. One cannot understand and apply the law, statutory or constitutional, without grasping the basic concepts that lie behind and above the law.

We judges, and especially judges of Supreme Courts, refer to these concepts, consciously or unconsciously, when we engage in the interpretation of statutes and constitutions. To the extent that we judges in Israel share some of these basic concepts and traditions with our U.S. counterparts, to the extent that the U.S. legal environment is similar to ours, the American legal experience is very relevant to ours.

Let me offer you some general examples. I shall start with the notion of democracy. The United States is a democracy, as is Israel. Democracies share certain common values. Democracy means, inter alia, respect for basic human rights. Our Supreme Court, basing itself on the fundamental premise that Israel is a democracy, held that Israel must of necessity recognize some basic human rights.[1]

Thus, following our constitutional experience, our Supreme Court declared that Israel recognizes freedom of expression,[2] freedom of the press,[3] freedom of demonstration,[4] freedom of movement,[5] freedom of association[6] and freedom of occupation.[7] Of course, in the United States some of these freedoms are embodied in the Constitution itself or in the Bill of Rights. We made these rights parts of our common law. They became, however, a source of individual rights, and establish the legal environment in which every statute should be examined.

Thus, every power granted by statute to the executive branch is interpreted against a background of these basic freedoms. Of course, not having a written constitution, a regular statute may prohibit or restrict these freedoms. But the statute must expressly state this. Clearly enough, what the statute states is only what the court says this statute states, and the interpretation of these statutes is conducted in the light of those basic rights.

In many cases, these basic principles or freedoms or policies clash with one another. Then, we are faced with a conflict and we must choose between alternatives or at least seek to obtain a balance.[8] And we have to balance not only on an ad hoc basis but on a principled basis.[9] And thus, we came up with some formulas quite familiar in the United States, such as "clear and present danger". United States cases are thus cited, discussed, distinguished, ruled upon and occasionally discounted. United States law articles are read. American law books are analyzed. Some are followed, some are not. One will find, in many of our cases, references to the First Amendment. Likewise, one can find references to questions of absolute rights, relative rights and the need to find a happy balance.

Let me give you some examples from judgements that I myself wrote, just in the last few years. The question arose: "Should we allow a political party whose ideas are antidemocratic (some even say racist) to participate in our election process?" There is no provision in our statutes dealing with such a question. Our Supreme Court said "yes", and we relied heavily upon U.S. cases in reaching that decision.[10]

Let me offer a further example. Dating back to the British Mandate, we in Israel have a regulation which provides for censorship of movies and shows. The statute says nothing about the discretion of the censorship board. The law says that there shall be a board, but the law does not specify which considerations the board should take into account in exercising its judgment. Cases have come before us bearing on this question. We said "Yes, the board has powers, but what is the measure of its discretion?" The board, we said, has to take into account, of course, public order, public peace, and public morals. But these are not the only considerations the board should take into account. The board should also give due account to the idea of freedom of expression. The outcome: the board may block the presentation of a movie or show only if it can be shown that there is a high probability of serious injury to public peace.[11] As one can see, we are coming very close to U.S. First Amendment cases.

Let me present another case involving the same party I mentioned before, which is claimed to be a racist and antidemocratic party. Our Broadcasting Authority, radio and television (which is similar to Britain's BBC), is a statutory body. The Broadcasting Authority decided to provide coverage of this party, only to the extent that it is a news item. It was decided not to give the party broadcasting privileges. For example, the Broadcasting Authority does not broadcast any political talk shows that include this party's representatives. The party came to us. They claimed their freedom of expression was being infringed and they cited many U.S. cases, First Amendment cases, concerning freedom of expression. We upheld the party's right to freedom of political expression.[12]

I mentioned some First Amendment examples. Of course, they are not the only ones. Belief in the dignity of the human being is a basic principle both countries share.[13] Thus, cases on the Fourth Amendment, such as search and seizure, the Fifth Amendment and the rights of the accused, are very relevant as part and parcel of the general environment in which we interpret our statutes.

Let me move into the area of the separation of powers. This idea of the separation of powers is not exclusive to a written constitution, or to a presidential system of government. Its main aim is to strengthen the liberty of the individual. We share that aim. Thus, we can adopt and adapt some of the U.S. jurisprudence relating to the separation of powers, checks and balances, and the independence of the judiciary.

Let me give an example. The speaker of the Knesset (the Israeli parliament) decided that according to his interpretation of the bylaws of the Knesset a one-man party may not ask for a vote of no-confidence. (Our parliament is run by regulations or bylaws which our parliament itself has established.) One such party took the matter to court. We assumed jurisdiction and gave our own interpretation to these parliamentary regulations. Our interpretation differed from that of the speaker. We quashed his decision and ordered him to allow this one-man party the right to present non-confidence motions to the Knesset.[14] Citing *Marbury* v. *Madison*, *Nixon* v. *the United States*, *Powell* v. *McCormick*, and other U.S. precedents, we determined that it is the duty and obligation of the Supreme Court to say what the law is.

The concept of the rule of law, what is called in America "government under the law," is not exclusive to a written constitution. It is a concept we share. Thus, citing U.S. cases and experience, we have developed this concept in our own country, taking into account our own circumstances.

Let me give an example. Israeli forces occupy the West Bank. This is a military occupation. Israeli law does not apply to the West Bank. The occupation of the West Bank is carried out according to international law. The question came up before our Supreme Court: Should the Court review cases arising from Israeli occupation of the West Bank? In short, should we control the executive branch and the military in their operations in the West Bank?

Because we embrace the concept of the rule of law, and of government under law, we decided that we shall exercise jurisdiction.[15] We thus exercise judicial control over our military operations in the West Bank quite extensively. We have more than one hundred cases per year in the Supreme Court, mainly from Arabs in the West Bank, and we scrutinize our executive branch's activities in the West Bank, both in terms of international law and in terms of our own administrative law. Recent developments on the West Bank have highlighted the extent of our judicial control there.

One might ask: "Why should Israeli courts apply a concept of constitutional interpretation if there is no written constitution? The answer is that we do have certain statutes, which are called "Basic Laws." Those are not regular statutes. They are constitutional statutes in terms of content. Thus, for instance, they provide for the powers of the president. They provide for the powers of the executive and they determine how our parliamentary system operates, our system of elections, and so on. In their interpretation, we approach them as constitutional statutes. We cannot approach them as we do a simple statute. "It is a constitution we are expounding." Here the door opens to some of the best of American judgments on constitutional interpretation. I myself use many of these judgments when questions come up before our Court.

Let me give an example. We have recently had the following case: Does our president have the power to give pardon before conviction?[16] I came to the conclusion (though I remained in a minority on this question) that our president does not have this kind of power. I used American cases—not in order to show that the U.S. president has no power to pardon before conviction (because he probably does, according to my understanding of the literature)—but in order to learn how one approaches a constitutional question, as opposed to a statutory question. What I was intent on learning was the approach one should adopt in analyzing a constitutional text within the framework of a constitutional scheme. Of course if one compares the Israeli president and the U.S. president, and says the Israeli president possesses the same powers of pardon as the U.S. president has, one will reach, I submit, the wrong conclusion. Our president has different powers than the U.S. president. The U.S. president is, inter alia, the chief executive, and has responsibility for the execution, of the law, which our president does not. So here also I tried to make this distinction. We applied U.S. case law, not in order to find a solution to a specific problem, but in order to share some basic general notions.

Constitutional interpretation leads to constitutional theory, and to the role that a Supreme Court plays in the life of a society. These problems are not peculiar to a written constitution and to judicial review, though they are demonstrated most dramatically where judicial review of statutes is practiced.

We, in Israel, face the same problems as a U.S. court.[17] What is the proper role of public policy in our deliberations? When should we exercise self-restraint? When should we be active? Can we operate outside the consensus? What should be our relationship with our parliament? All these basic questions which arise in the United States, arise in Israel as well. And in order to solve our problems, while they are different from those of the United States, we can share, and we do share some basic ideas propounded in U.S. courts.

Perhaps this is the place to mention a major difference between the role of a supreme court within a society that has a written constitution, and the role of a supreme court within a society that has no written constitution.

First, in a system with a written constitution, there is, by definition, a written text from which the fundamental constitutional principles emanate. Where there is no written constitution, this text is missing. The importance of this difference, however, should not be exaggerated. The constitutional text is frequently ambiguous and open textured. More than the judge actually takes from the text, he inserts into it.

A second difference might arguably arise with reference to "formal legitimation." Judicial creativity in a system with a constitution is grounded in the constitution itself. This essentially means that such legitimation cannot exist where there is no written constitution. Yet this difference too is not really meaningful. On the contrary. When the creative judicial activity begins to move away from the core of the constitutional text and operates instead in its penumbra, the formal legitimacy of the judge's creation is weakened. One has the feeling that the judge is creating constitutional common law, appending it to the constitution, and illegitimately giving it constitutional weight. In this sense he is, in fact, creating a new constitution.

We, in Israel, who operate without a written constitution, are not faced with this problem. We do not pretend to give our rulings superior or superlative force. We are not capable of striking down a statute. Our decisions merely create precedent in whose context the statutes operate.

Third, in a system with a written constitution, there exists a severe problem of substantive legitimacy. Judicial law making represents an attack on majoritarian democracy. It is argued that it is undemocratic for an elitist, nonelected body, appointed for life and unaccountable to anybody, to impose its will over the people unless this will is expressed by the legislative body. This argument has less force in our system. The Supreme Court does not circumvent the will of our parliament. Indeed, our parliament always has the chance to read our judgments and to change them, if it does not like them. If the legislature finds it inappropriate to make such changes, no one can charge the Supreme Court with having acted against the will of the people.

Against this background, against these differences, one can understand the problem of the Supreme Court, and the dilemma of a judge of a Supreme Court, in a system which does not have a written constitution. In a sense, he enjoys greater freedom of action than his colleagues, who operate in a system with a written constitution. Our judge is not limited by constitutional text. He can fashion constitutional doctrines with greater ease. He can adapt the law to changing reality with greater flexibility. He is not open to the charge that his activity is antidemocratic to the extent that his colleagues are. We may point to democracy as a delicate balance between the rights of the individual and the will of the majority. This balance is maintained in our system. Whatever the court determines in matters of individual rights may be changed by the majority through the legislature.

Yet in a deeper sense, the judge who must work without a written constitution is far more constrained than his colleagues who act within the framework of a written constitution. First, there is no judicial review of statutes. The power of the judge to give expression to the fundamental principles of a system is limited. In a system with a written constitution, judicial activity is limited by the self-restraint of the judiciary. In a system such as ours, without a written constitution, judicial activity is dependent upon the self-restraint of the legislature.

Second, the judge faces a serious problem in his relationship with the legislature itself. The legislature has the constitutional power to change, by statute, not only the rulings of the court, but even the court itself, as well as its jurisdiction. The court does not derive its power from a constitution, and is not above the legislature. It derives its authority from the legislature itself.

One can thus realize the importance of the U.S. experience for Israel, and its limitations. We can, and should, learn the importance of a written constitution and the essential role it plays, and should play, in such a sphere as judicial review. At the same time, we can learn the dangers and pitfalls of a written constitution and of judicial review from the U.S. experience.

We should not imitate blindly. We should not (though we probably will) repeat your mistakes. There are topics that are clearly so different in the two countries that we should not bother to seek guidance in relation to them. Federalism is an excellent example. But there are other practices that we do share, yet we prefer not to follow the U.S. example. Thus, in the matter of appointing judges[18] or of according standing, our practices differ. We have enlarged the concept of standing far beyond what is accepted in the United States.[19] We have almost abolished the political question doctrine.[20] Moreover, we have not adopted the exclusionary rule, which precludes acceptance of evidence illegally obtained.

Given the basic ideas we share, we must use them differently. A question of constitutional validity in the United States becomes, quite often, a question of administrative powers in Israel. Constitutional questions are channeled into administrative tools. While U.S. administrative law is derived from constitutional concepts, our constitutional concepts are derived via our administrative law. In Israel, we are not concerned with the details and the technicalities of the U.S. constitutional scheme. We don't care if the exclusionary doctrine is derived from the Fourth Amendment or the Fourteenth Amendment. We don't care if it is a state question or a federal question. We don't care if it is a majority judgment or a minority judgment. It is the constitutional principle; it is the idea which we care about and which we adapt to our needs.

In this respect, we do not rely solely on U.S. case law. We also draw on European ideas and European constitutional law. And lately, we have gained insights from the Canadian experience. All of these reflect common ideas about the way a democracy should operate. They fashion a zone of democratic legitimacy in which we would also like to operate.

As is well known, Israel is an old nation yet a young democracy. After 40 years of independence, our constitutional birth is not yet complete. We operate under very special circumstances: military danger to our national existence, occupation, racial questions concerning minorities, state and church problems, the melting pot dilemma, and so on. We are engaged in creating our own foundations. As a judge of the Supreme Court, under these circumstances, I feel in a way that we are now the framers of our unwritten constitution. We look to the U.S. Constitution for inspiration and guidance. We know that it does not embody one single political theory, one idea. We know it sometimes uses vague and open-textured phrases. We know it gives discretion to judges, and we know that this discretion is not accepted by all.

All this may impose burdens and cause troubles for the American people. For us, this plurality in thought and practice is a source of inspiration. We know the problems. We are not imitating blindly. We try to choose the best of everything in the U.S. experience, to use those basic notions which are part of our mutual tradition and our commitment to democracy.

NOTES

1. H.C.J. (High Court of Justice) 73/53 "Kol Haam" v. Minister of Interior 7 P.D. 871; H.C.J. 153/83 Levi v. Commissioner of the Israeli Police Southern District 38(2) P.D. 393; E.A. (Elections Appeal) 2/84 Neiman v. Chairman of the 11th Knesset Election Committee 39(2) P.D. 225.

2. H.C.J. 399/85 Kahana v. Broadcasting Board 41(3) P.D. 255.

3. H.C.J. 73/53 "Kol Haam".

4. H.C.J. 153/83 Levi.

5. H.C.J. 448/85 Daher v. Minister of Interior 40(2) P.D. 701.

6. H.C.J. 253/64 Jaris v. Haifa District Governor 18(4) P.D. 673.

7. H.C.J. 1/49 Bejerano v. Minister of Police 2 P.D. 80.

8. E.A. 2/84 Neiman.

9. H.C.J. 73/53 "Kol Haam".

10. E.A. 2/84 Neiman.

11. H.C.J. 14/86 Laor v. Film and Play Review Council 41(1) P.D. 421.

12. H.C.J. 399/85 Kahana.

13. H.C.J. 355/79 Katalan v. Prison Board 34(2) P.D. 294.

14. H.C.J. 73/85 "Kach" Party v. Chairman of the Knesset 39(3) P.D. 141; H.C.J. 742/84 Kahana v. Chairman of the Knesset 39(4) P.D. 85.

15. H.C.J. 390/79 Duwaikat v. Government of Israel 34(1) P.D. 1; H.C.J. 69/81 Abu Ita v. Commander of the Judea and Samaria Region 37(2) P.D. 197; H.C.J. 306/72 Abu Hilu v. Government of Israel 27(2) 169.

16. H.C.J. 428/86 Barzilai v. Government of Israel 40(3) P.D. 505.

17. On those questions, see Aaron Barak: *Judicial Discretion* (New Haven, CT: Yale University Press, 1988).

18. A judge in Israel is appointed by the president. He is nominated by a statutory committee of nine members: The minister of justice, two members of Parliament, two representatives of the Israeli Bar Association, the chief justice, and two other judges of the Supreme Court. The president has no discretion but to appoint the nominee.

19. H.C.J. 217/80 Segal v. Minister of Interior 34(4) P.D. 429; H.C.J. 852,869/86 Alony v. Minister of Justice 41(2) P.D. 1.

20. H.C.J. 910/86 Resler v. Minister of Defense (not yet published).

16 The Influence of First Amendment Jurisprudence on Judicial Decision Making in Israel

David Kretzmer

INTRODUCTION

My intention in the present chapter is to review the standing of freedom of speech in the Israeli legal system and to isolate facets of this topic in which U.S. constitutional doctrine has had an overt effect on judicial decision making. I shall try to show that although the original model for the Israeli legal system was the English system, judicial decision making in the field of civil rights in general, and freedom of speech in particular, have been influenced by U.S. doctrine, rather than by prevailing English judicial attitudes.

I shall begin with certainly fairly obvious, but crucial, distinguishing features of the U.S. and British legal systems and point out why the Israeli system is closer to the British, rather than the U.S. model. I shall then briefly discuss the landmark decision in the *Kol Haam* case, which was inspired by U.S. constitutional jurisprudence, and how that decision opened the way for drawing the Israeli system closer to the U.S. model. Finally I shall describe the areas in which Israeli courts routinely rely on U.S. First Amendment jurisprudence.

FEATURES OF U.S. AND BRITISH SYSTEMS

The U.S. System

The most important feature of the U.S. system that interests us here is the existence of a formal constitution, and more specifically, a bill of rights which is an integral part of that constitution. A bill of rights fulfills two discrete functions in a legal system. First, it grants the rights recognized therein status as "legal principles," that is, principles which *must* be considered relevant by lawmaking and law-applying organs in all relevant cases.[1] Second, in the U.S. example at least, it grants such principles entrenched status, in other words, it places them on a higher normative plane than ordinary laws and guards them against encroachment by all branches of government, including the legislative branch. The First Amendment statement that Congress may make no law abridging the freedom of speech or of the press both grants recognition to freedom of speech and of the press as principles in the U.S. legal system, and determines that the democratically elected federal legislative body may not abrogate these freedoms. While not stated explicitly by the Constitution itself, implicit in this declaration is the notion that a statute enacted by Congress that abridges this freedom will not be valid.[2]

The British System

Britain has long been regarded as the almost unique example of a modern democracy which has no formal written constitution. This means not only that there is no entrenched superior norm which places restrictions on Parliament, but also that there is no written law at all which grants recognition to civil rights as legal principles.[3] Liberty of the subject, under the British view, "exists in the interstices of the substantive law."[4] The British courts do indeed refer on occasion to "public interests" such as freedom of expression,[5] but they do so in much the same way as they refer to a host of other "public interests" such as public order or public policy.

The above attitude of the British authorities on the status of civil rights in the British legal system is stated quite clearly in academic discussion of this topic. Thus, in the first comprehensive study of freedom of the individual under the British system, the late Professor Harry Street put the matter as follows:

This is how English law goes about its job of defining limits on our freedom. The citizen may do as he likes unless he clashes with some specific restriction on his freedom. The law does not say: "You can do that"; it says "You cannot do this," which means that you can do everything else except that which it says you cannot do. Whenever such a prohibition is made, the reason will be that some other interest is rated more important than that freedom on which it impinges.[6]

ISRAEL AND THE BRITISH MODEL

There are a number of reasons why the Israeli legal system would seem to be closer to the British rather than the U.S. model. In the first place, the Israeli political system resembles the British system. Like Britain, Israel is a unitary parliamentary democracy in which parliament, the Knesset, is supreme. Israel still has no formal constitution[7] and although a number of attempts have been made to enact a basic law on civil rights, these attempts have so far been unsuccessful.[8] Second, when the independent state of Israel was established the tradition of the law in force was distinctly British. The British Mandatory authorities which ruled the country for 30 years had not only made the rules of common law and principles of equity a major source of substantive law,[9] they had also turned the procedure of the courts into British procedure. The Supreme Court had been given original jurisdiction, as a high court of justice, to exercise judicial review over administrative action by issuing the traditional British prerogative writs of certiorari, prohibition, and mandamus. Furthermore, many of the judges at the time of the British Mandate were British and even non-British judges and members of the legal profession often received their legal training in Britain or at British colonial institutions.

Perusal of the decisions of the Supreme Court of Israel in a number of major constitutional cases that were heard immediately after independence shows that the court relied entirely on local precedent or British authorities.[10] In these first years after independence the Supreme Court certainly saw itself as a bastion of individual rights, but its perception of this task was to ensure that the executive did not interfere with the liberties of the individual unless authorized to do so under statute[11] and that when authorized to restrict basic freedoms the executive would comply strictly with all procedural requirements.[12]

Since the first years of the state the above approach has been abandoned. Basic civil rights, such as freedom of expression and the right to demonstrate, have been lifted out of the interstices of the law and granted status as accepted legal principles. While these principles do not enjoy a superior status to primary legislation of the Knesset and may be restricted, or even abrogated, by such legislation, they do enjoy the status of legal principles and not mere statements of political ideals or public interests. Thus, one function of a formal written constitution, that is, the declaration of those rights recognized by the legal system, has been partially filled by judicial legislation that relies heavily on U.S. constitutional doctrine. The rest of this chapter will be devoted to discussing how this change in approach was effected and showing where U.S. doctrine has had a mark.

THE *KOL HAAM* DECISION

Every discussion of the status of civil rights in the Israel legal system must start from the landmark decision of Agranat J. in *Kol Haam* v. *Minister of Interior*.[13] The extent to which this decision was influenced by U.S. jurisprudence of free speech has been thoroughly covered by the leading scholar of free speech in Israel, Professor Pnina Lahav,[14] and I have no intention here of covering the ground already covered by Professor Lahav in her comprehensive treatment of the subject. I shall therefore merely summarize in brief the significance of the *Kol Haam* decision for the present discussion.

The *Kol Haam* decision dealt with an order of the minister of Interior, issued pursuant to his authority under section 19 of the Press Ordinance, suspending publication of two daily newspapers for periods of 10 and 15 days. The reason for this decision was the publication in the newspapers, both organs of the lawful Israel Communist party, of harsh attacks on the government, following a report (subsequently denied) that Israel's ambassador in the United States had promised that in the event of war between the United States and the USSR, Israel would place 200,000 troops at the disposal of the United States. Section 19 authorized the minister to order suspension of a newspaper "if any matter appearing. . . . is, in his opinion . . . likely to endanger the public peace" and in a previous case involving the same newspapers the Court had refused to interfere in a matter which was regarded as entirely within the minister's discretion.[15] Agranat J. decided, however, that given the democratic character of the state (as seen in the Declaration of Independence and in the nature of the political institutions of government), freedom of speech must be regarded as a recognized legal principle. For the purposes of the case before him this meant that where possible it was incumbent on all bodies, administrative or judicial, to choose that interpretation of a statutory provision which is consistent with this principle. Agranat J. proceeded to hold that the word "likely" in section 19 of the Press Ordinance lent itself to two possible interpretations: a "bad tendency" interpretation and a "probable danger" interpretation. He dismissed the first interpretation as being totally inconsistent with the free speech principle, and held that the only acceptable interpretation of the section was therefore the "probable danger" interpretation, which strikes an acceptable balance between freedom of speech and conflicting interests of public security and public peace. As the facts of the case showed quite clearly that the interpretation on which the minister based his decision was the bad tendency one, Agranat J. held that the minister had acted without authority and that the suspension orders must be invalidated.

As already mentioned, the influence of U.S. freedom of speech doctrine on this historic decision has been discussed elsewhere.[16] There is little doubt that this doctrine was the main force behind the decision.[17] One could even go as far as to say that even if the court had never quoted another U.S. decision or author after the *Kol Haam* decision, the mere influence of this decision itself on Israeli civil rights jurisprudence would have justified the conclusion that the effect of U.S. doctrine on Israeli jurisprudence has been decisive.

FREE SPEECH AS A LEGAL PRINCIPLE

Two facets of the *Kol Haam* decision have had a pervasive influence on the development of civil rights jurisprudence in Israel. The first is the holding that freedom of speech is a recognized legal principle; not a mere "public interest," but an integral part of the Israeli legal system. The second is that the balancing test to be used in the case of a conflict between freedom of speech and public security or public peace is the "probable danger" test.

It is by no means an obvious conclusion that in a country which sees itself as democratic, freedom of speech must be regarded as a *legal* principle (as opposed to a political principle or ideal). One could in fact take the view that the question of whether a country is democratic or not is partly a function of the restrictions that country's laws place on freedom of speech (rather than Agranat J.'s view that freedom of speech as a recognized principle is a function of the democratic nature of the state). Britain is certainly a democratic country in which there is a high degree of respect for freedom of speech. Nevertheless, as mentioned above, the British courts have refrained from recognizing freedom of speech as a principle that forms an integral part of the legal system.

In countries with formal bills of rights or even ordinary civil rights legislation[18] the constituent assembly or legislature have turned civil rights into legal principles. The first major contribution of *Kol Haam* to Israeli jurisprudence is that what was achieved in the United States and other countries by adoption of a formal constitution or by parliamentary legislation was reached in Israel by judicial legislation. In one fell swoop Agranat J. abandoned the British model, prevalent before the *Kol Haam* decision, and adopted a model similar in many respects to the U.S. constitutional model.

What are the implications of the definition of freedom of speech as a legal principle, rather than a mere public interest? One answer, provided in the *Kol Haam* case itself, is that where possible statutory provisions restrictive of freedom of speech must be interpreted so as to minimize the restriction. A major example of the use of this facet of the legal principle was the attempt by Shamgar J. to incorporate into Israeli law the rule in *N.Y. Times* v. *Sullivan*,[19] regarding libel actions by public officials for criticism of their official conduct, by means of interpretation of a provision in the Defamation (Prohibition) Law, 1965.[20]

The main use of the legal principle of freedom of speech has been in the limits it places on administrative discretion. In two areas this has been particularly significant: permits for processions and censorship of films.

Permits for Processions

Under the Police Ordinance a permit is required for a procession or an outdoor meeting.[21] The ordinance provides that when a permit is applied for the district commander of the police may grant the permit, subject to such conditions as he thinks fit, or refuse the permit.[22] This would seem to imply that, according to accepted rules of Israeli administrative law, as long as the commander acts in good faith and without discrimination and bases his decision to refuse a permit on relevant police considerations (such as public order or traffic control) he is acting within his authority and there is therefore no place for judicial intervention. This was indeed the attitude taken for a long time by the Supreme Court.[23]

However, in 1979 the Supreme Court held that the discretion of the district commander must be viewed in the light of the principles of basic freedoms which are part of the legal system. Barak J. stated: "It is well-known that the law of the State of Israel recognises the basic freedoms of man, as accepted in enlightened countries. Freedom of assembly and freedom of procession are among these freedoms."[24]

The effect of this principle was that in granting a permit the commander was not doing the demonstrators a favor or awarding them a privilege. He was merely allowing them to exercise a basic right and he could therefore not deny a permit unless he could prove that there were weighty and substantial considerations of public order that prevented him from doing so.[25] In two subsequent cases the court went even further and held that the police may not refuse a permit on public order grounds unless they can show that the threat to public order meets the probable danger test.[26]

The decisions in the above cases illustrate the difference between the Israeli approach, based as it is on basic freedoms as principles that are an integral part of the legal system, and the traditional English approach, followed in the first years of the state's existence. In *Kent v. Metropolitan Police Commissioner*[27] an attempt was made to overturn a ban on processions in London imposed under the Public Order Act, 1936. The Court of Appeal showed not the least concern about the right to demonstrate and whether the commissioner had given sufficient (or any) weight to this right. One of the justices, Sir Denys Buckley, went as far as to say that the commissioner's reasons for his order seemed meager but that it was for the petitioners to show that there were no, or no reasonable, grounds on which the commissioner could have held that the planned procession would be likely to cause serious disorder.[28]

Censorship of Plays

Under a British Mandatory ordinance it is forbidden to hold a public performance of a play in Israel unless the play has received the approval of a special public board appointed by the minister of Interior.[29] The said ordinance in no way restricts the discretion of the board or provides what the legitimate considerations for disallowing a play are. In a major opinion the former attorney general, Professor Yitzhak Zamir, held that "although established to exercise power of censorship, [the board] must nevertheless be guided first and foremost by the principle of freedom of expression."[30] The attorney general went on to hold that "the performance of a play should be prevented only in extreme cases in which the performance entails a criminal offense, such as incitement or rebellion, or an outrage to the public's values and feelings that is so severe that it clearly outweighs the principle of freedom of expression."[31] This approach of the attorney general was recently accepted by the Supreme Court which overturned a decision by the board to censor a play dealing with the military government in the occupied territories. The court ruled that the board may only censor a play if it meets the probable danger standard laid down in the *Kol Haam* case.[32]

A recent decision by the president of the Supreme Court illustrates another application of freedom of speech as a legal principle. The Evidence Ordinance, as amended by a series of Knesset laws, recognizes a number of privileges against giving evidence for certain professions: lawyers, physicians, psychologists and religious ministers. During the Knesset debates on the legislation which formally established these privileges, it was suggested that a privilege be extended to journalists, so as to allow them to refuse to reveal their sources.[33] This proposal was opposed by the minister of Justice[34] and was not adopted in the legislation. In *Zitrin* v. *Disciplinary Court of Israel Bar*[35] Shamgar P. rejected the idea that noninclusion of a privilege in the statute meant that the Knesset had impliedly rejected such a privilege. He held that such a privilege was essential in order to protect the public's right to know, which is part and parcel of freedom of speech. Shamgar P.'s conclusion was that given the status of freedom of speech as a leading principle in Israel's constitutional system, journalists enjoy a qualified privilege not to reveal their sources.

As stated above, the Bill of Rights in the U.S. Constitution fulfills two functions: recognition of basic rights as legal principles and granting these rights preferred and entrenched status. As the above discussion reveals, judicial legislation in Israel, influenced to a decisive degree by U.S. constitutional doctrine, has fulfilled the first function: it has incorporated freedom of speech and other basic rights as legal principles in our legal system. Before proceeding to discuss the other aspect of the

Kol Haam case we must say something about the second function of the Bill of Rights.

Israel has a fair number of antidemocratic laws inherited from the British Mandate.[36] Some original Israeli statutes may also be regarded as abridgements of basic rights, such as freedom of religion[37] or equality.[38] On occasion, the Supreme Court itself has labelled a law as antidemocratic.[39] Nevertheless, all primary legislation remains valid and will not be declared invalid by the court on the strength of the argument that it is inconsistent with basic constitutional principles. These principles may therefore be termed "soft legal principles".[40] They fulfill the first function of the rights set out in the U.S. Bill of Rights; they do not fulfill the second function. It seems that until such time as Israel adopts a formal written constitution we will have to make do with these soft legal principles.

THE PROBABLE DANGER TEST

The prevailing test in the United States at the time of the *Kol Haam* decision for resolving the conflict between freedom of speech and public order or security was the clear and present danger test. Agranat J. refrained from adopting this test in the *Kol Haam* decision, but instead he opted for the probable danger test favored two years previously by Chief Justice Vinson in *Dennis* v. *U.S.*[41] He stated that the wording of the statutory provision that he had to interpret in the case before him—that the matter was *likely* to endanger the public peace—prevented adoption of the clear and present danger test.[42] The main difference that Agranat J. saw between that test and his probable danger test was that under the latter it is not necessary that the danger be immediate.[43] He nevertheless recommended that as far as possible the minister should follow the guidelines set out for use of the clear and present danger test in the leading U.S. Supreme Court decisions.[44]

The probable danger test was restricted, in the *Kol Haam* case, to the specific question which arose there, namely the interpretation of the word "likely" in section 19 of the Press Ordinance. In *Israel Film Studios* v. *Gerti*[45] the question before the court was whether the Film Censorship Board had acted within its powers when it censored part of a newsreel dealing with police conduct in the evacuation of a house in a slum area. The question was certainly not a question of statutory interpretation; it concerned the limits of administrative discretion. Nevertheless, Landau J. held that "the decision in the *Kol Haam* case rests on a wide ideological base which entirely fits the present case"[46] and that the probable danger test was therefore the appropriate balancing test for the Board to use in deciding whether to censor on grounds of public order. Since then it has become generally accepted that the probable danger test is the general, but not exclusive, test in Israel for balancing freedom of speech and conflicting public order or public security considerations.[47] Thus, for example, in *Levi* v. *Police Commander*[48] the court dealt with the threat to public order posed by a hostile audience as grounds for refusing a permit for a procession. It held that this threat could only be a legitimate basis for refusing a permit if, in spite of police action to eliminate the threat, there remained a threat to public order that met the probable danger test.[49] In the more recent case of *Kahane* v. *Broadcasting Authority*,[50] Barak J. refused to accept the argument that the racist nature of speech was sufficient reason for the statutory Broadcasting Authority to ban broadcast of that speech. The test, held Barak J., must be the general test of probable danger to public order.[51]

In the United States the clear and present danger test, and its offspring, the probable danger test, have served largely as the standards for judging incitement or advocacy of lawless action and the conflict between freedom of press and fair trial.[52] In Israel, however, the probable danger test, adopted from U.S. sources, has been extended and applied in situations in which it would be quite inappropriate in the United States. Furthermore, it is interesting that the probable danger test has gained acceptance in Israel at the very time that the clear and probable danger test has lost credence in the United States.[53] How can one explain this? I submit that three factors should be considered.

First, the lack of judicial review over primary legislation in Israel means that options open to the U.S. courts are not open to the Israeli courts. Israeli courts accept the validity of primary legislation, however restrictive of freedom of expression it may appear to be. This prevents them in most relevant contexts from accepting first amendment tests adopted in some spheres in the United States, such as the overbreadth test[54] or the vagueness test,[55] as these are essentially tests that relate to the validity of statutes which impose restrictions on speech. The only possible approach for a court in Israel, when faced with a statute that restricts speech or grants an administrative body the power to restrict speech, is to do what the court has in fact done, namely to hold that the statute must be interpreted in a way that balances the abridgement of speech with the interest which the statute protects, or that in wielding administrative discretion, freedom of speech must be given due weight. Thus, for instance, it seems quite clear that a U.S. court would hold the Israeli statute on censorship of plays unconstitutional. The Israeli Supreme Court could not do this, and it has stretched judicial review of administrative action to its utmost limits by holding that the seemingly unfettered statutory discretion to censor plays may only be exercised in case of a probable danger.

Second, the clear and present danger test was adopted in the United States at times of national crisis: during and immediately following

World War I and the Russian Revolution and during the Cold War. Its wane began only after these states of emergency, as perceived by the Americans themselves, at least, had passed.[56] In Israel we are still faced with a formal state of emergency and constant security and political crises.

Finally, and possibly most importantly, there is often a discrepancy between the theoretical balancing test and its application. In the United States the clear and probable danger test may have seemed a fairly liberal test from the theoretical point of view, but its application cast doubts on its efficacy as a credible balancing test. In the major cases the test was applied *against* speech in circumstances in which the objective observer finds it hard to accept that a clear and present danger really did exist.[57] In Israel, on the other hand, there is no doubt whatsoever that the probable danger test has on most occasions been used in order to prevent incursions on freedom of speech rather than to sanction them.[58]

BEYOND LEGAL PRINCIPLES AND PROBABLE DANGER: CONSTITUTIONAL DOCTRINE

The main influences of U.S. constitutional law on Israeli civil rights jurisprudence have been, without doubt, the acceptance since *Kol Haam*, of freedom of speech and other basic rights as recognized legal principles, and adoption of the probable danger test as the balancing standard in freedom of speech cases. The above discussion has traced the influence of this *Kol Haam* legacy on Israeli law. The effect of U.S. constitutional doctrine on Israeli civil rights jurisprudence is not restricted to the *Kol Haam* legacy, however. A perusal of Israel Supreme Court decisions reveals other influences, which, while not as dramatic and decisive as the *Kol Haam* legacy, certainly deserve mention.

Having established that freedom of speech is a recognized principle in the Israeli legal system, the courts have been called on to define the scope and boundaries of that principle. In doing so they have often relied on U.S. First Amendment jurisprudence, not, of course, as a binding source of law, but as a model from which our system can receive inspiration. I shall now review two instances in which an idea intimately connected with the First Amendment has been adopted by the Israel Supreme Court. I shall then deal with the use of U.S. authorities in defining the scope and boundaries of free speech.

The Fairness Doctrine

The U.S. Federal Communications Commission (FCC) has the statutory task of allocating broadcasting licenses for radio and television. The FCC "fairness doctrine" requires stations to assure fair coverage for each side in discussion of public issues. In *Red Lion Broadcasting Co.* v. *FCC*[59] the U.S. Supreme Court unanimously upheld FCC regulations based on the fairness doctrine which specified the circumstances in which free reply time had to be made available by licensees.

Israel's system of broadcasting is radically different from the U.S. model. Broadcasting is in the hands of the statutory broadcasting authority, a largely, though not totally, autonomous body, and not in the hands of private broadcasting licensees. As a public body acting under law the acts and decisions of the broadcasting authority are subject to the jurisdiction of the High Court of Justice. In two cases challenging decisions of the Broadcasting Authority that were brought before the Israel Supreme Court, sitting as a high court of justice, the court referred to the fairness doctrine.

In *Shiran* v. *Broadcasting Authority*[60] the petitioners attempted to halt the broadcasting of a series on the history of Zionism. They argued that the text gave insufficient weight to the role in Zionist history of Jews from Middle Eastern and North African countries. In refusing to interfere, the court referred both to the fairness doctrine and to the *Red Lion* decision. Shamgar J. pointed out that

in a free country biased presentation of ideas and views is not corrected by *prohibiting* the broadcast by a court order; on the contrary, rules should be made whose object is to preserve the communications media as a platform, from which there will be a free flow of *all* the various views, and not only the views of the employees or directors of the communications media and in the U.S. this trend finds expression in the fairness doctrine.[61]

The second decision, *Zichroni* v. *Broadcasting Authority*,[62] dealt with a directive of the managing committee of the Broadcasting Authority not to allow initiated interviews with public figures in the occupied territories identified as PLO supporters.[63] The petitioner argued that according to the fairness doctrine the Authority is bound to present balanced information to the public and that this includes the duty to present views, as put by the holders of the views themselves. The Supreme Court accepted the validity of the fairness doctrine as a criterion for judging the legality of the Authority's directives. It held that this doctrine obliges the Authority to present the different views on a matter of public interest, but that it does not require it to allow any given individual to present those views. The broadcasting station may decide by whom and how an opposition view will be presented. In summing up, the court stated: "The resolution of the managing committee . . . meets the requirements of the fairness doctrine, as it allows for presentation of complete information in a balanced and fair manner. . . ."[64]

In the present discussion the significant facet of these two cases is not really their outcome.[65] What is significant is the natural way in which the court accepted a doctrine so intimately connected with the First Amendment as a criterion for judging the standards of the Israeli statutory broadcasting authority. Having accepted the U.S. view of the centrality of free speech as a legal principle, First Amendment jurisprudence becomes an obvious model for Israeli judicial decision making.

Preferred Status of Speech

One of the basic premises of modern U.S. constitutional law is that "freedom of expression is so vital in its relationship to the objectives of the Constitution that inevitably it must stand in a preferred position."[66] In *Haaretz* v. *Electricity Corporation*[67] Shamgar J. made an attempt to incorporate this notion into Israeli common law.[68] While this view of Shamgar J. held the day in that appeal, in the further hearing of the case before five justices it was expressly rejected by Landau J. whose opinion was joined by three other justices.[69] In spite of the fact that Shamgar J.'s view was rejected in the *Haaretz* case, Shamgar J. has repeated the preferred freedom notion in later cases without meeting with opposition.[70] Significantly, in his opinion on the powers of the play censorship board,[71] the attorney general also cited the section from Shamgar J.'s opinion in the *Haaretz* case on the special status of freedom of speech. The most important application of the preferred status principle was in the recent decision of Shamgar J. in *Zitrin* v. *Disciplinary Court of the Israel Bar* mentioned above.[72] Shamgar J. relied on this principle to justify recognition of a qualified privilege for journalists against testifying about their sources.

It cannot be assumed that the courts in the above cases would have reached a different outcome had Shamgar J. refrained from repeating the preferred status view rejected in *Haaretz*. Nevertheless, as in the example of the fairness doctrine, we are witness once again to incorporation in Israeli jurisprudence of a doctrine which is intimately connected with the First Amendment.

BEYOND LEGAL PRINCIPLES AND PROBABLE DANGER: SCOPE AND BOUNDARIES OF FREE SPEECH

The First Amendment is cast in what appear to be absolute terms. It contains no exceptions to the restriction of Congress' power to make laws abridging free speech. Nevertheless, the absolute view of the First Amendment has remained a distinctly minority view. First Amendment jurisprudence recognizes various legitimate bases for placing restrictions on speech. The Israel Supreme Court frequently refers to this jurisprudence as a model of the legitimate boundaries on free speech. It also frequently, and as a matter of course, refers to U.S. decisions and learned writings as authority for various propositions.

Reference to U.S. decisions relating to legitimate limitations on free speech began in the *Kol Haam* decision, itself. Agranat J. quoted dicta of Justice Holmes and Justice Brandeis in *Schenck* v. *U.S.*[73] and *Whitney* v. *California*[74] regarding the acceptability of restrictions on speech in times of war or state of emergency.[75] Since then, reference to U.S. authorities both on the demands of free speech theory and its boundaries has become almost standard practice. I will restrict myself here to examples drawn from three cases dealing with the right to demonstrate and its limitations.

As mentioned above, in a series of decisions all written by Barak J., the Israel Supreme Court has recognized the right to demonstrate in the streets as a legal principle, and has subordinated unfettered statutory police discretion to license processions to this principle. In all these decisions the Court has been careful to draw both the limits of police discretion to deny a permit to hold a procession and the limits of the right to hold the procession. In doing so it has relied mainly, though certainly not solely, on U.S. decisions. In *Saar* v. *Minister of Police*,[76] the court quoted extensively from three leading judgments of the U.S. Supreme Court, as authority for the propositions that the right to protest in the streets "is not absolute, but relative,"[77] that regulation of the use of highways to assure the safety and convenience of the public is not inconsistent with civil liberties,[78] and that traffic considerations are legitimate grounds for regulating the right to protest in the streets.[79] In the second decision, *Levi* v. *Police Commander*,[80] the court had to contend with the hostile audience question. It once again cited a number of U.S. Supreme Court decisions and articles published in U.S. law journals as authority for a number of propositions: that public expression of ideas may not be prohibited because of their offensiveness,[81] that hecklers cannot be given a veto over speech,[82] on the necessity of balancing the right to demonstrate with public order considerations,[83] on the primary duty of the police to protect demonstrators,[84] that the right to hold processions belongs not only "to children with flowers in their hands to march in the streets of the town, but also to people with unconventional opinions whose very march causes annoyance and arouses fury"[85] and to the doctrine of the least drastic means.[86] Finally, in *Temple Mount Faithful* v. *Minister of Police*,[87] which dealt with a case on the borderline of the right to demonstrate and freedom of worship, the court cited two U.S. Supreme Court decisions[88] which support the view that freedom of worship is not an absolute freedom and may be subjected to considerations of public order.

It is important to stress that the reference to U.S. authorities is not peculiar to free speech or other constitutional law problems. Israeli courts frequently refer to U.S. and other foreign sources in their judgments on all types of questions, in all fields of law. One cannot assume that the U.S. sources cited in free speech cases are necessarily decisive in these cases or that the courts would not arrive at the same conclusions without them. Nevertheless, the frequent citation of these sources in a constitutional system which is ostensibly so different from the U.S. system is hardly insignificant.

CONCLUSION

Israel still lacks a formal constitution and a bill of rights. In this respect, its legal system remains similar to the British model. However, I hope that the preceding discussion has shown that when one ignores form and looks to substance one sees that First Amendment jurisprudence has had an appreciable influence on judicial decision making in this country. This has not brought us in line with the U.S. model but it has placed us somewhere on the spectrum between the U.S. and British models.

NOTES

1. The term "principle" is used here in the Dworkian sense. A principle does not dictate a particular result, as a legal rule does, but it must be considered relevant in determining the scope of applicability of rules.

2. Consider the following dictum in Marbury v. Madison, 2 L.Ed. 60 (1801): "Certainly all those who have framed written constitutions contemplate them as forming the fundamental and paramount law of the nation, and consequently, the theory of every such government must be, that an act of the legislature, repugnant to the constitution, is void."

3. See de Smith in *Constitutional and Administrative Law*, Harry Street and Rodney Brazier, eds., 4th ed. (Harmondsworth, England: Penguin, 1981). 447. We shall not be dealing with the status of the European Convention on Fundamental Freedoms and Rights to which Britain is a signatory and under which an individual may bring an action against the state before the Commission on Human Rights.

4. See Wallington, "Injunctions and the Right to Demonstrate" (1976) 35 *Cam.L.J.* 82.

5. See Boyle, "Freedom of Expression as a Public Interest in English Law" (1982) *Public Law* 574.

6. See Harry Street, *Freedom, Individual and the Law*, 5th ed. (Harmondsworth, England: Penguin, 1982).

7. On the history of the attempts to adopt a formal constitution in Israel, see Gavison, "The Controversy over Israel's Bill of Rights" (1985) 15 *Israel Yearbook of Human Rights* 113. A series of basic laws have been enacted which were originally intended to be chapters in Israel's formal constitution, but the Supreme Court has held that these laws have no inherent superior status and differ only

in name from other laws: see Negev v. State of Israel (1973) 28 P.D. I 640; Kaniel v. Minister of Justice (1973) 27 P.D. I 794.

8. These attempts are described in a booklet published by the Knesset Constitution and Law Committee.

9. Under Article 46 of the Palestine Order in Council, 1922 in the case of lacunae in the Ottoman law which remained in force after the British occupation, the courts were bound to apply English common law and principles of equity.

10. Three major constitutional cases heard in 1948 were Leon v. Gubernik, 1 P.D. 58; Zeev v. Gubernik, 1 P.D. 86 and Al-Karbutli v. Minister of Defence, 2 P.D. 5. The question in the Leon case was whether antidemocratic emergency legislation enacted during the time of the British Mandate was accepted in Israel, given the statutory provision that the existing law would remain in force "subject to changes arising from the establishment of the state and its authorities." The question in the other two cases was whether such legislation should be regarded as invalid in the light of the promise in the Declaration of Independence that "the State of Israel . . . will be based on principles of freedom, justice and peace in the light of the vision of the prophets of Israel." The only nonlocal precedent cited in the decisions in these three cases was a British decision (Carltona v. Commissioner of Works [1943] All E.R. 560, cited in the Leon case at p. 77).

11. See Bijerano v. Minister of Police, (1949) 2 P.D. 80. In this case the Minister of Police had tried to restrict the entrance to the vehicle licensing office of people who made their living by writing applications for others. The Supreme Court stated that "it is a basic rule that every person has the natural right to engage in work or in a profession of his choosing, as long as engaging in that work or profession is not prohibited under law" (ibid., 82). The Court went on to state that the act of the police could not be regarded as a regular police action but should be seen "as an act which denies one of the basic rights of the citizen, and that absent express or implied authority in the law, the [police] prohibition has no justification" (ibid., 84).

12. See Al-Karbutli v. Minister of Defense, note 10 supra. In this case the Court decided that as a person placed under administrative detention was entitled to apply to an advisory committee to review his case, failure to establish such a committee meant that the power of administrative arrest could not be exercised.

13. (1953) 7 P.D. 871.

14. See Lahav, "American Influence on Israel's Jurisprudence of Free Speech" (1981) 9 *Hastings Constitutional Law Quarterly* 21.

15. Kol Haam v. Minister of Interior (1953) 7 P.D. 166. For a discussion of this case and the factors that led to a change in the judicial attitude in the later case see Shapira, "Self Restraint of the Supreme Court and the Preservation of Civil Liberties" (1973) 2 *Iyunei Mishpat* 640; Lahav, p. 30.

16. See Lahav, note 14 supra.

17. Professor Lahav shows that of all the U.S. authorities the main source cited by Agranat J. was Zechariah Chafee, *Free Speech in the United States* (Cambridge, MA: Harvard University Press, 1941).

18. An example of a country with ordinary basic civil rights legislation was Canada before adoption of the Canadian Charter on Human Rights.

19. 376 U.S. 254 (1964). Under the rule set out in this case it is unconstitutional for a state to impose liability for libel in an action of a public official against a

newspaper unless the official proves that the defamatory material was published with actual malice, that is, either with knowledge that it was false or with reckless disregard as to its truth or falsity.

20. See Haaretz v. Electricity Co. (1974) 31 P.D. II 281. Shamgar J.'s view, which was the majority view in this appeal, was later rejected on a further hearing of the case before a bench of five justices. In this further hearing only Shamgar J. himself supported the view accepted in the appeal: Electricity Co. v. Haaretz (1977) 32 P.D. III 337. The decision in these cases is fully analyzed by Lahav.

21. Section 83 of the Ordinance defines a procession as "fifty or more persons proceeding together or assembling with the object of proceeding together from one place to another whether actually moving or not, and whether such persons are or are not organised in any formation." Meeting is defined as "fifty or more persons assembled for the purpose of hearing any speech or address upon any topic of political interest, or for the purpose of any discussion upon such topic." The writer has discussed the law regarding demonstrations elsewhere: see Kretzmer, "Demonstrations and the Law" (1984) 19 *Israel Law Rev.* 47.

22. See section 85 of the Police Ordinance.

23. See Raffel, "The Right to Demonstrate: A Comparative Study of Israel and the United States" (1976) 11 *Israel Law Rev.* 348, 357–58. And see Kretzmer, 65.

24. See Saar v. Minister of Police (1980) 34 P.D. II 169, 171.

25. In the instant case the court held that the considerations of the commander had not been of sufficient weight to justify denying the permit and it therefore granted an order against the police to issue the permit.

26. See Levi v. District Police Commander (1983) 38 P.D. II 393: Neemanei Har Habayit v. Minister of Police (1983) 38 P.D. II 449.

27. *The Times*, 15 May 1981. Under the above act the police commissioner may not ban a specific procession but may place a general ban on processions for a period not exceeding three months. In this case the ban had been imposed in order to stop processions by the racist National Front. However, the general ban also applied to an annual procession planned by the CND. The police commissioner refused to relax the ban so as to allow this procession.

28. See also Hubbard v. Pitt [1975] 3 W.L.R. 201. This case involved an action by estate agents for an interlocutory injunction against a demonstration outside their offices. Lord Denning suggested that the right to demonstrate and protest on matters of public concern should justify dismissing the application, but his view failed to impress the majority who upheld the injunction awarded by the high court. The right to demonstrate was not a relevant factor in their decision which was based on the rules laid down in a previous case by the House of Lords for granting interlocutory injunctions. The dissenting Lord Denning's support for the right to demonstrate is regarded as the strongest judicial support in Britain for recognition of this right as a legal principle: See Williams, "Freedom of Assembly and Free Speech: Changes and Reforms in England" (1975) 1 *U. of N.S. Wales L.J.* 97, 119. And see Wallington, note 4 supra. In CARAF v. U.K. (Application 8440/78) 21 D. and R. of European Commission of Human Rights 138, the Commission of Human Rights held that a flat ban placed on processions in London did not contravene Article 11 of the European Convention on Human Rights.

29. See Public Performances (Censorship) Ordinance. In the meantime, this ordinance has been suspended until 1992.

30. See Opinion of the Attorney General in the Matter of Censorship under the Public Performances (Censorship) Ordinance (1982) 17 *Israel Law Rev.* 511, 523.

31. Ibid.

32. See Leor v. Public Board for Censorship of Plays (1986) 41 P.D. III 421.

33. See (1968) 49 Divrei HaKnesset, 2723, 2728; 52 Divrei HaKnesset 2971–72.

34. See 49 Divrei HaKnesset 2728.

35. (1986) 41 P.D. II 337.

36. Major examples are the Defence (Emergency) Regulations, 1945, the Press Ordinance, 1933, and the Public Performances (Censorship) Ordinance.

37. For example, the Rabbinical Courts (marriage and divorce) Law, 1953 provides that all marriages of Jews in Israel will be conducted according to the law of the Torah. This forces even nonbelieving Jews to marry in a religious ceremony.

38. The above law regarding jurisdiction of the rabbinical courts may be regarded as an infringement of the right to equality of women. The law granting extra children's allowances to families of persons who have served at any time and for any period of time in the army may be regarded as discriminatory against Arabs who are not recruited for army service.

39. See, for example, the judgement of Landau D.P. in Al Assad v. Minister of Interior, (1979) 34 P.D. I 505, 513, in which he described Mandatory legislation which grants unfettered discretion to the executive to deny a license for a newspaper without giving reasons as "inimical to basic concepts of a democracy regarding freedom of speech and expression."

40. See the article of the present writer cited in note 21, p. 65.

41. 341 U.S. 494 (1951). On the influence of this decision on the *Kol Haam* decision see Lahav.

42. See the *Kol Haam* decision, p. 891.

43. Ibid., p. 890. This was the very reason for rejection of this test in the *Dennis* case: see Ely, *Democracy and Distrust* (Cambridge, MA: Harvard University Press, 1980), p. 108.

44. He referred specifically to the decisions in Schenck v. U.S., 249 U.S. 47 (1919); Abrams v. U.S., 250 U.S. 616 (1919); and Whitney v. California, 274 U.S. 357 (1927).

45. (1962) 16 P.D. 2407.

46. Ibid., p. 2418.

47. In one area the Supreme Court has rejected the probable danger test in favor of a more restrictive test. In interpreting the section in the law that deals with publication of matters likely to influence the outcome of a trial, the Supreme Court adopted the test of the reasonable possibility, rather than the clear and present danger test or the probable danger test: See Disenchuk v. Attorney General, (1962) 17 P.D. 169; Azulai v. State of Israel, (1982) 37 P.D. II 565. The court expressly rejected the approach of the majority in the leading U.S. case Bridges v.California, 314 U.S. 252, which applied the clear and probable danger test in this context.

48. (1983) 38 P.D. II 393.

49. Barak J. mentioned that the court had not always distinguished between the probable danger test adopted by Agranat J. in *Kol Haam* and the clear and

present danger test rejected by him. He stated that the difference between the two tests is not great and that some commentators even regard them as two formulae for the same test: ibid. In Zichroni v. Broadcasting Authority, (1982) 37 P.D. I 757, 780, Bach J. stated that the test adopted in *Kol Haam* was the clear and present danger test.

50. (1985) 41 P.D. III 255.

51. It would seem, however, that Barak J. widened the scope of the term *public order* by including therein offense to public sensitivities. The view that the racist nature of speech does not justify refusal of the Broadcasting Authority to broadcast it was rejected by Bach J. The third justice, Netanyahu J., refrained from taking a stand on this issue.

52. See Laurence H. Tribe, *American Constitutional Law* (Mineola, NY: Foundation Press, 1978), pp. 608–631.

53. The leading decision in the trend against this test is Brandenburg v. Ohio, 395 U.S. 444 (1969).

54. See Thornhill v. Alabama, 310 U.S. 88 (1940) in which a statute prohibiting all picketing was held invalid since it banned peaceful picketing protected by the First Amendment.

55. See Papachristou v. City of Jacksonville, 405 U.S. 156 (1971) in which a vagrancy statute was held invalid. The vagueness test is not strictly a First Amendment test but a general constitutional test: see Tribe, p. 718. In one case the Israel Supreme Court did interfere with an administrative decision that limited freedom of speech on grounds of vagueness. In Zichroni v. Broadcasting Authority, 36 P.D. I 757, the question concerned the validity of a resolution passed by the Managing Committee of the Broadcasting Authority that forbade broadcasting of initiated interviews with public figures in the occupied territories who identify with the PLO or regard it as the sole and legitimate representative of the Palestinians in those territories. The majority of the court refused to overrule this resolution on the basis of the argument that it placed a restriction on freedom of speech which did not meet the probable danger test. However, the Court held that the resolution was vague in that it did not define the terms "public figures" and "identifying with the PLO."

56. See Ely, pp. 107–08.

57. See ibid.: "The clear and present danger test has been the object of considerable liberal nostalgia, and on its surface seems at least moderately demanding. The problem is that the defendants in the three cases in which it was introduced all ended up going to prison for quite tame and ineffectual expression."

58. In only one major case was this test applied so as to allow an act curbing freedom of speech by the administration: See Omer International Inc. v. Minister of Interior, (1981) 36 P.D. I 228.

59. 395 U.S. 367 (1969).

60. (1981) 35 P.D. III 368.

61. Ibid., p. 378.

62. See note 53.

63. Ibid.

64. Ibid., p. 776.

65. The view of the majority in the Zichroni case is highly problematical. With

all due respect, it is submitted that in this case the better view was the dissent of Bach J., according to which the directive of the Broadcasting Authority was an unwarranted wide restriction on freedom of speech, that prevented balanced presentation of many matters and was an abridgment of the public's right to receive comprehensive and balanced information in the most direct manner.

66. See McKay, "The Preference for Freedom" (1959) 34 *N.Y.U.L. Rev.* 1182, 1184. This view was strenuously opposed by Frankfurter J., who in Kovacs v. Cooper, 336 U.S. 77 (1949), referred to talk of a preferred position of freedom of speech as a mischievous phrase. See McKay.

67. (1974) 31 P.D. II 28.

68. Ibid., p. 295: "Freedom of expression and a statutory provision which limits it do not have the same equal status; if it is consistent with the text one must at all times prefer the right [i.e. freedom of expression D.K.] over a statutory provision which tends to limit it."

69. See Electricity Co. v. Haaretz, (1977) 32 P.D. III, 343. Landau J. not only rejected the idea of a preferred freedom but expressed his opinion that in a clash between a *freedom* and a *right* (such as the right to reputation) the right was to be preferred.

70. See Neiman v. Chairman of Central Elections Committee, (1984) 39 P.D. II 233, 245–46; Miterani v. Minister of Transport, (1981) 37 P.D. III 337, 356–57; Zitrin v. Disciplinary Court of Israel Bar, see note 35 supra.

71. See note 30.

72. See note 35.

73. 249 U.S. 47 (1919).

74. 274 U.S. 357 (1927).

75. See *Kol Haam* decision, note 13, p. 880.

76. See note 24.

77. From the leading opinion of Justice Roberts in Hague v. CIO, 307 U.S. 496, 515 (1939).

78. Quoting from Cox v. New Hampshire, 312 U.S. 569, 574 (1941).

79. Quoting from Cox v. State of Louisiana, 379 U.S. 536, 554 (1965).

80. See note 26.

81. Quoting from Bachellor v. Maryland, 397 U.S. 564, 567 (1970).

82. Quoting from Kalven, *The Negro and the First Amendment* (Columbus: Ohio State University Press, 1965).

83. Quoting from Fortas, *Concerning Dissent and Civil Disobedience* (New York: New American Library, 1968).

84. Quoting from a number of sources: Chafee, *Free Speech in the U.S.* (1948); Hague v. CIO, note 77; and the dissent of Black J. in Feiner v. New York, 340 U.S. 315, 326 (1951).

85. Citing Terminiello v. City of Chicago, 337 U.S. 1, 4 (1949).

86. Citing Note, "Less Drastic Means and the First Amendment" 78 *Yale L.J.* 464 (1969).

87. (1983) 38 P.D. II 449.

88. Cantwell v. Connecticut, 319 U.S. 296 (1940) and West Virginia State Board of Education v. Barnette, 319 U.S. 624 (1943).

Comment _____

THE ISSUE OF RELIGION IN THE ISRAELI SUPREME COURT

Arnold Enker

It seems to me that some of the ideas that Madison promoted, as developed in Professor Mendelson's paper, and which were not accepted in the United States, might have a relevance for future development in Israel. I want to use as my example certain problems of religion and state in Israel.

Of course, Israel does not have a written constitution, and therefore we do not have a First Amendment which declares that Congress shall make no law with respect to the establishment of religion. Also, of course, Israel was intended to be a very different kind of society, culturally and politically, from the United States. It was intended to be a Jewish state, not a society in which religious and national identities are completely separated. And so, the notion of a high Jeffersonian wall of separation between state and religion certainly would not be the most apt metaphor with which to describe the Israeli scene. The problems concerning the relationship between religion and the state are quite different in Israel.

Given that setting, and realizing that there is no legal, political, or cultural limit to the power of the Knesset to legislate, it must be appreciated that merely because certain legislation is religious or promotes religious interests is not, in and of itself, an argument against its validity.

Judicial review of religious legislation in Israel, therefore, relates exclusively to a review of secondary legislation, that is, legislation by local governments—local ordinances—and legislation by ministers or by governmental agencies in the form of regulations. Here again, the fact that this secondary legislation is designed to promote some religious interests is not, in and of itself, a ground for invalidating the legislation. The issue becomes one of jurisdiction. Does the local government or the minister have jurisdiction to deal with this problem? Also, as with any review of secondary legislation, it is a question of the reasonableness of the enactment.

There is a substantial connection between this matter of jurisdiction and the question of reasonableness. Primary legislation, of the Knesset in the case of Israel, generally reflects the broadest possible consensus any given society can muster, and is therefore more likely to reflect a reasonable accommodation of all the interests at stake. On the other hand, secondary legislation often reflects a narrower range of interests and of issues. Local government in one part of the country may be very different from local government in another part of the country. Each local government reflects a particular majority or combination of political forces peculiar to itself. Local governments are subject to varying pressures, including the pressures of threats of violence and even actual violence.

The result is that local government regulations often do not accommodate as broad a range of interests and therefore do not have that assurance of reasonableness as does national legislation.

That is not to say that arrangements approved by the national government or by the parliament are of necessity reasonable and do not ever reflect particular narrow pressures. Given the peculiar electoral system here in Israel, in which we have proportional representation of all interests, clearly a very small political group can in some circumstances use its control of the balance of power to promote its own parochial program, whether this be in the religious, or any other sphere. But I would suggest that there are severe limits to how far that power can be exercised. Apart from the fact that you cannot ordinarily use violence to promote your legislative aims at the national level, there is also a severe limit as to how much of your program you can promote by using your control over the balance of power without prompting alterations in the political balance of power which gives you such control. And I think we have seen just such political developments in recent years in Israel.

Given this background, I think that many of the Supreme Court decisions in Israel reviewing the exercise of local government powers in the religious sphere, although articulated in terms of jurisdiction, cannot be really understood in those terms, without understanding them also in terms of the Madisonian concept to which Professor Mendelson adverts in his chapter. What the Court really is looking to in these situations is the reasonableness of the arrangement. Does the arrangement reflect a broad consensus? Does the arrangement reflect a fair balance and accommodation of the conflicting political interests?

I can give one or two examples. Some years ago, the Supreme Court of Israel heard a series of cases in which various local governments, in one guise or another and through the exercise of one power or another, sought to forbid the sale of pork in restaurants and butcher shops. One after another, the Supreme Court struck down these arrangements on jurisdictional grounds, in other words, that although the local governments involved had the authority to license local business operations, they did not have the jurisdiction to legislate in the sphere of religion. The Court reasoned further that even if we do not view this legislation as a matter promoting religion, but as promoting national ideals or nationalism (and many people do view pork not as a religious issue but as a symbol of Jewish nationalism and of the Jewish struggle throughout history for the independence of Jewish life and Jewish culture), nevertheless, this matter of promoting national ideals and national symbols also is a matter that should be dealt with by the national legislature rather than by local government.

Yet when it came to matters such as Sabbath and holiday closing laws, the Court did not take the same view. The Court sustained local legislation ordering the closing of stores and other enterprises on the Sabbath even though here, too, it was dealing with local legislation that concerned religion or national symbols. In fact, these laws defined the hours of required closure exactly as in the Jewish religious law rather than as one would expect to find in a secular law. I think one of the reasons for this result was that, although the particular legislation was local, it had a basis in national legislation in the sense that there was national legislation which defined what were the days of rest. This national legislation, too, fixed those days of rest in religious terms.

A later decision seems to me to illustrate this point even more sharply. In this case, the issue was: May a municipality order the closing of restaurants on Tisha b'Av evening? Tisha b'Av is the Hebrew date of the anniversary of the destruction of the Temple some nineteen hundred and seventeen years ago. It is a day of national mourning. Many municipalities, probably most, forbid the opening of restaurants and places of entertainment on the eve of Tisha b'Av. Is that legal? Now the national law I referred to a moment ago declaring days of rest includes the Sabbath and includes various other holidays. But it says nothing about Tisha b'Av. No national legislation declares that Tisha b'Av is a legal day of rest. The local ordinances at issue did not require that businesses close on that day, only restaurants and places of entertainment.

The Supreme Court held this local regulation valid. Why? Because, it said, this is not really a matter of religion. It is a matter of national consciousness relating to the loss of our national independence. Ah, but in the pork cases the Court had said that national issues and issues of symbolic nationalism were matters that require national legislation. How do you reconcile the two? I think the answer is that clearly there was no real political controversy in the country over the question of closing of restaurants and places of entertainment on Tisha b'Av. No particular concrete interest was being violated by the order of closure. The opposition to this ordinance was based on an ideological position committed to a complete separation of government from all national religious symbols, a position not shared by the overwhelming consensus of Israeli society, on this issue, at least. In other words, the Tisha b'Av legislation, although local, reflected a broad national consensus and was a reasonable accommodation of all substantial interests; it was not the result of some local pressure.

It is no secret that the controversy over the relationship between religion and state is one of the impediments to the adoption of a written constitution in Israel. Permit me to suggest a compromise based on Madison's views as elaborated by Professor Mendelson that may help solve the problem. Perhaps, in this area of religion and state, our proposed constitution may dispense with judicial review which could invalidate national legislation. If our legislative system can be made more stable and more responsive to the public will, national legislation in matters of religion will not be likely to stray far from the mainstream of national opinion and will usually accommodate all of the major interests concerned.

In this regard, issues of religion and state differ from other issues of individual rights. The danger that the national legislature may be too solicitous of governmental interests at the expense of private rights necessitates the offsetting influence of judicial review, in order to protect such individual rights. But in the area of religion and state, where the competing interests are different ideological commitments in the community, rather than governmental and individuals' rights, the national legislature is more likely to yield a balanced result.

In conclusion, then, a lesson we might learn from Madison's writings is that constitution making does not necessarily require that the courts always have the last say on interpreting the constitution. Judicial review of local legislation and of secondary legislation commends itself more than does such review of national legislation. For Israel, this distinction may offer an answer to the search for appropriate constitutional structures that will govern the relationship between religion and the state.

X SOCIAL CHANGE AND SOCIAL JUSTICE: A NEW ROLE FOR THE CONSTITUTION?

17 Of Courts, Judicial Tools, and Equal Protections of the Laws

Henry J. Abraham

Even the most passive and cursory observer of *la vie quotidienne* in the United States during the past half-century must have recognized—and do so contemporarily—that social change has been as dramatic as it has been inevitable and that much, if not most, of its catalytic thrust has been due to its constitutionalization by what Alexander Hamilton— in what must surely rank as one of the euphemisms of the ages— charmingly inaccurately styled as "the least dangerous" branch of the government, namely, the federal judiciary. With or without sophisticated quantification as demonstrable proof, there is simply no gainsaying that, led by the Supreme Court of the United States, the judiciary has been the engine of and for social change and social justice. At times, it has been true to the hallowed inscription atop its glorious facade at number one First Street, S.E., Washington, DC, namely, the mandate of "Equal Justice Under the Law"; at others, as Chief Justice Warren Burger (and his onomatopoetic namesake Raoul Berger) would charge Associate Justice William O. Douglas with craving, it has embraced the conceptualization of "Justice At Any Cost." Its preeminent tool, of course, has been the seminal Fourteenth Amendment to the Constitution. That celebrated Civil War Amendment became a part and parcel of the basic document in 1868; was rendered more or less nugatory in terms of social change and social justice by the triple blows of *The Slaughterhouse Cases*,[1] *The Civil Rights Cases*,[2] and *Plessy* v. *Ferguson*[3]; served as a handy rationalization for the defense of laissez faire "über Alles" for the following four decades; and commenced to be turned into a latter-day lever for the realization of my assigned topic for this paper as a result of the dramatic 1937 "switch in time that saved nine." If the judiciary's moving finger of time lives up to the implications of Associate Justice William J. Brennan, Jr.'s August 1986 exhortation to the American

Bar Association, all we really need to do to attain nirvana is to utilize *de maximus*, and uninhibitedly, the open-ended terminology of the amendment's Section 1, that is, its "privileges or immunities," "due process of law", and "equal protection of the laws" seductive generalities.

Of that invitational trio of potentially cataclysmic and catalytic founts of judicial activism, the Fourteenth Amendment's Equal Protection of the Laws Clause indubitably constitutes the most problematic aspect of constitutional law today. In many respects, examination of and reflection upon equal protection, and how the judiciary has struggled to define and apply its often shadowy emanations and penumbras, reveal the dynamism inherent in any notion of a living Constitution. I shall endeavor to trace the constitutional nexus between the old equal protection and the new, and essay some general suggestions about how this portion of the law can be viewed in relation, first, to the manifold aspects of civil rights and liberties and, second, to the Constitution as a whole— our Constitution, which is both written and elastic, both specific and general. It is, and it ought to be, our sacred institutional cow.

Following the great nationalist era of the Marshall Court (1801–35) and Taney's at least partially redressive states rights period (1836–64), the Supreme Court under Chief Justices S. P. Chase (1864–74) and Waite (1874–88) more or less declined to forge consistent—at least visibly consistent—constitutional law, their chief concern being the confirmation of state authority over individuals and federal authority over interstate commerce. Yet under Chief Justices Fuller (1888–1910), E. D. White (1910–21), Taft (1921–30), and the first seven years of Hughes (1930–37), the Supreme Court entered a span of time marked principally by a sanctimonious attitude towards private property and a jaundiced eye toward social-economic experimentation by legislatures, although there were some notable exceptions. The Justices of that 50-year period, as John R. Commons commented, "spoke as, the first authoritative faculty of political economy in the world's history." They justified their penchant, in the economic-proprietarian realm, to strike down state and federal laws as allegedly violative of substantive due process, by what they viewed as the inherent commands of the Fifth and Fourteenth Amendments. Although the Constitution makes no mention of such substance-oriented due process guarantees, having limited itself in both letter and spirit to procedural safeguards, the justices were more than willing to expand the umbrage of the Fifth and Fourteenth Amendments to render private property and marketplace activity inviolable. The memorable case of *Lochner* v. *New York*,[4] represents the apogee of the substantive due process doctrine: there the Court struck down (5:4) a New York statute limiting the workweek of bakery employees to 60 hours. The proprietarian, laissez-faire, rationalizing reasoning by Justice Peckham for the narrow Court majority is assailed in Justice Holmes's now legendary dissent:

The 14th Amendment does not enact Mr. Herbert Spencer's *Social Statics* . . . [A] Constitution is not intended to embody a particular economic theory, whether of paternalism and the organic relation of the citizen to the state or of *laissez-faire*.[5]

Out of this era of heightened judicial deference to private property and the open marketplace the Supreme Court subsequently crafted its initial definition and application of the equal protection of the laws.

This deferential attitude of course changed dramatically and drastically following the New Deal showdown between President Roosevelt and the Court that produced the seminal switch in time that saved nine. Changing judicial attitudes vis-à-vis equal protection greatly contributed to the modern Court's double standard posture of placing much greater scrutiny over legislative infringement of so-called "preferred" or "cultural" freedoms, while at the same time generally deferring to the legislature in economic-proprietarian matters. It was Justice Holmes's successor, Justice Benjamin Nathan Cardozo's majority opinion in *Palko* v. *Connecticut*,[6] which referred to "preferred freedoms" for the first time. That opinion was one of two catalysts that moved the Court towards the new equal protection jurisprudence. In *Palko* Justice Cardozo—the supreme stylist and jurists' jurist, whom fate permitted but six short years on the Court—distinguished between those rights that are and those that are not "implicit in the concept of ordered liberty." Enunciating and punctuating his neo-Jeffersonian dichotomy, he wrote that

we reach a different plane of social and moral values when we pass to . . . freedom of thought and speech [which] is the matrix, the indispensable condition, of nearly every other form of freedom.[7]

This rather quickly and widely embraced notion that certain rights and freedoms guaranteed by the Constitution are more fundamental to the political order than others is crucial to our understanding of how and why the Court later would erect the disconcerting varying levels of judicial scrutiny and attitudes towards certain clauses in the Constitution, and their relationship to legislative activity, be the latter one of approbation or interference. The Court's new conception of equal protection would come to lie at the center of this new dynamic judicial scrutiny. To what extent Justice Cardozo would approve what his "T" square dichotomy has spawned, is a fascinating *quaere*.

The second catalyst in the evolution of new equal protection came four months later with Justice Stone's famed Footnote Number Four—authored chiefly by his brilliant law clerk, Louis Lusky, with an important assist by Chief Justice Hughes—in *United States* v. *Carolene Products Company*.[8] Carolene itself is a nondescript case dealing with the Filled Milk Act of 1923 and the scope of Congress's legislative power over interstate commerce. The footnote consists of three paragraphs, the first of which was supplied by Hughes, who was eager to present a formal connection with constitutional text. It addresses the possibility of a narrower presumption of constitutionality when legislation appears ipso facto to be within a specific prohibition of the Constitution, particularly vis-à-vis the Bill of Rights and those portions therein understood to have been, or to be, incorporated within the Fourteenth Amendment's Due Process of Law Clause. This paragraph is an excellent articulation, in microcosm, of the new equal protection's abandonment of the old equal protection's presumption of legislative constitutionality and deference towards legislative judgment.

The Court's move from economic-proprietarian self-restraint to judicial activism in the civil rights and liberties sphere was historically dramatic and telling. The Hughes Court (1930–41) continued along a course much reminiscent of the nineteenth century substantive due process era, as it struck down no fewer than 16 pieces of New Deal legislation between 1934 and 1936. But finally in *West Coast Hotel Co.* v. *Parrish*,[9] Chief Justice Hughes and Associate Justice Roberts joined Brandeis, Cardozo, and Stone in at last providing a 5:4 majority upholding Washington State's minimum wage law for women and children. During the same term, the Court also upheld 5:4 in *National Labor Relations Board* v. *Jones and Laughlin Steel Corporation*[10] the constitutionality of Congress' New Deal milestone authorization of the National Labor Relations Act of 1935. Hughes had seen the handwriting on the wall of politics, and persuaded Roberts to go along with him. By virtue of the decision the Court's meddlesome approach towards state economic-proprietarian legislation, often under the guise of substantive due process, ended—only to be replaced by the still more meddlesome spirit of the double standard, largely fueled under the guise of the new equal protection. A new "Lochnerism" had come of age.

In analyzing such a complicated and convoluted entity as new equal protection which emerged in full force in the Warren era, it is often utilitarian to develop signposts to help maintain one's perspective and keep the sundry different aspects of equal protection in order. The two dominant aspects of new equal protection jurisprudence have been the Court's development of, first, varying suspect classifications and categories and, second, fundamental rights and interests. Indicative of the often amorphous nature of new equal protection is the fact that these two developments have arisen from totally different justifications, with totally different purposes, and with totally different results that often run directly counter to one another. Euphemistically, we might explain away much of the confusion as the inevitable result of dynamic, organic constitutional law operating within the framework of a living constitution. Other observers not so fond of the Warren Court's innovations in the realm of civil rights and liberties, in general, and the equal protection clause, in particular, are more forthright in calling a spade a spade, and in condemning the Court's seemingly endless gradations and inconsistencies as *ad hominem*—induced jurisprudence.

The first strand of new equal protection that must be addressed is the Court's creation of a suspect category/classification scheme. To the extent that they are at all consistently identifiable, the Court seems to have limited itself to four standard levels of review—rationality, heightened scrutiny, very strict scrutiny, and suspect scrutiny—in ascending order of stringency. As we shall see, however, the Court has not limited itself in applying different levels of review to different areas of jurisprudence under different circumstances, thereby producing infinitely different results. The key to keeping abreast of this suspect classification strand of new equal protection is to endeavor to analyze, separately, the relationship between particular areas of jurisprudence and the various standards of review. Such an approach allows us to trace the ebb and flow of the Court's review practices, in general, and as they relate to the equal protection clause, in particular.

The Court has consistently applied suspect category of review to legislation involving race, alienage, and nationality. One initial prerequisite for the invocation of suspect classification is the demonstration of purposeful discriminatory intent on the part of either the legislators or the legislation in question. In *Strauder* v. *West Virginia*,[11] Justice Strong had revealed the Court's evolving position on the content and purpose of the Fourteenth Amendment. Although *Strauder* only dealt with overt state discrimination against blacks, the Court subsequently has placed all legislative classifications based on race and ancestry, as they trace to *de jure* discrimination, under the suspect standard of review. The Court's expanding application of suspect classifications in this area is summed up well by Justice Black, who spoke for the six-member majority in *Korematsu* v. *United States*.

[All] legal restrictions which curtail the civil rights of a single racial group are immediately suspect. That is not to say that all such restrictions are unconstitutional. It is to say that courts must subject them to the most rigid scrutiny. Pressing public necessity may sometimes justify the existence of such restrictions; racial antagonism never can.[12]

Indeed, the most consistent aspect of new equal protection has been the triggering of suspect judicial standards of review on the part of legislation cutting across racial lines. *Brown* v. *Board of Education*,[13] of course, unanimously overturned the "separate but equal" doctrine outlined in *Plessy* v. *Ferguson*,[14] as a violation of the equal protection clause of the Fourteenth Amendment, and required the states to desegregate their public schools. The companion case of *Bolling* v. *Sharpe*,[15] also unanimously decided, imposed the same requirement on the federal government and the District of Columbia public schools, here as a violation of the Fourteenth Amendment's due process clause. In *Loving* v. *Virginia*,[16] the Court, again unanimously, struck down on equal protection grounds, Virginia's miscegenation law that forbade interracial marriages. Chief Justice Warren held for the Court that

the clear and central purpose of the 14th Amendment was to eliminate all official state sources of invidious discrimination in the states. There can be no question but that Virginia's miscegenation statutes rest solely upon distinctions drawn according to race.[17]

As noted earlier, the Court initially made invocation of suspect standard of review dependent upon determination of state discriminatory intent, *à la Strauder*, therefore reaching only *de jure* discrimination. But in what would be the last unanimous decision on the issue, in *Swann* v. *Charlotte–Mecklenburg Board of Education*,[18] the Burger Court blurred the distinctions between *de jure* and *de facto* discrimination and, at least in the desegregation realm, applied suspect classification to both. And, in *Keyes* v. *School District No. 1*,[19] Denver, Colorado, the now fractured Court pushed its mandate for school busing into those areas of the country untouched by state-mandated segregation. Perhaps surprisingly, in *Washington* v. *Davis*,[20] it seemed to revive the requirement of demonstrable proof of state discriminatory *intent*, by letting stand a qualifying test administered fairly by the District of Columbia Metropolitan Police Department that tended to hinder black applicants' chances for employment, thereby perpetuating *de facto segregation*. Not surprisingly, the life span of the "intent" test would be short, giving way on both the voting and affirmative action fronts in the early to mid–1980s, albeit practically never without large dissenting votes. Good examples are *Thornburg* v. *Gingles*,[21] in the voting sphere (5:4 on adopting a "result" rather than an "intent" test); and an entire string of closely divided affirmative action/reverse discrimination cases in 1985, 1986, and 1987 (usually 5:4 or 6:3).

The second and third most stringent levels of review employed by the Supreme Court in conjunction with equal protection are "very strict scrutiny" and "heightened scrutiny," respectively. It is in these two levels of review that the confusion, contradiction, and inconsistency of new equal protection jurisprudence is most acute and most prevalent. And probably the most problematic aspect of this utterly vexatious portion of new equal protection has been the development and application of appropriate standards of review in the so-called "benign" use of criteria affecting race and gender. On the "benign" use of racial criteria, the Burger Court launched the affirmative action litigation explosion in *University of California Regents* v. *Bakke*.[22] Justice Powell, writing for a highly polarized Court, in two separate 5:4 opinions, held that the use of strict racial quotas in university admissions processes was violative of the equal protection clause and Title VI of the 1964 Civil Rights Act, but that race could be used as a "plus" by admissions officers toward the compelling state interest of achieving a diverse student body. In *United Steelworkers* v. *Weber*,[23] Justice Brennan, for a five-member majority, extended the constitutionality of voluntary affirmative action plans in the private sector workplace in the face of the Civil Rights Act of 1964's Title VII's crystal clear statutory requirement of racially neutral hiring practices. Indeed, he read the "NO" of the statute to be spelled "Y-E-S." And in *Fullilove* v. *Klutznick*,[24] the Court (6:3) upheld one version of a congressionally designed and sanctioned voluntary affirmative action plan in the public sector workplace, here floor-enacted by Congress, notwithstanding the explicit strictures of Title VII. Since then a narrow majority of the justices has usually sanctioned race-conscious preferential treatment except in the instance of neutrally established seniority systems. It is thus fair to conclude that although the Court purports to apply rather stringent standards of review in "benign" racial classification cases—whether it be "heightened" or "very strict" scrutiny, or some combination therein—the Court, practically speaking, is applying a test far more akin to the rationality test of old equal protection in the area of affirmative action, *pace* the latter's indubitable movement into reverse discrimination.

Sex, alienage, and illegitimacy, although in varying degrees, have all also triggered heightened or very strict scrutiny. Thus, in *Reed* v. *Reed*,[25] appellant urged the Court to find *sex* a suspect category, which the 9:0 court promptly declined to do in favor of a version of the rationality test. In *Frontiero* v. *Richardson*,[26] four members of the 8:1 majority (Brennan, Douglas, Marshall, and White) wanted to invoke the test of "compelling state interest" to affirm the right of a female worker in the uniformed services to claim her spouse as a dependent for the purposes of increased remuneration, just as her male counterparts had always been able to do. But Justice Powell, joined by Chief Justice Burger and Justice Blackmann, plus Justice Stewart, speaking separately in concurring in the results in *Frontiero*, expressed the Court majority's unwillingness to place gender in the suspect category:

[It] is unnecessary for the Court in this case to characterize sex as a suspect classification, with all of the far reaching implications of such a holding. *Reed*, which abundantly supports our decision today, did not add sex to the narrowly limited group of classifications which are inherently suspect.[27]

It has not been added to that group to this day.

Along the *alienage* frontier, the Court has vacillated between applying the strict scrutiny level of review and, more recently, a standard of review much akin to the rationality test. In *Graham* v. *Richardson*[28] the Burger Court, *sans* dissent, thus applied strict scrutiny in holding that states could not deny welfare benefits to aliens. Additionally, in *In re Griffiths*[29] a divided Court utilized strict scrutiny in striking down Connecticut's law excluding aliens from law practice, and in *Sugarman* v. *Dougall*,[30] over Justice Rehnquist's dissent, it invalidated a New York law providing that only U.S. citizens could hold permanent positions in the civil service. Yet, the Burger Court in the late 1970s began scaling back the strictness of review in alienage cases. In *Foley* v. *Connelie*[31] it ruled 6:3 with Justices Brennan, Marshall, and Stevens in dissent, that New York could bar the employment of aliens as state troopers. And in *Ambach* v. *Norwich*[32] the Court upheld 5:4 a New York law that predicated employment as a public school teacher upon U.S. citizenship. Invoking a standard of review remarkably reminiscent of the rationality test, Justice Powell's majority opinion held that

the Constitution requires only that a citizenship requirement applicable to teaching in the public schools bear a rational relationship to a legitimate state interest ... The restriction is carefully framed to serve its purposes, as it bars from teaching only those aliens who have demonstrated their unwillingness to obtain United States citizenship.[33]

Here Justice Blackmann joined the *Foley* trio of dissenters in what had become a fairly predictable quartet of dedicatees to the highest standards of review.

In the realm of *illegitimacy* the Court has utilized a strange hybrid of heightened scrutiny and the rationality test. Without question the area of illegitimacy is presently the most inconsistent aspect of new equal protection jurisprudence. Almost all we can conclude with even a modicum of certainty is that the Court has remained unwilling to invoke suspect classification in illegitimacy cases, although it seemed to begin to walk along that road in *Levy* v. *Louisiana*.[34] Yet it soon commenced to waver, and in *Mathews* v. *Lucas*[35] it invoked something less than strict scrutiny in sustaining 6:3 a Social Security Act provision that had proved disadvantageous to many illegitimate children. In *Trimble* v. *Gordon*[36] it did, however, stop short (5:4) of relegating illegitimacy to an unmitigated rationality test. Dissenting Justice Rehnquist, not amused, admonished the Court for what he viewed as its ongoing penchant for bench-made jurisprudence, fraught with inconsistencies, through the new equal protection doctrine. As he noted,

More than a century of equal protection decisions have produced a syndrome wherein this Court seems to regard the Equal Protection Clause as a cat-of-nine-tails to be kept in the closet as a threat to legislatures which may, in the view of the judiciary, get out of hand and pass "arbitrary," "illogical," or "unreasonable" laws.[37]

The Court's dramatic jurisprudential shift in moving from the old equal protection to the new cuts directly across such Blackstonian notions of proper deference to the legislature.

The Supreme Court's second major strand of new equal protection—the development of the doctrine of fundamental rights and interests—does not disturb any of the trends we have noted in outlining the various suspect and subsidiary categories/classifications. Although the fundamental rights and interest doctrine has been far less prevalent in equal protection jurisprudence relative to suspect categories, its impact in further illuminating Justice Cardozo's first articulation of the "preferred freedoms" concept in *Palko*[38] (now a half-century ago) has contributed to the efficacy of the suspect categories themselves. The fundamental rights and interests strand has had particular impact in voting rights and access to ballot cases. Beginning with *Harper* v. *Virginia Board of Elections*,[39] in which the Court struck down the poll tax—Justices Black, Harlan, and Stewart dissenting—the right to vote was raised to "fundamental" status, and therefore entitled to greater judicial scrutiny. Justice Douglas, writing for the majority, held that "A state violates [equal protection] whenever it makes the affluence of a voter or payment of fee an electoral standard . . . the requirement of fee paying causes an "invidious" discrimination [that] runs afoul of the Equal Protection Clause."[40] Additionally, the notion of the fundamental nature of the right to vote played a role in the Court's significant decision in *Kramer* v. *Union Free School District No. 15*.[41] There the Court (6:3)—with the same three justices as in the *Harper* case in dissent—struck down a New York law that restricted participation in certain school district elections to those persons who own taxable real property within the district and/ or who are parents (or have custody) of children enrolled in the local public schools. Petitioner Kramer failed the state's test for participation

on both counts—he enjoyed his single, propertyless, childless status—
and the Court, with Chief Justice Warren delivering the opinion, ruled
that

> [the] issue is not whether the legislative judgments are rational. A more exacting
> standard obtains. The issue is whether Sec. 2012 requirements do in fact suffi-
> ciently further a compelling state interest. [The] requirements of Sec. 2012 are
> not sufficiently tailored to limiting the franchise to those "primarily interested"
> in school affairs to justify the denial of the franchise to appellant and members
> of his class.[42]

Finally, the Court has also struck down in a series of cases various
durational requirements placed upon the right to vote. In *Dunn* v.
Blumstein[43] it invalidated (6:1) Tennessee's three-month durational requirement because it unduly impinged upon voters' fundamental rights
to vote and travel. The fundamental rights and interest strand of new
equal protection has served the Court well in expanding the suffrage as
well as maintaining access to the ballot, notably, for example, in *Williams*
v. *Rhodes*,[44] in which Ohio's formidable third-party petition requirements
were struck down (6:3) under challenge by George Wallace's American
Independent party.

The Court has also utilized the fundamental rights and interests strand
of new equal protection in bringing to the fore other rights and privileges. In the seminal holding of *Shapiro* v. *Thompson*[45] the right to travel
received special—indeed unprecedently expansive—constitutional recognition, and down went (6:3) Connecticut's durational requirement
vis-à-vis eligibility for state welfare assistance despite Congress' statutory permission—a fact that caused Chief Justice Warren and Justices
Black and Harlan to dissent. Justice Brennan held, however, that "the
laws violate equal protection. The interests which appellants assert are
promoted by the classification either may not constitutionally be promoted by government or are not compelling governmental interests."
Nonetheless, the justices have demonstrably stopped short of charac-
terizing wealth discriminations as suspect, and in *Dandridge* v. *Williams*,[46]
the Burger Court, over dissents by Justices Douglas, Brennan, and Marshall, resisted any notion of viewing as suspect routine classifications
affecting "necessities."

It is assuredly correct to conclude that the inconsistencies and contradictions that have so often plagued the "suspect categories" strand
of new equal protection are also present in the "fundamental rights and
interests" doctrine. Yet, arguably, such difficulties almost naturally in-
here within any evolution in constitutional law theory and application
based upon the notions of "preferred freedoms" and "implicit rights"
on the frontiers of ordered liberty. Such is the never-ending dynamism
of civil rights and liberties jurisprudence in general and new equal pro-

tection in particular. It may well constitute the essence of a living Constitution—yet there is little doubt that it has compounded doctrinal confusion that renders both lay and professional analysis inordinately complex, even mystifying. No wonder that many a student of our "least dangerous" branch has wistfully craved for a return to the old equal protection "rational person" standard that put a premium on deference to the legislative process.

Now, it is not only appropriate, it is essential that any account of the aforementioned dynamics recognize that they could not have been accomplished absent a climate of firm support of fundamental civil rights and liberties in and by our polity; absent our Bill of Rights; and absent the incorporation of all but a handful of the latter's specific commands to the 50 states via Section 1 of the Fourteenth Amendment. A few words about the Bill of Rights' status and the incorporation process would seem to be in order to appreciate and understand the Constitution's evolving new role.

As we prepare to celebrate the bicentennial of the ratification of our hallowed Bill of Rights by the then requisite 11 states on December 15, 1791, we are justified, I am convinced, in viewing its current status with genuine pride. It not only lives: it does so in excellent health; it is in good hands under the aegis of the judicial guardianship to which our constitutional firmament has assigned it (even if more implicitly than explicitly). It represents a guardianship that enables us to sleep far more soundly and contentedly than if that guardianship were lodged in the hands of either, or both, of the executive and legislative branches—for they are all too close, indeed, to political passion and partisan division.

My colleague, Professor Robert A. Rutland, has told the story of the birth of the Bill of Rights over the memorable 15-year period from 1776 to 1791 with historical acumen, profound insight, and uncommon clarity.[47] He succeeded admirably in providing the account of how Americans came to rely on legal guarantees for their personal freedom; that the English common law, colonial charters, legislative enactments, and a variety of events in the 13 colonies were the chief elements contributing to the basic rationale for a Bill of Rights. But to create the latter was far from the presumably facile task, viewed by some rather naively as all but unanimously preordained. Much opposition abounded. Yet, ultimately persuaded by that trio of noble Virginians, Messrs. Jefferson, Madison, and Mason—who had to convince themselves of its wisdom—what we know today as our 462-word Bill of Rights, comprising the first eight articles of amendment to the basic document (or ten to some who prefer to include Amendments Nine and Ten), was born and submitted to the first Congress for its approval in April of 1789, with the young but politically savvy Madison as its floor manager.

Fully alive now to the need for its approval, Mr. Jefferson had written to Mr. Madison in March of 1789 that "The Bill of Rights is necessary because of the legal check which it puts into the hands of the judiciary.[48] What he meant was a legal check against the *national* government—he was not worried greatly about the states since they had their own Bills of Rights. It would fall to our fourth Chief Justice, another renowned Virginian, John Marshall, to be the first to adjudicate the question when, in 1833, in his thirty-third year on the Court, he authored the Court's landmark opinion in *Barron v. Baltimore*.[49] He spoke for an unanimous tribunal in ruling that the Bill of Rights applied only against the national government, emphatically *not* against the states. His holding commenced a history of litigation on the question of the Bill of Right's applicability to the states—a process variously known as "incorporation," "absorption," or "nationalization."

Citizens like Barron were destined to have no further recourse until the ratification in 1868 of the Fourteenth Amendment, probably the most controversial and certainly the most litigated of all amendments adopted since the birth of the republic. And be it noted that today, 120 years later, a live argument still rages whether Marshall's position is not in fact still the proper interpretation of the Constitution, regardless of the Fourteenth Amendment. That, for example, is the current administration's position. What, then, of that amendment? In and of itself it did not overturn the *Barron* precedent; it contains no such explicit purpose of language, and disagreement, as indicated, persists regarding the intention of its framers, particularly as to the extent, if any, of the Amendment's application to the several states. We know that with respect to the matter of the reach of the Bill of Rights, both the heart and the greatest source of confusion and controversy of the famed amendment is the well-known phrasing of the second, lengthy sentence of Section 1, which was chiefly composed by Republican Representative John A. Bingham of Ohio:

No State shall make or enforce any law which shall abridge the privileges or immunities of citizens of the United States; nor shall any State deprive any person of life, liberty, or property, without due process of law; nor deny to any person within its jurisdiction the equal protection of the laws.[50]

There is no disagreement that the second phrase, which was lifted verbatim from the language of the Fifth Amendment, thus was intended to provide guarantees against *state* infringement supplemental to the Fifth's mandate against federal infringement. What does cause major disagreement, however, can be illustrated by two questions: First, *did* the framers of the amendment intend to "incorporate" or "nationalize" or "absorb" or "carry over" the entire Bill of Rights through the wording of its "due process of law" clause, thereby making it applicable to the several states; and second, regardless of their intention, *should* the Bill of Rights be applied to the states, given the nature of the rights involved and the demands of the democratic society in which we live? It remains a live issue, indeed.

In the face of the many disagreements on the "intent" of the framers, some argue that their intent no longer matters, for the "felt necessities of the time" (Justice Holmes's celebrated phrase) and the inevitable growth of the Constitution, may a fortiori dictate the application of the Bill of Rights to the several states regardless of the framers' intention. However, since it is preferable to have historical data to back one's contentions, both the proponents and opponents of total or even partial incorporation continue to invoke history to this day. A great deal of published research on historical justification is available, yet there is no conclusive answer, for the evidence is not persuasive. What *is* certain is that since the Supreme Court first "incorporated" aspects of the Bill of Rights in 1925, the process has been sporadic; but it has proved to be increasingly embracing as well as continuous over the next four decades.

As the Supreme Court of the United States continues in its first term under Chief Justice Rehnquist—after 17 years under Chief Justice Warren Burger—no further provisions of the Bill of Rights have been incorporated since the double jeopardy clause in 1969. But, in effect, only a few still remain "out": grand jury indictment; trial by a jury in *civil* cases; excessive bail and fines prohibitions; the so-called right to bear arms; and the Third Amendment safeguards against involuntary quartering of troops in private homes. What is crucial is the increasing recognition and acceptance, both on and off the bench, that if there is anything at all national in scope and application under the U.S. Constitution, it is our fundamental civil rights and liberties. It is my firm conviction that those cherished rights are secure. That they are secure, notwithstanding recurrent crises, is a tribute to "We the People's" dedication to the crucial principle that eternal vigilance is the price of liberty.

Let me close with an overall caveat, however: Our Constitution is based on the hallowed imperative of majority rule with due regard for minority rights. Majority tyranny is barred, and so is minority tyranny. Hence, with an eye toward the towering and inconclusive struggle between President Abraham Lincoln and Chief Justice Taney, and paraphrasing that wise jurist, Robert H. Jackson, let us remember that excessively grandiose notions of majority rule are unacceptable; equally unacceptable are excessively grandiose notions of civil rights and liberties. Our system, based upon the separation of powers, division of powers, and an intelligent, workable relationship or line between individual and societal rights and privileges, is a system with the irreducible aim of striving for those noble words atop the portals of the Supreme Court's magnificent edifice, "Equal Justice Under Law." It does *not* read "Equal Justice at Any Cost and Hang the Constitution." On all levels and in all seasons our government must always remain a government of laws, not a government of individuals—even in the face of apposite pressures for social change and social justice.

NOTES

1. 83 U.S. (Wallace) 36 (1873).
2. 109 U.S. 3 (1883).
3. 163 U.S. 537 (1896).
4. 198 U.S. 45 (1905).
5. 198 U.S. 75–76 (1905).
6. 302 U.S. 319 (1937).
7. 302 U.S. 326–327 (1937).
8. 304 U.S. 144 (1938).
9. 300 U.S. 379 (1937).
10. 301 U.S. 1 (1937).
11. 100 U.S. 303 (1880).
12. 323 U.S. 214 (1944).
13. 347 U.S. 483 (1954).
14. 163 U.S. 337 (1896).
15. 347 U.S. 497 (1954).
16. 388 U.S. 1 (1967).
17. 388 U.S. 10 (1967).
18. 402 U.S. 1 (1971).
19. 413 U.S. 189 (1973).
20. 426 U.S. 229 (1976).
21. 54 LW 4877 (1986).
22. 438 U.S. 265 (1978).
23. 443 U.S. 193 (1979).
24. 448 U.S. 448 (1980).
25. 404 U.S. 71 (1971).
26. 411 U.S. 677 (1973).
27. 411 U.S. 692 (1973).
28. 403 U.S. 365 (1971).
29. 413 U.S. 717 (1973).
30. 413 U.S. 634 (1973).
31. 435 U.S. 291 (1978).
32. 441 U.S. 68 (1979).
33. 441 U.S. 80 (1979).
34. 391 U.S. 68 (1968).
35. 427 U.S. 495 (1976).
36. 430 U.S. 762 (1977).
37. 430 U.S. 777 (1977).

38. 300 U.S. 379 (1937).

39. 383 U.S. 663 (1966).

40. 383 U.S. 664–668 (1966).

41. 395 U.S. 621 (1969).

42. 395 U.S. 633 (1969).

43. 405 U.S. 330 (1972).

44. 393 U.S. 23 (1968).

45. 394 U.S. 618 (1969).

46. 397 U.S. 417 (1970).

47. Robert Rutland, *The Birth of the Bill of Rights, 1776–1789* (Chapel Hill, University of North Carolina Press, 1955).

48. Thomas Jefferson to James Madison, March 15, 1789, *The Papers of Thomas Jefferson*, Vol. 14 (Princeton, NJ: Princeton University Press, 1958), p. 659.

49. 7 Peters 249.

50. 14th Amendment, Section 1.

18 The Constitution, Economic Rights, and Social Justice

Martin Shapiro

The story of the Constitution, the Supreme Court, and government regulation of economic matters has been told many times. In its earliest years, and faithful to at least one of the intentions of some of the framers, the Supreme Court had used the contract clause and other constitutional provisions to create a constitutional doctrine of vested rights in property that served as a shield for business enterprise against intervention by state legislatures that sometimes fell under the influence of small farmers and shopkeepers. By the time of the Civil War, however, contract clause jurisprudence had waned. By the turn of the twentieth century, however, the Court had seized upon the commerce clause and the due process clause as new shields against regulation. Under the former it created the dreaded dual federalism. State regulation of business enterprise would be struck down as invading the sphere of commerce reserved to the federal government by the commerce clause. Federal regulation would be struck down as invading the sphere reserved to the states. The due process clause was then converted through a conspiracy theory of the Fourteenth Amendment into a protection for corporations rather than freed blacks. The doctrine of substantive economic due process, read into both the Fifth and Fourteenth Amendments, allowed the justices to strike down any regulation which did not appear to the Court to be reasonable in the light of laissez-faire economic theory.

The doctrines of dual federalism and substantive economic due process brought about a collision between the Supreme Court and the New Deal in the 1930s. The New Deal won. The New Deal Court dismantled both doctrines and announced that it would never again use the power of judicial review to protect economic rights although it would continue to exercise that power in defense of civil rights and liberties.

While subsequent courts have not had an unblemished record in defending civil liberties, they have stayed out of economic matters and have concentrated on attacking racial and other discriminations and protecting the rights of accused persons.

This often told story is only partially true, and it is winners' history concocted by the New Dealers themselves.[1] For there is hardly any distinguished constitutional commentator over 50 who is not himself a Democrat for whom the New Deal experience is the founding myth of his political consciousness. Like all winner's history, this history is told as the march of virtue rather than the play of politics. Let us first reintroduce the politics and then correct the history. The New Deal did, indeed, win. It captured the Court in 1937 with the Roosevelt appointments of Justices Black and Reed followed shortly after by Douglas and Murphy. Having captured the citadel of Republican conservatism, however, the New Dealers fell into a quarrel. Should the citadel that had served the enemy so stubbornly now be leveled? That was the position of those like Justice Frankfurter, Judge Hand, and Professor Freund who preached the doctrine of judicial self-restraint that dominated the American Academy until well into the 1960s.[2] Because judicial review had so well served conservatives, it ought now to be entirely abandoned by the Supreme Court on Democratic grounds. (Of course these New Dealers spelled Democratic with a small d rather than a capital as I do.) The other side in the quarrel said that, having captured the citadel, it was foolish to destroy it. Instead its guns should be turned away from the protection of Republicans and to the protection of Democrats. This insight is embodied in the "proffered position doctrine," the doctrine that the Court should not protect economic rights but should protect First Amendment Freedoms and the rights of minorities. When it is recalled that in American history it is almost invariably intellectuals of the left who need to invoke First Amendment free speech protections and that the New Deal coalition was built up in large part of religious, racial, and ethnic minorities, it becomes clear that the preferred position doctrine is simply the transfer of judicial benefits from Republicans to Democrats. It is important to remember that the battle between judicial self-restraint and judicial activism in behalf of civil rights and liberties that so long shaped U.S. constitutional debate was simply an in-house quarrel among New Dealers.

Now to a brief correction of the history.[3] To save time, I will deal only with the post–1937 period. First of all, it is simply not true that the Court entirely abandoned judicial review of economic regulation. In one field, the negative or dormant commerce clause, it continued to do just what it had always done and what the New Deal had complained so bitterly about, imbue some general words of the Constitution with a procompetition economic theory and impose its policy judgments under that theory on legislatures. It is not that New Deal constitutional commentators denied that this large area of the Supreme Court's business continued to flourish. It stayed in the casebooks and articles were written about it. New Deal commentators simply ignored the fact that the continued existence of this body of Supreme Court activity contradicted both judicial self-restraint and preferred position. Justices Black and Douglas feebly protested for a while but then simply gave up.

During World War II and its immediate aftermath the Court was very self-restrained about nearly everything. By the late 1950s it had been reactivated by two major U.S. sociopolitical movements, McCarthyism and the civil rights movement. Desegregation fit neatly enough into the preferred position doctrine's teaching about special judicial review for isolated minorities. Indeed the doctrine had been invented to provide a special excuse for that kind of judicial activism. At first glance the McCarthy cases did too. Most of them involved the First Amendment. Preferred position had called for review to enforce the specific prohibitions of the Constitution, such as Congress shall make no law . . . abridging freedom of speech. . . . " These cases deserve a closer look, however. They provided a route by which the Court got back into the protection of economic rights, but the economic rights of Democrats rather than Republicans, and in cases that could be labelled civil liberties rather than economic rights.

Some of the McCarthy era cases were criminal prosecutions for conspiring to advocate overthrow of the government. Many others, however, involved dismissals from government employment or the withholding of government services, benefits, or licenses because of alleged disloyalty to the United States. In the course of these cases the Court announced the demise of the right-privilege distinction, that is the notion that government employment and benefits were mere largesse that could be given and taken away at the government's pleasure. Instead the Court held that persons otherwise entitled to government jobs and benefits could not be deprived of them simply because of their political beliefs. Such deprivations constituted violations of the First Amendment or of the due process clause.

Such cases were, therefore, First Amendment cases. That is how they were grouped in the casebooks and taught to law students. Here again it was not that the obvious was denied. It was simply ignored. For these cases were not simply free speech cases. They also created a new constitutional economic right, the right to get a living from government, and invoked the Court's review powers to protect that right.

Later as this new right to government support by job or by social service payment spread beyond the McCarthy era cases to instances in which the rights deprivation was predicated on some other consideration than disloyalty, the expression "new property" was coined for it. Liberal commentators proclaimed that the Court should and did protect the "new property."[4] They did not conclude that therefore the Court should also go back to protecting the old. The preferred position doctrine stood unmasked. Judicial review was legitimate when it protected the kind of property that Democratic voters were most likely to have against the government threats they were most likely to receive. Judicial review was illegitimate when it protected Republican, that is corporate, property from regulation. All of the new property cases were resolutely classed as civil rights and liberties cases. Deprivation of the new property was deprivation of a glorious civil right. Deprivation of the old property was only the legislative alteration of a mere economic right of the sort that courts ought not to consider constitutionally relevant.

Many of the new property cases involved racial discrimination or rather blatant violations of procedural due process. They could be kept under a civil rights and liberties cover without their economic rights edges sticking out too far. When gender discrimination began to loom large in the Supreme Court business, it became harder and harder to ignore what was really happening. For the central feminist constitutional claim was to be let into the mainstream of U.S. economic life on the same basis as men. Some of their claims involved the new property, such as government pension benefits and employment. Others involved such traditional economic interests as the power to be a trustee. Feminists were not concerned with the distinction between new property and old property. They wanted it all. And they were not loath to use the old constitutional arguments, such as freedom of contract, to get the Supreme Court to knock down economic regulatory statutes such as wages and hours laws that had been passed to "protect" women but were now seen as hampering their employment opportunities. It had been precisely such laws that both judicial self-restraint and preferred position had been designed to protect from judicial scrutiny.

Gender discrimination, too, remains firmly packed into the civil rights and liberties part of constitutional law. It cannot be long, however, before somebody notices that when negative commerce, new property and both new and old property for minorities and women, that is for about two-thirds of the American population, are within the ambit of judicial review, judicial self-restraint in the economic realm is just about gone.

Indeed this whole story must be supplemented with the story of a major movement of the Warren and Burger Court years that has suffered many setbacks and has not yet reached its goals but is very much alive. The original New Deal of President Roosevelt was no more consistent and complete about its welfare policies than it was about anything else. The United States has still not instituted a full set of government guaranteed minimums of subsistence, housing, medical care, and education. President Johnson's war on poverty was a self-conscious attempt to move on from the established New Deal consensus on such partial measures as the U.S. Social Security system, which had been accepted by Democrats and Republicans alike, to a more complete set of welfare state minimums. President Reagan's continuous assertions that his conservative administration would not dismantle the social "safety net" bears witness to the continued basic consensus but also the continued struggle over how complete, how generous and how nationally uniform welfare minimums should be.

Given the incomplete development and uncertain political appeal of the welfare state in the United States, it was hardly surprising that during the 1960s U.S. liberals sought to "constitutionalize" the welfare state.[5] A number of advantages would follow if access to minimum subsistence, housing, and so on, could be turned into constitutional rights. First, once they were declared to be constitutional rights by the Supreme Court, they could not easily be taken away again by legislative action. Second, such rights are usually required by the Supreme Court to be nationally uniform and so would tend to bring the benefits of such states as Mississippi into line with those of such states as New York and California. Third, American history showed that, once declared, constitutional rights tended to exhibit both ratchet and expansion phenomena. They were almost never cut back by a new Supreme Court below the level they had achieved in an earlier one, and they tended to expand to their logical limits. Fourth, constitutional rights are trumps. Once a social or economic interest is magically converted into a constitutional right, it goes to the head of the priorities list. Government must fund it first before it gets to serving mere interests. Finally, moving the campaign for welfare minimums from the general political arena to the special political arena of constitutional law was tactically useful because constitutional debate was almost completely dominated by liberal democratic lawyers and judges. In no other sphere of U.S. life was New Deal ideology so dominant.

This push to constitutionalize the welfare state was directed at the Warren Court which was, of course, headed by a Republican appointee. There is not time here to unpack the political genealogy of Earl Warren. It is enough to say that he came not so much from a Republican tradition as from a Progressive tradition of endowing government with power to achieve practical benefits. At the time of the welfare constitutionalizing campaign, the Warren Court was already busy creating a number of positive constitutional rights to government services and enforcing minimum national standards in their delivery. The most famous example is, of course, the right to counsel in criminal cases. It was the Warren Court too that had finally buried the rights-privilege distinction and thus created the New Property.

We have already noted the tendency of constitutional history to be winners' history. If the welfare constitutionalizers had been victorious in the 1960s, we would now look back on a whole string of 1960s cases as first recognizing constitutional rights to at least subsistence,[6] housing,[7] and education[8] minimums. We would be noting that, just as the right to abortion was obliquely constitutionalized in *Roe* v. *Wade*[9] by announcing a constitutional right to privacy, the right to subsistence had been constitutionalized in *Shapiro* v. *Thompson*[10] by announcing a constitutional right to travel. We would weave together a series of desegregation decisions to show that, while a southern government might close down a swimming pool to avoid integrating it, it could not close down a school for that reason, thus showing that there was a constitutional right to schools but not to swimming pools.[11] In general, we would be showing that after the Warren Court declared that it would abandon judicial self-restraint and be very judicially active where fundamental rights were involved, it expanded its lists of fundamental rights to include many state-supplied benefits. We would also be arguing that as the Warren Court demanded more and more procedural due process when government sought to deprive someone of the new property, the Court had in fact turned the substance of the new property into constitutional rights. After all the actual essence of any substantive property right is not that it is absolute but only that the government may not take it away from you without going over very tough procedural hurdles.

The welfare constitutionalizers did not win however. Although a complete theory of constitutionalized welfare can be picked out of the scholarly writing and the briefs of the period, the Warren Court did not go very far in accepting it. The Court's decisions were of the kind that could later have been seen as the first, tentative, only semiconscious steps *if* the later big conscious steps had been taken, but standing alone they often are little more than archeological traces still waiting to be appreciated fully.

If the Warren Court did not go nearly far enough fast enough, the Burger Court largely cut off the campaign. *Goldberg* v. *Kelly*,[12] the case that had nearly constitutionalized subsistence benefits by setting very high procedural due process hurdles, was decided a year after Burger came on the Court. It was really a Warren Court decision with only Burger and one other justice dissenting. Within six years *Mathews* v. *Eldridge*[13] cut *Goldberg* way back and in *Arnett* v. *Kennedy*[14] Justice Rehnquist sought, not entirely successfully, to create an opening through which judicial protection of the new property could be aborted. The greatest signal of the arrival of the Burger Court, however, was *San Antonio School District* v. *Rodriguez*.[15] There the constitutionalizers had found an ingenious argument that used the equal protection clause of the Fourteenth Amendment to lever the Court into judicial activism in the area of school financing. The Burger court cut off the argument by declaring that it was not going to expand the list of fundamental rights the violation of which triggered judicial activism to include education.

Rodriguez signaled that the Court was not interested in further general conversion of government benefits into judicially protected constitutional rights. But please remember that the welfare minimums story is a smaller story within the larger story of the Supreme Court and economic rights, and that the Burger Court was active in protecting both the old and new property rights of women against gender discrimination.

Having told these several stories, we can now return to preferred position—that is, the doctrine that the Supreme Court should defend civil rights but not economic rights, and its current status. A few vigorous proponents of the preferred position remain, among them my distinguished dean and participant in this project, Jesse Choper.[16] Another is John Hart Ely[17] of Stanford. We now have the San Francisco Bay school of preferred position. And no doubt many constitutional scholars in their later fifties and beyond cling to preferred position out of New Deal habit and allegiance. Among most younger commentators, however, preferred position has become almost irrelevant because the whole issue of judicial self-restraint has become irrelevant.

The group of younger scholars who have made the biggest noise is, of course, the Critical Legal Studies movement. They teach that the interpretation of the Constitution, like the interpretation of any text, is problematic and that U.S. constitutional law is a bourgeois capitalist ideology. Like all law in contemporary technologically advanced societies, U.S. constitutional law is a weapon of alienating exploitation of the powerless by the powerful. The courts that administer it are part and parcel of a regime of political domination. Given that the movement denies the legitimacy of the whole of U.S. government, law, and politics, the issue of whether judicial activism is more or less legitimate than executive or legislative activism hardly arises. And given that the movement sees every quantum of social action as simultaneously economic and political, the distinction between civil rights and economic rights is meaningless. Until the New Jerusalem can be built in which both economics and politics will be replaced by communitarian love, constitutional lawyers ought to manipulate the system in any way they can to alleviate the suffering of the poor, but to do so in such a way as to hasten the disestablishment of the current order. Of course in such efforts no one should feel bound by old minor New Deal squabbles about shutting the Court down or switching its services from Republican to Democratic clients.

Less noisy but far more important to contemporary U.S. constitutional law has been the vigorous regrowth of what is sometimes called today the jurisprudence of values. Reviving themes that are as old as American history, this school teaches that the Constitution is a receptacle of public values, that constitutional litigation is a discourse about public values and that the Supreme Court does and should serve a role of moral leadership, advancing and concretizing the moral aspirations developed and revealed in that discourse.

While these themes are as old as American history, their current vitality is obviously fuelled by two recent developments. One is internal to constitutional law. For a younger generation of scholars it is not the New Deal court crisis but *Brown* v. *Board*,[18] the great school desegregation case, which is the shaping myth of their intellectual lives. Their principal task is not to legitimate the victory of the New Deal over the nine old men but to legitimate and move forward the liberal activism of the Warren Court.

The second lies beyond constitutional law in the broader world of philosophy, particularly moral philosophy. We have experienced the rise of a post-consequentialist ethics that rejects the concept of values as mere personal preferences and teaches that there are moral rights and wrongs, or at least betters and worses, that can be arrived at by moral discourse among persons of good will. Many constitutional scholars now see constitutional law and constitutional litigation as one form of this discourse.[19]

For the new jurisprudence of values commentators, the New Deal crisis and the preferred position doctrine, with its distinction between civil rights and economic rights, is now far in the historical past and largely irrelevant.[20] Most of them see no need even to straighten the whole thing out. They are content to see new property put in the civil rights and liberties part of the casebook. Indeed they are content to put all the property of women and minorities and other underdogs in that part of the book where judicial activism is recorded and praised and to assign old property owned by fat cats to that part of the casebook which describes what the old, bad Supreme Court once wrongly did. They are content not because they care about judicial self-restraint versus activism issues but because they have settled upon judicial activism in favor of certain values. Those values are to be achieved by uplifting the downtrodden, not protecting the fat cats. The Supreme Court ought to proceed toward social justice because that is the right thing to do. If it makes older commentators, still plagued by New Deal fetishes, happier to call the bread and butter of the poor civil and the bread and butter of the rich economic, no harm is done.

Thus although the movement of the Warren Court period to constitutionalize welfare minimums did not get very far, the calls for such a move have remained and today constitute a strong, living stream of constitutional commentary, particularly in the work of such leading scholars as Frank Michelman[21] and Lawrence Tribe.[22] They continue to repeat old and construct ingenious new arguments designed to encourage judicial intervention. And there is sufficient response from the

Supreme Court to keep hope alive. For instance, recently the Court has come very close to saying, indeed probably really has said, that public school education is a minimum right of every child residing within United States boundaries.[23]

More generally the movement toward constitutionalizing the welfare state is now at a kind of halfway house that is signalled by the constant use of the term "entitlement" in U.S. law and politics. Indeed that word had to be invented when liberals could not quite get the Supreme Court to create constitutional rights to government jobs and benefits but were able to get them so deeply embedded in statutes and so shielded by procedural due process rights that may be constitutional in nature that they could no longer be considered mere government policies to be altered at will. As the Reagan administration has shown, the major problem with entitlements from a liberal perspective is that, although conservatives cannot easily eliminate them, conservatives can cut their levels of government funding substantially. Much of the push to move welfare minimums from "entitlements" to rights is motivated by the desire to endow them with high budgetary priorities.

The paradigm here has been the conversion of the cruel and unusual punishment clause into a set of positive rights to welfare minimums. Because the courts have declared that prisoners have a constitutional right to minimally decent food, shelter, sanitation, and recreation, today we find courts ordering the financially responsible governments to provide money for those things no matter what the impact on the rest of their budgets. If only we could get all of the poor into the constitutional garb of the prisoners, we could get judges to order governments to spend their money on butter not guns.

Thus there is steady pressure from the moderate left pushing the Supreme Court toward converting welfare entitlements into constitutional rights and thus pushing the Court into the realm of economic rights at least for the downtrodden. For those who believe that the Court should participate in the jurisprudence of values, it makes little sense to truncate that participation by refusing to look at some of the most basic human values of all.

In dealing with the intersection of the jurisprudence of values movement with constitutional law, basically we have been tracing a continuous pressure that began with the preferred position doctrine itself, inspired the attacks on the rights privilege distinction in the McCarthy era, went on to constitutional protections for the "new property," was partially stymied in its attempt to get the Warren Court to include welfare minimums among fundamental constitutional rights, and continues today to try to turn entitlements into rights.

To this rather continuous movement must now be added a new and entirely different movement, from conservative rather than liberal quarters. The story of this new movement is important in part for its own sake but in part because the conjunction of liberal and conservative pushes on the Court to move it deeper into economic realms may result in the near future in economic rights being once again an openly acknowledged central feature of constitutional debate. This movement is a central component of the law and economics scholarship that has had a major impact on U.S. law in recent years. The combination of law with laissez-faire Chicago school economics practiced by a set of prolific law professors at the University of Chicago Law School is not the whole of law and economics scholarship but that component is what concerns us here. For it is in the process of generating a new constitutional theory designed to push the Supreme Court back into judicial review of government regulation of the old property—that is, government regulation of business. The theory begins with some borrowing from pluralist political theory. The legislative process is a struggle between groups. Thus most regulatory statutes, like other statutes, register the victories of some groups over other groups. Now the economics begins. Because regulatory statutes constitute group victories, although they purport to regulate in the public interest, typically what they really do is grant monopolies and assign monopoly rents—that is, levels of profit above the levels competition would yield. An example is the regulation of rates and routes of airlines. Under regulation U.S. airlines were protected from competition by the FAA. They enjoyed the economic prosperity that comes to those who are allowed to charge high prices in markets where their share is guaranteed. When deregulation occurred, the airlines had to compete, which drove down rates, drove the less efficient into bankruptcy and takeover and drove down the high wages that had resulted when the industry had been forced by organized labor to pass on some of its monopoly profits to its workers.

If many regulatory statutes are monopoly-granting statutes that create economic inefficiencies that cost the general public dearly, and the very nature of the legislative process makes this outcome inevitable, then perhaps courts should intervene to correct the pathologies of group politics.[24] Isn't there some way, somehow or other, that we could call such statutes unconstitutional? Indeed once upon a time there was such a way. It was called substantive economic due process and was identified with *Lockner v. New York*,[25] one of the most villified decisions in U.S. constitutional history. And it is what New Dealers, under both the judicial self-restraint and preferred position banners, promised that the Court would never do again. For under substantive economic due process, the Court claimed that old property had a constitutional right not to be *unreasonably* regulated by government. What was and was not reasonable was to be determined by the Court.

Given the vigorous and complete rejection of this doctrine by the New

Deal court and the condemnation of it by several generations of New Deal commentators, how can conservatives hope to revive it now? One solution is to pick another clause than the Fourteenth Amendment's due process clause on which the substantive economic due process of *Lockner* rested. One candidate is the equal protection clause which is now doing such useful duty protecting the property rights of minorities and women. Another is the long dormant contract clause.[26] On some recent occasions, the Supreme Court itself has even used the First Amendment to strike down government regulation that throttled free competition.[27] Some clause will be found. The question is whether the Court is really in the mood to impose standards of reasonableness based on theories of the economic efficiency of competitive markets.

Hasn't the Court forever abandoned that mood however? No, it hasn't. First of all, without any break in continuity at all the Court has always continued to strike down state regulations that unreasonably interfere with interstate business competition. In doing so it has continued to praise the glories of free market competition. These are the "negative" commerce clause cases referred to earlier. So the Court has continued to claim a competence to judge the reasonableness of economic regulations under a free competition theory.

Second, in the First Amendment cases noted above, even the recent Court has shown so much commitment to laissez-faire economic theory that it was willing for the first time to extend free speech rights to a whole new category of speech in order to strike down state bans on advertising that were designed to insulate certain businesses from price competition.

Third, as the Court continues to increase its protection of what are obviously economic rights of the new property no matter how often they are called civil rights, it becomes harder and harder for the justices to defend their denial of constitutional protections to the old property on the grounds that courts should have nothing to do with economic rights.

Fourth, and most importantly, if constitutional law is supposed to be a jurisprudence of values in which public values are enunciated and enforced, what value more concerns the U.S. public today than economic efficiency? Faced with foreign competition and an aging industrial sector, U.S. citizens are no longer sure that the golden goose of U.S. business will go on laying all the golden eggs we need no matter how much we throttle it with government regulation. Democrats used to laugh at the idiot Republicanism of an industrialist who said "What's good for General Motors is good for the country." Nobody laughs anymore, least of all Democrats courting the votes of labor union members. Now may well be the time for the public value of economic growth as well as the value of welfare minimums to enter the Constitution.

Thus what is remarkable today, some 50 years after a New Deal court announced that it was getting out of the economics business, is that, not only is it still in that business, but also that it is being pushed by both the left and the right to get much deeper into that business.

To illustrate my point, let me turn to a recent Supreme Court case— a case which 20 years from now may be studied as the foundation of a whole new economic jurisprudence for the Court or barely noted as a minor extension of "civil rights." Which it will be later depends, of course, on who wins and who writes the winner's history. The case is *City of Cleburne* v. *Cleburne Living Center.*[28] To understand it a little review and supplementation of what has already been said is useful. Before 1937 the Supreme Court had used the due process clause of the Fourteenth Amendment to review state economic regulation of property rights. It struck down "unreasonable" state regulations. The Court made its own independent judgments of reasonableness essentially based on a laissez-faire economic theory. Free market competition and freedom to dispose of one's own property as one pleased was the ideal. A state regulation that interfered with this economic freedom was, in the Court's eyes, unreasonable unless the state could offer an awfully persuasive special reason for such regulation. This was the dreaded substantive economic due process, associated with the great case of *Lockner* v. *New York* that the New Deal Court appointed by President Roosevelt promised never to do anymore. The philosophy of judicial self-restraint was based on viewing substantive economic due process as the very paradigm of undemocratic judicial policy-making, the rejection of which should lead to the rejection of all judicial review. And when preferred positionists said that the Court ought to presume the constitutionality of economic regulation and engage in independent review only of statutes impinging on civil rights and liberties, it was precisely substantive economic due process review that they were attacking. After 1937 the Court never again struck down a state economic regulation as substantively unreasonable and thus a violation of the due process clause. Its doctrinal vehicle for withdrawing was to presume the constitutionality of state economic regulation and then apply to it a "minimum rationality" test. Only if the state regulation could not have been enacted by any reasonable person would it be unconstitutional. No state economic regulation ever appeared that unreasonable.

The Fourteenth Amendment not only has a due process clause but an equal protection clause. It was under this clause that the Court created constitutional protections for blacks, women, and a number of other categories of disadvantaged persons. As equal protection jurisprudence grew in the 1950s and 1960s, a kind of marginal substantive economic equal protection that was in some ways parallel to the old substantive economic due process arose. The Court held that where a state regulation adversely effected the interests of racial minorities or women for instance, the justices would make their own independent judgment of the statute's constitutionality rather than presuming it constitutional. Instead of the rational basis or minimum rationality test, the Court would employ a "heightened" rationality test. It would require very very persuasive reasons indeed from the state for any statute that appeared to treat racial minorities or women unequally. The Court struck down many state statutes on constitutional equal protection grounds. This was certainly substantive equal protection, but it was generally seen as substantive civil rights rather than substantive economic equal protection. Yet when the state statutes struck down were those that limited employment opportunities, or the capacity to hold property, make contracts and inherit, surely we had substantive economic equal protection of traditional property interests. They just happened to be the particular property interests of minorities or women or illegitimate children rather than the general property interests of all.

In this preliminary to the *Cleburne* case, we need to note one more point. Particularly in gender discrimination cases, the Court frequently held that where statutes that treated persons unequally reflected racial or sexual "stereotypes," they would fail the constitutional test of "heightened" rationality that the Court employed for such statutes.

Now to the *Cleburne* Case. Cleburne is a small city in Texas that like nearly all U.S. cities had a zoning ordinance that specified what types of buildings could be built in various parts of town. Such ordinances are precisely the kind of state and local economic regulations inhibiting the freedom of traditional property holders that the New Deal Court had sworn it would no longer declare unconstitutional under a substantive economic due process approach. In this case the Court did hold that the zoning ordinance was precisely the kind of economic regulation that need pass only the "minimum rationality" test that it had been using since 1937 to uphold every state economic statute that came before it. For reasons we will get to in a moment, the Court invoked the equal protection clause rather than the due process clause, but it used minimum rationality or rational basis as its test under this clause as well. Then it proceeded to strike down the zoning ordinance as applied to a particular piece of property because the application was unreasonable. So now again after almost 50 years the Court has taken it upon itself to declare unconstitutional a state economic regulation that appears to the Court to be unreasonable.

Have the conservatives won? Are we back to the substantive economic due process of *Lockner* but now transposed to substantive economic equal protection? Not quite. Or perhaps only: Not yet.

At issue in the *Cleburne* Case was the challenge of a proposed operator of a group home for mentally retarded persons to a zoning ordinance that barred such homes from a particular district of the city unless a special use permit were granted. The Court struck this provision down as applied to the group home in question on the basis that the provision was based on an "irrational prejudice" against the mentally retarded and so could not satisfy even a minimum rationality test.

This case then represents a curious intersection of the pushes from the left and the right to move the Court back to the center of economic concerns. In one sense this is a welfare minimums, new property case. It is about constitutional protection for the new property right of the retarded to receive decent shelter and care. In another sense, however, the case says that some state economic regulations of old property can be so irrational that they will flunk the test of constitutionality employed by the Supreme Court for such regulations. The Court has returned to demanding that state economic regulation really be reasonable. The current court may not judge reasonableness by the same laissez-faire economic theory that the *Lockner* Court did. But it is back in the business of striking down unreasonable regulation.

Cleburne can thus be read in a number of ways. For conventional constitutional law scholars with no particular axe to grind, except perhaps the axe of preferred position, the case can be treated as simply a part of the standard civil rights and liberties jurisprudence of the Supreme Court. From this perspective *Cleburne* simply adds retardation to race, sex, illegitimacy, age, alienage, and others on the list of suspect or quasi-suspect classifications that trigger constitutional equal protection interventions by the Court. Such commentators will treat the case this way even though the Court explicitly says that retardation is not a quasi-suspect classification. To those who have been pushing the Court toward constitutionalizing the welfare state, this case will be another small step by the Court in recognizing that basic social services are constitutionally protected even though the opinion does nothing to acknowledge such a position. To those who want the Court to return to making its own independent constitutional judgments on the reasonableness of economic regulations impinging on traditional property rights and individual economic freedom, *Cleburne* will be treated as precisely that return. It will be seen as the first case to thoroughly dismantle the preferred position doctrine and bring the Court back to its rightful place as guardian of economic rights. The proponents of substantive economic whatever—due process, equal protection, contract—will take this view even though the Court was obviously more interested in the retarded than in the business entrepreneur who proposed to serve the retarded.

Ten or 20 years from now *Cleburne* may be one of the sainted cases that returned the Supreme Court to the protection of capitalist rights and freedoms or one of the sainted cases that established the constitutional protections of the welfare state, or it may be merely a minor incident in equal protection jurisprudence. Which will it be, of course, depends on who wins and so who gets to write the constitutional history. Whatever it turns out to be, however, *Cleburne* reminds us that the Constitution and the Supreme Court's judicial review remain central arenas in which U.S. citizens seek to work out their visions of economic policy and social justice.

NOTES

1. See Martin Shapiro, "The Constitution and Economic Rights" in M. Judd Harmon, ed., *Essays on the Constitution of the United States* (Port Washington, NY: Kennikat Press, 1978).

2. See J. Skelly Wright, "Professor Bickel, the Scholarly Tradition and the Supreme Court," *Harvard Law Review* 84 (1971):769–836.

3. See Martin Shapiro, "The Supreme Court's 'Return' to Economic Regulation," *Studies in American Political Development* vol. 1 (New Haven, CT: Yale University Press, 1986), pp. 91–141.

4. Charles Reich, "The New Property," *Yale Law Journal* 73 (1964):733–87.

5. See Frank Michelman, "Foreward: On Protecting the Poor through the Fourteenth Amendment," *Harvard Law Review* 83 (1969):7–108.

6. Shapiro v. Thompson, 394 U.S. 618 (1969).

7. Reitman v. Mulkey, 387 U.S. 369 (1967).

8. Griffin v. Prince Edward County School Board, 377 U.S. 218 (1964).

9. 410 U.S. 113 (1973).

10. 394 U.S. 618 (1969).

11. Compare *Griffin* with Palmer v. Thompson, 403 U.S. 217 (1971).

12. 397 U.S. 254 (1970).

13. 424 U.S. 319 (1976).

14. 416 U.S. 134 (1974).

15. 411 U.S. 1 (1973).

16. Jesse Choper, *Judicial Review and the National Political Process* (Chicago: University of Chicago Press, 1980).

17. John Hart Ely, *Democracy and Distrust* (Cambridge, MA: Harvard U. Press, 1980).

18. 347 U.S. 483 (1954).

19. Brian Berry, "And Who Is My Neighbor," *Yale Law Journal* 88 (1979):629–58. Frank Michelman "Foreword: Traces of Self-Government," *Harvard Law Review* 100 (1986):4–77.

20. Martin Shapiro, "Fathers and Sons: The Court, the Commentators, and the Search for Values," in Vincent Blasi, *The Burger Court* (New Haven: Yale University Press, 1983).

21. Frank Michelman, "Constitutional Welfare Rights and *A Theory of Justice*" in N. Daniels ed., *Reading Rawls* (New York: Basic Books, 1975). Compare Richard Epstein, "The Uncertain Quest for Welfare Rights," *Brigham Young University Law Review*, no. 2 (1985): 201–30.

22. Lawrence Tribe, *Constitutional Choices* (Cambridge, MA: Harvard University Press, 1985).

23. Plyler v. Doe, 457 U.S. 202 (1982); Goss v. Lopez, 419 U.S. 565 (1975).

24. Frank Easterbrook, "Foreward: The Court and the Economic System," *Harvard Law Review* 98 (1984–85):4–60.

25. 198 U.S. 45 (1905).

26. Richard Epstein, *University of Chicago Law Review* 51 (1984):703–51.

27. Virginia State Board of Pharmacy v.Virginia Citizens Consumer Council, 425 U.S. 748 (1976); Friedman v. Rogers, 440 U.S. 1 (1979).

28. 105 S. Ct. 3249 (1985).

19 The Constitution and Social Change: A Comment

Michael Walzer

For more than three decades now, the Supreme Court (in fact, the entire set of federal district and appeals courts) has been the dominant agency for social change in the United States, far outdistancing in both zeal and effectiveness the Congress, the parties, the unions, and interest groups of all sorts. Along with this extraordinary dominance goes a standard worry: that judicial activism on this scale stands at some remove from democratic politics and doesn't work to strengthen democratic institutions and practices. In the 1930s, a similar worry took a rather different form. Then the judges seemed too ready to constrain and inhibit a powerful democratic movement. So the issue was posed in terms probably closer to the intentions and anxieties of the founders: What can political majorities do (and not do)? What are the constitutional limits on the popular will? Now the judges seem to many U.S. citizens too ready to act in the absence of a democratic movement. The question is, What can *only* majorities do? What are the constitutional limits on judicial will?

The earlier formulation fits better with our standard view of constitutional democracy—animated by popular energies and interests, constrained by judicial wisdom. But let us grant that even wise judges might sometimes choose the path of animation. Just as Puritan radicals in the seventeenth century argued against "tarrying for the magistrate," so there are lawyers and judges today who argue against tarrying for the people. The language of rights prompts an impatience of just this sort. For if the wrongs of our society are such that rights are being violated, immediate remedies are called for, and the courts seem the appropriate remedial agencies. If the condition of children in segregated schools or of convicts in overcrowded prisons, or of women in discriminatory workplaces is not merely a matter of disadvantage or loss of utility, but rather a matter of injustice, then how can we wait for the slow workings of the democratic process, the difficult business of building a civil rights or prison reform or feminist movement, the painful compromises of legislative decision making?

The courts offer a quicker corrective—a cheaper corrective too, not only in terms of money but also in terms of time and energy. Victories in court don't require the mobilization of political forces; they are not the work of a party or movement; they don't depend upon lobbying or congressional logrolling. All that is necessary is a clever lawyer and a good brief. In the years since the Supreme Court's school integration decision of 1954, U.S. liberals have become highly dependent upon victories of this sort. Unable (mostly) to win elections or to put together legislative coalitions, liberals have increasingly resigned themselves to a passive role: not activists but litigants. In this role they have been extraordinarily successful, the beneficiaries of three decades of judicial activism. They have won victories far beyond their political base—and this over a very wide range of issues. Civil rights, school integration, school prayer, affirmative action in employment, criminal law, capital punishment, prison reform, electoral reform, abortion, censorship, and pornography: In all these areas (with only the partial exception of the first) victories have come not because of the political strength of the liberal left but because of the persuasiveness of its lawyers.

Victory also depends, of course, on the readiness of judges to be persuaded, and the Reagan years have brought large numbers of judges into the federal system who are radically unready. What is curious about the current period is that the battle continues to be fought in (and around) the courts. Conservatives also have not been able to build stable political movements or legislative coalitions. The hardest political decisions these days are always approached indirectly—not in open debate about the substance of the issues but in confirmation hearings on the merits of this or that judicial candidate. We have grown used to a peculiar linguistic code, where phrases like "the intentions of the founders" or "strict constructionism" or "judicial activism" stand in for largely unstated political arguments. Senators and congressmen, elected by the people, seem all too ready to hand over crucial decisions to appointed judges, even while they insist on their own role in the appointment process.

I don't mean that there have not been significant political mobilizations in recent years; there have been—and significant demobilizations too. But both mobilization and demobilization have tracked success and failure in the courts. If liberals ceased in the course of the 1960s and 1970s to be activists and became litigants instead, this was in large part because they were such successful litigants that they hardly needed to be activists. The courts induced in them a state of mind and feeling that might be called democratic laziness. Thus the political struggle to legalize abortion, which was being fought state by state through the legislatures, was effectively ended by the Supreme Court's decision in *Roe* v. *Wade*. What need was there to work at building and organizing popular support, if one had the support of the judges? Similarly, what need was there to regenerate the prison reform movements of an earlier period, if the courts could be persuaded to undertake the reform of prisons themselves? Organizations largely devoted to litigation, like the American Civil Liberties Union or the National Association for the Advancement of Colored People, still had to raise money to pay lawyers, but they did not require a lot of money, and fund-raising was pretty much the extent of their outreach. Liberalism proliferated staff organizations, not without memberships but without substantial and active political constituencies.

The case of the conservative right has been exactly the opposite. Whereas liberals, over a long period of time, won in the courts again and again and failed to build a movement, conservatives lost again and again and organized outside. In almost all the areas I listed above (and especially with regard to school prayer, capital punishment, and abortion), conservative activists have put together committees, alliances, even single-issue parties, at the local as well as the national level: an extraordinary proliferation of groups which "participatory democrats" from the days of the New Left might well envy. There can't be much doubt that these groups played a part in the Republican victories of 1980 and 1984. Reagan was significantly helped, and some senatorial contests decided, by a mobilization of indignant citizens in response to recent Supreme Court decisions.

But the political victories of the right have not been translated into legislative success. So conservative activists have been forced to tarry for the judges, waiting for old age, disease, retirement, and death to erode liberal majorities in the courts and for the appointment process to produce what the political process has not produced—a reversal of the judicial decisions of the 1950s, 1960s, and 1970s. It is important to stress that the political process didn't produce those decisions either, though they were also not the product of any deliberate effort to create a liberal bench. Perhaps the political "atmosphere" played a part; I am sure it plays a part today. But judges are only partly responsive to the politics of everyday life, against which they have, after all, been constitutionally insulated. When public policy is shaped by the courts, it is, once again, shaped indirectly, judicial deliberation on points of law replacing democratic debate on the issues as they are popularly understood. The U.S. right and left seem alike to have reconciled themselves to this replacement. But is it good for democracy?

Perhaps there is something to be said for protecting the political process from issues likely to be peculiarly divisive. Abortion is the best example: Politicians avoid it if they can and are grateful for a judicial resolution. On the other hand, had there been a clear-cut political decision in favor of legal abortion (the opinion polls still indicate massive popular support), the years of hostility and rancor might have been cut short. It is not at all obvious how such questions are best worked out. But it can't be right for the courts to act *in loco populi* every time the people are divided. I should think that this latter point would be clearest to citizens who stand with the liberal left: Social progress depends upon political mobilization. The best judicial decisions, the most eager judges, cannot create a stable or strong liberalism. They cannot build the infrastructure of belief, commitment, organization, and activism upon which liberal left politics ultimately depends. The judges can right particular wrongs; they cannot set a democratic society right without democratic participation.

Index

Abortion, 276–77, 283, 355, 356. *See also Roe* v. *Wade*

Abraham, Henry, 266

Adair v. *United States*, 202–3

Adams, John, 18, 185, 222

Additions to the Constitution, 282–83

Adkins v. *Children's Hospital*, 202–3

Administrative law, 293, 297, 299–302, 303

Adversarial system, 146–60

Advice and consent power, 26

Affirmative action: and the adversarial system, 149, 151–60; and collective benefit/harm, 125–31; and the color-blind principle, 114–15, 116–24, 151–60; and compensation theory, 155, 156, 159, 160; definition of, 155; and differential standards, 131–37; disadvantages of, 166; and economic disparities, 111–13, 117–24, 129–30, 136; and equality, 149, 151–60; and equal opportunity, 114–15, 117, 119–23, 133, 134; and equal protection, 326–27; and gender, 112; and government action, 117, 122–24, 130, 136; and group inequality, 110–17, 124–31, 155; and group preferences, 110, 111–12; and historical conditions, 110, 112, 117–24, 126, 127–29, 130, 136, 155,

157–58; and the impact of the Supreme Court, 165–67; and the individual, 155–56, 159, 166; and the Jews, 127; and laissez faire, 117, 120; landmark cases concerning, 151–60; and the "less qualified," 131–36, 156–57; and merit, 165–66; and the military, 132; as a moral response, 113; and the plateauing phenomenon, 133, 136; political/philosophical aspects of, 124–31; and preferential treatment, 131–36, 165–66, 327; as a process, 166; and quotas, 121, 127; and reverse discrimination, 133, 152–60, 326, 327; and segregation, 154; and social discrimination, 117–24, 136, 152–53, 159; and victims, 127, 152–60

Aid to schools, 74, 103

Alienage, 327, 328

Ambach v. *Norwich*, 328

Ambassadors, 26, 30

Amendments: and additions to the Constitution, 282–83; appropriateness of, 261–62; and constitutional change, 239, 257–64, 282–83; and the meaning of "to amend," 226–27, 238–39; number introduced, 283; and privacy, 220–27; and the structure/composition of govern-

Contributors

HENRY J. ABRAHAM   James Hart Professor of Government and Foreign Affairs, University of Virginia, Charlottesville; author of numerous constitutional law studies including *Freedom and the Court*.

AARON BARAK   Justice, Supreme Court of Israel; former Dean, Law School, Hebrew University; author of many legal studies including the book *Judicial Discretion* (1988).

NORMA BASCH   Professor, Department of History, Rutgers University, Newark, New Jersey; author of many writings including *In the Eyes of the Law*.

JESSE H. CHOPER   Dean, School of Law (Boalt Hall), University of California at Berkeley; author of *Judicial Review and the National Legal Process* and numerous other legal studies.

DANIEL J. ELAZAR   N.M. Paterson Professor, Department of Political Science, Bar Ilan University, Israel; Director, Center for the Study of Federalism, Temple University, Philadelphia; author of *People and Polity* and other books.

ARNOLD ENKER   Professor, Faculty of Law, Bar Ilan University, Israel; author of numerous writings on constitutional law including *The Suspended Sentence*.

MALCOLM FEELEY   Professor, School of Law (Boalt Hall), University of California at Berkeley; author of *The Impact of Supreme Court Decisions* and other works.

LOUIS FISHER   Senior Specialist, Government Division, Congressional Research Service, Library of Congress, Washington, DC; author of *Constitutional Conflicts between Congress and President* and other publications.

RUTH BADER GINSBURG   Circuit Judge, United States Court of Appeals, District of Columbia Circuit; author of many legal studies including the casebook *Sex-Based Discrimination*.

ROBERT A. GOLDWIN   Director, Constitutional Studies, American Enterprise Institute for Public Policy Research, Washington, DC; author of *How Federal is the Constitution?* and other publications.

LOUIS HENKIN   University Professor, School of Law, Columbia University, New York; author of *Foreign Affairs and the Constitution* and numerous other works on constitutional law.

DAVID KRETZMER   Louis Marshall Chair, Faculty of Law, Hebrew University of Jerusalem, Israel; author of *The Legal Status of the Arabs in Israel* and other books.

JACOB W. LANDYNSKI   Professor, Department of Political Science, Graduate School, New School for Social Research, New York; author of *Search and Seizure in the Supreme Court* and other works.

NATHAN LEWIN   Former Deputy Assistant Attorney General, Department of Justice; Partner, Miller, Cassidy, Larroca & Lewin, Washington, DC; has written extensively on constitutional law and has argued many cases before U.S. Supreme Court.

GLENN C. LOURY   Professor of Political Economy, John F. Kennedy School of Government, Harvard University, Cambridge; author of the forthcoming *Free at Last?* and other publications.

THEODORE J. LOWI   John L. Senior Professor of American Institutions, Department of Government, Cornell University; author of *The Personal President* and other works.

WALLACE MENDELSON   Professor, Department of Government, University of Texas at Austin; author of *The Constitution and the Supreme Court* and other works.

WALTER F. MURPHY   McCormick Professor of Jurisprudence, Department of Politics, Princeton University; author of *Congress and the Court* and other works.

MICHLA POMERANCE   Professor, Department of International Relations, Hebrew University of Jerusalem, Israel; author of *Self-Determination in Law and Practice* and other works.

FRANCES RADAY   Professor, Faculty of Law, Hebrew University of Jerusalem, Israel; has written extensively on the law including *Adjudication of Interest Disputes*.

DONALD L. ROBINSON   Professor, Department of Government, Smith College, Northampton, Massachusetts; author of *To the Best of My Ability: The Presidency and the Constitution* and other publications.

MARTIN SHAPIRO   Professor, School of Law (Boalt Hall), University of California at Berkeley; author of *Law and Politics in the Supreme Court* and other works.

SHLOMO SLONIM   Chairman, Bicentennial Conference Organizing Committee; James G. McDonald Chair, American Studies, Hebrew University of Jerusalem, Israel; has written extensively in the field of American constitutional history.

JAMES L. SUNDQUIST   Senior Fellow emeritus, The Brookings Institution, Washington DC; author of *Constitutional Reform and Effective Government* and other works.

MICHAEL WALZER   Professor of Social Science, Institute for Advanced Study, Princeton, New Jersey; author of *The Company of Critics: Social Criticism and Political Commitment in the Twentieth Century* and other books.

GORDON S. WOOD   Professor, Department of History, Brown University, Providence, Rhode Island; author of *The Creation of the American Republic 1776–1787* and other publications.